SLAPPs

Getting Sued for Speaking Out

SLAPPs

GETTING SUED FOR SPEAKING OUT

George W. Pring

AND

Penelope Canan

TEMPLE UNIVERSITY PRESS

Philadelphia

Temple University Press, Philadelphia 19122

Published 1996
Printed in the United States of America

∞ The paper used in this book meets the requirements of the American National Standard for Information Sciences—Permanence of Paper for Printed Library Materials, ANSI Z39.48–1984
Text design by Gary Gore

Library of Congress Cataloging-in-Publication Data

Pring, George W. (George William), 1942–
SLAPPs : getting sued for speaking out / George W. Pring and Penelope Canan.
p. cm.
Includes bibliographical references and index.
ISBN 1-56639-368-X (cloth : acid-free paper). — ISBN 1-56639-369-8 (pbk. : acid-free paper)
1. Freedom of speech—United States. 2. Petition, Right of—United States. I. Canan, Penelope, 1946– II. Title.
KF4770.P75 1995
323.4'7'0973—dc20 95-13610

Chapter 6: Excerpts from the June 19, 1990, study "Public Attitudes Toward Siting Residences for People with Chronic Mental Illness: A Study Conducted for the Robert Wood Johnson Foundation Progam on Chronic Mental Illness" are used by permission of DYG, Inc.

To Kitty Pring and Lily Canan Reynolds

Contents

Preface

The court perceives this [lawsuit], with a great deal of alarm, as part of a growing trend of what have come to be known as "SLAPP suits." (The term . . . was coined by two University of Denver . . . professors, Penelope Canan and George W. Pring.) . . . The filing of such suits has seen increasing use over the past decade. . . . The wholly lawful exercise, by citizens in a community, of the right to petition their local government to follow a certain course of action . . . should be vigorously protected and should not expose individuals to suit by persons unhappy with the results of such petitioning.

—U.S. District Judge Charles R. Norgle Sr.
in *Westfield Partners, Ltd. v. Hogan,*
740 F. Supp. 523, 524–26 (N.D. Ill. 1990)

Short of a gun to the head, a greater threat to First Amendment expression can scarcely be imagined.

—N.Y. Supreme Court Judge J. Nicholas Colabella
in *Gordon v. Marrone,*
155 Misc. 2d 726,736,
590 N.Y.S. 2d 649, 656 (Sup. Ct. 1992)

Great discoveries often come from an unexpected shock. Our discovery of SLAPPs came when they dropped—like Newton's apple—on our own heads in the late 1970s. For the environmental lawyer in Denver, it was the shock of having the tables turned and his environmental clients sued by the governments and polluters they opposed. For the sociologist then in Hawaii, it was the shock of having herself and her university threatened with a lawsuit for criticizing a publicly funded research program.

As it turned out, these were not unique experiences. We discovered case after case in which people were being sued just for talking to government, circulating a petition, writing a letter to the editor, speaking at a school board meeting, or testifying in a public hearing. We observed what happens to committed, public-spirited citizens suddenly confronted with a lawsuit, summonses, depositions, attorneys, and the trauma of a multi-million-dollar damage claim hanging over their lives. We saw the "role reversals" as community leaders were frightened into silence, supporters dropped out, resources drained away, campaigns foundered, and community groups died.

Our paths converged at the University of Denver. In 1983 we were introduced by law professor Joyce Sterling, a colleague and an expert in both our disciplines, who delighted in seeing "a lawyer and a sociologist interested in the same lawsuits." The more we shared our common concern, the more excited we became about this unstudied type of case. Initially, we saw such suits as attacks on traditional "free speech" and regarded them as just "intimidation lawsuits." As we studied them further, an even more significant linkage emerged: the defendants had been speaking out in government hearings, to government officials, or about government actions. Spurred by a prescient student article in the *Michigan Law Review,*[1] we realized this was not just free speech under attack. It was that other and older and even more central part of our Constitution: the right to petition government for a redress of grievances, the "Petition Clause" of the First Amendment. This refocused us dramatically, and from that time on we have concentrated on just that one subset of intimidation litigation: the cases we have named "Strategic Lawsuits Against Public Participation" in government, or "SLAPPs."

With that focus, we saw these lawsuits as more than an unaddressed legal phenomenon. We began to see their more ominous social and political implications, not only for the individuals and organizations under attack, not only for the issues and communities involved, but also for the future of "citizen involvement" or "public participation" in American democracy. Why were they happening? Who was filing them and against whom? Who was being sued? What was motivating them? Were they a new phenomenon? If so, why suddenly now? How numerous were they? How widespread? Were they increasing? Were they succeeding? If so, we began to wonder, could they not threaten that greatest of all democratic safeguards—the core reason for the First Amendment—an informed and involved citizenry?

To answer these questions, we initiated the Political Litigation Project at the University of Denver in 1984. With funding from the Hughes Research and Development Fund and the National Science Foundation, we carried out the first nationwide study of SLAPPs. We wanted to learn all we could about their legal aspects and their nonlegal aspects as well—their psychological, sociological, economic, and political ramifications. Our research approach therefore had to be interdisciplinary, multifaceted (combining both quantitative/statistical and qualitative/interview methods in hundreds of cases), and pioneering (amazingly, no one had ever studied lawsuits threatening the right to petition or communicate one's views to government). We examined hundreds of cases and interviewed nearly a thousand participants—on all sides—to get a complete, balanced view. We transformed that information into detailed computer coding and ran extensive comparative analyses of the participants, political activities, substantive issues, legal claims, judicial processing, and outcomes of the SLAPPs.

Phase I was a thorough statistical analysis of a diverse range of 100 SLAPPs. We studied the key legal documents, court filings, exhibits, and media coverage available in each case, and coded all information about participants, issues, claims, judicial processing, and outcomes. These computerized data gave us the basic "legal statics" of SLAPPs, characteristics that have remained virtually unchanged by the subsequent addition of hundreds more cases to the database and the almost daily telephone calls from SLAPP parties, legal counsel, government officials, researchers, and journalists over the past 10 years. Phase II involved in-depth interviews with 93 SLAPP filers, targets, and observers in 11 high-profile cases, chosen to represent the diversity of issues, communities, and participants we had found in the legal statics. These data enabled us to create a "model" of cross-institutional (political-legal) disputing. Phase III tested the model in 241 cases, through telephone interviews and lengthy follow-up questionnaires covering 268 filers, targets, observers, and a control group. We explored the causes and effects of SLAPPs through direct survey questions and cross-checked by using hypotheticals or "vignettes." (Annotated details of the study methodology, findings, and conclusions are provided in the Appendix.)

On the basis of our years of study, we conservatively estimate that thousands of SLAPPs have been filed in the last two decades, tens of thousands of Americans have been SLAPPed, and still more have been muted or silenced by the threat. We found that the legal system is not effective in controlling SLAPPs. We found that SLAPPs profoundly affect the outcomes of future political disputes as well as those that trigger them. We found that filers of SLAPPs rarely win in court yet often "win" in the real world, achieving their political agendas. We found that SLAPP targets who fight back seldom lose in court yet are frequently devastated and depoliticized and discourage others from speaking out—"chilled" in the parlance of First Amendment commentary. In short, we found that SLAPPs can and do eliminate or warp public political participation.

Our study confirms that these suits are a growing legal threat for concerned Americans who speak their minds on issues of importance to their communities, state, or nation:

- every citizen who takes a stand on a public concern;
- everyone who has ever been tempted to "fight city hall";
- everyone who has ever worked in a political campaign;
- everyone who has ever felt like speaking up on a neighborhood issue;
- everyone who supports a cause;
- everyone who has ever stepped on powerful toes;
- everyone who cares if government "by the people" works in America.

Over the years we published our study results widely, and many others have written about them. But professional journals, conferences, expert testimony, media, and classrooms have limited audiences. What was really needed, we thought, was a comprehensive but easily understood book—useful to lawyers, researchers, judges, public officials, legislators, politically active citizens, community leaders, the suers and the sued—a book to describe and explain a significant legal practice that now touches us all and to suggest solutions for the problems it raises.

The result is, we hope, a "Handbook on SLAPPs" for Americans who do not want to be cut off from public issues or from those who govern them. Chapter 1 defines and describes the phenomenon; Chapter 2 explains the constitutional legal issues involved. The next five chapters cover the most common types of SLAPPs: lawsuits spurred by opposition to real estate developments (Chapter 3); by criticism of public officials (Chapter 4); by speaking up for the environment and against polluters (Chapter 5); by "not in my backyard" responses to locally unwanted land uses, from group treatment homes to toxic dumps (Chapter 6); and by taking a stand for consumers', workers', women's, and others' rights (Chapter 7). Finally, Chapters 8, 9, and 10 lay out our recommendations and methodologies for "curing" SLAPPs.

We have tried to expose and analyze a legal practice that seriously undermines American democratic principles of government. We hope that the real-life stories, findings, and recommendations in this book will illuminate the problem, help us find a balanced cure, lead us back to the public-political forums in which we all belong, and demonstrate that political freedoms in America—just as much as in the independent republics of the former Soviet Union, the Balkans, Latin America, and elsewhere—demand daily vigilance, protection, and, above all, use. A government that does not hear from the governed, that loses touch, that ceases to be (in Abraham Lincoln's great phrase) "of the people" and "by the people" will not long remain "for the people."

We owe an immense debt to the many who have inspired, assisted, supported, and criticized our work over the years. Our heartfelt thanks go to Dean Emeritus Robert Yegge and the Board of Trustees of the Hughes Research and Development Fund—Millard Ruud, Victor Rosenblum, and Richard Schwartz—for first seeing the potential; to Felice Levine and the National Science Foundation for their generous support; to University of Denver Law Deans Dan Hoffman, Ed Dauer, and Dennis Lynch and to Sociology Department Chairs Peter Adler and Charles Cortese for their unfailing backing; to Susan Stein and her staff of OMNI Research and Training, Inc., Denver, for helping plan and execute the complex research projects; to Eve Pell, whose journalistic prowess blazed the trail; to the many lawyers (on both sides) who have contributed to our practical understanding of SLAPPs, including Robert Abrams, Fred Altshuler, Joe Belluck, Phillip Berry, William Bethke, Joseph Brecher, Patrick Canan, William Chapman, Mark Chertok, Nancy Cohen, Marina Corodemus, Wallace Craig, Eunice Edgar, Deborah Ellis, Morton Galane, Mark Goldowitz, John Grzybek, Henry Kaufman, Tom Lamm, David Letvin, Bill Lockyer, Nick McGrath, David Miller, Ralph Nader, Brian Pendleton, Sandy Pooler, Michael Rubin, Diana Sawaya-Crane, David Sive, Nancy Stearns, Rudy Stegemoeller, John Voorhees, Ralph Wegis, Gene Wong; to our law professor colleagues across the country for their many contributions (often by way of disagreement that has caused us to rethink our views), including Albert Alschuler, Richard Brooks, Alan Chen, Harry Lawson, Marty Margulies, Julie Nice, John Reese, Nick Robinson, Steven Shiffrin, Rodney Smolla, Ralph Stein, Joyce Sterling; likewise, to our social science colleagues, including Robert Brisson, Ronald Cohen, Paul Colomy, Edmond Costantini, Shari Seidman Diamond, Troy Duster, Bryant Garth, Peter Gregware, Michael Hennessy, Robert Kidder, Martin Kretzmann, John Means, Neal Milner, Michael Musheno, Marvin Olsen, Nancy Reichman, Reid Reynolds, Joseph Schneider, Malcolm Spector, Philo Washburn, Stephen Yeazel, Frances Zemans; to the legions of University of Denver Department of Sociology and College of Law students who served as Hughes Scholars and research assistants, particularly Kristen Koroloff Auger, Ellen Buckley, Danna Burlingame, Karen Caldwell, Leslie Kline

Capelle, Colleen Carlson, Douglas Carson, Jon Cross, Brandee DeFalco, David Doran, Shawn Gour, Nina Hammon, Lucy Hawley, Kevin Hecht, Barbara Jensen, John Kennedy, Simon Krause, Laurie Larson, Kirk Leggatt, Michael McGurrin, Marylin Mockensturm, Brenda Myers, Joanne Radmore, Kevin Ryan, James Saffell, Gloria Berndt Satterfield, Barry Schwartz, Phylis Solnick, Geoffrey Sweitzer, Vicky Thomas-McGuirk, Patricia Wellinger; to the administrative, computer, and secretarial professionals who supported us throughout these years of study, including Deborah Bradford, Lora Coven, Jennifer Evans-Moore, Bruce Hanson, Stacy Hogg, Esther Jones, Lora Lee, Dorene Miller, Carol Taylor, Tamera Trueblood; and, finally, to the hundreds of individuals on all sides of SLAPPs who shared their stories with us, patiently describing experiences and emotions that ranged from outrage, fear, and sadness to camaraderie, celebration, and hope—proof that robust political debate is still possible and still cherished. All these and many more were, in Hotspur's words, "the very life-blood of our enterprise,"[2] in agreement and disagreement, and only the authors are to blame for any imperfections in the resulting corpus.

SLAPPs

Getting Sued for Speaking Out

1 The Onslaught of SLAPPs

We shudder to think of the chill . . . on . . . freedom of speech and the right to petition were we to allow this lawsuit to proceed. The cost to society . . . is beyond calculation. . . . Competing social and economic interests are at stake. To prohibit robust debate on these questions would deprive society of the benefit of its collective thinking and, in the process, destroy the free exchange of ideas which is the adhesive of our democracy. . . . It is exactly this type of debate which our federal and state constitutions protect; debate intended to increase our knowledge, to illustrate our differences, and to harmonize those differences. . . . We see this dispute . . . as . . . more properly within the political arena than in the courthouse.

—West Virginia Court of Appeals
in *Webb v. Fury*,
282 S.E. 2d 28, 43 (W.Va. 1981)

A new breed of lawsuits is stalking America. Like some new strain of virus, these court cases carry dire consequences for individuals, communities, and the body politic. Americans by the thousands are being sued, simply for exercising one of our most cherished rights: the right to communicate our views to our government officials, to "speak out" on public issues. Today, you and your friends, neighbors, co-workers, community leaders, and clients can be sued for millions of dollars just for telling the government what you think, want, or believe in. Both individuals and groups are now being routinely sued in multimillion-dollar damage actions for such "all-American" political activities as circulating a petition, writing a letter to the editor, testifying at a public hearing, reporting violations of law, lobbying for legislation, peacefully demonstrating, or otherwise attempting to influence government action. And even though the vast majority of such suits fail in court, they often succeed in the "real world" by silencing citizens and groups, with potentially grave consequences for the future of representative democracy.

As a nation, we have prided ourselves on having, in the U.S. Supreme Court's words, "a profound national commitment to the principle that debate on public issues should be uninhibited, robust, and wide-open."[1] Our system encourages us to speak out, to petition, advocate, criticize, lobby, and argue. The American Revolution was fought for the freedom to criticize the Crown. We have resisted censorship, Nazism, McCarthyism, and suppression of thought and belief in all forms. From city hall to Congress, neighborhood to nation, soapbox to sit-in, picket lines to prime time, Americans feel they have a "right" to speak out on important issues, to each other and to their government officials. We accept the risk of equally public and hard-hitting rebuttal from the other side, but we assume that the system, which encourages us to speak out, will protect us when we do.

That assumption is no longer valid. The ominous new risk for those who express their views to the government is that opponents—not content with rebuttal in the same public forums—will drag citizens out of the political arena and into the courthouse with staggering personal lawsuits. The "chilling" effect this new breed of cases on public debate and citizen involvement is already significant; the possible effect on the future of our society and its public-participatory form of government is even more threatening.

The University of Denver's Political Litigation Project—an interdisciplinary project of the Department of Sociology and the College of Law—has been studying and reporting on these lawsuits for more than 10 years.[2] We have found citizens being sued for

- writing a letter to the president of the United States opposing a political appointment;[3]
- testifying against a real estate development at a zoning hearing;[4]
- reporting violations of environmental laws to federal agencies;[5]
- complaining to a school board about unfit teachers;[6]
- filing a complaint with a government safety, consumer, civil rights, or equal employment office;[7]
- recommending county acquisition of open space;[8]
- reporting official misconduct;[9]
- demonstrating peacefully for or against government action;[10]
- testifying before Congress or a state legislature;[11]
- reporting a violation of law to health authorities;[12]
- filing a nonmonetary, public-interest lawsuit against the government;[13]

- lobbying for local, state, or federal legislation;[14]
- campaigning for or against a ballot issue;[15]
- reporting workplace sexual harassment to government authorities;[16]
- rating judicial candidates for the voters (on the part of a bar association);[17]
- collecting signatures on a petition.[18]

When we began studying these cases, there was virtually no recognition—by the legal profession, courts, academia, government, or the public—of their similarity or linkage.[19] The tendency was (and often still is) to view them as unrelated and to apply conventional legal labels: a "libel" case, a "business interference" case, a "conspiracy" case. Looking deeper, we found what they had in common: every case was triggered by defendants' attempts to influence government action—the exact activity covered by the Petition Clause of the First Amendment.

We coined the name "strategic lawsuits against public participation" in government, or SLAPPs, to call attention to these cases in an emphatic way, to illuminate simultaneously both their cause and effect, and to encourage lawyers, judges, government leaders, and parties to look beyond labels and deal with them as a new, unitary type of litigation. The acronym is now widely used by judges in court opinions,[20] by lawyers and academics,[21] in the media,[22] and even on television's *L.A. Law.*[23]

Though we have called these a "new breed" of lawsuits, the type actually appeared first in the political infighting of our young country shortly after the Revolution, when there were scattered cases of citizens being sued when they criticized corrupt government officials. But courts generally made short work of these early attempts to squelch public debate and reform.[24] The practice seems not to have caught on with the private sector—corporations, developers, and the like—and largely died out until some 150 years later. SLAPPs were "reborn" in the political activism of the 1960s and 1970s; they grew and multiplied in the 1980s; and in the 1990s they are a major threat to involved citizens. By no means limited to extremists, radicals, or professional activists, they have struck thousands of typical, middle-class, middle-of-the-road Americans in just the last few years. They are found in every state; they erupt at every government level, in every type of political action, and on every public issue of consequence. And even though many have failed in court, their victims are now legion: in the last two decades, we conservatively estimate that thousands have been sued into silence, and that more thousands who heard of the SLAPPs will never again participate freely and confidently in the public issues and governance of their town, state, or country.

Cases in Point

Betty Johnson scarcely viewed herself as politically active—she was, in her own words, "just a housewife"—the night she attended her first city planning commission meeting in her Denver, Colorado, suburb of Louisville.[25] She was motivated to go because she had heard that a large residential development was being proposed for the vacant farmland next to her house. Sitting quietly in the audience, she was surprised at the "pro-growth" bias of the commission. She found herself agreeing with a dissident city councilman who was urging a "moratorium" on further annexation and development pending a study of what urban sprawl was doing to their town. The planning commission turned a deaf ear.

Aroused, Betty Johnson started looking into growth issues in Louisville. She researched, asked questions, and conducted a poll in her neighborhood, finding that 93 percent of her neighbors supported a building moratorium. She went back to the planning commission with her data—and hit a stone wall: "Basically, they said, 'Thank you, now go back to your dishes.' [My own] councilman . . . told me I was 'a special interest group.'" The planning commission and city council went on to approve the development of Klubert Warembourg's 92-acre farm, abutting the Johnsons' house. American Continental Corp., a huge national developer doing business as "Medema Homes," planned a 400-home residential development on that land.

Betty Johnson and her neighbors were stunned that the city's leaders would go against the clear desires of their citizens, but this was only their first shock. The neighbors regrouped and like generations of Americans before them, decided to circulate a petition, gather signatures, and force a popular election to overturn the city go-ahead. They succeeded: two weeks after they filed their petitions and before an election could be held, the city council caved in and repealed Medema's approval. Johnson and her friends congratulated themselves. They felt they had "worked within the system" and won. A few days later. however, "I was in New Orleans for a funeral, and my brother-in-law called and said that he had read in the newspaper that four folks had been sued for an 'undetermined amount.' And my name was one of them! I was freaked out! Was I going to lose my house? I thought, 'They can't do that!'" But real estate developers and property owners like Medema Homes and Klubert Warembourg can and do. They had not only sued the city and city officials—a normal and unobjectionable appeal step for those denied government permits—but had named as defendants the four residents who were the official circulators of the petitions, charging that the citizens' act of petitioning their city government had violated the developers' "constitutional rights" to develop the land and constituted "restraint" of their business.[26]

The citizens were "terrified." None had ever been sued; they could not afford the legal fees; and the city refused to defend them. Fortunately, the American Civil Liberties Union of Colorado stepped in. Its legal director, David Miller, was outraged at this violation of First Amendment rights, calling it a "tactic aimed at silencing legitimate citizen participation in local government annexation proceedings." He and the ACLU took on the residents' defense without charge. Judge Michael Enwall agreed with the victims, and a record-short four months after the suit was filed, he dismissed it with a stinging rebuke for the developers:

> The activity which is the subject matter of this litigation is . . . political, protected, First Amendment activity. . . . I don't know how any activity could be more First Amendment activity than that engaged in by the individual defendants in this case. The existence . . . of this lawsuit has a chilling effect on that activity. . . . [The citizens'] motive in filing . . . petitions is irrelevant. . . . I find that those [lawsuit] claims are frivolous and groundless. The law is so overwhelming, it is so undisputed, that it would seem to me to be impossible for the [developers] to file [this lawsuit] seeking monetary damages against these individuals . . . in good faith.[27]

The developers eventually dropped their suit against the city as well and soon abandoned the project.

But did the citizens really "win"? "I won't circulate another petition, and my husband wants me to get out of [community issues]," one resident admitted. Another, who felt "defenseless," might participate in civic activities in the future, but "I don't want my name on anything." The community was polarized: some onlookers were "mad," "disgusted," and ready to fight; others withdrew from public involvement. Betty Johnson admits that she was stressed and frightened; she attributes her divorce in part to the strains of the SLAPP. But, paradoxically, it also turned her on politically; she subsequently ran for and was elected to the Louisville City Council on a slow-growth slate.

Many SLAPP victims do not fare that well either in court or afterward. While Betty Johnson was slugging it out with Medema Homes, a similar developer-community debate was occurring only a few miles away. "Protect Our Mountain Environment," or POME, a local environmental group in the foothills west of Denver, was shocked by a proposal from developer Gayno Inc. for a huge 507-acre residential-commercial "new town" in a pristine alpine meadow north of Evergreen. POME leaders testified against county approval and, when the county commissioners granted a go-ahead over their objections, filed the customary appeal.[28] In response, the developer filed a $40,000,000 suit accusing the group, individual leaders, and even their lawyer of "conspiracy" and "abuse of process."[29]

The lawsuit dragged on for nearly four years, taking a tremendous toll in stress, lost time and work, and mounting legal costs. POME's leaders ceased being environmental watchdogs in their community and withdrew from public life; some literally moved out of town. Popular support for POME faded, contributions dried up, and the organization died. Ironically, the development has never been built, and in 1995 community and county leaders are completing plans to acquire and preserve the property as open space—exactly what POME wanted in the first place. Still, a decade later, environmental campaigns in that county can be withered by the phrase: "Remember *POME*" (for more on the case, see Chapter 3).

The two Colorado cases are anything but unique. Consider the diversity of issues, locations, and participants in these typical SLAPPs.

In 1995, residents of West Covina, California, protested to the city about operations at a 583-acre landfill. The landfill countered with a federal court lawsuit against the group "RACOON" (Residents Against Contamination of Our Neighborhoods), twelve neighbors, and city officials, claiming that the protests violated the company's "civil rights."[30]

Even while Congress was wrestling with "tort reform," the tort reform movement was SLAPPed. A Sapulpa, Oklahoma, attorney filed a 1995 class action on behalf of the state's trial lawyers against "Citizens Against Lawsuit Abuse," sponsors, and newspapers, alleging that their campaign for a state referendum to limit lawsuits "libels" lawyers.[31]

Two retirees in Huntington Beach, California, spoke out before the city council against "inflated" city pensions. Two city policemen testified against them, using language that the citizens regarded as personally threatening. When they filed protests with the city, they were promptly sued for unspecified damages by the two cops.[32]

In 1994 a Dallas, Texas, resident wrote city officials complaining that a city contractor was dumping building waste next to his property. The contractor promptly sued the resident for $90,000 plus punitive damages for "libel."[33]

An anthropology professor fought to preserve an ancient Indian village found on his California State University campus, before the university buried it in apartment buildings and retail stores. He wrote letters to government officials protesting lack of compliance with California's Environmental Quality Act and was sued for $570,000 by the university's consulting firm for "negligent interference with contractual relations," "libel," "slander," and "trade libel."[34]

Pennsylvania parents, alarmed over reports of unsafe school buses, voiced their concerns at a school board meeting. The bus company filed a $680,000 suit for "libel" against 68 parents.[35]

In 1992 a North Kingston, Rhode Island, homeowner reported to government authorities her concern that a local landfill was contaminating the area's drinking water. The owners sued her for "defamation" and "contractual interference."[36]

Collier County, Florida, taxpayers opposed a housing development at public hearings and in letters to the county commissioners. The developer sued them for $1,000,000 for defamation and "abuse of right to speak."[37]

In 1991, an Iowa county sued "all . . . persons protesting . . . [this] fiscal year budget and future such budgets."[38] The county dismissed the action three months later.

Long Island, New York, residents testified against a proposed residential development on the beach. The developer sued 9 groups and 16 individual residents for $11,200,000 for "libel," "prima facie tort," and "conspiracy."[39]

Baltimore neighbors protested a liquor license renewal for a controversial tavern. The owner filed an $8,000,000 suit against them for "business interference."[40]

The Beverly Hills League of Women Voters successfully campaigned against sale of city property for a high-rise condominium. The builders sued the League's leaders for $64,000,000 for "libel."[41]

The Sierra Club appealed the government's plans to clear-cut a California wilderness. A logger countersued for money damages for "interference with contract."[42]

Conservative religious parents complained to school authorities about a liberal grade school teacher in a suburb of Denver. The teacher won a $250,000 jury verdict for their "defamation."[43]

A South Carolina woman filed a sex harassment complaint against her male supervisor, which the federal government found valid. He retaliated with a $1,500,000 lawsuit for "defamation," "invasion of privacy," and "malicious abuse of process."[44]

Peaceful demonstrators protested a California nuclear power plant. The county responded with a $2,891,000 lawsuit, demanding that demonstrators repay its costs for arresting and jailing them.[45]

A Maryland homeowner filed an official complaint with the state over a shoddy home improvement job. The contractor retaliated with an $800,000 suit for "libel."[46]

And these are just the tip of the iceberg. SLAPPs are now occurring not only in the United States but in Canada, Australia, England, and Singapore.[47] Their message is unmistakable: There is a price to be paid for voicing one's views to the government. The price can be a multimillion-dollar personal lawsuit, which, even if successfully defended, can mean enormous expense, lost time, insecurity, risk, fear, and all the other stresses of extended litigation. That is an ominous message for every American, because SLAPPs threaten the very future of "citizen involvement" or "public participation" in government, long viewed as essential in our representative democracy.[48]

The Definition: What Are "SLAPPs"?

Most lawsuits intimidate. Many are strategic, not just tactical. Many are motivated by retaliation, or filed to stop particular behavior, punish certain speech, or counter political activities. And many pressure tactics other than lawsuits are used to suppress political behavior. Our first challenge, then, was to decide exactly what we meant by "SLAPPs": what we wanted our study to cover and what not. To focus our research, we devised a clear-cut, objective definition. The key to defining SLAPPs, we found, did not lie either with the parties' subjective motives or good faith or with who was right or wrong on the merits. Contrary to what one might expect, we found "good" people who file SLAPPs without intending to harm constitutional rights, and "bad" people who get SLAPPed yet still merit constitutional protection.

We asked, "Why do we care about these cases?" The answer, we concluded, lay in their cause and effect: we care about them because they happen when people participate in government, and they effectively reduce future public participation. It is the single element of reaction to political action that distinguishes SLAPPs from the everyday retaliatory lawsuits seen in the business, labor, contract, and other arenas. Our definition focuses on that key factor: whether defendants were engaged in activity covered by the Petition Clause, which is both the cause and the effect that should concern us. Our definition thus avoids subjective judgments about "motives" or "intent," "good or bad faith," "truth or falsity," "rightness or wrongness." The real value at stake is, quite simply, whether our nation will continue to encourage, to protect, and to be a government "of the people, by the people, and for the people."

To qualify as a SLAPP for our study, then, we required that a lawsuit meet one primary and three secondary criteria. Primarily, it had to involve communications made to influence a governmental action or outcome, which, secondarily, resulted in (a) a civil complaint or counterclaim (b) filed against nongovernment individuals or organizations (NGOs) on

(c) a substantive issue of some public interest or social significance. These criteria provide a neutral, manageable, easily applied definition whereby even opponents can agree whether a case is a SLAPP or not. Although the Petition Clause covers even more (criminal cases, government officials, private interest petitioning), this four-part definition captures the core of "self governance" that our Constitution's drafters sought hardest to protect (see Chapter 2).

Here are the rationales for our criteria. *Lawsuits only:* We recognize that there are other tactics for suppressing political opposition—employment sanctions (the "whistleblower" syndrome, for example), boycotts, societal shunning, physical violence, and many other pressure tactics can be used and have been studied—but what surprised and intrigued us was that no one had studied the use of litigation to achieve political intimidation. *Petition Clause only:* Certainly lawsuits are used to attack many other forms of constitutionally protected actions and beliefs—rights of speech, press, association, religion, equal protection, due process, on and on—but these have been extensively studied, whereas no one had empirically examined the use of lawsuits against Petition Clause–protected activities. *Civil cases only:* Criminal prosecutions can be similarly used to suppress political activity, and individuals have contacted us about their "criminal SLAPPs." They are beyond the scope of what we could accomplish in this research but certainly merit study. *NGOs only:* Government officials and employees are also protected by the Petition Clause, but other citizens are far less protected. Government personnel have different and more diverse legal protections, in-house legal resources, public financial backing, social supports, job expectations, differing career impacts. Moreover, lawsuits against government personnel have already been extensively studied. *Substantive issues only:* By focusing on "issue" politics, we exclude election campaigns for political office, but do so only to keep the study manageable; many election-to-office SLAPPs came to our attention, making this another area that deserves study. *Public issues:* Concededly, the Petition Clause also protects the self-interested (even venal and greedy) seeker of private, personal advantage, and concededly, in many cases it is hard to distinguish between self-interest and public interest. Our personal sympathies, however, are with the effect of litigation on issues of societal and political significance, more common to us all, and without being overly compulsive about it, we have attempted to focus on the cases that evidence attributes beyond simple self-interest.[49]

To denote SLAPP parties we have found it clarifying to use the terms "filers" (rather than "plaintiffs") and "targets" (rather than "defendants") for, respectively, the initiators and the objects of SLAPPs. The majority of

SLAPPs are new case complaint filings, where the filers are the plaintiffs and the targets are the defendants; some SLAPPs, however, reverse these customary labels by being filed in a defendant's counterclaim or cross-claim,[50] making filers and targets clearer designations.

The Process: How SLAPPs Work

We found that a SLAPP typically evolves in three stages as the dispute moves back and forth between the political and judicial arenas. In the first stage, citizens develop a position about some public concern, then communicate their views to some government decision-maker: official, employee, agency, or voters. This is classic "political" behavior protected by the Petition Clause of the First Amendment of the U.S. Constitution. In communicating a position, however, the citizens are opposing someone else's interests or plans, and that opposition makes enemies.

In the second stage, the enemies reach a point where they have "had enough" opposition and file a suit that targets defendants precisely because of their political, Petition Clause–protected activity (whether mentioned or not). This immediately "transforms" the situation in three ways that are advantageous for filers, disadvantageous for targets. "Dispute transformation," by characterizing the targets' conduct as some technical, legalistic injury (such as libel, business interference, or conspiracy), efficiently transforms the dispute from a political controversy into a legal one. "Forum transformation" moves the dispute from a public forum (where it can be politically resolved) to a private judicial one (where only the technicalities can be addressed). Finally, "issue transformation" shifts the emphasis from citizens' perceived injuries (deriving from a new housing development or the like) to the filer's claimed injuries (from slander, restraint of business, or whatever). These transformations serve to suppress the issue of who is right in the underlying dispute; they block solution.

The third stage is the disposition of the case. If the targets counter with a claim of constitutional political rights, they typically win dismissal. They have succeeded in retransforming the "private" and "legal" action back into a "public" and "political" one by reminding the court that First Amendment political rights ordinarily outweigh personal injury claims and, indeed, that claims of injury from another's exercise of First Amendment rights are generally rejected. But if the targets (or their lawyers, or the court) fail to recognize the case as a "political" one, no retransformation occurs, and the case is settled or adjudicated as though it were an ordinary legal dispute. When this happens, the targets typically lose—both in court and in the real world.

Perhaps the best description of SLAPPs comes from New York trial judge J. Nicholas Colabella; they are, he says,

> suits without substantial merit that are brought . . . to "stop citizens from exercising their political rights or to punish them for having done so" [citing authors' study]. . . . SLAPP suits function by forcing the target into the judicial arena where the SLAPP filer foists upon the target the expenses of a defense. The longer the litigation can be stretched out, the more litigation that can be churned, the greater the expense that is inflicted and the closer the SLAPP filer moves to success. The purpose of such gamesmanship ranges from simple retribution for past activism to discouraging future activism. Needless to say, an ultimate disposition in favor of the target often amounts merely to a Pyrrhic victory. Those who lack the financial resources and emotional stamina to play out the "game" face the difficult choice of defaulting despite meritorious defenses or being brought to their knees to settle. The ripple effect of such suits in our society is enormous. Persons who have been outspoken on issues of public importance targeted in such suits or who have witnessed such suits will often choose in the future to stay silent. Short of a gun to the head, a greater threat to First Amendment expression can scarcely be imagined.[51]

The "game" of SLAPPs is nothing if not paradoxical, however. Sometimes, as in Betty Johnson's case, it backfires, and the targets are provoked to even more determined and successful opposition. Some SLAPPs so shock the conscience of the community that it rises up to defeat the filers' plans. And more and more targets are suing back, winning multimillion-dollar jury verdicts against the filers for violating their political and civil rights—the cases we call "SLAPPbacks." Nevertheless, the lives of most SLAPP targets are dramatically altered and the political lives and futures of untold others in the community influenced by the "ripple effects"—predominantly the recommendation of those affected that others not speak out or participate in government decision-making.

Why Not SLAPPs? Sympathy for Filers

"There are two sides to every question," Protagoras teaches us, and that has presented our greatest set of challenges. "Doesn't the First Amendment's Petition Clause apply to the filer's lawsuit as well?" we are asked. "Doesn't the Seventh Amendment guarantee filers 'the right of trial by jury'?" "Aren't there cases where the filers have no choice but to sue or where targets deserve to be sued?"

SLAPPs may be a lopsided phenomenon but not one-sided. The answer to all those questions is a qualified yes. Citizens' constitutional right to political speech is not absolute; no constitutional right is. Other citizens also have constitutional rights: to sue, to go to trial, to have their plans and reputations protected. But neither are those rights absolute. When two sides each have fundamental constitutional rights, they must be balanced, must somehow be qualified or limited so that each does not cancel out the other. Courts strike this balance in the overwhelming majority of SLAPPs (appropriately, we believe) by finding for the targets. This is because targets are generally seen as representing not only their own personal interests and injuries (like filers) but also (unlike filers) the additional, broader concerns of continued public participation in government, the viability of the representative political process itself.

Let's conjure up the most unsympathetic case we can against citizen petitioners, brought by the most sympathetic filer. Here is a composite of the toughest hypotheticals thrown at us.

People Concerned about AIDS, Inc. ("People"), a nonprofit, charitable corporation, purchases a building in a mixed residential-commercial area of town. People is a small, local, primarily volunteer organization, funded by individual donations and small grants and dedicated to providing a hospice for AIDS victims in the terminal stage of their condition. The building had been used for 30 years as a nursing home for the elderly, housing 25 patients. Gloria Goodworks, volunteer president of People, is a respected health-care professional with years of experience providing care for AIDS victims; she lost her own son to the disease in 1990. She is delighted with the building's ideal layout, comparable past use, and location in a community that in the past has supported other AIDS-treatment facilities.

Goodworks anticipates opposition but believes that cooler heads will ultimately prevail in this educated, socially conscious community. To her surprise, Bob Bigot, a retired resident on the same block, becomes very upset when he hears of the proposal and undertakes a vicious, dishonest, but ultimately successful campaign to block People's proposed hospice.

Bigot prints up a letterhead for a newly invented organization, Neighbors Opposed to Sickness ("NOS") and goes to work. He first circulates a petition in the neighborhood, drumming up hundreds of signatures in opposition and signing up hundreds of members for NOS; he then presents the petitions to the city zoning board at public hearings on the occupancy permit. Bigot tells neighbors that People plans to house 100 patients, build new wings, and have a walk-in clinic. He asserts that the hospice will attract "drug addicts, gay people, minorities, and violent criminals." He spreads rumors that People is a radical, extremist political organization, and Goodworks an inept bleeding heart. Bigot manipulates the local newspapers and TV and generates a number of anti-hospice stories. He files anonymous complaints about People with the U.S. Environmental Protection Agency, the state's Department of Health, and the county tax assessor. A substantial number of his statements are outright lies or matters he has no reason to believe.

After numerous meetings in the neighborhood and before various government bodies, most of which are dominated by Bigot and his cohorts lambasting People and Goodworks, the government officials yield to the political pressure and deny the required permits. Goodworks is personally devastated; she feels that her reputation has been hopelessly besmirched. People, as an organization, is devastated; it concludes that there is no way to beat this "tyranny of the majority" or to persuade local officials to allow an AIDS hospice after this debacle. AIDS victims and their families who have been counting on this facility are devastated; many have nowhere else to go. Goodworks consults her brother-in-law, a lawyer. His advice: "Sue."

People and Goodworks then jointly file a state court money-damages lawsuit against Bigot, NOS, and (not knowing all those involved) "100 John and Jane Does." The suit charges that the defendants have "defamed" the plaintiffs, committed "civil rights discrimination," engaged in "unlawful conspiracy," induced "breach of contract," interfered with plaintiffs' "future economic expectancies," and caused "restraint of trade."

This hypothetical case reverses the usual SLAPP stereotypes: Filers are sympathetic, and their project is worthy; the chief target appears reprehensible, and his campaign is based on lies. Two observations: First, this is a classic situation and not anomalous; second, even lies need protection if we want "citizen involvement" in our political governance. Let's examine the story from these two perspectives.

First, this not-so-hypothetical case represents some actual SLAPPs detailed in Chapter 6. In the *Adult Blind Home* case, residents were sued for blocking the conversion of a home for the blind into a home for the emotionally disturbed; the court dismissed the home's suit. In *Hotel St. George Assocs. v. Morgenstern*,[52] a hotel for AIDS victims SLAPPed neighbors for alleged false reports about it to government authorities, as well as for race discrimination; the court dismissed the case. Targets' prejudice was blatant in *Weiss v. Willow Tree Civic Ass'n:* Ramapo, New York, neighbors blocked Hasidic Jews from building a housing development with a vile lobbying campaign against "the peculiar way of life of 'these people'"; the court, while evidencing its disgust for the defendants, nevertheless dismissed the Hasidic congregation's SLAPP. Clearly, the issue in these decisions was not the filers' sympathetic positions, the merits of their proposal, or the bad faith and untruths of the targets. Those were not determinants; bigger issues were at stake.

Second, protecting lying and bad motives may not seem attractive or altruistic until one thinks what the alternative implies. The alternative is censorship, judicial censorship of the political process. Constitutionally, we do not protect Bigot because he is a nice guy or right on the issues, any more than we protect Nazis marching through Skokie, Illinois, or Ku Klux Klan ravings or flag burnings because we like the message. Rather, we protect them because any other rule would fail to protect the rest of us. In the SLAPPs context, if we were to make lying an exception to Petition Clause protection, every filer would claim that every target "lied," and even the most blatant SLAPP could not be dismissed short of a full-scale trial on that fact issue. Moreover, for political issues, it is the function and duty of the political process, not the courts, to provide a full and fair forum in which truth can be separated from falsehood, emotion from reason, wisdom from foolishness (see Chapter 2).

Now, let's turn up the lights on the Goodworks-Bigot hypothetical. Its sympathetic filer had every bit as full access to the decision-makers—neighbors, the zoning board, other government agencies—as did Bigot. She had every opportunity to get her proposal "accepted in the competition of the [political] market." She had full opportunity in the government hearings (and through media and public relations) to counter the rather easily rebuttable lies Bigot spread about her future clients. Even had those been not lies but real concerns that warranted public consideration, the filer still had access to an open political process for challenging, by way of zoning appeals, the government's decision. She still had numerous location, operation, and service alternatives, which the neighbors did not.

Why did she lose? Obviously, Bigot and the neighbors strongly opposed her development as inappropriate for their community and sought a government-denial outcome (as they had every right to do). Obviously, the political representatives were responsive to the community (as they should have been). It is not obvious that either would have responded differently if Bigot had told no lies. No proposal to change the status quo deserves more political opportunity than People got, let alone a judicial opportunity to punish the opposition. That is just substituting "Tyranny of the Judiciary" for "Tyranny of the Majority."

Thus, the hypothetical supports our position; it is a success story for the political process. We will not always like the issue outcome; we may even like a filer's proposal. But our country's representative democracy does not guarantee outcome. At best, it guarantees process, and that process has the greatest legitimacy when the greatest number of viewpoints are encouraged to contribute to it. "Representative" democracy has no more basic tenet. That is the central reason why SLAPPs are wrong: wrong shifting of political issues to court, wrong chilling of public participation in governance, wrong censoring of the Right to Petition. The constitutional right at stake is the fundamental, but little studied, right to petition the government for a redress of grievances, the Petition Clause of the First Amendment. The next chapter surveys the confusion of U.S. Supreme Court decisions on this most fundamental right, pinpointing the sounder ones that can lead us out of the confusion and solve the SLAPP problem.

2 The Constitution's Great Safeguard

The Right to Petition

If liberty and equality . . . are chiefly to be found in a democracy, they will be best attained when all persons alike share in the government to the utmost.

—Aristotle, *Politics,* Book 4

"Public participation" or "citizen involvement," always central to democracy, as Aristotle attests, has been a hallmark of American political life from its beginnings.[1] Our constitutions, laws, institutions, and political style encourage all citizens to petition, lobby, debate, campaign, testify, complain, litigate, demonstrate, and otherwise "invoke the law"[2] to promote or discourage action by those who govern us. The encouragement given to political participation may well make it the most fundamental constitutional right. At the same time, ironically, it may also be the most taken for granted and ignored.

The Theory Behind "Open Government"

"The right of the people . . . to petition the Government for a redress of grievances" concludes the U.S. Constitution's First Amendment. It stands shoulder to shoulder with the great rights of free speech, press, and assembly. Collectively, they are the "interrelated components of the public's exercise of its sovereign authority"[3] over that government which "we the people" have created to serve us. Actually, the right to petition is far older than its better-known cousins. Its roots run deep in many cultures. It appears in the earliest English laws of more than 1,000 years ago.[4] In 1215, in a field called Runnymede, it gave birth to the Magna Carta.[5] By the seventeenth century it was a firm fixture in English law.[6] It was vigorously asserted in our American colonies a full decade before the Revolution,[7] figured prominently in the Declaration of Independence,[8] and appeared in eight state constitutions even before the Bill of Rights added it to the U.S. Constitution in 1791.[9] Some admirers even claim that it is the "original" political right.[10]

Over the years, the right to petition has been stretched far beyond its literal language of "petitions," "redress," and "grievances." Today, it covers any peaceful, legal attempt to promote or discourage government action[11] at any level (federal, state, or local) and in any branch (legislative, executive, judicial, and the electorate).[12] Protected activities include all means of expressing views to government: filing complaints, reporting violations of law, testifying before government bodies, writing letters, lobbying legislatures, advocating before administrative agencies, circulating petitions, conducting initiative and referendum campaigns, and filing lawsuits. It even protects peaceful demonstrations, protests, picketing, and boycotts aimed at producing government action.[13] We exalt this political-participation right as "inspired by . . . the ideals of liberty and democracy,"[14] "among the most precious of the liberties safeguarded by the Bill of Rights,"[15] one of the "fundamental principles of liberty and justice which lie at the base of all civil and political institutions,"[16] "beyond question,"[17] implicit in "the very idea of government."[18] We have even canonized it as one of the international "human rights."[19]

This Petition Clause, a host of related laws,[20] and our political ethos encourage Americans to debate, campaign, lobby, testify, complain, litigate, demonstrate, and otherwise speak out on public issues; they even make doing so a test of good citizenship. As one court succinctly put it:

> Citizen access to the institutions of government constitutes one of the foundations upon which our republican form of government is premised. In a representative democracy, government acts on behalf of the people, and effective representation depends to a large extent upon the ability of the people to make their wishes known to governmental officials acting on their behalf.[21]

The Petition Clause recognizes that the "word of the represented"—your word and ours—is a vital part of controlling the way government affects our lives. The right does not hinge on whether the citizen is right or wrong, wise or foolish, well intentioned or mean spirited.[22] That way lies government censorship. The right assumes that error and abuse will happen and relies not on censorship but on the competitiveness of truth in a free market of ideas. As the great Justice Oliver Wendell Holmes Jr. put it: "The ultimate good is better reached by free trade in ideas . . . [and] the best test of truth is the power of the thought to get itself accepted in the competition of the market. . . . That at any rate is the theory of our Constitution."[23]

The justification for the petition right lies in the fact that it is a two-sided coin. On the one hand, it protects individuals and groups who communicate with government; on the other, it also protects the government, providing an "early warning system" or "safety valve" against voter dissatisfaction, civil unrest, and revolt. In the eloquent words of Holmes's contemporary Justice Louis Brandeis:

> Those who won our independence believed . . . that public discussion is a political duty. . . . They knew that . . . it is hazardous to discourage thought, hope and imagination; that fear breeds repression; that repression breeds hate; that hate menaces stable government; that the path of safety lies in the opportunity to discuss freely supposed grievances and proposed remedies; and that the fitting remedy for evil counsels is good ones. Believing in the power of reason as applied through public discussion, they eschewed silence coerced by law—the argument of force in its worst form.[24]

A lawsuit is also a two-sided coin (or perhaps a two-edged sword). On the one hand, we have always viewed litigation as one of the key ways citizens can effectively petition their government to solve their grievances; on the other, we recognize that litigation can also be a force for suppressing that same citizen involvement. As the U.S. Supreme Court has said:

> A lawsuit no doubt may be used . . . as a powerful instrument of coercion or retaliation. . . . Regardless of how unmeritorious the . . . suit is, the [target] will most likely have to retain counsel and incur substantial legal expenses to defend against it. . . . Furthermore . . . the chilling effect . . . upon a [target's] willingness to engage in [constitutionally] protected activity is multiplied where the complaint seeks damages in addition to injunctive relief.[25]

These "two-sided" paradoxes were recognized even in the political lawsuits that flourished briefly in the cutthroat political climate of early nineteenth-century America. In *Harris v. Huntington*,[26] an 1802 case and the earliest SLAPP we found, five citizens of Shaftsbury, Vermont, petitioned the state legislature not to reappoint Harris as a county justice of the peace, because he was "a quarreling, fighting, and sabbath-breaking member of society . . . [with] a wicked heart." "Wicked-hearted" Harris promptly sued them for $5,000 for libel. The court, despite some concerns about the citizens' truthfulness, held that their petition was absolutely privileged and resoundingly dismissed the case:

> Our English ancestors have ever held the privilege of petitioning the King and Parliament for redress of grievances as an inherent right; and their Courts of Law have

> ever . . . discountenanced prosecutions declarative of such petitions as libels. . . . If this right of petitioning for a redress of grievances should sometimes be perverted to the purposes of defamation, as the right of petitioning with impunity is established both by the common law and our declaration of rights, the abuse of the right must be submitted to in common with other evils in government, as subservient to the public welfare. . . . No action can be maintained for a libel, upon a petition for redress of grievances, whether the subject matter of the petition be true or false.[27]

Similar early cases were also struck down,[28] and the type largely disappears from the reported cases until the political activism of the 1970s.

Some judges today can be equally vehement about the new wave of SLAPPs. In tossing out one case, the West Virginia high court sermonized:

> [We] shudder to think of the chill . . . were we to allow this lawsuit to proceed. The costs to society in terms of the threat to our liberty and freedom is beyond calculation. . . . To prohibit robust debate on these questions would deprive society of the benefit of its collective thinking and . . . destroy the free exchange of ideas which is the adhesive of our democracy.[29]

Today, your right to participate in government is not only recognized by the Constitution and judges like these but also encouraged by our legislatures with diversity of laws unmatched by any other nation on earth. From "Administrative Procedure Acts" to "Freedom of Information Acts" to "Government in the Sunshine" laws to "Citizen Suit" provisions, our laws invite every American to believe in participation in government, to act on that belief, and to practice it.[30]

Despite all this, the right to petition could qualify as the "unknown soldier" of the Bill of Rights: enshrined, dutifully praised on state occasions, but often neglected. Compared with the Constitution's more famous guarantees of free speech, press, religion, and so on, the Petition Clause has scarcely been a household word. There is scant literature analyzing it.[31] It is rarely taught in law schools.[32] There are few Supreme Court cases on it.[33] And it is seldom thought of or relied on by the politically active (often, it turns out, not even by their lawyers), perhaps because "the right to petition appears so much a part of everyman's constitutional instinct that he is hardly aware of its existence at the time he is most involved in an exercise of the right."[34] We frequently found that those involved fail to recognize a Petition Clause issue even when it is staring them in the face. SLAPP filers and their attorneys are often unaware they are violating people's rights and shocked and denial-prone when confronted with the fact.

Targets and their attorneys likewise often overlook the constitutional issue, and even judges are frequently blind to the political rights tangled in their scales of justice.

Yet even courts that recognize them sometimes allow SLAPPs to continue, because the majority of judges view no constitutional right as absolute; instead, they see all rights situationally, as having some limits or qualifications. A minority of courts do view petitioning as absolutely protected,[35] but the majority, including the U.S. Supreme Court, do not; even when recognizing that a lawsuit is attacking Petition-Clause-protected rights, they will struggle to find a "balance" between the target's and filer's rights. The balance is normally struck in favor of the target's Petition Clause rights, but not without qualification.

But courts have had trouble articulating what the "qualification" is. Just as in the free speech arena of pornography (protected) versus obscenity (unprotected), courts have failed to agree on a single, clear-cut standard for petitioning activity that is "over the line" and unworthy of protection. Some judges have refused to protect targets whose government petitioning was done out of "malice,"[36] or was a "sham,"[37] or intended to "harass."[38] Not only are such tests vague and inconsistent; they raise a subjective "fact quagmire"—targets' mental state—and create field days for discovery and delay through full-scale trial. Finally, the U.S. Supreme Court cut through this Gordian knot in 1991 in *City of Columbia v. Omni Outdoor Advertising, Inc.*[39]—albeit not without some prior, inconsistent opinions that require attention first.

The Supreme Court and the Fact Quagmire

The Supreme Court's 1970s–1980s handling of SLAPPs reminds one of the fable of the blind men and the elephant, where trunk, limb, side, and tail were each thought to be a separate animal. Instead of seeing the phenomenon whole, the Court dealt with lawsuits against Petition Clause–protected activity disconnectedly, as an "antitrust" case[40] or a "labor" case[41] or a "defamation" case.[42] The problems with this approach were twofold: first, the Court developed inconsistent rules for each type; second, it fell squarely into a fact quagmire that prevented early adjudication without trial—even as other federal and state courts were seeing the whole "elephant" and developing effective dismissal precedents.[43]

Bill Johnson's Restaurants v. NLRB: No "Right to Sue"

Labor troubles triggered the Supreme Court's first modern SLAPP encounter, in 1983. "Unwarranted sexual advances" and "a filthy restroom for women employees" spurred Phoenix waitress Myrland Helton to try to unionize her co-workers at Bill Johnson's Big Apple East Restaurant in 1978.[44] She was promptly fired. She came back swinging, filing an unfair labor practice charge with the National Labor Relations Board (NLRB), which agreed with her and issued a complaint. She and her cohorts then picketed the restaurant and handed out leaflets urging a customer boycott. The restaurant manager threatened to "get even" with them "if it's the last thing I do."[45]

Five days later the restaurant filed a classic SLAPP in state court against Helton and the other demonstrators, alleging libel, business interference, and related injuries and demanding an injunction, compensatory damages, and $500,000 in punitive damages. In court, Helton countered with a suit of her own—a SLAPPback—against the restaurateurs' suit, alleging abuse of process, malicious prosecution, wrongful injunction, libel, and slander. The Arizona trial judge dithered and let both suits survive, first granting a partial restraining order against the waitresses (later lifted), then dismissing some but not all of each side's charges, determined to have a trial on the cross-claims of libel.

The waitress filed another unfair labor complaint with the NLRB, charging that Bill Johnson's suit was illegal retaliation against her legally protected unionizing. The NLRB agreed again and ordered the restaurant to dismiss its lawsuit. The U.S. Court of Appeals affirmed, agreeing that the employer's suit "lacked a reasonable basis in fact" and was "filed to penalize Helton [and] the picketers for engaging in protected activity."[46]

A unanimous U.S. Supreme Court fully agreed with the NLRB and Court of Appeals that such a lawsuit can be "a powerful instrument of coercion or retaliation," that "regardless of how unmeritorious the . . . suit" the defendant will "incur substantial legal expenses to defend against it," and that "the chilling effect" upon people's willingness to engage in legally protected activity is particularly severe when they are sued for substantial money damages.[47] And so, the Court unanimously—reversed, striking down the NLRB order and letting the SLAPP continue in state court! Yes, it allowed a corporation "to carry out the threat to 'get even' and to chill the waitresses' federal rights with a coercive lawsuit."[48] Why did the Court do it, when it so clearly saw the state suit as what we now call a SLAPP?

Actually, the Court had a very understandable reason: it felt that for federal bureaucrats to order a halt to a state court lawsuit was inappropriate because—except in very carefully limited circumstances, not met in this case—that would "usurp the traditional fact-finding function of the state-court jury or judge."[49] For the NLRB to order a lawsuit stopped, the Supreme Court said, the suit must have both "retaliatory motive" and "lack of reasonable basis,"[50] and these must be clear on the record without the NLRB's holding its own "de facto trial,"[51] as if it were the court.[52] So, despite its clear sympathy with the targets' rights, "weighty countervailing considerations"[53] moved the Court to allow the filer's suit to continue. The first, a consideration in all SLAPPs, was that lawsuits should be dismissed with care, because the very same Petition Clause that protects targets also gives filers a "right of access to the courts," a right to sue; lawsuits are, after all, one of the key ways we have of petitioning our government for redress of grievances. Although the right to sue is not an absolute right, as we will see, the Supreme Court thought that federal agencies certainly should be "sensitive to these First Amendment values" before ordering parties to dismiss their lawsuits.[54] The second consideration, not involved in SLAPPs in general, was the need for federal agencies to defer to "the substantial State interest 'in protecting the health and well-being of its citizens' ";[55] this is not typically a factor in SLAPPs, because it is the state or federal court itself dismissing the lawsuit, not Washington bureaucrats. Thus, *Bill Johnson's* sits on the books as an anomaly: An undismissed SLAPP, but only because the dismissal order came from forces outside the court, appearing to usurp the court's function.

Bill Johnson's is very helpful, however, in squelching the tired argument that "SLAPPs can't be dismissed, because filers have a First Amendment right to sue." The Supreme Court expressly put this argument to rest: "Suits based on insubstantial claims—suits that lack . . . a 'reasonable basis,' . . . are not within the scope of First Amendment protection."[56] This is because the values justifying Petition Clause protection are not met, according to the Court:

> Such suits are not within the scope of First Amendment protection: "The first amendment interests involved in private litigation—compensation for violated rights and interests, the psychological benefits of vindication, public airing of the disputed facts—are not advanced when the litigation is based on intentional falsehoods or on knowingly frivolous claims. Furthermore, since sham litigation by definition does not involve a bona fide grievance, it does not come within the first amendment right to petition." . . . Baseless litigation is not immunized by the First Amendment right to petition."[57]

It was "considerations analogous to these" that led the Court eventually to the more successful handling of SLAPPs—but not until after it had floundered fully into a failure mode in *McDonald v. Smith.*

***McDonald v. Smith:* The Failure Model of "Actual Malice"**

Two years after the less-than-resolute treatment of a SLAPP in *Bill Johnson's,* the U.S. Supreme Court slipped the rest of the way into the fact quagmire in *McDonald v. Smith,* reminiscent of the politico-bashing cases of the 1800s. In 1980, shortly after Ronald Reagan was elected president, attorney David Smith of Burlington was under consideration for appointment as U.S. attorney for North Carolina. Local resident Robert McDonald, who had had run-ins with Smith, wrote two letters to President Reagan opposing the appointment (and apparently sent copies to every other Washington official he could think of).

These were not calm, deliberative, or very credible letters. They spewed a breathtaking barrage of insult and invective, even for the no-holds-barred world of politics. McDonald wrote the president that Smith had "an extremely unsavory reputation," was "known as 'Mad Dog' Smith," had committed "the most reprehensible conduct of any attorney," had "fix[ed] a [drunk driving] charge," had "tremendous lack of regard . . . for the law, . . . civil rights . . . and our system of justice." He was guilty of "criminal contempt, . . . conspiracy to fraud, . . . blackmail, . . . perjury," and was "contemptible, a liar, and basically dishonest."[58] McDonald even accused the candidate of being "the only attorney advertising for business in the classified section" of the Yellow Pages.[59]

When "Mad Dog" Smith did not get appointed, he bit back with a $1,000,000 libel suit, based entirely on the two letters to the president. McDonald was defended by one of our country's eminent civil liberties lawyers, Bruce Ennis of Washington, D.C., but to no avail. The courts all refused to dismiss, rejecting McDonald's argument that he had an "absolute immunity" from suit because of the Petition Clause. In its unanimous opinion in 1985, the Supreme Court held that the U.S. Constitution does not confer an absolute immunity from libel, slander, or defamation for petitioning with the government.[60] While confirming that "the values in the right of petition as an important aspect of self-government are beyond question,"[61] the Court held that communicating with government confers only a "qualified" right.

At first blush, the qualification the case articulates may sound reasonable: To be protected by the Petition Clause, the petitioner must not act out of "actual malice" (knowledge of falsity or reckless disregard of the truth). The Court thus adopted for the Petition Clause the same test it has used since 1964 in the free press area, the famous standard established in *New York Times v. Sullivan.*[62] The case was ordered back down for a trial, during which Smith could attempt to prove that McDonald acted with "actual malice" and, if so, recover damages from McDonald. (Smith ultimately failed to prove his case, and *McDonald* was dismissed a number of years and thousands of dollars later.)

The Supreme Court was reluctant to adopt an "absolute immunity" that would make the right to petition more favored than free speech and a free press. On the other hand, adopting the "actual malice" standard—as the qualifier or exception allowing SLAPPs—thrusts citizen-petitioners into the same "fact quagmire" the press tends to suffer under the not-so-very-protective standard set by *New York Times v. Sullivan.*[63] It is very easy to allege "actual malice" but very difficult to prove or disprove such a subjective fact question, short of a full-scale trial with in-depth witness testimony. The exception therefore actually defeats its intention, making it extremely difficult for defendants (press or petitioners) to win pretrial dismissal, stop the chill, and protect their constitutional rights. Worse, the *New York Times v. Sullivan* "actual malice" standard applies only when the alleged defamee is "a public figure." Does this mean that *McDonald*'s use of it is similarly limited, and that if the SLAPP filer is a "private" person, the standard is just the normal state defamation standard of "negligence"? If so, private SLAPPers would have an even easier time overcoming the right of petition.[64]

The Court clearly failed to think through the practical results of its copycat ruling. Perhaps the best rebuttal had already been formulated 13 years earlier by the federal trial judge in *Sierra Club v. Butz:*

> [W]hen a suit . . . is brought against a party whose "interference" consisted of petitioning a governmental body to alter its previous policy a privilege is created by the guarantee of the First Amendment. This court, however, does not believe that the privilege should depend upon malice. . . . This court is persuaded that all persons, regardless of motive, are guaranteed by the First Amendment the right to seek to influence the government or its officials to adopt a new policy. . . .
>
> Moreover, this court believes that the malice standard invites intimidation of all who seek redress from the government; malice is easy to allege . . . and therefore in most cases even those who acted without malice would be put to the burden and expense of defending a lawsuit. Thus, the malice standard does not supply the "breathing space" that First Amendment freedoms need to survive.[65]

Other courts have agreed, establishing an "absolute" privilege for petitioning under their state constitutions.[66]

The muzzy *McDonald*-malice approach for taking away Petition Clause protection flies in the face of two other crucial considerations: First, to be competent, government needs all the input it can get; second, if it is competent, government can sort the wheat from the chaff without the help of court censorship. Fortunately, savvy lower courts have found a number of ways to get around *McDonald*,[67] and in a parallel series of cases the U.S. Supreme Court itself has built a far better approach to SLAPPs in, of all places, the antitrust arena—the "*Noerr-Pennington* doctrine," which eliminated fact quagmires and culminated in the *Omni* success model.

The *Noerr-Pennington* Doctrine and the "Sham" Exception

As early as 1961 the Supreme Court found itself dealing with a SLAPP in *Eastern Railroad Presidents' Conference v. Noerr Motor Freight, Inc.*[68] The railroaders had conducted a vicious, deceptive, no-holds-barred lobbying and publicity campaign to block deregulation of their chief competition, the trucking industry. The truckers sued the railroaders, alleging (with good reason) that the campaign was an attempt to restrict competition and thereby a violation of the Sherman Antitrust Act.

The Supreme Court disagreed, holding that the railroaders' constitutional right of petition immunized their activities from antitrust liability, regardless of their evil "purpose" or "intent":

> The right of the people to inform their representatives in government of their desires with respect to the passage or enforcement of laws cannot properly be made to depend upon their intent in doing so. . . . At least insofar as the railroads' campaign was directed toward obtaining government action, its legality was not at all affected by any [illegal] purpose it may have had.[69]

In other words, petitioning the government is protected, even if done for an illegal purpose or with the intent to violate the law. The Court went further, immunizing the publicity campaign as well, since it was related to the petitioning, even though the railroaders' publicity "deliberately deceived the public and public officials."[70] This was an astonishing shot in the arm for the right to petition, particularly given that such unattractive, mercenary interests were involved.

Yet despite this sweeping language, the Court stopped short of holding *all* petitioning to be absolutely privileged. It drew the line at "situations in which a publicity campaign, ostensibly directed toward influencing governmental action, is a mere sham to cover what is actually nothing more than an attempt to interfere directly with the business relationships of a competitor."[71] Thus was born the "sham exception"—the antitrust equivalent of the "actual malice" exception in the defamation area—allowing SLAPPs to be filed against "sham" petitioning.

The second step of what has become known as the *Noerr-Pennington* doctrine came four years later in *United Mine Workers v. Pennington.*[72] In that case, the union and large coal companies were accused of conspiring to drive small mines out of business by petitioning federal agencies to boost minimum wages and limit government coal purchases to companies who could afford the higher wages (the large, unionized companies, naturally). Again, the Supreme Court sided with the less than scrupulous petitioners, ruling that "joint efforts to influence public officials do not violate the antitrust laws even though intended to eliminate competition."[73] At that point, *Noerr-Pennington* made the right to petition look absolute, except for the ticking time bomb of the as yet unapplied "sham exception."

A sham was finally found in 1972, although it took a particularly wild case to do it. In *California Motor Transport v. Trucking Unlimited,*[74] every time the plaintiff trucking company tried to expand to a new state, the entrenched defendant truckers would flood the state licensing agency with frivolous objections to the license applications, not with any expectation of succeeding but simply in order to impose expense and delay. The Supreme Court held that these "baseless, repetitive claims" were not protected petitioning; instead, they were the opposite of genuine petitioning, blocking another petitioner's "meaningful access to adjudicatory tribunals" or right to petition and thereby "usurp[ing] the [government's] decisionmaking process."[75] But even though the Court found defendant's petitioning to be a "sham," it provided little guidance for what "sham" meant. Apparently, petitioning would still be protected even if done with illegal intent or purpose, but not if the intent was simply to prevent someone else's ability to petition government.

A decade later, in 1982, the *Noerr-Pennington* doctrine took a great leap out of the antitrust arena when the Supreme Court applied it in a famous civil rights case, *Nat'l Ass'n for the Advancement of Colored People v. Claiborne Hardware Co.*[76] A major NAACP strategy throughout the South in the 1960s was to press for adoption of local city-county antidiscrimination laws. The town of Claiborne, Mississippi, resisted, and the NAACP instituted an economic boycott of local merchants to pressure the city council to adopt civil rights laws. The local hardware and 16 other white-owned businesses filed a $3,000,000 business-interference SLAPP against the NAACP and other activists. The local jury not surprisingly sided with the merchants and ordered the NAACP to pay $3,500,000 in damages; the devastating jury verdict was affirmed by the Mississippi Supreme Court.

The U.S. Supreme Court reversed, and what a reversal it was! Contrary to its muddled handling of *Bill Johnson's* the year before or *McDonald* a year later, with civil rights in issue the Court torched the Claiborne SLAPP, holding that the Noerr-Pennington doctrine applied and protected indirect petitioning of government through boycotts of private businesses. The Court even excused violence by the petitioners:

> [T]he boycott clearly involved constitutionally protected activity . . . the established elements of speech, assembly, association, and petition. . . . Through the exercise of these First Amendment rights, [targets] sought to bring about political, social, and economic change. Through speech, assembly, and petition—rather than through riot or revolution—[targets] sought to change a social order that had consistently treated them as second-class citizens. . . . It is not disputed that the major purpose of the boycott in this case was to influence governmental action. . . . The First Amendment does not protect violence. . . . In this case, however, [targets'] ultimate objectives were unquestionably legitimate. . . . The taint of violence colored the conduct of some of the [targets] . . . [but] a massive and prolonged effort to change the social, political, and economic structure of a local environment cannot be characterized as a violent conspiracy simply by reference to the ephemeral consequences of relatively few violent acts.[77]

The *Omni* Case: A Success Model

The best means of managing SLAPPs and protecting Petition Clause activity is early, fair, effective court dismissal review. The problem has been, as noted above, how to articulate a simple, objective rule or test for what actions should be dismissed, what petitioning actions immunized. The test must be easy to apply and not based on subjective-fact, dismissal-defeating questions about either filer's or target's "intent," "good faith," "malice," "purpose," "motive," "sham," and the like. In 1991 the U.S. Supreme Court finally succeeded in articulating such a test in *City of Columbia v. Omni Outdoor Advertising Inc.*[78]

Omni was an antitrust dispute between two competing billboard companies. Omni Outdoor Advertising, a newcomer, was trying to gain a foothold in the Columbia, Georgia, market but was blocked by the bigger, already established Columbia Outdoor Advertising firm (COA), whose owners had "deep roots in the community, and enjoyed close relations with the city's political leaders."[79] To keep Omni out, COA successfully lobbied its friends on the city council to adopt ordinances restricting new billboards; since COA's signs were already in place, it was largely unaffected, but the new ordinance blocked Omni's ability to get its signs up. COA did not play with white gloves on, either; it contributed funds and free billboard space to city officials[80] and, according to its rival, spread "untrue and malicious rumors about Omni and attempt[ed] to induce Omni's customers to break their contracts."[81]

Omni fought back by suing the city and COA for antitrust violations, just as the political losers in *Noerr, Pennington,* and *California Motor Transport* did. Omni's lawsuit charged that COA's city council petitioning was a "sham," designed only to interfere with Omni's business, and indeed, the courts found that COA "indisputably set out to disrupt Omni's business"[82] to protect its monopoly position. The jury took a dim view of COA's politicking and awarded filer Omni a $2,200,000 verdict. The trial judge disagreed, sided with the target, reversed the jury, and dismissed the case; a divided court of appeals reversed the judge and reinstated the jury verdict; finally, the U.S. Supreme Court reversed again, ruling that the trial judge was correct, not the jury, and that the case should have been dismissed.

The Supreme Court opinion was written by Justice Antonin Scalia, certainly not a liberal free speech advocate.[83] It addresses the Petition Clause issue in Part III, the only part joined unanimously by all nine justices,[84] strengthening the *Noerr-Pennington* line of cases and dramatically curtailing the troublesome "sham" exception. Speaking in language applicable to all SLAPPs (not just antitrust cases), *Omni* rules it "irrelevant" that a private party's political motives are selfish" because the Petition Clause "shields . . . a concerted effort to influence public officials regardless of intent or purpose."[85] The *Omni* opinion expressly limited the "sham" exception[86] to just one situation in the future: that in which "persons use the governmental process—as opposed to the outcome of that process"—as a "weapon."[87] Thus, dismissal of a SLAPP should be granted in all cases except where the target's activities are " 'not genuinely aimed at procuring favorable government action' at all."[88] If a target is seeking "a government result," the case should be dismissed, and it does not matter if target's motives are impure or target uses "improper means."[89]

This "outcome versus process" test is logical and consistent with the purpose of the Petition Clause. It requires SLAPPs to be dismissed whenever the target's petitioning seeks an outcome of a governmental process (that is, actual legislation, rulings, or other government action or inaction). Only if that is not the case can the SLAPP be allowed to continue, and then only if the target's petitioning uses the governmental process solely as an end in itself (that is, it invokes the costs, delays, and inconveniences of the government procedure only, without regard to outcome).[90] The *Omni* test for protecting Petition Clause activity can be stated simply. Genuine government petitioning is not deemed to be aimed at the opposition (although it may nonetheless have an impact on their interests); it is deemed rather to be aimed at the government with the intent to produce a desired outcome. The Rhode Island attorney general's office has advanced this helpful "toward-government/toward-plaintiff" description in defending that state's anti-SLAPP law.[91] Thus, under *Omni,* the key is an objective, outcome-focused standard, not a subjective, intent-focused one. As long as target's petitioning is aimed at procuring favorable government "action," "result," "product," or "outcome," it is protected and the case should be dismissed, all nine justices agreed.

This is cause for celebration. The Supreme Court has created a maximum-protection standard for Petition Clause activity which sweeps away the most troublesome arguments on dismissal, the fact-quagmire issues.

The question remains, should the *Noerr-Pennington-Omni* doctrine be applied to SLAPPs outside the antitrust area? A few think not,[92] but courts have overwhelmingly applied the doctrine in many areas outside antitrust. The U.S. Supreme Court itself relied on it in the *Claiborne Hardware* civil-rights / restraint-of-trade case discussed above, and other federal and state courts have used it to "protect citizens' communications with the government in a variety of cases,"[93] recognizing that

> while the doctrine arose in connection with antitrust cases, it is fundamentally based on First Amendment principles. More than one court has held that the doctrine is a principle of constitutional law that bars litigation arising from injuries received as a consequence of First Amendment petitioning activity, regardless of the underlying cause of action asserted by the Plaintiffs.[94]

Recent Supreme Court statements concur with the spread of the doctrine outside the antitrust cases, as trial courts have noted:

> In Professional Real Estate Investors, the Supreme Court . . . wrote: "Whether applying Noerr as an antitrust doctrine or invoking it in other contexts . . . ." 113 S. Ct. at 1927. This statement indicates the [Supreme] Court's view that Noerr-Pennington is not limited to the antitrust arena. In support, the Court cited, among other cases, NAACP v. Claiborne Hardware Company. . . . Thus Professional Real Estate Investors and Claiborne Hardware support the proposition that Noerr-Pennington immunity is a constitutional, not an antitrust, doctrine."[95]

Moreover, there is nothing to stop a state court from adopting the *Noerr-Pennington-Omni* approach as a matter of state law. Some states that have adopted anti-SLAPP laws have wisely incorporated that approach.[96] Even without a statute, the doctrine can be applied to interpret the Petition Clause in the state's own constitution.

SLAPPs: More Than a "Legal" Problem

The constitutional implications of SLAPPs, though profound, are only a starting point. Understanding SLAPPs requires understanding more than their "constitutional" or "legal" aspects, for these are not ordinary "lawsuits"; they operate in much broader realms. Filers seldom win a legal victory—the normal litigation goal—yet often achieve their goals in the real world. Targets rarely lose court judgments, and yet many are devastated, drop their political involvement, and swear never again to take part in American political life.

These suits are not ordinary because they do not use the courts as an end in themselves, as a normal decision-making body. Rather, they use court leverage to empower one side of a political dispute and to transform it, unilaterally. You may think you are speaking out against a city zoning permit for an unwanted toxic waste dump in your town. Then, suddenly, "city hall" becomes "courtroom"; "zoning" becomes "slander"; "permit denial" becomes "$1,000,000 in damages." The magic wand of a SLAPP has conjured you away from the place where your issue could be resolved, completely changed what issues can be discussed, and increased the stakes with a wholly unexpected monetary risk. Normally thought of as the protectors of constitutional and political rights, courts are being used, in SLAPPs, to transform public political disputes into private judicial disputes, to the unfair advantage of one side and the disadvantage of the other.

So, who is waving this magic wand? Who are the targets? What causes one side to want to transform a public, political-arena dispute into a private, judicial-forum one? And what are the effects? The next five chapters answer these questions by unfolding true stories of all the major SLAPP types, and the lessons behind them.

3 Real Estate SLAPPs

Developers, Land Use, and Growth Turning Up the Heat

I have no doubt there are unscrupulous developers who do use these types of lawsuits to suppress opposition, and I agree the courts should be on guard for it. [Citizen] input is necessary, but the process becomes distorted when there are deliberate attempts to inflame the community with erroneous information about the proposed development.

—A real estate developer's attorney
in *SRW Associates v. Bellport Beach Property Owners,*
No. 24211/84 (Sup. Ct., Suffolk County, N.Y., filed Oct. 26, 1984);
129 A.D. 2d 328, 517 N.Y.S. 2d 741 (dism. July 13, 1987)

When you are served and you call your attorney and you're told that you immediately have to come up with $1,000 in defense fees, it's devastating. I'd never been in court before this happened. I'd never even had a traffic ticket.

—A SLAPP target, in *SRW Associates v. Bellport Beach Property Owners*

What New York newspapers now label "the trend"[1] of real estate developers suing their community opponents got under way in the early 1980s. Real estate SLAPPs are now the largest single category we found, over one-third of all such cases. As one experienced New York attorney explains it: "New York has been prime grounds for SLAPP suits—perhaps because of the supposedly aggressive (and presumably, therefore, litigious) characteristics of its citizenry. Indeed, the problem has been perceived as sufficiently serious to warrant the enactment of legislation . . . because New York State courts, by and large, did not act with sufficient alacrity and firmness to discourage SLAPP suits."[2] One of the earliest and truly classic SLAPPs proves him right.

A Classic Real Estate Developer SLAPP

SRW Associates v. Bellport Beach Property Owners is a mirror of all SLAPPs.[3] For two years, the residents of East Patchogue and other communities in Brookhaven Township on Long Island's south shore had been fighting high-density "cluster" and "multifamily" residential developments on their beaches. Patchogue means "turning point" in the language of its First Inhabitants, and the 1980s proved to be just that for the residents. Patchogue for many is the "American ideal." Just over an hour from downtown Manhattan, with large undeveloped land tracts, unspoiled beaches, and a stunning view of Great South Bay, it still preserves its rural flavor. "Development" may not be an entirely dirty word in this suburban transition zone, but "dense development" and "loss of beaches" are fighting language.

SRW Associates, a local real estate partnership, owned a wooded forty-acre tract in East Patchogue, its 1,500 feet of glorious beachfront for all practical purposes a public playground. In 1982, SRW proposed to build "Land's End at East Patchogue" there: 44 multifamily condos. Opposed by residents, the plan was rejected by the township planning board. For two years, the property lay vacant. SRW continued consulting with officials and trial-ballooning plans with the locals. Bowing to residents' demands for conventional, detached private homes, SRW submitted just such a design, only to be turned down a second time by the planning board. Ironically, the board had done a 180-degree turnaround and now, contrary to the citizens, wanted SRW to go back to a "cluster" development: Although that would mean denser housing, it would provide more open land and preserve the beach. To residents' dismay, SRW gave the planning board what it wanted: a "cluster zoning" proposal for 36 luxury homes, grouped more closely than they would have been on the separate one-acre lots favored by the residents. The third time was the charm; in two weeks, SRW had planning board approval.

Galvanized, residents launched a campaign against final approval. With the decisive Brookhaven Town Board hearing scheduled for October 3, 1984, nine local civic and neighborhood groups banded together and placed an ad in the local newspaper, published a position statement, passed out leaflets, put notices in mailboxes, and got the local radio station to play the issue up. Their publicity urged residents to come to the town hearing and make their feelings known to government officials. But they made one misstatement that gave the developer a hook on which to hang a SLAPP: they described SRW's proposal as "multiple-family housing," when in fact it was a grouping of detached, single-family houses.

The October 3 hearing was great theater. As more than 300 residents jammed the hearing room, SRW's local attorney vehemently attacked the residents' mischaracterization of the project as "multifamily":

ATTORNEY FRED BLOCK: Now, I consider that to be irresponsible . . . unfair . . . reprehensible. . . . I hope none of you have been misled by that advertising. . . . That is a LIE! . . . That is a lie, that is irresponsible! This is not a multiple housing application! . . . Now, let me tell you what the merits of this application are, and let's see how responsibly you can deal with the merits. You don't like to hear that, but you must hear that! (*murmuring from audience*)

[BROOKHAVEN TOWN] SUPERVISOR ACAMPORA: Okay, come on, Freddie. Don't scream at the people.[4]

SRW produced its own petition bearing the signatures of 400 residents in favor of the project, and six locals got up their courage and testified in support of SRW. "I think I know how General Custer felt when he was surrounded by the Indians," one said apprehensively.[5]

Then, the "Indians" came on, to applause and cheers. Nine community leaders testified vigorously against "Land's End." They raised standard development concerns, such as "downzoning," "preserving the environment," "poor taste," tax base, life style, sewage, and traffic. Significantly, they did not oppose all development of the property, just development other than the prevailing one-house, one-acre model. A show of hands at the end of the meeting was overwhelmingly against SRW. The board got the message and unanimously denied SRW's proposal. The relief of the plan's opponents was short-lived. Ten days later SRW filed an $11,250,000 state court lawsuit against nine area civic and homeowner groups and 16 of their leaders.[6] The suit zeroed in on the opponents' Achilles heel, the technical mischaracterization of the project as "multiple housing." In its "claims" or "causes of action," SRW's complaint characterized the injury three different ways, each a classic, often-used basis for SLAPPs. The residents were alleged to be guilty of (1) "libel" (an injurious falsehood in writing), (2) "prima facie tort" (intentional infliction of harm by otherwise lawful acts), and (3) "conspiracy" to libel (a group plan to defame).

The shock was immediate. "We . . . felt that SRW was suing not because they thought they could win, but because they wanted to intimidate people from speaking out in the future," the targets' Manhattan attorney, Harriet Dorsen, told the *New York Times*.[7] SRW's attorney, Fred Block, countered in *Newsweek*: "My clients feel there ought to be a limitation on every person's right to speak out. You can't misrepresent the facts."[8] Another SRW attorney, Richard Hamburger, said the citizens deserved to be sued because they made "deliberate attempts to inflame the community with erroneous information."[9]

Who was right? Was the developer's SLAPP simply "intimidation," as targets charged, or was it appropriate punishment for "misrepresent-[ation]," as the filers claimed? The answer lies in the record of the October 3 town board hearing, which discloses that SRW had full opportunity to correct any misstatements about its development and not only did so but even forced the opponents to concede in their testimony that it was not "multiple housing."[10] Did SRW need a second forum? Was anyone still confused by any "misrepresentations" after that hearing? Did the town board really vote "no" because of confusion over SRW's designs? And if SRW's goal was to build, why did it not sue the town board, whose decision it needed to have reversed in order to build? In short, did SRW deserve—in addition to the public hearing—a "day in court"?

What a "day" in court SRW had: It was three years before the targets finally won dismissal. The targets' attorney had promptly filed the one-two punch that has come to characterize successful SLAPP defense: (1) a motion for dismissal or summary judgment against the suit for violating the citizens' First Amendment rights; and (2) a counterclaim or counter-suit against the filers (a SLAPPback), for abuse of process—that is, for filing a "frivolous and groundless" lawsuit "to harass defendants and to intimidate defendants into refraining from further opposition to SRW's application and from the further exercise of defendants' First Amendment rights."[11] Thus, from the outset, targets successfully characterized the case as a political matter and invoked the First Amendment—the essential strategy of "retransformation." The filers' SLAPP had transformed the community political dispute into a legal one, and targets had to transform it back into a political one in order to prevail in court.

Filers countered with two standard SLAPP tactics. First, they sought court permission to file an amended complaint (to try to cure defects pointed out by targets). Second, they filed a motion to dismiss the targets' SLAPPback. Each of these moves extends the original case and requires targets to file more responses.

On April Fool's Day, 1985, the trial court judge denied each side's motion to dismiss the other's case. While recognizing that a constitutional issue existed, the trial judge conservatively opted not to deal with it at this preliminary stage but to keep the cases alive and give both sides more time to develop their suits. Recognizing this for what it was, a victory for SRW, the targets immediately filed an appeal, but that took another two years to brief, argue, and decide. Not until July 13, 1987, did a unanimous appellate court resolve the case in a "plague on both your houses" fashion: It dismissed both suits. Ducking the constitutional and political issues, the appeals court dismissed SRW's SLAPP, ruling that the town hearing had cleared up any possible misunderstanding and that any injury to SRW was caused by the town board's decision, not by the targets; it dismissed the targets' SLAPPback, ruling that it did not meet certain technical requirements under New York law.

The lawsuits marked a bitter "turning point" for Patchoguians. The targets were chilled, and few others in the community would ever again be as likely to speak out against development. Donna Gallo summed up their experience in a word: "Devastating."[12] But the filers were affected as well. Although they ultimately built the development, they had sacrificed time, resources, and community relations in the process and would be unlikely to resort to a SLAPP in the future. As SRW attorney Richard Hamburger summed it up:

> The [appeals court] decision is saying that no matter how false, no matter how malicious are the representations, there are going to be protections from liability as long as the developer has a chance to be heard before the municipal body. Based on that, I would now advise a developer that he can't sue, and that he has to grin and bear it.[13]

Other New York developers, however, ignored that advice, and their state became a hotbed of real-estate SLAPPs. In 1983, for example, the developer of an office and shopping center in rural North Salem sued local residents, a farm company, and an attorney for $8,000,000—charging libel, slander to property, interference with business, and prima facie tort—over their court appeal of the town's approval and their media opposition (the development would cause "cancer-causing materials in [residents'] water supplies").[14] Again, the trial court would not fully dismiss the SLAPP, and an appeals court finally had to reject it three years later.

In Suffolk County a developer sued the leaders of a Greenlawn civic association for $1,033,168, plus "treble damages," for "malicious prosecution" because in town meetings and court the association challenged its cluster development.[15] Once more, the trial court would not dismiss, and it took an appeals court (after some four and a half years) to dismiss all the charges.

In 1987 when Terra Homes, a Nassau County developer, tried to build a two-house project in Wantagh, residents lobbied government agencies and protested with circulars, ribbons on trees, and signs accusing the company of "Terra-rizing" the neighborhood. Terra then sued seven of the residents for $6,652,000, alleging interference with property, contract, economic advantage, and business, as well as defamation, and two counts of trespass.[16] The case was finally dismissed after almost five years.

Also in 1987 a Brooklyn developer filed a SLAPP counterclaim for $10,000,000 and treble damages against a block association and 20 property owners for opposing the sale of city property to him for construction.[17] That same year a Brooklyn neighborhood association, its officers, and 25 "John Does" were sued for over $44,500,000 after they filed an environmental lawsuit against the city for approving filers' 13-story condominium project opposite historic Prospect Park—and this time the trial court took only two months to dismiss the SLAPP.[18]

In 1988 a Westchester County developer filed a libel suit for $14,500,000 against a North Salem civic group and 10 residents because of their newsletter article and letter to the town board;[19] they had accused the developer of "terrorism" for suing town officials personally after they vetoed his proposed 134-room hotel in a residential area. The trial court dismissed the SLAPP, and the appeals court affirmed.

Also in 1988 two New York City developers countersued two neighborhood improvement groups and 53 individuals for $200,000,000, alleging property and contract interference.[20] The targets had circulated a letter and filed a court appeal challenging the city's lease of property under the Queensboro Bridge for the developers' shopping mall. The trial court dismissed the SLAPP, the developer appealed, and the parties finally worked out a settlement.

In 1990 a citizens' group in Windsor, appealed town approval of a "luxury condominium project." The developer held a "distress sale" of the property, then SLAPPed the citizens' group and the town for deprivation of civil rights and abuse of process.[21] In 1992 the trial court summarily dismissed.

In a first-of-its-kind SLAPP, one New York developer sued to revoke the tax-exempt status of the Nature Conservancy. The trial court instead found the suit to be in "retribution against the Conservancy for opposing his development plans for the area around the Mianus Gorge, and an effort to chill the Conservancy's future exercise of its First Amendment Rights."[22] This was apparently the first New York state court decision squarely tackling a SLAPP as a constitutional issue, rather than dismissing it on nonconstitutional grounds.

A Rash of SLAPPs

New York state is not unique, of course: Real estate SLAPPs filed throughout the country have involved swank condos in Beverly Hills and low-income housing in Chicago, seaside restaurants in Massachusetts and shopping centers in backwoods Missouri, marinas in Washington and swampland developments in Florida, strip mines in West Virginia and toxic waste dumps in Louisiana, pipelines in South Dakota and yoga camps in Michigan. All represent disputes over the development of land and concomitant growth. (Some represent unique subsets—"toxics and health hazards," "destruction of wilderness," "neighborhood threats"—for which we have created separate chapters, focusing this chapter on the most common SLAPP-starter of all: standard residential / commercial growth.)

California, not surprisingly, has had its share. Each case has much in common with the others, allowing generalizations and predictability, but each has its own special lessons to teach as well.

McKeon: Filers Finance Their Future Foes

Several lessons can be learned from one of the earliest SLAPPs we found, a California developer's suit against Sierra Club volunteers: (1) Even large, powerful groups are not immune; (2) courts' reluctance to grant pretrial dismissal can greatly prolong the chill of a SLAPP; and (3) a SLAPPback can be a very effective cure, putting a price tag on the SLAPP strategy.

Since 1970, Sierra Club leader Bruce Kennedy and other Sacramento area environmentalists had vigorously opposed the breakup of scenic Elliot Ranch, outside the state capital. McKeon Construction Company planned to subdivide the 5,380-acre open space into residential "ranchettes." The environmentalists were successful in lobbying against local government approval, so on April 6, 1972, McKeon filed an $80,000,000 lawsuit against Kennedy, four other environmentalists, and other unnamed "conspirators."[23] The complaint charged conspiracy to interfere with "prospective economic advantage" (lawyerese for "future profits"), injure business reputation, and defame. What were the targets' violations of law? The court papers complained only of statements "made and published to local government agencies." Surprisingly, some SLAPPs do not bother to hide the fact that government petitioning is the only "injury" claimed.

Since the Sierra Club itself was not named, the targets had to hire their own attorneys, but the club raised $25,000 to cover part of their legal fees and submitted a friend-of-the-court brief in their support. "The charges were absurd, the main point [of the suit] being intimidation and making the defendants pay the cost of hiring attorneys," target Kennedy explains.[24] For two years, the trial court was like gumbo. Three times the targets presented motions to dismiss the complaint ("demurrers" in the Dickensian jargon of the California courts). The first time, the developer's attorneys quickly refiled a corrected complaint, without even waiting for the court to rule against them. The second time, the court gave the developer "leave to amend" (another chance to rewrite the complaint and cure defects, a common way SLAPPs are inadvertently prolonged by routine court management). The third time, in 1974, the court finally had had enough and dismissed the case "without leave to amend."

In the meantime, the filer had pursued another common lawsuit tactic—"discovery." Typically, this involves taking the depositions of targets (oral cross-examination of individuals under oath with a court reporter taking down each word) and requesting the production of documents (demands for targets' files). Blocking such "fishing expeditions" put targets through rounds of additional filings, briefs, and hearings, including one appeal. Eventually, the court of appeals affirmed the trial court's dismissal but did so on technical state law grounds, not dealing with targets' "constitutional smoke screen," as the developer called it.[25] On July 6, 1977, after four years of litigation, the California Supreme Court denied a hearing, and the case was over.

The targets promptly filed multimillion-dollar countersuits against McKeon and its four lawyers, charging malicious prosecution and abuse of process.[26] These "SLAPPbacks" charged that the developer's suit was designed solely "to frighten and intimidate not only the [environmentalists] but other persons . . . so that [they] would cease . . . speaking out at public meetings . . . and otherwise exercising their constitutionally protected rights."[27] The countersuits worked like a charm. The developer demurred, but the targets' complaints survived. Faced with going to trial, the developer's side paid a "substantial" out-of-court settlement (confidential, but rumored to be in six figures), a classic example of how SLAPP-happy filers can end up financing their own opposition.

***Maple Properties:* Not Seeing the Forest for the Trees**

Surely the most infamous California real estate SLAPP is *Maple Properties/Okun;*[28] the case certainly spent enough time in the public limelight to earn that dubious distinction. Among its many lessons: Courts do not handle SLAPPs well by keeping their hands on them. This long-running SLAPP started in an industrial zone in Beverly Hills. For years, the area had served as an "out-of-sight" location for the city's municipal services (garbage trucks, police car parking, maintenance shops, and the like), keeping the clutter out of the city's swank residential neighborhoods. But in November 1978 the city council approved a land exchange whereby it gave the area to Maple Properties, a Los Angeles real estate developer, and rezoned it so that Maple could build condominiums there. The Beverly

Hills League of Women Voters, the Committee to Save Beverly Hills (CSBH), and other residents geared up for a NIMBY ("not in my back yard") fight—to prevent not the condos but the spread of the displaced city facilities: "These indispensable city services . . . must be contained in the Industrial Area for they are unpleasant neighbors. We cannot afford to allow developers to take over the only suitable location within our city for these vital needs."[29]

League members and others gathered enough signed petitions to force a series of elections in 1979 on the land swap and rezoning. The campaign was juicy. City officials and the developer accused the activists of being "just a dozen ladies," elitists, vested interests, and anti-elderly-housing activists.[30] The residents countered that the mayor was in the pay of the developers and the whole deal smacked of "a John D. MacDonald novel of Florida land wheeler-dealers mired up to their necks in deception of the public."[31] The citizens won the elections, resoundingly rejecting the city-developer plans, and it appeared that the "condo caper" had been laid to rest. But a few months later, in September 1979, the developer filed a $63,555,000 suit against league president Betty Harris, CSBH chair Joann Ruden, resident Erwin Okun (all in their own names), and 1,000 "John Does."[32] Not suing (or even mentioning) the groups they represented appeared a deliberate attempt to cut them off from organizational support.

The SLAPP was southern California at its most flamboyant. The developer's complaint is one of the most lengthy, complex, and repetitive we have seen. Its 10 different legal claims included three counts of libel (for an election flyer and two letters to the editor), one count of slander (for election speeches), one discrimination charge (because Maple's partners included "Iranians"), one charge of interfering with future profits, and four counts of conspiracy (planning with others) to do all of the above. Over the next six years of litigation, even at pro bono reduced rates, legal fees for the three targets would escalate into the tens of thousands of dollars.

The targets may have made their fatal mistake at the outset: They promptly filed demurrers (to dismiss the complaint) but did not raise any of the obvious constitutional issues. Instructed and now wiser, the developer just amended and strengthened its complaint. Targets demurred again, again on nonconstitutional grounds. Their failure to emphasize the Constitution coupled with their detailed technical responses to each facet of the filers' complaint proved disastrous—paving the way for the courts' later obsession with the legal-technical "trees" instead of the overall political-constitutional "forest"—and turned the lawsuit into a six-year quagmire. After several more rounds of lengthy briefs, on April 24, 1980, the trial judge dismissed six of the ten counts, but with four of the filer's libel and conspiracy claims surviving, naturally the SLAPP survived. This illustrates one of the significant tactical problems in these cases: Targets have to prevail 100 percent to "win," whereas filers can lose all but one count and still keep the suit alive.

Disappointed, the targets took their case (now named *Okun*) to the California Supreme Court. After a one-year wait the high court heard oral argument and seemed to grasp the political dimensions of the case; Chief Justice Rose E. Bird wondered aloud whether people would have to consult a lawyer before writing a letter to a newspaper,[33] and Justice Stanley Mosk asked if a suit against 1,000 John Does would not chill political activity in a town.[34] Despite these good auguries, the California Supreme Court's June 1981 opinion was another "almost victory" for targets. It relied on and fell into the "fact quagmire" of *McDonald v. Smith* and *New York Times v. Sullivan* (see the criticism in Chapter 2). Rather than focusing on the macro constitutional-political problems, the lengthy, lukewarm opinion labors through an analysis of why each of the targets' statements was not done with "actual malice" or otherwise did not meet all the minute technical requirements of a libel.

Even with all counts thrown out, the SLAPP was not over. Amazingly, four of the seven justices agreed to allow the developer "leave to amend" (yet again) one of the ten legal claims. The other three justices could see that only a shutout wins a SLAPP for targets, and they were outraged that the political chill would be allowed to continue.[35] Nevertheless, the case went back down to the trial court and was dragged out for almost three more years. Even after the developer's remaining complaint was fully dismissed without further leave to amend, Maple Properties appealed, seeking to open all issues again. In August 1984 the court of appeals ruled for targets on all issues and, moreover, set a precedent by ordering the filer's attorneys to pay targets $20,000 in sanctions for a "frivolous" appeal. The developer nevertheless appealed yet again to the California Supreme Court and then the U.S. Supreme Court, until finally its last appeal was rejected in 1985 and the case closed—after six grueling years.

Reliance on *McDonald/New York Times* and losing the forest among the trees had resulted in disaster. As one scholarly article noted in dismay:

> If New York Times is applied . . . the case may be resolved along the lines of Okun v. Superior Court. Okun is a SLAPP defendant's worst-case scenario because the suit took . . . years to resolve. . . . The extended time frame and cost of the litigation penalized the defendants for petitioning the government. . . . Okun illustrates

that the New York Times doctrine leaves room for all of the potential harms of SLAPP suits.[36]

California had just positioned itself to be a mecca for real estate SLAPPs, and they flooded in: suits over beachfront subdivisions,[37] high rises for the elderly,[38] wetlands,[39] S&Ls,[40] hotels,[41] county master plans,[42] and sweeping no-growth moratoria.[43] It would be nearly a decade before California passed legislation to stop the flood (see Chapter 10).

Repeat Players and Developers' Motives

Instructive cases have occurred throughout the country. The *Warembourg–Medema Homes* SLAPP in Colorado (Chapter 1) has the distinction of being a twin: The same law firm simultaneously filed an identical SLAPP for another developer against residents of another Denver suburb.

Dubbing itself "the Carnation City" for its major product, Wheat Ridge, Colorado, is a typical American suburb. In 1980 its population of 30,293 was predominantly white middle class, its landscape was largely residential and undeveloped, and growth was a polarizing force in the community's politics. The Einarsen property, a three-block strip along one of Wheat Ridge's busiest thoroughfares, had been a source of town controversy for decades. Since purchasing it in 1941 the Einarsen family had tried to develop it without success, first residentially and then, as the character of the neighborhood changed, commercially. In 1977 city zoning refusals erupted in a lawsuit, which the Einarsens lost, and their development plans went on hold. In April 1983, however, the Einarsens emerged with a surprise victory: city approval of a "planned commercial development" on the property. Members of the surrounding Westhaven Homeowners Association, previously successful in blocking nonresidential development of the property, had mixed emotions. Nancy Snow, a former city council member, remembers that not all the association members were against development, but long-standing frictions with the Einarsens sparked a petition drive.[44] Soon they had enough signatures to force a citywide election to rescind the city go-ahead.

The same law firm that filed the *Warembourg* SLAPP in nearby Louisville was retained by the Einarsens. They hired a consulting firm to "counterpetition" and gather signatures for them, and they challenged the association's signatures in a trial-like hearing before the city clerk. Nancy Snow recalls the ordeal:

> [The filers' attorneys] served subpoenas on a lot of people for the hearing—on those who passed petitions [and those who signed] and felt "misled." Others were really "raked over the coals." Panic followed. A lot of elderly people were scared.

. . . The cross-examination was devastating for some, especially some of the older women, who are, as a group, against excessive [government] zoning. A few really didn't know the issues and [the developer's attorneys] nitpicked at some things like "where the clip was on the clipboard." . . . The hearings were frightening for a lot of people. . . . Everybody was mad. . . . About 40–50 people changed their minds [and withdrew their signatures]. I knew one elderly lady who couldn't sleep because of the hearings. It was painful.

After five grueling days of hearings, the city clerk upheld the antidevelopment petitions. That put the issue on the ballot, to be decided by majority vote of the townspeople. Before the election could be held, the Einarsens sued city officials and the three residents listed as "representatives" on the petitions.[45] The three residents were surprised and "scared"; they "saw it as a tactic to get us to stop petitioning."[46] But the SLAPP also made people mad, even neutrals. "I was flabbergasted," states Nancy Snow, "surprised, . . . angry and horrified. Especially when I found out that the [lawsuit] claims were word for word from the [Warembourg] suit. I considered it harassment. The charges were outrageous."

The election was a disaster for the neighbors. The pro-Einarsen forces won handily, and the filers kept their commercial zoning. After the election, when it was too late, the SLAPP was dismissed on Petition Clause grounds. Having won the election, the developers did not appeal, but their attorney stated, "If the election had failed, we would have continued with the case."[47] As is typical of SLAPPs, the filers lost in court but won in the real world. Still, it was "a victory so expensive that it really wasn't a victory."[48] The land remained unsold and undeveloped. Variously blamed by observers were "the tough real estate market," a high price, and "the bad name" the property had acquired through its history of zoning fights.[49] Years later it still had a big "for sale" sign and no buildings. Other developers also suffered from the political militancy the SLAPP stirred up. Frustrated with the city leadership, the neighborhood association got active in politics and elected a new majority to council, and the zoning board was mostly replaced, with one of the targets even becoming a member.

Atypically, all participants interviewed profess not to have been chilled by the experience; targets, city officials, and filers' attorney all report they would "do it again" and had "no regrets." Of course, willing interviewees may exclude those who feel otherwise in any given case, and they may overstate their future courage as well. As the attorney representing the targets reminds us, even her more heroic clients were "devastated" and "exhausted" by the SLAPP,[50] and the memory of those feelings may undercut their future political involvement.

Why do real estate interests and their attorneys file SLAPPs? Attorney

Scott Albertson, who represented both developers in these twin Colorado cases, was quite forthright with us: He pointed out that his developer clients were used to suing local governments over development denials but "had never sued private citizens before." He was concerned that petition circulators might be "indispensable parties," required to be named along with city officials, although there was no Colorado law on that point (for discussion of "indispensable parties," see the *Adult Blind Home* case in Chapter 6). Whether the citizens should also be sued for real dollars was another question entirely: "Whether to assert damage claims is a difficult decision. My client had to recognize that there were no cases in Colorado in which citizens had been held [financially] liable in a case like this. The possibility of prevailing was remote." So, what made them go for the citizens though their wallets?

> I can't say specifically what Medema said to us, but we did discuss the risks of bad press, . . . the risks of claims being dismissed and attorneys fees being awarded. . . . They weren't looking to line their pockets with gold from litigation. They hoped . . . to come up with a plan . . . suitable to the city and the citizens. Medema had probably spent a half a million dollars on engineering and development plans for that property. Their ultimate goal was to [develop] the property.

As these candid comments show, the developers' view of SLAPPs is very different from that of the targets. Filers can be motivated by deeply held feelings about vested private property rights, obligations to investors, the value and necessity of growth, the contribution that developments make to the economy, the need for honesty in dealings, the need for sanctions against those who misrepresent the truth or otherwise operate in perceived bad faith, and so on. Even though many developers' representatives state that SLAPPs are counterproductive and should not be used in the future, Mark Chertok, an attorney who has represented both developers and citizen opponents, throws cold water on that faint hope: "SLAPP suits are still viable weapons in the arsenal of real estate developers in certain circumstances, and may serve to chill effectively the First Amendment rights of citizens."[51] He believes SLAPPs can be a "success" for developers, if several key factors are present: the filer has a good reputation; the dollars at stake are high; the targets stoop to personal attacks; and the targets are relatively unsophisticated individuals, not backed by larger entities.[52] Other deterrents are possible, however.

A Protective Precedent

The lawsuit destined to create one of the strongest anti-SLAPP precedents in the country ended disastrously for its actual victims. Yet the state supreme court opinion it generated has become a model followed by other defense attorneys, judges, even legislatures, thereby protecting many other SLAPP victims.

The *Protect Our Mountain Environment* or *POME* case (highlighted in Chapter 1) began inauspiciously enough for the targets. In 1977 a Denver-area developer, Gayno Inc. (later to become Lockport Corporation), proposed to build a 507-acre residential-commercial development in a pristine alpine meadow near the Rocky Mountain foothills town of Evergreen, 35 miles west of Denver. POME, its attorney, and other residents campaigned against county zoning approval and failed. They then filed a nonmonetary court appeal against the county, which also failed (and even resulted in a $2,000 sanction against the residents for a "frivolous" procedures). The animosity engendered between the lawyers for the two sides, observers agree, had significant bearing on the filing of the SLAPP.

On April 1, 1981, the developer filed suit, demanding $40,000,000 from POME, its leaders, and their lawyer,[53] charging them with abuse of process and conspiracy in bringing their "dilatory and baseless" court appeal. For two years, the case went badly for the targets in the trial court, which steadfastly refused to dismiss and at one point even temporarily entered a default judgment against the residents. Discouraged, POME changed lawyers, engaging Frank Plaut—an experienced zoning and trial lawyer and former president of the Colorado bar association—and his new law associate, Nancy Cohen, who, while in law school, wrote with Professor Pring, co-author of this book, an early article on SLAPPs.

In what was then a bold strategy but has since become standard practice across the country, the new counsel filed a direct appeal with the state supreme court, leapfrogging the trial and appeals courts by asserting that constitutional rights were being denied by the continuation of the SLAPP. The ACLU, the League of Women Voters, Common Cause, and a Denver neighborhood group leaped into the fray, requesting Professor Pring to file a friend-of-the-court brief supporting dismissal. The Colorado Supreme Court accepted the case and on February 21, 1984, handed down a unanimous opinion that cut directly to the political-constitutional issue:

> The First Amendment to the United States Constitution guarantees "the right of the people . . . to petition the government for a redress of grievances." Citizen access to the institutions of government constitutes one of the foundations upon which our republican form of government is premised. In a representative democracy government acts on behalf of the people, and effective representation depends to a large extent upon the ability of the people to make their wishes known to government officials acting on their behalf. The right to petition has been char-

acterized as one of "the most precious of the liberties safeguarded by the Bill of Rights."

. . . It cannot be denied that suits filed against citizens for prior administrative or judicial activities can have a significant chilling effect on the exercise of their First Amendment right to petition the courts for redress of grievances. . . . Damage to other persons and society, however, can also result from baseless litigation instigated under the pretext of legitimate petitioning activities. . . . Accommodation of these competing concerns can best be achieved by requiring the suing party, when confronted with a motion to dismiss predicated on the First Amendment right to petition, to demonstrate the constitutional validity of his claim.[54]

The court adopted what was for that era an attractive way to avoid most of the fact quagmire of *McDonald*'s malice test and the then *Noerr-Pennington* sham exception (discussed in Chapter 2) by switching the burden of proof to the filer. (Chapter 8 analyzes *Omni's* improvement over *POME.)*

Despite this resolute ruling, it took another year in the trial court before the filers finally dropped the last vestiges of the case. In one sense, everyone lost. The development died without a shovel being turned, a victim of the withering Denver economy. POME died as an organization, and its leaders dropped out of the political process. Citizens in Jefferson County still think twice about speaking out, and locally, "Remember POME" has the opposite force of "Remember the Alamo."

Yet in another sense there were many winners. A decade later, in 1995, the meadow is still the pristine home of elk, deer, and mountain lion and is being acquired by a "partnership" of the community, the recreation district, and the county open space program, while Gayno is finally building its mega–shopping center three miles away.[55] The Colorado Supreme Court decision offers Coloradans in their civic outspokenness one of the strongest protective precedents in the country. Other states have followed suit, both in court opinions and legislation. And despite their caution, Jefferson County residents have recently been embroiled in a number of development fights, including a Chicago millionaire's proposal for the state's largest open-pit gravel mine in a near-wilderness canyon on Denver's doorstep.[56]

The real estate development SLAPPs found across the country, particularly where economic conditions favor development and growth, have so much in common that they often appear to be the same case. The scene may change from downtown to suburbs, from rural areas to commercial zones; the proposed development may be single homes or high rises, subdivisions or malls. But the circumstances are always the same: Landowners and builders want to develop property; residents are opposed to the change; the residents' opposition before government agencies is effective or about to be; then the developers, losing ground in those public forums, take the dispute to court, where they typically lose their case but succeed in silencing the citizens and winning development approval in the real world. The pattern is not unique to real estate SLAPPs. As the following chapters show, SLAPPs come in a thousand shapes and sizes, but all have identifiably similar causes and effects—and require the same solution: In the words of the California Supreme Court dissenters in *Maple Properties:* "In the preservation of the free exercise of speech, writing and the political function, the early termination of [such a] lawsuit is highly desirable. We should discourage attempts to recover through the judicial process what has been lost in the political process."[57]

4 The Ultimate SLAPP

Public Servants Turning on the Taxpayers

If one wants to be a public servant in a free society, he must develop a thick skin. If the First Amendment means anything, it means that a citizen has a right to criticize, even unjustifiably, the conduct of those operating the government. If the government itself can decide which criticisms it will tolerate and which it will not, by its courts freely allowing government officials to bring actions against citizens expressing grievances, then an essential aspect of our freedom is impaired.

—Dissent in *Berkey v. Delia,*
287 Md. 302, 341–42, 413 A. 2d 170 (1980)

The First Amendment's Petition Clause was designed with one overriding goal: to keep representative government in touch with those it represents. In the real estate developer SLAPPs of the last chapter, citizens first communicated with government, then other citizens attacked that communication with lawsuits. But there is an even more worrisome prospect. What if the government officials and employees themselves want to punish those communications? What if our public servants sue their citizen masters merely for communicating criticism of their government performance, projects, policies, peccadillos, or outright improprieties? Would that not be the supreme denial of all that the right to petition government protects? Would that not be the ultimate SLAPP?

Unfortunately, such suits against citizens, taxpayers, and voters are a very definite reality—in fact, next to real estate development SLAPPs, we found them the most numerous. Police sue citizens who file misconduct complaints against them. Public school teachers sue parents for complaining to the school board or administrators about teacher competence or conduct. Worst of all, elected and appointed officials and bodies—county commissioners, city council members, sewer districts, recreation boards, government attorneys, governors, and even IRS agents—sue their own constituents, typically for no more than standing up in a public meeting and criticizing a pork-barrel project or the conduct of a public official. Each of these varieties—police, school, and public official SLAPPs—has its own characteristics and lessons to teach, but the three also have enough in common to show a path for diagnosis and ultimate cure.

The Police SLAPP

> *Our society vests its law-enforcement officials with formidable power, the abuse of which is often extremely detrimental to the public interest. Citizen complaints . . . serve a public function of vital importance . . . through which abuses may be reported to the proper authorities, and the abusers held accountable.*
>
> —The Maryland Court of Appeals in *Miner v. Novotny*, 304 Md. 146, 498 A.2d 269, 274–75 (1985)

SLAPPing the "Good Samaritan"

"Trouble with the law" was the furthest thing from Lora Fellin's mind as she and a girlfriend left a New Year's Eve jazz concert on the edge of Milwaukee's inner city and headed home at 12:30 A.M. on the first day of 1979. A social worker in the public schools, the quiet, diminutive Milwaukee native had no prior police or court experience, and her attitudes about the police were positive. What she saw next would change all that. According to Fellin, as they walked to her car, they saw a young African American being pursued out of "a redneck bar" by a group of white patrons.[1] She saw them kicking him as he lay on the sidewalk and immediately sized it up as "a racial confrontation." The youth broke free, and fled with the mob of whites at his heels.

Before the observers could call the police, a squad car cruised by and caught up with the group. Fellin felt she should report what she had seen to the officers, but as she approached them, she found the youth down on the ground, handcuffed:

> I saw both police officers kick and shake him . . . as he was screaming and trying to avoid their blows. One officer then walked away while the other officer continued to kick the man several more times in the head, side and chest. The man's face and head were . . . bruised and bleeding.

She rushed over and objected, whereupon one of the officers ordered her to leave "at the count of ten" or he would arrest her too. Shocked, she stood her ground, and the officer took her by the arm and told her she was under arrest. When her girlfriend came to her defense, the officers finally backed off and allowed her to go. But before she left, she got the injured youth's name.

Thinking that she was doing the "humanitarian thing," she wrote a letter to Third District Police Captain Joseph Kalivoda, describing the incident and reporting without mentioning names, that the officers "physically abused the man . . . for no logical reason [and] acted in a deplorably undignified and unprofessional manner."[2] She sent copies to the district attorney, several city officials, the Milwaukee police union, the ACLU, and a prominent black radio commentator.

The police officers involved saw the situation differently. Patrolman William Welter, 6'4" and a seven-year veteran of the force, and his partner, David Clark, reported that the youth "started to fight with us,"[3] so with the aid of some of the white patrons they subdued and handcuffed him on the ground. His injuries, they said, had been inflicted entirely by the bar patrons. Patrolman Welter viewed Lora Fellin as interfering:

> She started yelling, "The man has rights. You have no right to do this. You have no right to do that." . . . [W]e told her you have to get out of the street or you could be arrested for a pedestrian violation and in interfering with our arrest. She got the guy totally riled up again. . . . It took four of us to get him in the van. . . . We talked to her a little bit and recovered our composure . . . and we just advised her to be gone.

Welter had reason to be upset when Fellin's complaint letter came in. Even though he was not named, he knew it would be obvious to anyone who checked the arrest logs which officers were involved, and this was not the first brutality complaint filed against him, since he was, by his own admission, "aggressive." Also, he was about to sit for the upcoming sergeant's exam and felt that another complaint could hurt his chances for promotion. Yet he was "cleared." The city's fire and police commission ruled that only a victim could legally complain, not a "third party" like Fellin. The city district attorney's office investigated but concluded there was no criminal conduct by the police. Significantly, in a February 13, 1979, letter the DA's office nevertheless praised Fellin for reporting: "I am satisfied that you had no reason in the world to pursue this complaint other than to seek justice and tell the truth. . . . Please do not let this discourage you from continuing to be as good a citizen as you have demonstrated yourself to be."[4] Later, she appeared as a witness for the youth, and the charges against him were reduced to mere misdemeanor disorderly conduct.

That appeared to end it—until December 1980, nearly two years later, when Patrolman Welter filed a $50,000 libel suit in state court against Lora Fellin, based solely on her complaint letter to the police department.[5] His reasons: "This is sitting in my [employment] folder which is very damaging to my character. It's alleging that I am a brutal person. It's having an effect on my career. I haven't been able to [get promoted]." Admitting to his "fair share" of complaints over "unjustified force," he was concerned both about promotion and whether other police would continue to work with him. He also felt he owed it to other officers to take a stand against "false complaints": "I was hoping that this [lawsuit] would get enough publicity and that she would be found at fault so that it would lessen the number of complaints on officers." So, the policeman was obviously aware that his suit could "chill" and hoped the chill would extend to other citizens thinking of complaining in the future.

Fellin was astonished but not overwhelmed. She had felt "a personal and moral obligation to report the incident." Her parents suggested that she contact the ACLU, and Eunice Edgar, executive director of the Wisconsin ACLU, immediately saw the First Amendment implications of the suit. She had no trouble persuading ACLU volunteer attorney Robert J. Lerner to take on the defense pro bono. He too was surprised that a police misconduct complaint could trigger a lawsuit, because citizen complaints are "fairly common" and generally "not very successful." But "as a lawyer," he said, "I loved it. I thought I had a case I was going to win. . . . I have always enjoyed . . . taking on the establishment or whatever. That's part of the fun of being a lawyer. . . . I never thought there was much merit to the case. I was always fairly confident we were going to win.[6]

Meantime, having already spent some $1,200 of his own money on legal fees, Welter went to his police union, the Milwaukee Police Association, for financial help. He got it. As Bill Kruger, head of the union, explained to us: "Part of the benefits, if you will, of being a member of the [police union] is that if you find yourself the defendant in a [lawsuit] brought . . . by a citizen, by the department, by anybody, you are entitled to legal counsel free. . . . [And] we have never denied an officer [legal] representation that wants to file suit."[7] Although conceding that it is "not common" for police to sue over complaints, Kruger justified such suits on the grounds that most brutality claims are self-serving, plea-bargain ploys: "The majority of the time the complaints are made by people who . . . have been arrested and feel that a complaint is going to help them avoid being charged in the city district attorney's office." Patrolman Welter's lawyer (also the union's in-house counsel) was aware that suing citizen complainants raised problems: "People should be able to express their concerns without fear that there will be some kind of retribution legally or otherwise."[8] So, how did he justify filing this suit? His rationale, a view commonly expressed by SLAPP filers, was that the target in this case had gone beyond mere government petitioning: "Instead of just contacting the Fire and Police Commission or the Police Department or the District Attorney [with her complaint] . . . this person sent it out to all kinds of reporters and . . . other unrelated officials in city government." In the eyes of the policeman and his attorney, then, going public (even though such complaints are of public concern and on the public record) was enough to place her outside Petition Clause privilege.

Going public also made the case go badly for Fellin in court. In April 1981 her motion to dismiss was denied because of the very common "catch-22" that the *McDonald/New York Times* approach imposes on judges. Despite recognizing complaints like hers as privileged, the judge felt he could not dismiss without determining whether she had lost the privilege by acting out of "malice"—a fact question that he believed required a trial. Hence the catch-22: no protection from trial without a trial! Over a year later a new judge was routinely assigned the case and promptly dismissed it. But Fellin won no constitutional precedent; the dismissal was based on the narrow (and questionable) ground that a libel suit requires the plaintiff's name to be mentioned in the offending document. Fellin's letter had mentioned no names. Welter did not appeal, and the SLAPP was over.

Neither of the parties was satisfied with the outcome, but both expressed calm resignation—which is atypical, given the antagonisms and emotion in most of the police SLAPPs we uncovered. Welter was disappointed that he did not get "the lesson for [future] unfounded complaints" he wanted, but "that's one for the bad guys," he shrugged. He eventually made sergeant in 1987, and, yes, he would sue citizen complainants again. Lora Fellin was "glad it was over," expressed satisfaction with her attorney and the legal system, but still felt like a "victim." Would she file a citizen complaint again? Her answer was vague and evasive. Could she handle another lawsuit? "No. This was enough."

Street SLAPPs

Most police SLAPPs do not end so quickly or calmly, but then, most involve not "good Samaritans," like Lora Fellin, but persons actually being arrested and charged, just as the Milwaukee police union leader believed. Many such persons, however, turn out to be not serious criminals but simple traffic offenders. Parking, speeding, and accident tickets, as innocuous as they seem, generate the most police SLAPPs, and a significant number of these result in victory for the police in court and out.

In 1986 Gary Reinartz and his father were stopped by Santa Clara, California, city policeman Dennis Grilli for speeding in a school zone. Words ensued, then a scuffle. The Reinartzes claimed the policeman struck the father; the policeman claimed they struck him and arrested the two for assault and battery. The next day the son telephoned the Santa Clara Police Department and complained. The phone call triggered a formal investigation, which exonerated the policeman. Yet the following year, to the Reinartzes' surprise, they were sued by Grilli for defamation.[9] The targets moved for summary judgment, had it denied, tried an appeal, and were again denied relief. Finally, in 1989, they made a payment of $1,000 to the policeman to dismiss the SLAPP, on their lawyer's advice that it would cost more than that to litigate it.

A pullover in Alameda, California, resulted in an altercation and the arrest of a passenger in the car for drunk and disorderly conduct. The passenger then filed a lawsuit against the city and arresting officer Robert Villa, alleging violation of civil rights, assault and battery, false arrest, and infliction of emotional distress. The city settled the case with the passenger. Three years later the policeman sued the passenger and his attorney for malicious prosecution. The trial court dismissed the action because the policeman had not won the first suit, and an appeals court affirmed in 1992, ending the two-year SLAPP.[10]

Debra Lee Wurm was stopped in her hometown of Brooklyn Park, Minnesota, for a traffic violation. She filed a formal complaint afterward that the patrolman had "harassed, vilified and made sexually derogatory comments" to her.[11] Two months later the traffic charges were dropped in return for her agreement to drop the complaint against the officer. She was wrong to think that settled the matter: the officer SLAPPed her for $50,000 for defamation, and the case was still pending three years later.[12]

Steven W. Holloway was arrested in St. Charles, Missouri, for careless driving and complained that he was beaten during the arrest. He filed first a brutality complaint with the St. Charles Police Department, then a federal court suit against the arresting officer and the city. Six weeks later, according to the ACLU, which followed the case with concern, the charge against him was upped from careless driving to "felonious assault on a policeman," and he was rearrested.[13] That assault charge was dropped after investigation, and after Holloway lost his federal court suit, the matter seemed a standoff. But then the arresting officer filed a $600,000 SLAPP against Holloway both for libel (his citizen complaint) and for malicious prosecution (his federal court suit).[14] The SLAPP was "not vigorously pursued," however, and died after Holloway moved away without leaving a forwarding address.[15]

North Olmsted, Ohio, residents complained at a city council meeting about a certain city policeman and an alleged "quota" system for speeding tickets. They were sued for $1,500,000 by the officer in question, who dropped the suit when the targets signed a letter of apology.[16]

One of the cruelest police SLAPPs was a Warwick, Rhode Island, case in which the widow of a man killed in a high-speed police chase was sued by one of the policemen who pursued her husband to his death. Patrolman Kenneth Anderson saw a 26-year-old local, who had a juvenile record, on what he thought was a stolen motorcycle. He gave chase, and the motorcyclist, attempting to pass a car on the right, died in a grinding crash. The motorcycle proved not to be stolen, witnesses disputed the officer's version of events, and the widow asked the FBI to investigate. For contacting the FBI, the patrolman sued her for $50,000 for defamation.[17] The Rhode Island ACLU leaped to the widow's defense, the press had a field day drubbing the police, and the SLAPP was dropped a few months later.

Of course, one's sympathies can frequently lie more with the police than the "victim" (except, of course, for the chilling effect on others). For example, a Norwalk, Connecticut, city policeman observed a car illegally parked in front of the local supermarket and honked his horn. The owner, Flora Lippe, emerged from the store and let the officer have—in the court's words—"a verbal barrage," calling him "clown," "big fat ape," "stupid son of a bitch," and so on;[18] reportedly, she also kicked and flailed at him with her pocketbook and topped it all off by filing a police brutality complaint, sending copies to the local newspaper.[19] The officer filed a defamation SLAPP, and a sympathetic jury awarded him $4,000, most of which was reversed by the appeals court. The policeman finally dropped the case after some six years.

Woe to the cop who stops a speeding shrink! A Maryland psychiatrist who was ticketed for speeding formally charged his arresting officer with being "mentally deranged, . . . psychopathic and/or pathologically sadistic," and demanded a "mental evaluation" of the policeman.[20] The officer SLAPPed the psychiatrist for $120,000 for libel and slander.[21] The target won a pretrial dismissal, but the appeals court reversed for the policeman, the state supreme court affirmed, and on remand the psychiatrist paid the policeman a confidential out-of-court settlement for his off-the-couch diagnosis.

Non-Traffic Police SLAPPs

Miscellaneous other situations also trigger police SLAPPs. After an Oklahoma man got caught watering his yard during an emergency water-rationing day, he filed a brutality complaint against the police who tried to stop him;[22] the police filed suit, but the water bandit eventually got the case dismissed. The owner of a topless bar in Charleston, South Carolina, was SLAPPed for reporting a county deputy to the FBI as "a crooked cop" who tried to solicit a bribe,[23] but the officer dropped the case on the day it came to trial.

Efforts at prison reform have engendered other SLAPPs. Attica Prison guards sued Ellen Yacknin, a New York Legal Aid attorney, for $15,500,000 because of her critical exposé of prison conditions, which was distributed to state government officials.[24] The guards' suit was dismissed on summary judgment, and Yacknin, undeterred, continued her crusade for prisoners' rights. Unlike Yacknin, however, prison reformers in St. Petersburg, Florida, were clearly chilled by a SLAPP. When the Florida Clearinghouse on Criminal Justice made public a report to government authorities about parole officers who were "abusive" in delaying prisoners' release dates, one of the parole officers sued.[25] Even though the Clearinghouse won a dismissal, it will publish no more studies for government officials and the public, the *St. Petersburg Times* reported in an angry 1983 editorial, because of the "intimidation effect" of the suit.[26]

Demonstrations and picket lines are additional sources. For example, the Teamsters and their officials were SLAPPed twice by Eugene, Oregon, policemen after the union had written the governor, the police chief, the mayor, and the media, criticizing police brutality at a strike.[27] The union targets initially got the cases dismissed, but an appeals court reversed and sent them back for trial, pressuring Teamster officials into an undisclosed settlement with police.

Another case finally settled out of court occurred when fearful neighbors in a small town in Maine told the police chief of a certain police detective's "violent temper" and requested that he not be allowed to bring his gun home. The detective and his wife promptly sued six of the neighbors.[28] The jury awarded the detective $36,000; the court of appeals reversed, leading to a confidential settlement.

Seeking a Solution

Not all police-SLAPP victims are blameless, of course; some cases support the police view that citizen complaints are filed by malefactors just seeking leverage to reduce legitimate charges against themselves. Still, even if these cases are not the small percentage we found them to be, is the proper cure even for unjust complaints to encourage private lawsuits by the police against citizens? Maryland courts and others that have looked carefully at the problem have taken a hard line against police SLAPPs. Other states might well consider the Maryland model.

Harford County Deputy Sheriff John J. Miner stopped Joseph A. Novotny and charged him with driving while intoxicated. The deputy claimed that Novotny spit in his face. Novotny filed a police brutality complaint; Miner was exonerated but then SLAPPed Novotny with a $1,500,000 suit for defamation, intentional infliction of emotional distress, and abuse of administrative procedures for filing the police complaint.[29] But the Maryland court laid down the law:

> It matters not that [the citizen's] complaint may have been made without substantial justification, or that it was unfair or malicious, or that it was motivated by self interest, or that it was likely to cause professional injury to [the police officer], or even that [the citizen] was pleased by the prospect of causing such injury. . . .
>
> In this country the right of the people to complain to responsible governmental officials about the manner in which the complainant believes himself or herself to have been abused by public officials and other public employees is a fundamental, constitutional one expressly reserved to the people. The First Amendment, as we have seen, expressly reserves to the people the right "to petition the Government for redress of grievances." If that right is denied, our government will no longer be representative of the will of the people, which representation is the cornerstone of our republican form of government. . .
>
> [The police officer] probably feels that he has been maligned by [the citizen], and that the complaint was used . . . as a ploy to compel [the officer] to drop the charges. . . . Even if that be true, the constitutional right to petition cannot be made subservient to hurt feelings, bruised egos, or tarnished reputations. The First Amendment does not provide that only truthful petitions for redress may be filed.[30]

Maryland thus protects its citizens by eliminating sticky fact questions about their "truthfulness," "motives," "malice," or "intent." These quagmires, in which filers can sink motions to dismiss and extend the chill of the SLAPP through trial, are simply ruled out of order, allowing the merits of the case to be decided by an early judge-only motion.

California law, by contrast, contains a provision authorizing a peace officer to bring a defamation action against any citizen who files a police misconduct complaint if the complaint is (1) "false," (2) made "with knowledge that it was false," and (3) also made "with spite, hatred, or ill will."[31] California may be a leading civil rights jurisdiction that purports to encourage and protect civilian complaints, but this law drastically—perhaps unwittingly—negates that support, for every police officer would view his or her case as meeting those three criteria. They are, in short, not limits on but enticements to police SLAPPs and, by turning on fact questions, a barrier to their pretrial dismissal. It remains to be seen whether this unfortunate statute is effectively negated by California's 1992 "Anti-SLAPP Law" (see Chapter 10).

California's schizophrenia is illustrated by its leading cop SLAPP, *City of Long Beach v. Bozek*.[32] In 1974 Richard Bozek, complaining of a beating and false arrest, unsuccessfully sued the city and two of its police officers. Five years later the city and the two officers filed a $500,000 suit against Bozek for filing his suit. The California Supreme Court saw the constitutional implications of the case clearly enough:

> [Such a suit] would generate a potentially chilling effect of considerable dimension upon the exercise of the right to petition the government through the courts for a redress of grievances. . . .
>
> The right encompasses the act of filing a lawsuit solely to obtain monetary compensation for individualized wrongs, as well as filing suit to draw attention to issues of broader public interest or political significance. . . .
>
> If the courts were to condone the imposition of civil sanctions, even if only for statements made with actual malice, a severe chilling effect would result on the legitimate exercise of the right to express beliefs freely when those beliefs appear to be derogatory of the governing authorities. . . . [If such suits are allowed], the institution of legitimate as well as baseless legal claims will be discouraged. . . . The bringing of such suits against the government is absolutely privileged and cannot form the basis for imposition of [court] liability.[33]

Yet what did the California court actually do? It dismissed the city's half of the SLAPP against Bozek but allowed the policemen's portion to survive. The case survived Bozek as well, at least financially; it was finally discharged as a contingent debt when he went bankrupt.

Official Encouragement of Police SLAPPs

An even more pervasive and daunting problem is overt official and quasi-official support for police SLAPPs. Alan J. Azzara, an ACLU volunteer attorney in Mineola, a Nassau County suburb east of New York City, has defended a number of targets and reports that filing police SLAPPs was "part of a standard practice Nassau County police were engaged in [in the 1970s and 1980s], through the police [union]."[34] Such cases, he recalls, were routinely dismissed by the court and not appealed; their intent, he believes, was "to bring an end to the filing of [citizen] complaints" against police.

That practice may have ended in Nassau County, but there is nevertheless evidence of widespread official support for police SLAPPs.

- "Sure, there's a trend nationwide of police suing citizens who make false accusations against them," a California attorney representing some 20 police organizations admits.[35]
- The ACLU reports that the New York City police union "promise[d] to sue anyone who brought a police complaint that the civilian review board later found to be unsubstantiated."[36]

- Investigative journalist Eve Pell cites a number of such suits and their official encouragement and notes that a police publication, *Police Plaintiff,* keeps track of SLAPPs and reports on them.[37]
- A leader of the International Brotherhood of Police Officers (IBPO), the largest national union of police, makes no bones about it: "We were getting tired of people making false accusations against police officers. We had to go to court."[38]
- The editor of IBPO's magazine, *Police Chronicle,* concurs: "Oh sure, we've been encouraging our members to sue [citizen critics]. . . . We started fighting back right away; and where we have struck back, the number of police brutality complaints dropped sharply."[39] He attributes his union's success in attracting membership in part to the fact that it offers its 52,000 members free legal services.[40]
- In 1981, when a Dearborn, Michigan, couple filed suit alleging police brutality in a traffic case, not only did the policemen counter with a $10,000,000 SLAPP, but the chief of police himself served as their lawyer.[41] The SLAPP was dismissed only after targets left town and dropped their lawsuit against the police and city.

Society vests its police with "formidable power," as the courts have noted.[42] Police SLAPPs will continue as long as they receive a neutral response (let alone encouragement and financial support) from police higher-ups, government officials, and police associations, lawyers, and unions. Until these authorities and our laws and judges make it clear that such suits are unacceptable, they may well continue to censor the message by censuring the messengers.

The School SLAPP

> *One of the crosses a public school teacher must bear is intemperate complaint addressed to school administrators by overly solicitous parents concerned about the teacher's conduct in the classroom. Since the law compels parents to send their children to school, appropriate channels for the airing of supposed grievances against the operation of the school system must remain open.*
>
> —The California Court of Appeals in *Martin v. Kearney,* 51 Cal. App. 3d 309, 124 Cal. Rptr. 281, 283 (1975).

Our schools have always been a focus for controversy. Our children are precious to us, and few things more important than the values we want them to learn. What parent has not criticized his or her child's education at some point? What teacher has not felt his or her professional actions, academic freedom, or entire career threatened by an unjust complaint?

The disputes triggering SLAPPs in the schools range from the trivial to the titanic: from humiliation over a B+ to attacks on teacher incompetence, charges of racism, and outrage over religion.

School SLAPPs, like other types, follow a pattern. Parents develop a concern for their children's sake and report it to school authorities, expecting change. Then they are sued, usually by a teacher—although there is a subset of school SLAPPs not filed by teachers. A school bus company sued parents for complaining about unsafe brakes; a school board sued taxpayers for opposing a bond issue; a standardized test company sued parents for criticizing its test questions. Even teachers themselves have been sued for criticizing their school administration or union.

By far the most numerous school SLAPPs we found, however, were classic teacher-versus-parent lawsuits in which antagonism is fueled by a sense of powerlessness on both sides. Parents feel they are up against a system designed to preserve the status quo, but teachers also feel hamstrung and vulnerable, as pointed out by a lawyer who specializes in representing teachers (and who filed the *Cole v. Lehmann* suit discussed below):

> To say that anti-SLAPP reform [in schools] is merely a matter of returning issues to the "free marketplace of ideas" ignores the ability of sensational lies to gain media play and the power of organized campaigns to ruin individual careers and lives. . . . [Teachers] as [public] employees . . . may be handcuffed by the limits on their First Amendment rights and unable to take part in a no-holds-barred debate. Thus there is no "free market-place" or "level playing field" in such disputes.[43]

Parents win teacher SLAPPs most of the time (with some standout exceptions), as demonstrated by the following spectrum of cases, from the almost laughable contretemps over grades to community-polarizing disputes over race and religion. School SLAPPs show that no teacher, no matter how excellent, is immune to attack and that no parent who speaks out, no matter how justifiably, is immune to a SLAPP.

Appealing an Unappealing Grade

Question: How much difference is there between an A – and a B+? Answer: Enough for a four-year-long SLAPP. In Ann Arbor, Michigan, a disappointed Jonathan Martel came home from his high school honors English class in 1980 with a B+. Under the announced grading formula, his tests should have averaged an A–. When he tried to point out computation mistakes to his teacher, Dr. Marcia Swenson-Davis, she told him her decision was final; they had words, and the boy went home feeling "humiliated."[44]

Jonathan's physician father, Dr. William Martel, was incensed but pursued the complaint procedure set out in the school's "Fair Treatment Policy for Parents, Students and Employees of the School District" by first meeting informally with the teacher and her principal. The doctors locked horns: Swenson-Davis said the parent had "attempted to intimidate" her;[45] Martel said the teacher had engaged in "emotional behavior" and "precipitously walked out" of the meeting.[46] The father moved to the next step of the school's grievance procedure, filing a formal complaint with the principal. It accused the teacher of "unfairness, insensitivity, and unprofessional conduct."[47] Conceding that "the difference between A– and B+ is, indeed, small," he wrote, "[for my son] the issue is important and there is also a matter of principle here.... I would be remiss in my parental and civic responsibilities were I not to take this action" (a recurrent parental theme in teacher SLAPPs).[48] The outcome of the formal hearing that followed was almost laughably chicken-in-every-pot. In the student's favor, the hearing officer ruled that the teacher had been "insensitive" and had definitely miscalculated the grade.[49] In the teacher's favor, he ruled that she was "not unprofessional," and although he recommended that she "reconsider" the grade, he would not order it changed. The teacher did not appeal, but she felt marked by the administration as a "teacher who needs help" and soon was seeing a psychiatrist.[50]

That fall, the teacher sued the parent.[51] Swenson-Davis sought undisclosed damages for libel and intentional infliction of emotional distress, specifically identifying Martel's official complaint letter to school authorities as the cause.[52] Like the police unions, her teachers' union provided the funds for her lawyer. Caught in the middle, the Ann Arbor School Board made the tough and unusual decision to side with the parent (few schools take a position in teacher SLAPPs, we found). School authorities authorized their lawyers to intervene in the suit in support of Martel because of the need "to assert and defend the public's interest in the viability and integrity of [the school's] ... procedure for resolving complaints ... without fear of reprisal through a libel suit ... [whose] chilling effect ... nullifies ... open debate and reasoned, impartial conflict resolution."[53] School authorities feared that the effect of the SLAPP would spread: "Community members have expressed their concern ... that this lawsuit will have a chilling effect on parents' willingness ... to register legitimate complaints about teachers."[54]

The trial court dismissed the suit the court of appeals affirmed, and the state supreme court refused to reconsider, but the case consumed nearly four years in court. The appeals court majority ducked the constitutional issue, preferring to dismiss the case on the state law privilege for communications between parties who have a common interest. Irritated at this pusillanimous approach, one appeals judge separately wrote:

> It is patently ridiculous that courts should be required to countenance claims of libel and intentional infliction of emotional distress from everyday ordinary communication of the sort belabored in these proceedings. . . . This case should have been peremptorily dismissed on First Amendment grounds as containing free expressions of opinion. . . . We question the competence of our professionals daily in every conceivable form of communication and it is our absolute right to do so publicly in matters of opinion, let alone in the course of quasi-judicial school district complaint procedures. This matter should have received the shortest shrift possible: "However pernicious an opinion may seem, we depend for its correction not on the conscience of judges and juries but on the competition of other ideas."[55]

Another B in high school English got an even pushier Florida parent SLAPPed for $550,000 and an injunction.[56] In 1980 Joseph Nodar was upset that his son was making Bs rather than As and became "frustrated" in talking with two of his teachers.[57] For months thereafter the father telephoned school officials up and down the chain of command; he wrote to them, to the school board, and finally to the governor; and he spoke out at a school board meeting. His criticisms were blunt: The teachers had "victimized" his son, condoned cheating, were "unqualified," and were teaching "nothing that will enable these children to take an SAT test or any college examination."[58] The school board took no action, but a month later one of the teachers, Patricia Galbreath, sued Nodar for defamation.[59]

The teacher won the early rounds: the jury awarded her $10,000, and the court of appeals affirmed. In a stinging rebuke, however, the Florida Supreme Court "quashed" the verdict and tossed the case out, ruling that a parent has a constitutional privilege to criticize teachers as long as there is no "malice" involved. The months of irate phone calls, flood of letters, and invective at the public meeting were not enough, the Supreme Court ruled, to show "malice." Given this parent's verbal overkill, it is hard to imagine facts that would support a successful teacher SLAPP in Florida. Perhaps that is just the signal the Florida Supreme Court wanted to send.

The "Incompetent" Teacher

Carping about teacher competence may rank among the all-American pastimes, but it is not taken lightly by the criticized educator. Ten parents and students in Nassau County, New York, found this out the hard way in 1982 merely by signing a petition to a school board. The petition criticized East Norwich–Oyster Bay teacher Steven Weisman's conduct as "unsatisfactory,"alleging he had skipped class, struck a student, insulted a parent, threatened bodily harm to a female parent, accused a student of lying, and made ethnic slurs. The parents sent the petition to the school board and the local paper.

Within a month all the signers were defendants in a $450,000 libel suit brought by the teacher.[60] Had they not sent the petition to the newspaper, the SLAPP would have been over quickly, for Justice Beatrice S. Burstein correctly saw that the act of petitioning school officials had to be protected:

> The lines of communication between parents and school authorities must be kept free and open. Ever mindful that 'the threat of being put to the defense of a lawsuit . . . may be as chilling to the exercise of First Amendment freedoms as fear of the outcome of the lawsuit itself,' this Court holds that defendants' petition to the Board of Education is absolutely privileged.[61]

But despite her insight that a petition to school authorities was protected absolutely, the judge reasoned that the identical petition released to the public or the media was protected only if there was no "malice." Ignoring the "public interest" in the issue, the judge treated the identical petitions as two legally different items, depending upon who was reading it and, worse, placed the burden on the defendant parents to disprove their own "malice." Since their simple dismissal papers did not present volumes of facts proving lack of malice, the parents were bound over for trial on that issue alone. Here is another example of the catch-22 judicial reasoning: The judge recognized the importance of stopping the chill but blindly contributed to its continuance. In this case, it continued for six years before the parents eventually won summary judgment and the threat of trial was over.

California has been more protective of parents. Families in a Los Angeles suburb complained that the typing teacher was rude, abusive, and unfair in grading. When the teacher sued, both the trial and appeals courts made short work of the SLAPP by saddling the filing teacher, not the parents, with the burden of proving "malice" when the parents' moved to dismiss.[62] The teacher failed to prove malice, and the case was dismissed. Some courts avoid the "malice" quagmire by declaring an absolute immunity for critics of schools, regardless of motive. That is one way to avoid the long wait for a full-scale trial. Others, such as California and Colorado courts, place the burden of proof on the filer. Whichever side must (dis)prove a difficult, subjective fact issue can be expected to fail more often than not. Saddling SLAPP filers with the requirement that they demonstrate facts entitling them to continue seems logical and fair to a growing number of courts.

Racism, Schools, and SLAPPs

Racial issues have plagued our schools since the very beginning of public education in America.[63] From the *Plessy v. Ferguson*[64] "separate but equal" case of 1896 to the great school desegregation case of *Brown v. Board of Education*[65] and its progeny, issues of schools and race have been fought out in our courts. Perhaps it should come as no surprise that they sometimes manifest themselves in SLAPPs.

Dorothy Stevens, who is white, had been the principal of Mollison Elementary School in Chicago from the day it opened in 1962. By 1980 its student body had become predominantly black. That year Dorothy Tillman, an African American, was elected president of the Mollison PTA and

> launched the [PTA] on a crusade to remove Stevens as principal. Tillman and supporters occupied Stevens's office at the school for three days running and served her with an "eviction notice"; they organized a boycott that (they claimed) kept more than 80 percent of the students out of school; they distributed handbills, picketed the school, and delivered tirades against Stevens at meetings of the Board of Education.[66]

The campaign worked. Within months, Stevens was sent to another school; she would retire a few years later. Tillman, "by then a well-known figure,"[67] was elected to the Chicago City Council.

A few months after her removal the principal sued Tillman and nine other PTA parents for discrimination against her on the basis of her race, for defamation, and for interference with her contract.[68] The standard charges were based on targets' demonstrations, boycotts, and speeches, all of which had been aimed at getting the school board to act. Pretrial dismissal motions failed. In Chicago's crowded courts the case finally limped to trial in September 1986, nearly six years later. A few minor claims were dismissed, but the key civil rights and defamation charges went to a jury. In allowing the case to continue, the federal judge demonstrated one of the most difficult problems in dealing with SLAPPs quickly and effectively, a judge's "programming" against dismissing a case without a full-scale trial:

> The court . . . is uncomfortable with the prospect of deciding this constitutional issue based merely on the record before it. . . . The court abides by the settled prin-

ciple that if it has doubts about whether to grant a motion for [dismissal], the better practice is to deny the motion and let the jury return a verdict.[69]

When in doubt, this seems to say, protect a filer's right to sue, not a target's right not to be sued.

Ironically, the jury found that the parents had committed defamation yet awarded the principal only $1.00. She appealed but got no relief from the court of appeals. There, Judge Frank Easterbrook ruled that "accusations of 'racism' . . . [have] been watered down by overuse, becoming common coin in political discourse."[70] He concluded:

Stevens was a public official. . . . Her performance as a public official was open to public comment. . . . The statements in question either were made at meetings of the Board of Education or were part of a campaign to influence the Board. . . . [They] are equally protected. The first amendment prohibits efforts to ensure "laboratory conditions" in politics; speech rather than damages is the right response to distorted presentations and overblown rhetoric. A campaign to influence the Board of Education is classic political speech; it is direct involvement in governance, and only the most extraordinary showing would permit an award of damages on its account.[71]

This protection did not depend on whether the parent had been fair, truthful, or correct. In fact, Judge Easterbrook was critical of the target as well but did not let that sway his judgment: "No doubt Stevens suffered injury at Tillman's hands. No doubt Tillman's methods were crude. . . . The jury found that Tillman uttered quite a few falsehoods, and the discourse was neither dispassionate nor reasoned. . . . [But Tillman] was within her rights under the first amendment."[72]

In a very similar Massachusetts case,[73] a substitute physical education teacher SLAPPed members of a "Parents Council" appointed by the federal court to oversee desegregation of the Boston schools.[74] The parents had written school officials to demand dismissal of the white teacher because of a fight with a black student. Charges of racism again flew in both directions. The teacher was forced out, and she filed a $300,000 SLAPP for defamation. But she did not stop there. Her lawyers got a state judge to grant "attachment" of the targets' homes—an extraordinary procedure that ties up title and blocks any sale or mortgage of real estate; attachment is generally used only in extreme cases where a judge determines that the plaintiff is likely to win and the real estate is the only way the damages will be paid. In this instance, the federal court overseeing the school's desegregation snatched the case away from the state court, for interfering with desegregation, and dismissed it (together with the parents' nightmare of losing their homes) a little over one year later.

Religion, Schools, and SLAPPs

Certainly one of the most controversial issues facing education in America is the role of religion in the schools. The U.S. Supreme Court has generally ruled that like oil and water they are not to be mixed, but those rulings seem only to have fired the concern of some that schools are thereby teaching values not merely neutral but negative to their beliefs. Polarization between conservative, fundamentalist Christian parents and schools is a growing battlefield for minds and values and a perfect launching pad for teacher SLAPPs.

Northglenn, Colorado, a working-class suburb of Denver, provided a rich case study, combining a classic religion-in-school SLAPP, a truly "sympathetic" filer (like the hypothetical AIDS worker in Chapter 1), and a devastating loss for the target parents.[75] In 1984 William and Arlene Lehmann and their daughter Pam were members of the fundamentalist New Life Fellowship Church. Like any parents during the first week of school, they asked Pam about her new classes and teachers. Her report about one in particular raised their eyebrows. Pam informed her parents that teacher Jan Cole had engaged the class in "relaxation exercises," discussed "firewalking," and led students in confessing "bad things they had done" while holding hands in a circle.[76]

A veteran teacher at Malley Elementary, Jan Cole was highly respected by her peers and had never before had difficulty with parents.[77] She was also progressive and innovative and did engage her students in relaxation periods while listening to Vivaldi flute compositions, in visualizing scenes they were going to write about, and in discussing other cultures and their practices (including firewalking).[78] But Arlene Lehmann was alarmed by her daughter's reports:

> It was in my mind that this was some kind of exercise in hypnotism. . . . I was very concerned . . . because children are very susceptible. . . . My studies . . . indicated to me that hypnotism must develop out of a religious exercise used in Egypt and therefore had its roots in the occult religious practices, and I didn't feel it had a place in the classroom.

For the fundamentalist Lehmanns and others, relaxation resonated as "hypnotism," visualization as "projecting souls out of bodies," firewalking as "New Ageism," and flutes as "instruments of the Devil."[79] The Lehmanns requested a meeting with Cole and the principal; they were treated courteously but were given no indication that things would change. They promptly withdrew their daughter from Malley and enrolled her in a parochial school.

Meanwhile, in another New Life Fellowship family, Sandy Montoya's daughter Jessica came home with similar accounts of Jan Cole's class. The mother consulted her pastor, who put her in touch with the Lehmanns. The Montoyas and Lehmanns met, shared concerns, and agreed to work together, even though the Lehmanns' daughter was no longer in that school. During the winter and early spring of 1985 they contacted a number of conservative educators and religious groups. Among these was Bill Jack, state director of the Caleb Campaign, a fundamentalist Christian youth ministry concerned with school issues. Jack believed that it was "a matter of parents' rights to determine what is taught to their children."[80] He told the parents of "the threat of 'the New Age Movement' "—a liberal, one-world, all-religions-are-good ethic that he believed was sweeping the country—and he advised them that public school educators were in a "conspiracy" to indoctrinate children.

Sandy Montoya, the Lehmanns, and other parents, abetted by Jack, began a campaign of calls, writing, meetings with school officials, and door-to-door parent organizing about Cole's teachings and methods. When the accusations escalated to "witchcraft" and "satanism," the alarmed principal warned the parents against "slander."[81] The press had a field day sensationalizing the case: "Angry Parents Put Heat on Firewalking Holistic Instructor" read one headline.[82] Obviously, their campaign was not all nice, neat Petition Clause–protected activity. One incident, among many, that really rankled the pro-teacher forces was described by Cole's lawyer:

> Well after the Lehmann child was no longer in public school, Ms. Cole's class and others went to an outdoor education facility for an overnight trip. . . . Mrs. Lehmann called the camp director, himself a fundamentalist [and not a government official or employee], and told him that her child was coming [to] the camp, that Jan Cole was a satanist and that Mrs. Lehmann feared for the "safety" of the children. The camp director was alarmed and observed Ms. Cole closely. . . . He concluded the accusation was unwarranted [in fact, he testified for the teacher at the trial] and was not pleased he had been lied to about Mrs. Lehmann's child. On the other hand, he found Ms. Cole unguarded in how she expressed herself and thought she was easily misunderstood by these parents. . . . [Linking "satanism" with "safety"] implied much more than a religious dispute over a handful of teaching techniques.[83]

One of the major problems in this case was that the school district had no organized process or forum in which parents could air and educators defend against complaints about teachers[84] (such as the Ann Arbor schools, for example, used to good effect in *Swenson-Davis v. Martel,* discussed above). In June, however, the school did put together a hearing of sorts before its Policy Council Subcommittee on Controversial Issues (which had previously dealt only with textbooks). The subcommittee decided that the teacher should not give "holistic" health or medical advice to students, not engage students in meditation or yoga except with parental permission, and reconsider talking about her firewalking experiences; on the other hand, it determined that she was not teaching personal religious beliefs and that the rest of her actions were proper. The board of education reviewed the decision and concurred.[85] With some misgivings, the teacher accepted the decision, but the parents did not and stepped up their campaign.[86] Their unwillingness to accept the school's decision made further confrontation inevitable.

By the time of the hearing the teachers' union, the Colorado Education Association (CEA), had provided Cole with a lawyer—William Bethke, an experienced civil rights attorney—and was willing to bankroll her SLAPP. This evidenced a significant split between the state and national teachers' unions, as Bethke explains:

> [The National Education Association] would not give financial support to any slander or libel suit by a teacher against parents. In part this reflected failure in or backlash from previous suits. In part it was consistent with NEA's policy of pursuing the greatest possible degree of First Amendment freedom for teachers themselves. It was far more common for NEA to hear from teachers fired because they said something controversial than it was to hear teachers complaining about the controversial statements made by parents.[87]

Attorney Bethke himself was torn at first:

> For my part, the prospect of filing a defamation suit was unsettling. Personally, I was a near-absolutist on First Amendment issues and, in any event, I recognized the substantial barriers we would face both politically and legally. The CEA legal defense fund—made up mostly of teachers—had no such hesitation and authorized a suit.[88]

The CEA was willing to break ranks with the NEA rule for three reasons, according to Bethke. First, Colorado lacked mediating processes other than courts for teacher disputes, so litigation was "viewed by CEA as the ordinary process for resolving disputes"; second, recent cases had curtailed teachers' free speech rights on public issues,[89] making them feel that others should be under similar constraints; third, educators across the country were beginning to have "serious concern about the activities of the religious right," and Northglenn "was turning into a hotbed of religious right activity."[90] On September 4, 1985, the day the board of education formally adopted the hearing recommendations, the Cole suit was filed against the Lehmanns and Sandy Montoya.[91]

All the main actors seemed heavily influenced by others. What finally decided Jan Cole to sue? She states:

> There was a series of events, they just wouldn't stop, and the stuff in the classroom . . . every day I dealt with something about it. . . . My principal said, "You've got a lawsuit on your hands." And I said, "I don't want to sue anybody." And then he told me what was happening then to him because of it. I called my brother, who is an attorney in California, and he quietly said, "Sue."[92]

The pressure on Cole had been intense: she had spent several weeks thinking of suicide and had entered counseling.[93] Finally, she gave in and filed the lawsuit to "stand up, not only for my own self, but for other children's rights, and other parents' rights who didn't believe like [the Lehmans and Montoyas] did. And for academic freedom." Conversely, her attorney blames outsiders for putting pressures on the targets: "I don't think we should underestimate the extent to which the parents were influenced by their own religious advisers. . . . Their lawyers kind of took the back seat to the pastors and the advisers of a religious nature."[94] The targets, in turn, blame the teachers' union. Marlene Gresh, attorney for the Lehmanns, states: "I don't think the CEA should have funded a lawsuit. I think it was inappropriate . . . taking a position so adverse to the parents. The CEA should not take a position that parents voicing concerns of this nature should be sued."[95] But the union saw it as a major precedent, a test case, as one CEA spokesperson put it: "The methods of the teacher were questioned, elements of academic freedom [were] involved, and it apparently had some organized effort. It wasn't a parent filing a complaint. It was obviously an organized effort."[96]

Legal strategies were significant factors in the filer's win and the targets' loss. Filer attorney Bethke's strategy was to keep the case narrowly focused on the parents' untrue or defamatory statements outside the hearing process and the resulting harm to the teacher.[97] The targets played right into his hands: they wholly failed to seize the high ground by claiming that constitutional issues and political rights were at stake. Instead, the parents backtracked on the "satanism" and other extreme statements, insisting that they had been misunderstood, though refusing a complete retraction.[98] They forfeited the chance to "retransform" the case. Playing the hand they were dealt, the targets' attorneys' relied on narrow, nonconstitutional state law issues, only to see their motions to dismiss denied. That strategy cost them the case.

On March 20, 1987, the jury returned a verdict for Jan Cole, awarding her $110,500 in compensatory and punitive damages ($83,000 against the Lehmans and $27,500 against Montoya). The parents appealed, still on technical, nonconstitutional law grounds. At that point, Concerned Women of America became involved in Montoya's defense and her appeals brief for the first time finally raised her constitutional rights, including the Petition Clause. But it was too late. To her dismay, her insurance company insisted on settling the case with Cole for $10,000, before the appeal was decided. "It was a matter of economics," she believes; had she refused to settle, the insurance company said it would stop paying for her defense.[99] The Lehmanns' appeal also resulted in an out-of-court settlement by their insurance company.

This is one of the few known devastating jury verdicts against targets. Why did the teacher win? What made this SLAPP so unusual? Several lessons stand out. First, the parents' campaign made the teacher's First Amendment rights and career appear to be under attack, so "her suit looked like an effort to 'defend' herself, even though she was taking the offensive."[100] Second, one of the reasons we argue that misstatements and even lies should not take away the Petition Clause protection is that once such a case is allowed to go to trial, it is predictable that a judge or jury will react negatively to such unappealing actions. Third, although we argue that even non-petitioning activity deserves protection if it is an integral part of the overall petitioning effort, when a filer's attorney focuses, as here, only on "the least protected, most outrageous statements,"[101] courts will often succumb to the catch-22 of protecting some but not all actions—and it takes only one for the filer to win. Last, and perhaps most important, this is one of the few times we have seen targets literally throw away their First Amendment defense by denying having made the statements; failure to retransform is fatal.

What was the fallout of this case? The parents are still frightened to talk about it. They expressed "fear" and "intimidation," and our interviews with them several times stopped in tears. Fundamentalist Bill Jack confirms: "The parents are still frustrated and concerned, but they don't want to speak. So is justice served? No. Justice came out perverted." The psychological chill was augmented by the financial one, as Arlene Lehmann reported:

> It's been hard on us financially. We have to scrape and scrimp to get a loan to keep our house secure. Our [catering] business has suffered from it on account of our parties have gone down from the schools that are friends with [Cole's principal]. . . . So, it has hurt us financially. . . . If we ultimately lose, we may lose our home.

Moreover, the chill was community-wide, according to the targets' attorney Marlene Gresh: "My very cynical viewpoint of the result of this case is that it shut up parents. And they have very effectively done that. They have shut up parents in Adams County." Bill Jack agrees:

There were [other] such parents [with similar concerns], but they were intimidated by the lawsuit. . . . [I]t had a chilling effect on the entire community. Any parent who now wishes to voice objections to . . . techniques they find offensive to them personally, or objectionable, or poor teaching techniques, in the backs of their minds they're thinking, "I'm not going to speak because I'll get sued."

But Bethke, the filer attorney, sees it very differently:

Notably, filing [the case] did not stop the actions against Jan Cole, though it did change their character. The [three] named defendants stopped making public comments. But several parents who had not been sued began an intrusive process of observing Jan's classroom, taking notes, day after day. . . . Ms. Cole told me recently that the 1993–94 school year was the first one in which there were no significant problems with parents since 1984–85. In other words, despite the suit, parents have been complaining about Ms. Cole, year after year, for a full decade.[102]

Montoya's religious willingness to do it again supports that

I would go through the whole same thing again, because I can stick by my beliefs, and my rights. I mean it's got to start and stop some place. And I refuse to let somebody intimidate me [so] that I can't do anything. I mean, this is supposed to be America, land of the free. Why can't I say something without fear of reprisal like this? But, if that's the cost, fine. I'll go down that road.

Filer Jan Cole seems to have suffered most of all:

It has been the most painful experience of my life, and the most draining, just because it's gone on for years. And the hard thing, it took me a whole year just to accept what was happening. I didn't understand. I just didn't understand. And it's like the death of yourself. I was suicidal for a while. . . .

If I ran for President of the United States, I would expect criticism . . . but as a teacher you're usually sensitive, caring. . . . And this hurts a lot. I mean, we aren't set up politically to take this sort of thing. . . . I mean, all of my belief systems were challenged, and I'm still in limbo about a lot of things.

In this instance, moving the religion-in-schools debate from the public political arena into the courts appears to have left only victims. Another case involving unsympathetic parents ended differently. A Memphis, Michigan, life science teacher and one of her pupils filed a $1,000,000 SLAPP against parents who complained to the school board about the teacher's sex education class.[103] The parents' role "was not a pretty one," and the school board "panic[ked]" and fired the teacher, according to U.S. Court of Appeals.[104] Nevertheless, the court threw out a jury verdict against the parents, because the case violated their constitutional right to petition. The court justly left the unsupportive school district to pay for the teacher's demonstrated suffering.

Standardized testing provoked a SLAPP in Texas when some students complained to their parents that the questions were anti-Christian and anti-patriotic. The parents' request to see the tests was denied on the basis of a confidentiality agreement with the test publishing company, Riverside Publishing. After the parents lost a state court battle to enjoin the tests, Riverside sued them in federal court for "patent infringement," alleging that the parents had printed pamphlets revealing some of its questions.[105]

The religion-in-schools fight may be only warming up. In hundreds of school districts across the nation, according to education, "vigorous campaigns" are underway to control what students read, what courses they take, and what teachers teach.[106] Conservative religious groups call for more "parental involvement" and "respect,"[107] while their liberal opponents cry "censorship" and complain of "attacks on the freedom to learn."[108] Conservative school watchdog groups sponsor training sessions for parents on how to fight secular humanism, global education, sex education, evolution, situational ethics, drugs, and "immoral behavior"; how to influence or get elected to school boards; and how to change school curricula.[109] According to the leader of one such group: "We get local people involved. Parents should have a voice."[110] We can expect religion-in-school SLAPPs to escalate, the louder and more effective those "voices" become.

Other School-Related SLAPPs

Parents may be sued for criticizing any aspect of schools, not just teachers and books. In a SLAPP that takes the prize for gall, a Pennsylvania school bus company sued 68 parents for $680,000 because they filed safety complaints with the school board.[111] Over several years, parents in the Johnstown area had been hearing from their children of frequent school bus breakdowns, loss of wheels, flames shooting out of the steering column, broken turn signals, even loss of brakes.[112] They circulated a petition asking the school board to "conduct an immediate investigation" and "begin negotiations as soon as possible with other [bus companies]."[113] The bus company immediately sued every signing parent, citing "the . . . petition to the . . . School District . . . and to various other state agencies and officials" as an act of defamation. A more literal assault on the right to petition could hardly be conjured up. The court agreed and, a year later, dismissed the suit for violating "the citizen's right to petition the government for redress of grievances."[114] The court's decision pinpointed the illogic of SLAPPs when there is a more appropriate, nonjudicial forum in which a filer could exonerate itself: "Urging an investigation, in which the government may independently evaluate and redress the claims, is precisely the kind of exercise which the First Amendment is designed to protect."[115] The bus company did not appeal.

An Ohio school district filed a $494,582 SLAPP against the leader of the PTA and his attorneys for challenging in court the legality of a bond issue.[116] Some six and a half years later the court dismissed the SLAPP, on technical grounds, just as it was to go to trial.

Teachers themselves can get SLAPPed for exercising their rights to petition. Professors at West Texas State University used a campus newspaper to criticize their university president (a public official) to government higher-ups and the public, whereupon the president sued his professors.[117] The president quickly rethought his position and dismissed the lawsuit two months later, but the chill remained. In Massachusetts the teachers' union sued a public school teacher for $50,000 for "deformatory" [*sic*] statements.[118] The target teacher had been campaigning to get rid of the union by urging other teachers to report union violations to the state labor commission[119]—classic Petition Clause–protected activity. Again, the filer thought better of it and voluntarily dismissed after only two and a half weeks.

Solutions

School SLAPPs, like all SLAPPs, stem from citizens' willingness to bring their problems to the open, public forums that authorities provide for dispute resolution. In some schools, however, a mediation forum is either nonexistent, inadequate, unsupportive, or, worse, threatening to one side or the other. That deficiency drives parents to engage in protests other than petitioning and drives teachers to remove the dispute to a judicial forum.

Surprisingly, teachers who sue their critics appear to generate less judicial sympathy than do the police; at least more of the police SLAPPs we found survived and resulted in legal victories for filers. Judges seem to express more shock and outrage that a teacher would sue parents than that a police officer would sue accused lawbreakers. The real world consequences, to the extent we can trace them, also seem less favorable to teachers: More teachers than police officers seem to feel hurt, unvindicated, and victimized afterward.

Two things are certain: The parental instinct to protect children and their own values guarantees continued pressure on our schools; and the greater that pressure, the more academics will be tempted, in Jan Cole's words, to "stand up for their rights" by filing SLAPPs. The solution we see from studying the cases is for all involved—schools, teachers, unions, parents, PTAs, and courts—to "trust the system." First, schools must provide effective forums for dispute resolution and then insist that parents and teachers respect them and confine themselves to them, as the Ann Arbor schools did. Second, "outside" pressure groups such as teachers' unions, parent-teacher associations, and religious bodies should refuse to support actions by parents or lawsuits by educators that circumvent or weaken the public mediation system, following the example of the National Education Association. Finally, the courts need to do their share by refusing to become arbiters of school-parent problems through the "back door" of personal injury, money-demanding SLAPPs, as the U.S. Court of Appeals in Chicago and the Florida Supreme Court have done. Working in this way, schools, parents, other concerned groups, and courts can solve disputes without resorting to lawsuits that infringe on constitutional rights.

The Public Official SLAPP

> *[We have] a profound national commitment to the principle that debate on public issues should be uninhibited, robust, and wide-open, and that it may well include vehement, caustic and sometimes unpleasantly sharp attacks on government and public officials.*
>
> —The U.S. Supreme Court in *New York Times v. Sullivan,* 376 U.S. 254, 270 (1964)

> *[County officials] seek to muzzle defendant by haling him into court and requiring him to defend a position he asserts in public. Only the deliberately ignorant would consider involuntary submission to litigation to be less intrusive into the sphere of constitutional freedom than meek submission to a direct order. Like the auto da fe, litigation lasts longer and is more painful than mere silence.*
>
> *. . . In publicly voicing his objections to [the county's actions], defendant has engaged in the most protected and encouraged form of expression known in this country. [The U.S. Supreme] Court has recognized that expression on public issues "has always rested on the highest rung of . . . First*

> *Amendment values." "[S]peech concerning public affairs is more than self-expression; it is the essence of self-government." There is a "profound national commitment" to the principle that "debate on public issues should be uninhibited, robust, and wide-open."*
>
> *. . . By instituting this lawsuit, [the county] has impermissibly sought to chill, indeed freeze, defendant's protected political speech because of his disagreement with [the county's] activities. . . . I find this suit to be frivolous, groundless and vexatious. . . .*
>
> —U.S. District Judge John Kane
> in *Board of County Commissioners of Adams County v. Shroyer,*
> 662 F. Supp. 1542, 1544–46 (D. Colo. 1987).

SLAPPs filed by police officers, teachers, and other public employees certainly raise gripping concerns. But even worse are those filed by elected and appointed public officials: governors and legislators, mayors and county commissioners, government attorneys and judges, and all the other federal, state, and local government leaders. Are these not the exact decision-makers with whom the First Amendment encourages us to communicate? Is not informing, influencing, supporting, and even "vehemently attacking" these officials "the essence of self-government," as the Supreme Court and Federal Judge Kane remind us? If our own government officials lash back with lawsuits against their citizens/voters/taxpayers, the very people the First Amendment directs to listen are attacking those it encourages to speak. The early nineteenth-century SLAPPs were of this type: citizens were sued for complaining to their governors or legislatures about corrupt sheriffs, justices of the peace, and the like (see Chapter 2). The courts made short work of those suits, but public official SLAPPs have come back with a vengeance, even though the citizens have typically done no more than stand up and criticize the officials' policies, programs, or practices. Is this not then the *ultimate* ultimate SLAPP?

We see two overlapping types of politician SLAPPs. In the first and simplest form the citizens criticize the conduct, competence, or criminality of specific officials, and those officials file a SLAPP. These cases span the spectrum of sympathy, from those exposing out-and-out government crooks to those in which the citizens' criticisms appear very unjust. One of these latter—sympathetic official versus unsympathetic citizen—led to the famous (and mishandled) *McDonald v. Smith* (discussed in Chapter 2). In the second and more complex form, citizens criticize a government-supported project or plan, and the government responds with a SLAPP. These cases involve everything from projects for clean water to proposals for dealing with toxic waste; from jails, airports, and nuclear plants to the Equal Rights Amendment. Here the citizens are uniformly viewed as "obstructionists," no matter how much more thoughtful their campaigns than the government's logrolling and pork-barreling. In court, the citizen-targets appear to win or achieve dismissal of the majority of both types of politician SLAPPs. Far more problematic, in the real world it seems that targets lose and government filers win a disproportionate amount of the time. On the other hand, politicians are taking a huge risk in SLAPPing, because this can lead to the hardest-hitting of all SLAPPbacks, a citizen suit under the Civil Rights Act (as discussed in Chapter 9).

Fingering Graft, Greed, and Grievances

Criticizing our politicians may be another all-American pastime, but it can quickly backfire into the "wronged official" SLAPP, as a classic Pennsylvania case shows. Growth in Towamencin Township, just north of Philadelphia, was "frozen" on August 9, 1984, by a state-imposed building ban, because the township's overloaded sewage treatment plant was flooding homes, streets, and nearby streams with raw sewage. After the announcement, however, residents learned that 83 more building permits had mysteriously been issued, each dated August 8, the day before the ban took effect. Among those who stormed into the next township supervisors' meeting and charged officials with illegally "backdating" the permits to help developers circumvent the ban was Robert Smith, president of the Concerned Citizens Association, a civic watchdog group. In a heated debate with the township's attorney, Frank Jenkins, Smith insisted, "You should have told [the building inspector] to date them [August] 14th instead of the 8th." Three months later Jenkins sued Smith for slander because of that one word—"you."[120]

Smith was shocked by the suit, since by then township officials had admitted that they had falsified the permits to avoid the ban and had been fined $14,000 by the state.[121] Smith also admitted to being intimidated by his adversary, who was a government attorney, former state legislator, former county commissioner and sheriff, and upcoming chair of the county Republican Party. Worse, Smith discovered that the judge assigned to the case was Jenkins's former law partner and the former town attorney who had actually approved the eighty three permits.[122] Smith felt the suit was

> definitely an attempt to try to silence and threaten the Concerned Citizens or anyone else from speaking up at Towamencin meetings . . . to take away the freedom of speech and expression at any public meeting, which is every American's con-

> stitutional right. It is frightening to realize that a solicitor of a municipality could threaten and intimidate citizens with a nuisance lawsuit to control and silence free speech. . . . I fought in World War II for just this reason—to be able to stand up in a public meeting in the United States without getting shot or sued![123]

Jenkins denied that this was his aim; instead, like many filers, he claimed that the case was appropriate vindication for false accusations: "I've taken a lot, and I don't have to take that."[124]

Smith filed an answer, moderating his meeting statement somewhat: by "you," he said, he meant Jenkins's law firm collectively, not Jenkins individually.[125] Later that year the state supreme court removed the judge from the case as a "material witness" and transferred the lawsuit to another county. Then, in 1987, less than two months before the trial date, Jenkins dismissed his suit. In one interview he said he dropped it because Smith's original answer was a "retraction";[126] in another he said he didn't want to "waste the time of the township employees," and his own, driving to court in another county.[127]

The SLAPP was over. Smith, who spent over $10,000 defending against it, professed to be undaunted, and his government watchdog group was still active. But he was worried: Jenkins remained a political power in the county, and "a lot of people are afraid to talk up these days."[128] Because "someone has to file a retaliatory lawsuit to show that this is not fair,"[129] Smith then turned the tables: He filed a $150,000 federal court SLAPPback against Jenkins for "interfering with, chilling, and denying" his constitutional rights.[130]

Town Attorney Jenkins's SLAPP was no isolated instance; government attorneys seem to thrive on suing their constitutents. For example, a Texas SLAPP exploded after Brewster County citizens complained about some of their officials, including the county attorney. Biding her time, the county attorney waited two years and then in 1991, after resigning, sued the citizens.[131] Although she dropped the suit two months later, she has maintained the right to refile it at any time, thus keeping the chill alive.[132]

The borough attorney in Slippery Rock, Pennsylvania, sued a local husband and wife for slander.[133] The couple had testified at a borough meeting that the attorney should be fired for conflict of interest because he was "one of the biggest landlords in the borough" (and also was suing them on a busted land deal).[134] After two years, both his SLAPP and the targets' SLAPPback were dismissed. Similarly, the Deerpark, New York, town attorney sued a junkyard operator[135] for sending letters to town officials, the bar association, and a local newspaper claiming that the attorney should disqualify himself from advising on the junkyard's permits, since they were already suing each other over a real estate deal.[136] The target countered with a SLAPPback; the trial court dismissed both cases; and the appeals court affirmed three years later.

Government officials other than attorneys also SLAPP their share of citizens. In 1990 a New York county supervisor sued several of his constituents for defamation because they questioned his "unconventional" land dealings and asked the district attorney to investigate.[137] The trial court sided with the targets, dismissing the case and ordering the politician to pay their attorneys' fees; the appeals court affirmed, ending the SLAPP in a little over three years. When the commissioners of North Versailles Township, near Pittsburgh, approved construction of a candy factory in a residential neighborhood, an affected resident called them "criminal" at a township meeting, and they sued him for $50,000.[138] The citizen countered with a civil rights violation SLAPPback;[139] the commissioners folded and dismissed their lawsuit, and the township's insurance company paid a $10,000 settlement to the citizen.[140] A defense contractor was sued by a federal employee for sending a letter critical of his management to his government superiors. The trial court granted the target a directed verdict (a verdict ordered by the judge because the party with the burden of proof failed to prove its case) affirmed on appeal.[141]

We also found a number of cases in which those seeking government positions—the "wannabes" of politics—SLAPPed those opposing their appointment or election. In a virtual replay of *McDonald v. Smith* (see Chapter 2), a candidate for New Hampshire Commissioner of Health and Welfare sued a local resident for $250,000 for writing to state officials that he was "scandal-tainted" and "incompetent," that he "disregard[ed] the law" and had a "weakness for . . . vested interests."[142] The citizen finally won a jury verdict and was dismissed, but the appointment went through.

In 1992, opponents of a judge up for reelection in a southern Colorado county wrote letters to the editor turning the judge's name, Keohane, into "Cocaine" and calling him "the best judge money can buy." After losing the election, the judge sued 13 of his detractors; he won a $20,000 verdict against the most vocal, a city councilman, but lost against all the rest.[143] The widespread practice of "rating" judges up for election has made even powerful bar associations SLAPP targets. In one example, a losing candidate sued the Los Angeles County Bar Association for rating him "unqualified" in its election report to the voters.[144] The trial court dismissed the case with dispatch, and the dismissal was affirmed on appeal.

Opposing Public Works Projects

If the foregoing cases suggest that politicians become SLAPP-happy when their personal reputations are attacked, observe them when their favorite projects, programs, plans, or pork barrels are criticized. These "government-project" SLAPPs are triggered by citizen opposition to dams, toxic waste incinerators, utilities, jails, roads, airports—even proposed lion hunts. One of the earliest presented us with a rich in-depth study: the case of *City and County of Denver Acting by and Through Its Board of Water Commissioners v. Andrus.*[145]

In the arid West, "making the desert bloom" has been a pioneer philosophy for so long it approaches religion—but not a peaceful one. As the western adage goes, "Whiskey is for drinkin'; water's for fightin'," and for 150 years those fights have ended up in court.

The Denver Water Board, a huge government agency responsible for the City and County of Denver's water supply, has frequently been at the center of controversy as it has spun its network of dams, reservoirs, and pipelines throughout the South Platte River Basin, even spanning the Continental Divide to import Colorado River Basin water from western Colorado. In the 1950s, foreseeing the metropolitan area's growth, the board began planning for the new Foothills Treatment Plant southwest of the city. Designed to double the amount of water Denver could treat, the plant would necessitate new dams and diverted rivers. Although one would scarcely expect objections to pure drinking water, Foothills became a symbol of the "big dam era," over which many would go to war. To the Denver Water Board and its allies (state and local government officials and water-short suburban real estate developers), Foothills symbolized the duty to assure adequate water supplies to meet the inevitable growth of the metro area. To local environmentalists and their allies (national environmental groups and some federal officials), it symbolized the converse: a huge water buildup that would not only devastate pristine mountain environments but would itself fuel unbridled urban growth. The stage was set for an immensely bitter "chickens and eggs" debate over the relationship of water and growth in a semiarid region. The two sides, it seems, had opposite interpretations of the phrase "living within our environmental means."

The board's 1950s plans prompted two decades of relatively innocuous land acquisition and designing. Little controversy surfaced until the passage of the National Environmental Policy Act of 1969 (NEPA)[146] required federal agencies to prepare detailed environmental impact studies (EISs) on major federal actions significantly affecting the quality of the environment. Foothills was a city project, but Denver needed rights-of-way over federal land managed by the U.S. Bureau of Land Management (USBLM) and U.S. Forest Service (USFS) and a permit from the U.S. Environmental Protection Agency (USEPA), and that meant complying with

NEPA. In 1974, when the board applied for an extension of an existing right-of-way, USBLM announced that NEPA required it to study the whole Foothills project before approval. A draft EIS was released in 1976, but, following highly critical public hearings, chagrined Washington officials conceded its inadequacy and withdrew it. A new EIS study was laboriously started in February 1977. One month later the frustrated Denver Water Board filed a "reverse NEPA" lawsuit, demanding a court ruling that NEPA had already been complied with and that federal approval was required.[147] Its first complaint (of the *five* it would eventually file) named only federal agencies and officials as defendants; the suit was not yet a SLAPP.

The newly appointed USEPA regional administrator, Alan Merson, was a long-time Colorado political figure and environmentalist. He opposed the project for two reasons:

> One was . . . the direct environmental effects of the project. The damming of the South Platte River and the effects on a free-flowing stream, . . . a high-quality coldwater trout fishery . . . of considerable value recreationally. . . . [The second was] what is the justification for it? . . . [It] didn't appear terribly persuasive because . . . the water was going for lawn watering. Denver had not appeared to have made any kind of serious conservation effort. . . . Denver's need for the water . . . didn't seem to overbalance the environmental damage, . . . [which] had to be viewed in terms not only of what would happen in the canyon but in terms of the secondary impacts, . . . the growth impacts of bringing in water . . . in southwestern Denver.[148]

Environmentalists saw an even more frightening prospect. They viewed the treatment plant as just a "foot in the door" for a long-feared Denver Water Board project just upstream: the Two Forks Dam.[149]

From the board's perspective, however, its ability to provide adequate water supplies was being compromised by federal government and environmentalist know-nothings. As the board's attorney, Jack Ross, complained, "One of the frustrations about the whole controversy . . . [was] non-utility people attempting to tell utility professionals how to do their business. . . . The federal agencies . . . don't know utility operations. . . . The people who opposed the project were not utility people."[150] Board employees such as Ed Ruetz went to great lengths to douse the "water fuels growth" and "Two-Forks-dam/foot-in-the-door" arguments:

> Some of the objection . . . was in anticipation of some day a Two Forks being built. [It was an] anti-growth attitude. There was a very simple little syllogism [used by environmentalists], very invalid . . . but nonetheless . . . popular and very con-

vincing. . . . It went something like this: Population growth in the Denver area is bad for the environment. Right? . . . The only way this town is going to grow is if it has enough water. Right? Shut off the water and you stop growth. Right? Wrong![151]

Meanwhile, a new draft EIS was produced, and more vitriolic public hearings were held in the fall of 1977. The board's lawsuit against the federal government was assigned to U.S. District Court Chief Judge Fred Winner, who—in a development we have seen elsewhere—urged the board's attorneys to combine "all interested parties" in the suit, presumably so that the issues regarding Foothills could all be controlled in one action. The Denver Water Board would later assert that it included the environmental defendants "at the strong suggestion of the court."[152] So, in an amended complaint filed in February 1978, the board added as defendants four local and national environmental groups and three local citizens, solely because in the federal government NEPA hearings they "had testif[ied]" and "submitted written comments" opposing the project.[153] Now the case had become a SLAPP. Six months later, other environmental groups filed a nonmonetary lawsuit against the federal government in Washington, D.C., challenging the legal adequacy of the final Foothills EIS. Water Board lawyers promptly added these groups too as defendants in the Denver case,[154] bringing the total to 14 groups and four individual environmentalists.

How did the board determine what environmentalists to sue? Attorney Ross stated candidly: "Well, it isn't hard to do. All you do is listen to people who complain about [Foothills]. That's how you identify [defendants]." Individuals and groups, with their files, were subpoenaed by the board for sworn depositions.[155] Targets, despite being experienced political advocates, were frightened and outraged that they could be grilled and their files gone over, simply because they had participated in federal government hearings on the project.

At this point, U.S. Representative (later U.S. Senator) Tim Wirth offered to mediate the dispute, and the Colorado ACLU agreed to represent the targets who wanted out (some wanted to stay in and fight). Judge Winner, in two separate hearings in December 1978, denied dismissal, and an emergency appeal was not acted on by the Tenth Circuit U.S. Court of Appeals. Two months later, in February 1979, all parties agreed to a settlement, through Congressman Wirth's mediation. The board appeared the big winner: The settlement canceled both lawsuits, approved the EIS, and allowed Denver to proceed with construction of the first phase of the Foothills plant.

Why did the environmentalists settle? One of the targets, John Bermingham, a former Republican state legislator and former chair of the State Land Use Commission, cited two reasons: "We were running out of money to pay the lawyers. . . . And then there was political pressure through the offices of Tim Wirth, Congressman, to settle the thing."[156] Target Bob Weaver of Trout Unlimited admitted to a third reason:

> We had become very isolated politically. All the members of the congressional delegation, the governor, everybody at the time had decided to support the Foothills project, . . . even [politicians] who were our friends. . . . Politically, the [board] had developed a very strong coalition . . . of metropolitan area governmental entities and developers. . . . Politically you can't afford to go against it. I think Tim Wirth was the same way.[157]

All the environmentalists got, according to one bitter defendant, was "out." Still, targets did get three precedent-setting commitments from the board: to undertake a water conservation program, to expand the citizens' role in future water decisions, and to apologize for the SLAPP:

> The [Denver Water Board and its members] hereby recognize that the environmental defendants have asserted their opposition to . . . Foothills . . . in good faith and within their Constitutional and statutory rights. The Denver Water Board and its members assert that they joined these environmental defendants at the strong suggestion of the court in good faith and without any intent to interfere with their constitutional and statutory rights. [We] . . . now recognize that . . . the environmental defendants are not proper parties to this litigation.[158]

Judge Winner did not approve of the settlement; even though he agreed to dismiss the case at the board's request, he would not sign the agreement.[159]

The Foothills case is a clear example of a government filer winning both in court and in the real world. These proved costly victories for Denver, however, leading a decade later to the defeat of its next big project. In the 1980s, as environmentalists had feared, the Water Board proceeded with plans for the massive Two Forks Dam on one of the state's finest blue-ribbon trout streams, southwest of Denver. The dam was opposed by much the same coalition, but this time its older and wiser members were more effective in wooing political support away from the board early on. In a surprise coup they persuaded the just-installed George Bush administration to veto federal support for Two Forks early in 1989. No SLAPPs have been filed or threatened, and the Two Forks plan remains a casualty of the water wars today.

Opponents of various other public works projects and schemes have been sued by government officials, with varied results. In 1988 a western Colorado county denied two Denver suburbs a permit for their proposed water export project in a wilderness area.[160] The thirsty suburbs then sued the county and also named as defendants several environmental groups, an association of commercial river rafting companies, a ski area, and a county historical society simply for testifying against their project at the county hearings. The targets all elected to stay in the fight, and they won: The Colorado Court of Appeals upheld the county's ban on dams, and the Colorado Supreme Court denied further review in June 1995.[161]

In 1992 the San Joaquin Hills Transportation Corridor Agency was preparing to build California's first toll road and sued the environmental groups who objected that a required environmental impact study had not been prepared. The road-builders lost all around: The trial court dismissed the SLAPP and ruled that the EIS was needed before the project could go forward.[162]

Incineration plants, like lightning, have struck a number of times. Across the bay from San Francisco, the West Contra Costa Sanitary District filed a $42,000,000 SLAPP against critic-in-residence Alan LaPointe and 490 unnamed "John Does" for opposing the district's plans for a massive waste-burning and energy-generating plant in 1988.[163] LaPointe had prompted two grand jury criminal investigations of the district, given adverse testimony before government agencies, and filed a test-case lawsuit to reform district practices; these acts the suit characterized as interference with prospective economic advantage and conspiracy to interfere. The California attorney general intervened in support of LaPointe, as did the media.[164] The trial court dismissed, awarding LaPointe $23,000 in attorneys' fees, and LaPointe filed a successful SLAPPback (see Chapter 9). In 1989 two upstate New York counties sued scores of their own citizen-taxpayers who had filed a court challenge against county revenue bonds being used to finance a waste-to-energy plant; the counties SLAPPed them with a $1,500,000 counterclaim.[165] Burnt by the adverse publicity and scathing editorials,[166] one county sheepishly backed out of the suit, but it took two years and the court of appeals to pull the plug on the other.

In 1984 a governmental rural electric utility in Colorado filed a $1,200,000 countersuit against some of its own member-consumers (see Chapter 7) who had filed a test case to oust the incumbent directors and reform the utility's practices. The directors' SLAPP was in the courts for five years; the targets won technical victory after victory, but the filers ultimately won in the real world by grinding down their opponents and maintaining control of the utility.

To promote voter approval and lure the new Denver International Airport, Adams County funded a promotional campaign. A local political gadfly called the use of public funds "illegal" in public meetings and media statements. The county commissioners sued the citizen, prompting the outraged dismissal by U.S. District Judge John Kane, quoted above.[167]

After imposing a moratorium on mountain lion hunting for 16 years, in 1988 California officials wanted to lift it and allow nearly 200 of the animals to be killed. All the Mountain Lion Preservation Foundation did was testify in government hearings against lifting the ban, but that was enough to spur the state Department of Fish and Game to sue it, ostensibly to "resolve the issue," but media and political outrage peppered the state agency into dropping the case.[168] Two years later, targets and other wildlife advocates succeeded in passing Proposition 117, banning mountain lion hunting in California, but in October 1995 Governor Pete Wilson signed a bill putting it back on the ballot, reopening the risk of SLAPPs.[169]

Politician SLAPPs do not always concern the government's own projects; sometimes the government tries to protect private business ventures by SLAPPing their critics. Probably the most notorious of these cases occurred when the National Organization of Women urged a convention boycott in Missouri until the legislature approved the Equal Rights Amendment.[170] The state of Missouri sued, calling the boycott a restraint of trade and intentional infliction of economic harm on Missouri tourist businesses; NOW called it legitimate political lobbying. NOW won. The trial court granted pretrial dismissal, the appeals court affirmed, and the U.S. Supreme Court let the dismissal stand. NOW then filed a SLAPPback against the state for interference with its constitutionally protected political rights.[171] But both sides lost: NOW failed to get enough votes for the ERA, and Missouri had to pay a confidential settlement to get NOW to drop its countersuit.

Antinuclear demonstrators protesting the Diablo Canyon power plant in San Luis Obispo County, California, got nuked themselves with two massive SLAPPs.[172] A conservative legal foundation, pronuclear groups, and plant employees spearheaded the suits against the demonstrators. When the first SLAPP was thrown out of court, the plaintiffs persuaded the county to sue the protesters for the costs of police protection and cleanups caused by their demonstration.[173] That SLAPP was also dismissed, and filers were ordered to pay $20,000 in attorneys' fees to the protesters for a frivolous appeal.

In sum, SLAPPs by public officials cover the entire gamut of political issues and are virtually an index of current events. Significantly, we found them most prevalent at the local government level. State-filed political SLAPPs are few, and federal political SLAPPs almost nonexistent. This tracks a key finding: the great majority of SLAPPs are filed by locals against locals, suggesting that they are not a strategy most Goliaths need.

Though not notably successful in court, politician SLAPPs clearly do discourage citizens who, expecting to remain in the political arena, find their legitimate political comment a magnet for high-cost court entanglement. The chill on politically active Americans, as well as on others who might contemplate public involvement, is palpable, even among the most resolute. No one condones intemperate and untruthful citizen demagoguery, but SLAPPs as a cure are worse than the disease. Lawsuits do not weed out "the crazies"; rather, they wilt the resolve of legitimate participants in America's political life and threaten a future when even what is right will go without defenders.

5 Eco-SLAPPs

Turning the Tables on the Environmental Movement

Parties whose interests are threatened . . . have jeopardized the . . . future effectiveness of citizen enforcement of environmental protection laws by devising a new litigation strategy—the assertion of a multi-million dollar counteraction . . . against the environmental[ists].

—*Michigan Law Review* (1975)

The 1960s sowed the seeds of environmentalism in America, and the 1970s saw it flower. The seeds were postwar affluence, population, urbanization, technology, and our growing chemical dependency (exposed in Rachel Carson's *Silent Spring*);[1] campaigns over wilderness, dams, and pesticides; and intense media attention.[2] In 1969 the first modern environmental protection law, the National Environmental Policy Act,[3] expressed a national commitment that blossomed into a political force in the 1970s. The dry words of the *Michigan Law Review* (quoted above)[4] indicate the reaction and suggest the tensions of the era: the competing forces, the fervid ideological disputes, and the dollars at stake.

The 1970s opened with the Santa Barbara oil spill, the first "Earth Day," and a deluge of new environmental laws and programs. Environmentalists found legislative and other government doors springing open to them. The new laws created public participation opportunities that had never before existed, authorizing and encouraging citizens to report violations, sit on government boards, testify at public hearings, file enforcement actions, lobby agencies, and sue both government and polluters.[5] Income tax deductibility helped bankroll environmental litigation and "public interest" law firms. Courts opened their doors ever wider to environmental protection actions brought by citizens and groups as "private attorneys general."[6] The government's rationale for expanding the citizen role was doubtless part altruism, part political posturing, and part self-serving recognition that government enforcement resources would be insufficient without citizen aid.[7] Environmentalists, from the longhaired counterculturists and "little old persons in tennis shoes" to paid professionals, accepted the new challenges with gusto.

The backlash was swift. By the early 1970s, SLAPPs had emerged to "counteract" the new environmental movement.[8]

These eco-SLAPPs, like the other varieties, all prove to be variations on the same model. In the first stage, environmentalists petition government over a problem caused by the plans, projects, policies, or programs either of the government itself or of private parties. Their lobbying can be directed toward the legislature (for a new law or a repeal) or an administrative agency (to change its position); if that fails, it can become judicial "lobbying" (such as entering a nonmonetary "law reform" suit against the government, or seeking a court order to change the government's policy, plan, or decision). In the second stage, opposition interests are aroused (sometimes private parties benefiting from the government's decision, sometimes the government itself). They see direct debate about alleged injuries to the environment as counterproductive or insufficient for their purposes. Instead (or in addition), they sue for money on the grounds of injuries allegedly being caused them by the environmentalists' petitioning. These quintessential strategic lawsuits against public participation occur in every environmental area, but three issues—wilderness, pollution, and animal rights—best illustrate the eco-SLAPP.

SLAPPs in the Wilderness

Wild, untamed natural areas have always provoked paradoxical reactions in the American mind, a strange amalgam of fear, desire to dominate, and deep aesthetic appreciation.[9] With "the end of the frontier," the late 1800s gave birth to a preservation movement in America, a new land ethic encouraged by the works of Thoreau, Emerson, Whitman, Muir, Olmstead, Teddy Roosevelt, the Hudson School of Art, and others. The U.S. government began a massive set-aside program, reserving hundreds of millions of acres for national parks, forests, and other special preservation purposes. In 1964 America became the first nation in history to recognize through law the need for wilderness in its past, present, and future.[10]

Wilderness preservation was the first great battle of the fledgling environmental movement. Leading national groups (the Sierra Club, the Wilderness Society) and local volunteers by the thousands lobbied for congressional protection for natural areas. Even in the 1990s, with some 90,000,000 acres (4 percent of U.S. land) designated as wilderness, the battles are still fierce between preservationists and their opponents, principally the timber, mining, and livestock industries and their local supporters. Those powerful opponents, perhaps not surprisingly, soon discovered that the courts could add to their clout against the preservationists.

The Sierra Club: First and Foremost

Among its distinctions, the Sierra Club can count itself the nation's leading SLAPP target, with at least 10 suits against it, yet a very atypical one: Instead of the local environmentalists and small groups usually targeted, these SLAPPs have taken on a real Goliath. The Sierra Club, with its multimillion-dollar annual budget, hundreds of thousands of members, 100-year existence, extensive courtroom experience, and even its own law firm (the Sierra Club Legal Defense Fund) would seem unchillable—and indeed it has won dismissal of all SLAPPs filed against it. Yet despite all its resources, even its volunteers can be intimidated, its funds diverted, and its campaigns lost in the real world, just like those of the smallest, poorest neighborhood group.

The spectacular wilderness areas of California have been a battleground between the Sierra Club and timber/mining/ranching interests since the nineteenth century. One of the great modern battles triggered what we believe is the first officially reported eco-SLAPP and one of the best reasoned to date—*Sierra Club v. Butz.*[11] In 1965 the U.S. Forest Service opened for logging a virgin 3,500-acre area near what was to become the Salmon-Trinity Alps Wilderness in the far northwest corner of California. The contract was awarded to Humboldt Fir, the largest employer in the region, but it did not begin logging immediately. In 1970 the Sierra Club awoke, began objecting to the Forest Service that the proposed logging was "illegal," and requested that the area be kept in wilderness. The government denied the request, and in 1972 the club appealed, filing a federal court challenge to overturn the government's decision.[12]

Three days later Humboldt Fir filed a counterclaim demanding an injunction, $750,000 in actual damages, and $1,000,000 in punitive damages against the Sierra Club. Humboldt claimed to have been driven into bankruptcy and—in an unashamedly literal attack on the Petition Clause—charged "interference with contract" because the Club "orally and by letter and by administrative appeal proceedings and by the complaint herein, engaged in a calculated course of conduct to induce the Forest Service . . . to refuse to continue its performance of the said contract."[13] The club promptly filed a motion to dismiss, plainly worried about the "drastic monetary liability,"[14] and objecting strenuously to the violation of its political rights:

[Humboldt's] claim is that the presence of a timber sale contract . . . chokes off [the Sierra Club's] freedom to address the Government with their views as to the best use of the public lands in question. If such a fanciful notion bore any resemblance to the law, it would stifle any effective effort to remedy the myriad environmental abuses that spring from government projects. . . . It would mean that any citizen who beseeched the Government to end oil drilling in the Santa Barbara Channel or to halt the SST project would be subject to the same kind of potential liability to Union Oil or Boeing. . . . It would be difficult to imagine a cruder attempt to deprive ordinary citizens of their right . . . to communicate with their Government and petition it for redress of grievances.[15]

The Sierra Club's decision to focus on political-constitutional issues rather than the breach-of-contract camouflage was quickly rewarded: The U.S. District Court dismissed Humboldt's counterclaim in a near-record four months. One of the very first federal court opinions to rule SLAPPs unconstitutional, *Sierra Club v. Butz* remains a landmark precedent today:

The First Amendment provision guaranteeing the right of the people to petition the government for a redress of grievances . . . is a basic freedom in a participatory government, closely related to freedom of speech and press; together these are the "indispensable democratic freedoms" that cannot be abridged if a government is to continue to reflect the desires of the people.[16]

The court saw clearly the risk of such suits and its own critical role in controlling or perpetuating them:

This court cannot be too careful in assuring that its acts do not infringe this right. . . . [The U.S. Supreme Court has said that] "fear of damage awards . . . may be markedly more inhibiting than the fear of prosecution under a criminal statute. . . . Erroneous statement is inevitable in free debate, and . . . it must be protected if the freedoms of expression are to have the 'breathing space' that they 'need . . . to survive.'" Under a less strict rule, the [Supreme Court] feels: "would-be critics of official conduct may be deterred from voicing their criticism, even though it is believed to be true and even though it is in fact true, because of doubt whether it can be proved in court or fear of the expenses of having to do so. . . . [This would] dampen the vigor and limit the variety of public debate. It is inconsistent with the [U.S. Constitution]."[17]

The opinion went further to state that even "malice" should not undercut the protection—contrary to what the U.S. Supreme Court would say 13 years later in *McDonald v. Smith* but like its protective approach in *City of Columbia v. Omni Outdoor Advertising, Inc.* (as discussed in Chapter 2).

Since then, the Sierra Club or its members have been targets in at least nine other eco-SLAPPs, not always ending so well. The club has been twice sued for opposing logging: by a timber company on the Mission Indian Reservation east of Los Angeles;[18] and by an Alaskan Native Corporation in the nation's largest forest reserve, the magnificent coastal rain forest of Alaska's Tongass archipelago.[19] Its efforts to protect rivers provoked two more: a commercial river rafting company SLAPPed the club over a new river management plan for the Grand Canyon in 1978;[20] Oregon water interests sued the club in 1994 for trying to remove a dam from the Rogue River.[21] Fighting residential, resort, and road developments in wilderness areas triggered three more: the *McKeon* SLAPP and SLAPPback outside Sacramento (Chapter 3), the *Perini* SLAPP and SLAPPback in Squaw Valley (Chapter 9), and a county's SLAPP when the club tried to stop it from widening the Burr Trail in Utah's canyonlands into a two-lane road.[22] Just publishing a book, *Environmental Justice and Communities of Color*, got it sued by New Mexico landfill operators for libel.[23] Finally, even opposing a small expansion of an existing seaside hotel in Mendocino got the club sued for $3,250,000.[24]

Seeing the litigious Sierra Club itself as the target of lawsuits raises a very important point. We are often asked, "If targets can file a lawsuit, what's wrong with filers doing it?" The answer lies in the relief sought by the suit. Our study includes as SLAPPs the countersuits and counterclaims filed against an initial lawsuit brought by the target—but only when the target's original lawsuit can be classed as pure "government petitioning": in short, a suit seeking to change a government policy, action, decision, or plan, not to acquire money damages. The countersuit or counterclaim is classified as a SLAPP because it has completely different goals or effects—not a government result or outcome but monetary compensation from the target. It thus injects a collateral issue, changes the stakes, and diverts attention and resources from the real public dispute needing resolution.

Litigation is protected under the Petition Clause, but pure lobbying, nonmonetary, public-interest cases merit greater solicitude than private-interest money cases because they involve the very kind of "private attorney general" citizen participation in government that is at the core of First Amendment concern and of Congressional policy in the health, safety, and welfare area. Targets petition courts to alter another government authority's decision. SLAPP countersuits and counterclaims seek to cut off citizens' access to courts to petition government outcomes, just as other SLAPPs seek to cut off access to achieve outcomes from our legislatures and agencies.

"Eco-Guerrillas"

Radical, "monkey-wrenching" environmentalists[25] are even more frequent targets of SLAPP threats and filings than the Sierra Club, particularly those who engage in "direct action"—picketing, demonstrations, sit-ins, blockades—to stop logging and change government timber policy. In 1982, after efforts to protect the Pyramid Area of Oregon's Willamette National Forest through litigation or wilderness legislation had failed, the U.S. Forest Service awarded Willamette Industries a large timber contract in the natural area. Bloodied but unbowed, Earth First!—a radical "eco-guerrilla" group—and local wilderness supporters escalated the protest in what has become a familiar drama in the Pacific Northwest. They lined the logging road with picket signs, called in the media, and formed a "human chain" across the road, temporarily blocking the loggers' access. The blockaders and some innocent bystanders were arrested and tried by the county for misdemeanor criminal trespass and similar charges. Some were found guilty, some not guilty, and for some the charges were dropped. The guilty had to pay fines and make monetary restitution to Willamette Industries.

Not satisfied with that, the logging company filed a SLAPP against Earth First! plus two local wilderness groups, 31 named individuals, and 50 "John and Jane Does."[26] Charging nuisance and intentional interference with contractual relations, it sought more money damages and an injunction against further "interference." The industry got a boost when the targets' attorneys failed to defend on constitutional grounds or to characterize the blockade as a form of government petitioning.[27] Some defendants were dismissed or never served, but the jury nailed the others: a $12,800 verdict against one local group, $100–200 verdicts against four individuals, and a $13,500 default judgment against the nine remaining defendants; their appeals were rejected. One target did file a SLAPPback,[28] but it went nowhere.

In 1990 Earth First! founder Mike Roselle described the logging industry's intense retaliatory tactics (of which SLAPPs are now an integral part):

> When we got involved in old growth [timber preservation] ten years ago, the older [environmental] groups said we couldn't organize in these sparsely populated timber communities. . . . We went out there, got arrested, beat up, sued, run over by bulldozers, and we'd come back. We slowly won grudging respect from the loggers. They'd never seen a Sierra Clubber out there. We were accessible, and even if they didn't agree with us, they knew where we drank, they knew where we lived. The communities themselves became less afraid of us, and that's where the timber companies reacted and tried to portray us as a very violent, secretive,

almost cultish force. But that's kind of a rear-guard defense action against us, and it's not working.[29]

Land Trusts

At the opposite end of the environmental spectrum from radical action groups like Earth First! and often called "the real estate arm of the environmental movement," land trusts are government or nonprofit charities that preserve nature by acquiring land. They range from well-known national groups such as the Nature Conservancy and the Trust for Public Land to local community preservation groups. Land trusts, it is said, favor three-piece suits over lawsuits; their tools are the donation, the deal, and the deed.[30] Yet even these ultra-businesslike groups are not immune to SLAPPs.

The Nature Conservancy (TNC) has been SLAPPed multiple times. In 1974, with six of its workers, it was sued for $2,790,000 by seaweed-farm developers in the scenic San Juan Islands north of Seattle.[31] What had TNC done? To quote the complaint, it had "inventoried" the "potential natural areas" in the county, identified lands that should be preserved (including the filers'), and turned the study over to the county government as a recommendation. The trial court dismissed, and the court of appeals affirmed, but not until this SLAPP over a simple government study had dragged on for over four years. In 1988 TNC was sued again, along with two local land trusts and individuals, for supporting state acquisition of the Lake Minnewaska resort and natural area in upstate New York.[32] The bankrupt owners sued for $36,000,000, because they had hoped to get more from a private developer than they would from the state. The trial court dispatched the case in six months. TNC was also on the receiving end of a first-of-its-kind SLAPP, a New York developer's suit to revoke the Conservancy's tax exemption for opposing a housing project on the rim of scenic Mianus Gorge, TNC's very first preserved area (Chapter 3).

TNC is not alone. In 1990, when the Big Sur Land Trust in California tried to buy a pine-eucalyptus grove annually visited by millions of migrating monarch butterflies, negotiations broke down, and the owner decided to develop. After stormy public hearings his city building permit was denied, and the owner sued not only the city but the land trust and others who testified against him.[33] The environmentalists were dropped from the suit after a few months, but it slowed their preservation efforts. Big Sur and other land trusts report numerous instances in which they have been threatened with SLAPPs, typically by developers competing for the same property.

In a fine bit of irony, Colorado environmentalists got SLAPPed for keeping county "open space" funds from being spent on a new jail. In 1980 Jefferson County, immediately west of Denver, was under federal court orders to build a new jail to alleviate overcrowding. To get funds, the county scheduled an election on its proposal to siphon off tax dollars from its nationally famous Open Space Program, sparking "a bitter, circus-like battle between the county and Plan Jeffco, Inc.,"[34] the citizen group that had sparkplugged creation of the program. The county promptly dragged Plan Jeffco and its officers into their jail case as "third-party defendants" and asked the court to enjoin their opposition campaign.[35] The federal court quickly dismissed the organization,[36] but three of its officers decided to tough it out; they counterclaimed and won a court order forcing the county to present both sides of the issue in the election campaign. The funds switch was defeated at the polls, and new jail space was built, but not at the expense of open space.

"Pollution-Buster" SLAPPs

Today's pollution control laws authorize and encourage citizens to report, testify, and even file lawsuits against the government and private industry for violations.[37] Paradoxically, citizens who do so are at risk because "many polluters and developers continue to find it easier to use the court system as a weapon of intimidation, than to try making their cases with the public."[38] Pollution-buster SLAPPs are a decided risk for anyone who takes these laws seriously.

Spotlighting Polluters

The most famous of these cases is *Webb v. Fury*.[39] In 1980, Rick Webb was a thirty-one-year-old "bearded, college-trained, blue-denimed vegetarian" and "self-styled back-to-the-land emigrant."[40] He was also the leader of two local environmental groups in his West Virginia coal region. Through their newsletters and direct contacts he reported DLM Coal Corporation to the federal government for pollution and fish kills at its strip mine, making it expressly clear that his reports were an "attempt to implement EPA's established Public Participation Policy."[41] One federal inspector described the company as "a high violator where almost every time we make an inspection we write a notice of violation,"[42] and the EPA finally issued a formal notice of intent to revoke DLM's license (a revocation later blocked by the company in federal court). Webb was promptly sued by the coal company for $200,000 for "defaming" it in his reports to the government.[43]

The suit sent shock waves through the environmental community nationwide. Webb's attorney, David Grubb, himself a state environmental leader, saw the stakes as very high:

We feel like this might be an effort to tie up the environmental movement. . . . Tying up citizen complaints would effectively halt the environmental movement. . . . And so far, it has already had somewhat of that effect. We've had to take away from other things to defend this suit, instead of taking new actions, we're defending old ones. . . . In order to be faithful to all the environmental groups in the nation, we have to put together a tremendous group of attorneys, and we have to win a decisive victory.[44]

But DLM's attorney, Donald H. Vish, defended the SLAPP: "This is certainly a case of first impression as to whether an environmental group can attempt to inflict an environmental death penalty, capital punishment on a corporation."[45] And among others who cheered the coal company's action was Raymond M. Momboisse, head of the Washington office of the Pacific Legal Foundation, an industry-supported, conservative law foundation soon to be involved in bringing other SLAPPs. He stated: "There have been tremendous losses suffered by private industry and by members of unions who lost their jobs through needless environmental complaints. . . . Frankly I'm surprised [a SLAPP] hasn't been tried before."[46] A year later, Pacific Legal was representing filers in SLAPPs against nuclear plant demonstrators in California (see below), and its midwestern sibling, North Star Legal Foundation, would soon file a SLAPP against antiwar demonstrators in Minnesota (Chapter 7).

Unprepared for the outpouring of national interest over the case, Attorney Vish admitted:

We're astonished at the attention [the lawsuit] has attracted. We think it's being given a purpose that it doesn't have, and an effect that it doesn't have. . . . Some would like to say this is some kind of counter-attack on environmentalists. That simply is not the way we see it. We regard it solely as a private suit. There really isn't anything else behind it. . . . D.L.M. has no grievance with environmentalists.[47]

After the trial judge refused to dismiss the case, Webb's appeal to West Virginia's highest court set a national precedent against SLAPPs; in unusually indignant language, the court castigated the lower court for failing to dismiss promptly:

[The trial court decision against dismissal] invades the unique constitutional guarantee of the right to petition the government for a redress of grievances contained in the First Amendment to the United States Constitution.

The right to petition . . . is "among the most precious of the liberties safeguarded by the Bill of Rights." It shares the "preferred place" accorded in our system of government to the First Amendment freedoms, and "has a sanctity and a sanction not permitting dubious intrusions." Indeed, . . . the right to petition is logically implicit in and fundamental to the very idea of a republican form of government.

[A court should] prohibit a case from proceeding to trial when the remedy of appeal is manifestly inadequate to protect against the chilling effect. . . . If it appears that the [targets'] conduct falls within the class of absolutely privileged petitioning activity, the mere pendency of the [lawsuit] will threaten [their] free exercise of their right to petition government and the denial of the motion to dismiss by the [trial] court . . . [is] error.[48]

The court ruled that the West Virginia state constitution provided even more protection for petition activity than the U.S. Constitution—an absolute, unqualified privilege.[49]

Even the one justice who dissented (rejecting blanket absolute immunity) concluded that this suit was outrageous:

In the case before us we have ordinary citizens who are being sued by a well financed corporation for activities which appear to be not only constitutionally privileged but statutorily solicited and welcomed [by government]. While the [filer] here in effect can spend unlimited amounts on superb legal talent, [targets] in this and similar cases will be hard pressed to hire legal counsel at all. The potential for chilling legitimate first amendment rights when there is anything less than absolute immunity is awe inspiring. . . . The key for solving this dilemma is finding a device which will screen legitimate first amendment activity from irresponsible or sham first amendment activity.[50]

The case was over in one year. The coal company kept operating, but under a sharper government eye, and Rick Webb had the last word: The SLAPP had "spotlighted the [environmental] problem better than we ever could have done."[51]

The Terrifying World of "Toxic Torts"

Webb v. Fury is cloned frequently when citizens report polluters.[52] But there are even more frightening prospects. Since World War II the growth of the chemical, petroleum, nuclear, and transportation industries has created new toxic risks—chemical, physical, mechanical, radiological, or biological—for all Americans.[53] The human injuries can range from the toxic to the cancerous, from damage to the fetus to permanent genetic mutation through all future generations. The property damages can range from diminished value to multimillion-dollar cleanups, from temporary uninhabitability to cataclysmic destruction. Countless human activities once thought safe turn out to involve deadly places or products, and new risks are born daily in labs and factories and on Madison Avenue. "Once safe" examples include farm and home pesticides (such as DDT) that turned out to be long-lived carcinogens; medical drugs and devices (thalidomide, DES, the Dalkon Shield, 1950s radiation treatments for acne); hazardous waste landfills (Love Canal and "the Valley of the Drums"); mining and mine waste (radioactive tailings piles throughout the Southwest and heavy metals leaching into rivers from Appalachia to Sutter's Mill); long-neglected air pollutants; once common household products, food additives, clothing-industry chemicals (such as cancer-causing Tris in infant sleepwear). More recently, there has been growing concern over non-ionizing electromagnetic radiation (from ordinary household wiring, electric home appliances, power lines, utility substations, and radio/TV transmission towers).[54]

The sad truths are that everyone is a target for toxic exposure, and that everyone who protests is a potential SLAPP target. One whistleblower found himself sued by no less than the Shell Oil Company. In 1981 Shell made polybutylene resin for use in household water pipes. Raymond J. Leonardini, attorney for a California plumbers' union council (and formerly a top California state consumer official), became concerned over a lab report showing DEHP, an animal carcinogen, in the pipe material. Leonardini submitted the report to the state agency that was determining whether to approve polybutylene pipes for home use. The revelation stopped the state proceedings cold; a full environmental study was ordered. Shell's response was to sue for an injunction to silence Leonardini and the lab.[55] The lab folded quickly, settled with Shell (without admitting error), and was dismissed. Leonardini would not budge. He moved to dismiss the suit as censorship of his constitutional rights, whereupon Shell voluntarily withdrew its case, claiming the lab's cave-in was vindication. Outraged at this highhandedness, Leonardini promptly filed a SLAPP-back against Shell for maliciously prosecuting him and won a staggering $5,200,000 jury verdict (Chapter 9)—a very expensive warning for anyone considering eco-SLAPPs in the future.

Nevertheless, these cases continue to be filed, as a group that joined an already-filed government lawsuit against a polluter found out. In 1987 the Environmental Protection Agency filed an enforcement action against Environmental Waste Control, Inc. (EWC) and two managers, alleging toxic waste law violations at its Rochester, Indiana, landfill. Supporters To Oppose Pollution, Inc. (STOP), a local environmental group, intervened in the federal court suit, raising an additional 14 violations and asking for an injunction. The landfill company then counterclaimed against the environmental group for unspecified dollar damages, charging only that STOP had met with, written to, and testified before federal and state government officials.[56] Even though the environmentalists had voluntarily entered the judicial arena, they were there only to make a nonprofit petition for pollution cleanup. The landfill's counterclaim subjected them to a different and unexpected risk—huge personal monetary damages—but they hung in and won. The judge shut down both the SLAPP and the landfill, and ordered the company to pay over $2,700,000 in penalties to the government.

The antinuclear arm of the environmental movement has also defended its share of suits. A leading example is the $2,891,000 *Abalone Alliance* politician SLAPP (Chapter 4), in which antinuclear, antiwar, and environmental groups and individuals were sued for their 1981 political demonstration-blockade of the Diablo Canyon nuclear power plant in California. Twice dismissed for lack of proper plaintiffs, the filers persuaded the County of San Luis Obispo to join them, alleging that the demonstrators added to police costs. Eventually, the targets' dismissal was affirmed on appeal—but not until 1986. The conservative Pacific Legal Foundation filed a companion SLAPP on behalf of the plant workers, claiming lost wages, mental anguish, and interference with business. The trial court dismissed some counts, but targets despaired when, after three years in court, it allowed filers a chance for a fourth amended complaint. They appealed unsuccessfully and eventually had to come back and face the music in the trial court. Finally, however, a different judge dismissed the SLAPP completely in 1986.

Across the country another antinuclear group and its public relations firm were sued for $4,500,000 by an electric company.[57] In the November 1982 general election, Maine voters had a clear-cut choice: to vote for or against "an Act to prohibit the generation of electricity by nuclear fission within five years." The Maine Nuclear Referendum Committee had worked to get the moratorium on the ballot and campaigned hard that fall, with radio and TV spots about increased leukemia in southern Maine (site of the state's only nuclear plant) and the dangers of radioactive waste. Four weeks before the election the Maine Yankee Atomic Power Company sued, claiming defamation. The antinuclear forces won in court: The SLAPP was dismissed less than three months after the election, and the utility paid them $4,500 in attorneys' fees to drop their SLAPPback. But the utility won in the real world: The moratorium was defeated at the polls.

Animal Rights and Wrongs

From the first, America has been schizophrenic about animals. Massachusetts Puritans in 1641 forbade "Tirranny or Crueltie towards any bruite Creature" even as they were hacking a civilization out of wilderness habitat and setting the turkey on the road to Thanksgiving stardom. We make folk heroes of the likes of "Buffalo Bill" Cody, who contributed to the virtual extinction of a living species in one generation; we send others to jail for poaching single, unendangered animals. And although the Humane Society of the United States estimates that a typical major city records 5,000 animal abuse complaints a year, only 10 to 20 are prosecuted, and less than 10 percent of these result in jail terms.[58]

The current "animal rights" movement was inspired by Peter Singer's 1975 book *Animal Liberation*,[59] and in their efforts to protect both domestic and wild animals, advocates have become increasingly activist.[60] So have their opponents. Polarization is strongest in two areas: the fur garment industry, and laboratory research.[61] Not surprisingly, animal protectors are among the hardest-hit SLAPPs targets spanning the animal rights spectrum. Yet the typical SLAPP victim, we found, was a mature, respectable pillar of the community, not a wild-eyed, radical extremist.

Let the Fur Fly

SLAPPs are the fashion industry's newest fashion. Listen to Bob Harrowe, columnist for *Fur Age Weekly*, urging SLAPPs against "anti-fur forces":

> I agree that fighting back on the legislative front is important. I also agree that promoting the fashion elegance of furs is important.
>
> But both of these measures are defensive. In no way do we leave a single scar on the enemy, even when we win. The antis simply come back again with new proposed legislation, against which we have to expend our energies and financial resources as a defense . . . again.
>
> . . . Cleveland Amory . . . goes on TV and announces matter-of-factly that "People trap because its KIND OF FUN to TORTURE animals"—and we slink away with our tails between our legs.
>
> Why can't we face him in court—and make him back up such a ridiculous statement, or pay for the damage he has done to the industry and every man or woman who traps for a living. . . .
>
> The question of damage? Obviously, his intention was to end trapping, which is the source of all or part of a trapper's income. And how would you like your neighbors to sneer at you as a guy who gets his jollies TORTURING animals?
>
> Wake up you defenders of the fur industry—and learn that you can never win a war defensively. Only a solid "offensive" blow to the "gut" can bring victory.[62]

His call was heard. The Fur Retailers Information Council a year later reported that it was "now moving ahead with legal action against those who publicly slurred specific furriers by name, and [we] will be monitoring advertising messages. Video film and photographs of demonstrators furnished by furriers and the news media are being turned over to the Department of Justice."[63]

The earliest animal rights SLAPP we found, and one of the longest ever, was a 1976 suit against the Utah State Humane Society and its director for trying to improve conditions at a local dog pound.[64] From 1971 to 1975, according to the court, the targets "repeatedly contacted city and county officials to complain about cruelty and unhealthy treatment of the dogs in the [government] pound, but no action was taken."[65] Despairing, in 1976 the Humane Society launched a media campaign, urging vacationers to boycott the tourist-dependent town "in order to create public pressure upon government officials to make improvements."[66] The pressure was felt. Eight town businessmen sued the society for "intentional infliction of harm to plaintiffs' businesses," even though they recognized that targets were "motivated by their . . . political . . . beliefs relating to city and county government."[67] The Humane Society was enmeshed in the SLAPP for nine years and made two trips to the Utah Supreme Court before winning a ruling that the "secondary boycott" was protected by the Petition Clause—despite the fact that it brought "incidental injury to parties concerned—because it was "designed to influence governmental action."[68]

A 1991 case highlights the dark side of zoos and aquariums. Boston activists filed test cases against the New England Aquarium, challenging its authority to transfer dolphins born in captivity to other facilities, asserting that doing so disrupted the social lives and values of these intelligent marine mammals.[69] "Kama," one of the dolphins, was named a plaintiff in the suit. The aquarium countered with a monetary SLAPP against the activists (not including Kama), claiming that some of their statements were "false."[70] Some two years later, Kama's lawsuit was dismissed by the court, whereupon the aquarium dropped its SLAPP.[71]

Have you ever seen a starving horse, an injured dog, or another abused animal on someone else's property? Would you call the Humane Society or the county animal control? That is all it takes to get sued in Michigan, a hotbed of animal SLAPPs. In 1980, Detroit-area farmer George Dienes filed a damage action against a newspaper, a TV station, the Michigan Humane Society, its lawyer, and two Does.[72] The Humane Society, after receiving a report of starving cattle on Dienes's farm, had followed standard practice in filing with the court and obtaining a search warrant. Then its attorney, a veterinarian, TV and radio reporters, and state troopers went to the farm and found cows in extremely poor condition. According to Sienna La Rene, the Humane Society's lawyer, "Under that coat all you got is bones, just skeletons, most of them."[73] The Humane Society's insurance company handled the targets' defense and paid the farmer a confidential settlement (rumored by others than the parties to be in four figures) for "nuisance damages"; further, the Humane Society agreed not to prosecute him, not to file a SLAPPback, and to release him from all liability if he would dismiss his SLAPP.[74] The society defends the settlement: The filer was in financial difficulty and it was better, in their view, for him to spend money on his animals than on lawsuits; Dienes phased out his operation, and "it worked out fine for the animals."[75]

Animal rights activists are not always the victims. Indeed, they file their own share of SLAPPs, and apply all the pressures of the most mercenary filers, as the following antitrapping cases show.

In 1981, during a bitter fight over a proposed state ban on leg-hold traps, Friends of Animals, Inc., filed two $2,000,000 suits, back to back against the Connecticut Trappers Association.[76] The first SLAPP claimed that the Friends had been defamed by the Trappers' spreading a "rumor" in government circles that Friends had faked photos by trapping animals themselves.[77] When the Trappers' president countered that Friends were "trotting around a three-legged dog down south and claiming it was injured by a leg-hold trap when it was really injuried [*sic*] by a lawnmower,"[78] the Friends promptly filed a second defamation SLAPP. Once the targets began discovery, however, the filers withdrew both suits, whereupon the Trappers responded with the SLAPPback[79] and snapped up a confidential settlement (reportedly substantial) from the animal protectors.[80]

An almost identical $1,250,000 SLAPP was filed by animal rightists after they lost an Oregon antitrapping election.[81] Oregonians Against Trapping had campaigned hard for a 1980 ballot prohibition on trapping, but fighting just as hard on the other side was the national pro-hunting/trapping Wildlife Legislative Fund of America, as well as state groups such as Oregonians for Wildlife Conservation. The trappers won the election by a solid majority,[82] and the disappointed antitrappers sued the national group, its state and national leaders, and their public relations firm, alleging violations of election laws through "false statements" in "letters, posters, publications, and advertisements in opposition to Ballot Measure 5."[83] After a trial and a hung jury, the judge finally ruled the state election law unconstitutional and threw the SLAPP out in 1985, awarding the target trappers $22,000 in attorneys' fees, but the pro-animal filers had kept the case going for four years.

Laboratories and Lawsuits

New York has established a resounding precedent, protecting animal (and all other) activists from SLAPPs. It came about in "one of the longest, most bitter, and expensive libel suits in the history of New York State,"[84] pitting one of the world's largest international drug companies against two animal protectors and a medical journal. First Amendment expert Anthony Lewis says when it comes to "vexatious litigation—abusive, inflated, meritless lawsuits," this one is "my candidate for the prize in outrageousness."[85]

Dr. Shirley McGreal, chair of the International Primate Protection League (IPPL) in Summerville, South Carolina, has an extensive track record of fighting for apes, monkeys, and lemurs. She persuaded the late Prime Minister Indira Gandhi to ban the export of rhesus monkeys from India and has changed the practices of several American university primate programs that she considered inhumane. In 1983 she published a letter in the *Journal of Medical Primatology,* castigating Immuno AG—a multinational drug company based in Austria—for planning to establish a facility in Sierra Leone, Africa, for hepatitis research using chimpanzees, an endangered species. Journal editor J. Moor-Jankowski, himself a medical researcher with whom McGreal has not always agreed, prefaced her letter with an editorial note stating that he had shown the letter to Immuno and invited the company to submit a rebuttal. Immuno's lawyers wrote back, terming the charges inaccurate and threatening suit, but when, after an extended wait, Immuno had not offered a response for publication, the editor printed the McGreal letter alone. On October 11, 1984, the drug giant filed a 57-page complaint against Moor-Jankowski, McGreal, and the journal's publishers and distributors, alleging defamation and demanding $4,000,000 in actual and punitive damages. The letter to the editor was, at most, a very indirect communication to government, but significantly, the complaint also objected to numerous instances in which either McGreal or Moor-Jankowski had contacted government officials in the United States and abroad to complain about Immuno's activities. That made it a SLAPP.

The case began badly: Efforts to dismiss were rebuffed by the trial judge, Justice Beatrice Shainswit, and McGreal was subjected to 14 days of grueling depositions by Immuno's attorneys, who even inquired into her "sexual acts."[86] Immuno also submitted affidavits, denouncing McGreal, from animal industry sources with whom she had crossed swords. She was horrified that a lawsuit could have "all this filth flying around."[87] Soon, only Moor-Jankowski was left in the case. Paying Immuno "substantial sums" to dismiss them, the other targets settled—even, over her strenuous objections, McGreal: "My insurance company, having spent $250,000 to defend me, paid Immuno $100,000 to drop the case against me. But I signed no papers, and I refused to retract what I saw was the truth."[88]

In 1987, Moor-Jankowski moved for summary judgment, only to be turned down yet again by Justice Shainswit. Although complaining about the parties' "massive" filings (over 4,000 pages), she still ruled that unresolved fact issues about Moor-Jankowski's "actual malice" required a full-scale trial.[89] Moor-Jankowski appealed, and in one of the most indignant and unflattering reversals of a trial judge on the books, the New York Appellate Division unanimously struck down Shainswit's decision and dismissed Immuno's entire case:

We think that [Justice Shainswit's] analysis was flawed in several respects. . . . The factual assertions upon which McGreal's opinions rested were evidently true. . . . Contrary to the assumption [in Shainswit's] opinion, the truth or falsity of the assertions made in the McGreal letter was not a matter necessarily to be reserved for trial. . . .

The importance of summary adjudication in . . . libel litigation cannot be overemphasized. Libel actions are notoriously expensive to defend, and, indeed, "The threat of being put to the defense of a lawsuit . . . may be as chilling to the exercise of First Amendment freedoms as fear of the outcome of the lawsuit itself.' . . . To unnecessarily delay the disposition of a libel action is not only to countenance waste and inefficiency but to enhance the value of such actions as instruments of harassment and coercion inimical to the exercise of First Amendment rights. . . .

That [Justice Shainswit] . . . was evidently reluctant to apply the ordinary summary judgment criteria . . . is regrettable. It is disturbing that [Immuno] had, by threatening legal action, managed to delay publication of the McGreal letter for almost a year, and that it succeeded in coercing what [Justice Shainswit] referred to in [her] decision as "substantial settlements" from all but one of the original defendants for the obvious reason that the costs of continuing to defend the action were prohibitive.[90]

Such outraged criticism of a judge is rare in judicial circles. The appeals court was clearly convinced, from facts already in the record, that "Dr. McGreal's comments . . . were . . . eminently fair . . . statements of opinion," "quite simply true," "absolutely protected," and "statements which [Immuno] utterly failed to show . . . false."[91] Moreover, "the law of libel was not properly used by [Immuno] as an instrument for . . . suppression."[92]

Immuno appealed to the state's highest court, the New York Court of Appeals, which agreed unanimously on December 14, 1989, that the case should have been dismissed at the outset. Moreover, in the process it broke new First Amendment protection ground for all New York activists:

Pure opinion—however misguided or vituperative—is entitled to the absolute protection of the state and federal constitutional free speech guarantees. . . . However pernicious an opinion may seem, we depend for its correction not on the conscience of judges and juries but on the competition of other ideas. . . .

Most importantly, for many members of the public, a letter to the editor may be the only available opportunity to air concerns about issues affecting them. . . .

. . . The public forum function of letters to the editor is closely related in spirit to the "marketplace of ideas" and oversight and informational values that compelled recognition of the privileges of fair comment, fair report and immunity accorded expression of opinion. These values are best effectuated by according defendant latitude to publish a letter to the editor on a matter of legitimate public concern—the letter's author, affiliation, bias and premises fully disclosed, rebuttal openly invited—free of defamation litigation. . . .

This case—having already engendered thousands of pages of a litigation record and "substantial" settlements from all other defendants—exemplifies that the "threat of being put to the defense of a lawsuit . . . may be as chilling to the exercise of First Amendment freedoms as fear of the outcome of the lawsuit itself." . . . We have therefore stressed the particular role and importance of summary judgment, where appropriate, in libel cases.[93]

Shirley McGreal and her International Primate Protection League had won court vindication, after the fact. She continues her campaigns on behalf of all primates—sadder, wiser, poorer, and a shade less confident. The headlines in a typical issue of IPPL's newsletter seem undaunted: "Animals Starve at Teheran Zoo"; "Hong Kong Monkeys Face Problems"; "Gorilla and Chimpanzee Poaching in Uganda"; "Monkeys Die at M.I.T."[94] But the SLAPP ordeal has taken its toll in funding, insurability, and confidence in the protection of the judicial system, and McGreal today continues her crusade under the shadow of the next SLAPP.

And her co-defendant, the editor? Commentator Lewis's outrage is a fitting epilogue for this SLAPP:

No award now could really cure the injury of this case to our legal system—or to Dr. Moor-Jankowski. His legal expenses so far exceed $1 million. He has spent most of the last seven years on law instead of medical research. Open debate, crucially important to science, has been chilled. And all that for a letter to the editor. The right way, the American way, to challenge such a letter is to answer it. Dr. Moor-Jankowski in fact asked Immuno to reply. Instead it sued. Somehow our law must make clear—to giant foreign companies among others—that in this country we honor and protect free speech.[95]

Still, Shirley McGreal fared better than five animal welfare advocates in Michigan for whom "the American way" was a cruel joke, costing them over $800,000 and nearly nine years in a nightmare SLAPP.

Dr. Mary Lou Durbin, a middle-aged special education teacher, served as a volunteer for the Michigan Humane Society and other animal welfare groups in 1980. Cathy Blight, then in her early thirties, was an unemployed commercial artist, married with two children, and president of the Livingston County Humane Society. George Regan and his wife, Linda, and Wanda Glodowski were also residents of Livingston County, east of Detroit.

Hodgins Kennels in Howell, the county seat of Livingston County, was owned and operated by a husband and wife, Fred and Jan Hodgins. In the words of the Michigan Court of Appeals:

> [The Hodginses] are state and federally licensed dealers who receive or purchase unwanted animals from municipal and county dog pounds, specifically Garden City and Monroe and Livingston Counties. These animals are those which have not been adopted, are unclaimed, or about to be put to death. The animals then undergo certain conditioning which includes shots, worming treatments and quarantine. [They] then sell these animals to hospitals, universities, and drug companies for use in medical research, experimentation, teaching, surgical and medical procedures, pharmaceutical testing, and toxicology studies.[96]

The Hodginses viewed their work as a cause:

> The use of live animals for medical research, testing, experimentation and teaching is indispensable to the . . . state's medical schools, . . . hospitals and medical facilities. . . . The discovery of insulin, drugs used in the control of tuberculosis, bubonic plague, smallpox, rabies, diphtheria, syphilis, . . . hypertension, . . . heart by-pass surgery, are examples of developments which would not have been possible without the use of live animals. The alternatives, in many cases, . . . are to try untested drugs and techniques directly upon human subjects, to abandon the research, or to conduct it outside the United States.[97]

Animal advocates, of course, disagreed. In a letter to the *Livingston County Press* Cathy Blight wrote:

> Mr. Hodgins has his own reasons for defending the practice [of selling county shelter animals for research], mainly a substantial loss of income. He failed to mention he is the local animal dealer who purchases dogs and cats from the shelter for $1 to $1.50 each and resells them to labs for anywhere from $25 to $50 each. Not a bad mark-up. He is understandably worried about losing business.[98]

Were the Humane Society advocates anti-science Luddites or extremists? Blight continued:

Preventing cruel and unnecessary animal experiments would not "endanger the furthering of valuable research." On the contrary, such measures would only enhance the credibility of results obtained and insure more accurate findings.

Before you write this off as another letter from an "unrealistic, bleeding-heart animal lover," let me say that I am 100 percent in favor of medical research as a valuable tool in saving human lives. My brother has multiple sclerosis, so I know from experience what research can do. But I am also 100 percent against the use of animals. Sound like a contradiction in terms? Not if you have studied what goes on in the research community.

A noted research scientist from England [discussing noncomparability of dog and cat results with human, cell culture alternatives, and England's ban on animal experimentation] said the use of animals was an incredible waste of life, not to mention time and money. Results from such experiments were more often than not inaccurate and useless.[99]

Providing insight on why targets focus their petitioning on local government, she concluded: "[This newspaper] suggests we concentrate our efforts on legislation and leave the labs alone. For years the Humane Society of the United States has been doing just that. But the legislative process is painstakingly slow. Meanwhile, we will continue to work at the local level."[100] And work they did. That same year, Mary Lou Durbin spoke out at public meetings of the Garden City Council and the Monroe County Commission, against sending pound animals over to Hodgins Kennels. The Regans also testified before the Garden City Council, and both local governments soon stopped the practice. The Livingston County Humane Society put out a flyer urging an end to animal sales in that county as well, and Wanda Glodowski testified before the Livingston County Commissioners.

The Hodginses then sued Garden City and the five advocates for unspecified damages, charging defamation, tortious interference with business relations, and conspiracy.[101] Singled out were the targets' lobbying of government bodies, Blight's letter to the editor, and the Humane Society's flyer. The dog dealers complained that the animal advocates had falsely accused them of cruelty, "petnapping," "vast profits," "bribes," and conducting "a furtive and sinister business," in order to cause "termination of [the kennel's] business relationship" with the governments.[102]

The case went to trial and was a disaster for the animal advocates. The filers shrewdly put "American Medical Research" on trial instead of the right to petition, with scientists and academics testifying that animals were needed for their research. Filers succeeded in characterizing targets as motivated to put them "out of business."[103] The jury strongly sided with the kennel owners, awarding them a staggering $329,739 in damages against the city and the advocates.

Durbin and Blight appealed and a clearly filer-sympathetic appeals court reversed on a technicality but was overturned by the Michigan Supreme Court, which reinstated the filers' victory. In fact, the filers collected a reported total of $835,000 in settlements. Among the relatively few court victories for SLAPP filers, this one sets a record for its huge dollar recovery; no other case comes close (except for the Immuno's cash settlements before it lost on appeal to the last target holdout). Immediately after the jury verdict, Garden City settled with a payment of $260,000 to the Hodginses, and the Regans agreed to pay $35,000. After the appeals, Durbin's insurance firm agreed to a $525,000 settlement (of which Durbin paid $125,000, most of her savings from 30 years as a Garden City teacher).[104] Blight, the last to give in, finally agreed to pay $15,000, with funds raised by animal rights groups and individuals (including Cleveland Amory). She felt she could not go on because "your life comes to a screeching halt. You can't get credit, you can't get insurance. The first thing they ask you is if you have any [court] judgments. I always had to answer yes."[105]

Were the targets chilled? After the case was settled, Blight told the press she was reluctant to talk: "I don't want to upset them [the filers]. I don't want to make them angry. I don't want them to come after me again. It angers me tremendously. I should be able to talk to you. I should be able to talk."[106] Durbin still finds it hard to believe: "I didn't say anything against the dog dealer. I didn't slander him or libel him. I talked against the issue, and felt that what I was doing was within my constitutional rights."[107]

The Hodginses declined to respond to press inquiries, but their attorney, Nancy Kahn, said in a letter to the media:

> This lawsuit was filed because false statements were made about the plaintiffs and their business. Those statements were very damaging. The jury agreed and their verdict has been upheld by the highest court in Michigan. . . . Now that the plaintiffs have repeatedly proven that the statements made about them were false, they should be left alone.[108]

They did not leave others alone, however. In 1982, a year after filing the Durbin-Blight suit, they filed another SLAPP against the vice-president of the Humane Society of St. Clair County, north of Detroit, and the publisher of the *Port Huron Times-Herald*.[109] During a campaign to get the county pound contract away from the Hodginses, the vice-president had written a letter to the editor stating that some dogs were ending up as "training animals" in illegal dog fights. The letter had its intended effect: The county canceled the contract. But the Hodginses promptly sued for $500,000; a default judgment of $70,000 in punitive damages was entered against the Humane Society officer, who did not defend the case; and the jury ruled both defendants liable to the Hodginses for $130,000 in "actual" damages. The Michigan Supreme Court again upheld the verdicts.

In 1988 the Humane Society of America distributed nationwide a poster headed "BEWARE! Protect Your Pet!" Lab prices were so high, it asserted, that some animal dealers would "resort to stealing pets from owners." Attorney Nancy Kahn sent out letters to locals suspected of "distributing" the posters, stating that even though Hodgins Kennels was not named, the poster created an "inference" that it was stealing because it was the only animal dealer in the area: "If you persist in this activity, Hodgins Kennels will have to seriously consider alternatives such as litigation."[110] As a result, the national Humane Society advised the Michigan volunteers "to stop distributing the materials" and apologized for the "embarrassment."[111]

The targets' attorneys in the *Durbin-Blight* SLAPP still feel that the courts missed the real issues. As Blight's ACLU attorney, I. W. Winsten, put it:

> This case involved fundamental First Amendment freedoms. What the Hodginses were attempting to do was intimidate their opposition. . . . The thing that's most frightening about this is that Cathy Blight is like a lot of people we know: a good American who got involved in her community on a particular issue and got saddled with a huge lawsuit.[112]

The assessment of Michael Walter, Durbin's lawyer, can serve as the epilogue for this chapter:

> The spooky thing is, these are not the animal-rights terrorists, if you will, breaking into governmental labs or disrupting fur shows. These are people petitioning government for a change in policy, advocating change through letters to the editor. I thought that was the American way. I still do.[113]

6 "Not in My Backyard" SLAPPs

Care Homes, Landfills, and Other "LULUs" Turning Up on Our Doorsteps

I hope you never have to handle a [neighborhood] association of do-gooders, but if you do, here are some tips.

First, try to get along with them. Offer them $50 as a donation for their projects. Accidentally make the check out to the president or leader. . . . When this check comes back from the bank, keep it with your valuable documents. If, at a later date, the do-gooders threaten you, claim you have been blackmailed by them. Threaten to call the media and tell them how the leader said he would keep the neighborhood gang off your back for $50. . . .

If the above does not work, threaten them with lawsuits for harassment and loss of income. . . . Sue the leader personally. Sue the organization. Sue all! Once they find out that you are not going to take their abuse without fighting and that they are going to have to pay a lawyer and take time off from work, they will leave you alone. They are basically gutless and will give up easily. You can intimidate them through our courts. That's the American way. God bless America!

—A. Kane, *Care and Feeding of Tenants* (1981)

Some people will do almost anything that is legally permitted to thwart the creation of [objectionable facilities] near their homes or cities or towns. Some residents will press their claims in neighborhood meetings, before administrative panels and before the courts. . . . Citizen[s] . . . that will use any and all available means to halt the construction of a garbage dump or some such thing do more than try the patience. . . . They may also prevent a much-needed [facility] from being built. But the proper response is surely not to rescind the citizens' right to petition the government. No matter how much the [facility] is needed . . . eliminating such a fundamental right is far too high a cost to pay.

—*Albany* (New York) *Sunday Times Union* (1989)

Every day in America some new facility is proposed in a community by a landowner, developer, government agency, or nonprofit charity. It may be a very small project: a driveway, tennis court, radio antenna. It may be larger: a bar, church, nursing home, fast food franchise, dance hall, video arcade, low-income housing, mental illness or drug addiction treatment center. Or it may be larger still: an office park, quarry, factory, recycling center, medical waste incinerator, or toxic waste dump. Frequently, reaction to the proposal is predictable: protesting citizens, an aroused community, pressured officials, intense opposition, spiraling costs, delays, and potential defeat of the project.

This scenario has public officials, planners, service providers, and developers wringing their hands over the "NIMBY" ("not in my back yard") syndrome in America today.[1] Acronyms breed, and NIMBY has spawned yet another: "LULU," for "locally unwanted land uses." The common NIMBY reaction to LULUs leaves developers and officials wondering whether any change is ever acceptable to existing neighborhoods and community groups, while beleaguered neighbors wonder whether "outsiders" in pursuit of a fast buck will ever stop trying to change their communities for the worse. This mutual frustration and distrust explodes into one of the most fertile fields for litigation, making NIMBY SLAPPs against neighbors and neighborhood groups a standard-issue risk for those dealing with government about facilities and problems in their communities.

The most frequent NIMBY SLAPPs are those involving residential-commercial real estate developments (Chapter 3), and at the other end of the spectrum are the eco-SLAPPs (Chapter 5), whose issues affect more than just one community or neighborhood. This chapter surveys the spectrum of LULUs in between, the localized community disputes resulting in SLAPPs that share this distinguishing mark: However civic-minded the surface objections, at the core targets are also concerned about their own property values, personal safety, aesthetics, and life-style. But to highlight the self-centeredness of the targets of NIMBY SLAPPs is not to denigrate them or their right to advocate their cause. The First Amendment's Petition Clause was not created to encourage only altruistic, selfless, civic-minded discourse. Its drafters had just fought and killed in a bloody revolution because their previous government taxed their businesses, confiscated their properties, and jailed their persons—all "without representation," without a safe chance to be heard. NIMBY protesters are successors to that legacy. They are people who feel personally attacked and threatened and, on that basis, have the strongest reason of all to insist on being heard. Like the message or not, these people and their concerns are a big part of what the First Amendment was designed to protect.

A national study of the NIMBY syndrome by the Daniel Yankelovich Group (DYG)[2] reveals important insights for SLAPPs. That study found NIMBY campaigns widespread (14 percent of those surveyed reported their neighborhood involved in at least one during the previous five years) and fairly successful (in 50 percent the facility in question was stopped); they also involve significant numbers of us (6 percent reported actively opposing and 8 percent supporting a facility).

Not all projects generate the same level of NIMBY hostility. The DYG study finds a three-tier hierarchy of acceptability. Tier 1 (least objectionable) comprises schools, day-care centers, nursing homes, hospitals, and medical clinics. A majority of those questioned "would welcome" these (from 65 percent for schools to 57 percent for clinics), and only a small minority would oppose them (12–15 percent). Tier 2 (more objectionable) includes group homes for the mentally retarded, homeless shelters, alcohol and drug treatment centers. Less than a majority "would welcome" these (45–40 percent, a significant drop), and opposition doubles (21–31 percent). Tier 3 (most objectionable) involves shopping malls, group homes for the mentally ill or AIDS patients, factories, landfills, and prisons. There is a real plunge in those who "would welcome" such facilities (36–37 percent), and opposition skyrockets (40–85 percent).

What causes NIMBYism? The DYG study found that demographics strongly influence negative reactions, with income the single best predictor of opposition. Project opposers are disproportionately higher-income ($50,000 and up), male, older (60 or more), well-educated professionals; they are predominantly white, married homeowners living in large cities. Project supporters are more likely to be lower-income (under $25,000), female, younger (under 30), less well-educated persons in service jobs; they tend to be single, nonwhite renters. "Neutrals" (a significant group of persons not registering strong feelings about the project either way) have a profile very much like "welcomers." Interestingly, the study found that geographic region, length of time in the neighborhood, and having children are *not* key factors. Moreover, the conventional wisdom that preserving property values is the key NIMBY stimulus has been overstated; threats to physical well-being are more salient.

What modern American attitudes and values cause many up-scale individuals to oppose even socially desirable projects such as schools, day-care centers, and clinics? The DYG study found that the current social climate in the United States "reinforces" NIMBYism. Seven social trends contribute. First, the eroding psychology of affluence: The belief that current and future economic well-being can be taken for granted has been replaced by a more pessimistic belief that individual success, though still possible, is not automatic or available to everyone. Second, the emergence of a two-tiered society: Disillusionment with the failure of egalitarianism ("the Great Society") has led to a growing acceptance of self-reliance, mastery, and rewarding winners ("social Darwinism"), even if this means that some fall by the wayside and we become more a classist, have/have-not society. Third, risk aversion: Americans are less willing to take chances, in their personal finances, in the foods they eat, in exposure to environmental hazards, in the consumer goods they buy. Fourth, less tolerance: The 1960s–1970s acceptance of different life-styles is waning, and in a climate of limited economic resources pluralism is being replaced by parochialism. Fifth, hunger for affiliation: As tolerance for difference diminishes, a desire for connectedness with others is increasing, manifesting itself in recommitment to family, ethnic or racial or religious groups, neighborhood, and community. Sixth, more time at home: Particularly for Americans under 50, the home is emerging as an even greater focus; "cocooning" (stress response), reduced spending, and relationship maintenance are seen as key reasons. Seventh, more child-centeredness: The woman's dilemma—to work outside the home or not—is a growing force, increasing her workload, stress, child-centeredness, and need for day care. The SLAPPs that follow NIMBY protests, within the three escalating tiers from least to most objectionable projects, reinforce these findings to a large degree, although not without some surprises along the way.

The Least Objectionable LULUs

Tier 1 projects—schools, traditional child and elderly care, and medical facilities—may be the least objectionable statistically, but these and even more minor projects can generate vicious disputes, polarization, and retaliatory SLAPPs—seemingly out of proportion to their relative benefit or size. We have yet to find a smaller, more trivial development leading to a SLAPP than the new driveway that was enough in Berkeley, California. Neighbors protested that change in their "designated landmark" neighborhood and finally sued the city to appeal the permit, later dismissing their case when the driveway was built. At that point they were SLAPPed for $7,007,000 by their driveway-desiring neighbors for malicious prosecution and emotional distress.[3] The filers eventually dropped the suit.

Recreation facilities can be SLAPP-starters too, as was a tennis court in the affluent Rice Island community on Boston's South Shore.[4] When the Lowry Bells received a permit to build a tennis court on their seaside property, their surrounding neighbors objected, most particularly the Peter Mazzas. Mazza filed objections with the building inspector, police, and local court (arguing wetlands destruction, traffic, noise, and lights); he offered to buy the property and, failing that, allegedly threatened "that he had 'connections' and would do 'anything,' 'at any cost,' to prevent the [Bells'] construction of any tennis court."[5] After three years of protests, hearings, restraining orders, and being cursed in the street,[6] the Bells sued the Mazzas for money damages for violation of their civil rights. The trial court dismissed the SLAPP, but the filers won reversal in the appeals court because the targets' alleged "threats, intimidation, and coercion," were said to overcome their Petition Clause rights.[7] The case settled, the Bells built their court, the Mazzas moved out—and the Bells also left town shortly thereafter.

A lawyer who opened an office in his home in Chico, California, opened himself up to an injunction lawsuit by the county and his neighbors, since businesses were excluded from that residential zone. The lawyer and his wife filed a $764,000-plus cross-complaint against county officials and 12 neighbors.[8] The jury sided with the lawyer, awarding him a $650,000-plus verdict; the shocked trial judge reversed the verdict, however, and even ordered the lawyer to pay targets $30,000 in attorneys' fees. The appeals court affirmed, noting that "private citizens' communications to zoning officials" even to "persuade the officials to engage in allegedly unconstitutional zoning activities" are "not actionable" because they come under the right of petition. In an amusing about-face the County of San Luis Obispo—itself the filer of an earlier SLAPP against antinuclear demonstrators (Chapter 4)—joined 88 other counties and cities in filing a friend-of-the-court brief in this case, to urge that citizens' rights to petition be protected from the "fundamental danger" of SLAPPs.

Churches too may be unwelcome in residential communities. Take one example with a happier than usual outcome. The Jehovah's Witnesses have created some of our most protective First Amendment legal precedents, fighting for their rights to freedom of speech and religion,[9] but they filed a classic SLAPP against the First Amendment rights of others in a 1987 Colorado case.[10] For years, the Witnesses sought to build a new church in a fast-gentrifying commuter area southeast of Denver. Finally, frustrated by opposition, the congregation sued zoning authorities, a homeowners' association, and residents for opposing their zoning application. The ACLU (which has represented Jehovah's Witnesses in other civil liberties cases) contacted the filers' attorneys, expressing concern over the SLAPP filing, and to their credit the Witnesses promptly dismissed their suit against association and neighbors while continuing their proper judicial appeal against the government zoning authorities. Today, they have several churches in the area.

The elderly, despite the debt we owe them and the fact that more of us are joining their ranks every year, are not warmly welcomed by many neighborhoods, and developers of elderly housing, retirement complexes, and nursing homes have resorted to SLAPPs in a number of cases. A particularly unsympathetic case for targets is the often cited *Gorman Towers v. Bogoslavsky,*[11] in which Fort Smith, Arkansas, landowners sued neighbors for $1,700,000 for opposing their 150-unit high rise for the elderly and handicapped. The targets were anything but fair; the court found they had spread "false derogatory rumors about [the] proposed housing project"[12] and had "without rational basis" persuaded the city to rezone filers' property to exclude high rises.[13] Despite real sympathy for the filers and disgust with the targets, however, the U.S. Court of Appeals upheld dismissal of the SLAPP, ruling that the neighbors had "absolute immunity" because their "real purpose [was] to induce governmental action, [not to] injure plaintiff directly."[14] The elder-care home had to be built elsewhere.

More Objectionable LULUs

Tier 2 projects such as group homes and treatment centers for the mentally ill, developmentally disabled, homeless, and substance dependent raise the NIMBY ante. Predictably, a majority of the neighborhood will oppose these facilities, according to the DYG study—to the distress of many, given the desirability of community-based treatment for such illnesses and conditions, in lieu of the "out of sight, out of mind" institutional penal approaches of the past. But the modern move to shift away from large, impersonal institutions and disperse patients to smaller, less-restrictive, in-community residences often leads to "bitter local clashes" in which "the mentally retarded, homeless, elderly, disabled and incarcerated [are seen as] today's 'parasites' [instead of as] our children, brothers and sisters, aunts and uncles, parents and grandparents."[15] And those clashes lead to SLAPPs, as illustrated by a case that generally fits the SLAPP model but has enough non-SLAPP aspects to make it worth exploring in detail.

The Adult Blind Home Case: The "Indispensable Parties" Problem

Since 1940 the stately old Denver building with its Grecian pillars, built at the turn of the century as a tuberculosis hospital, had housed the blind, another group once routinely institutionalized. By the 1980s, however, policies of deinstitutionalization and public acceptance had moved the visually impaired into the mainstream—and the nonprofit Adult Blind Home (ABH) into bankruptcy. In 1984 the ABH thought it had found the perfect buyer: the REDI ("Rehabilitating Emotionally Disabled Individuals") Corporation wanted to use the building as a residential treatment center for about 40 people with depression and other mental health problems. REDI was delighted with the ABH building, as a representative explained:

> It was the finest facility of its kind that I had ever seen. It was in outstanding shape and the buy was just incredible . . . $300,000 for a building of that size and where we have difficulty getting a building a third that size for the price. It was magnificently clean . . . up to every single code. . . . It would serve us extremely well, extremely well.[16]

REDI assumed that after 80 years the neighborhood had accepted the building as a group home. Moreover, with Denver's exclusionary zoning, "there were no other options. There are no other ones on the market, and we can't build one." REDI was hot to deal.

The old building overlooks a beautiful village green that gives the neighborhood its name, "Highland Park." On Denver's near north side, it is an area of squat brick bungalows and a few stately mansions—a neighborhood in decline with a mix of older, established lower- and middle-class families, ethnic groups (predominantly Hispanics and Italians), transients, and some young professionals; "gentrification" had come to Highland Park a few years before, only to be frozen by the sagging Denver economy. This combination of older natives and younger, educated activists provided a fertile mix for the coming clash and was well represented in the five neighborhood advocates who were SLAPPed by ABH and REDI. Richard Miles was a college-educated 1960s antiwar activist and self-described "poor dumb starving artist,"[17] with a wife, a small daughter, and another child on the way; he would become the acknowledged "catalyst" of the opposition.[18] Husband and wife George and Wavia Tullar were lifelong "involved" residents of Highland Park, high school graduates, now near retirement. Marie Clark, a professional health-care worker, was single and a newcomer to the neighborhood. Don Koza, a college-educated building contractor living outside the neighborhood, was concerned about his latest condominium project across the park from ABH. Each of the five had a strong sense of community, some involvement with activism, concerns about the neighborhood's decline, and a personal economic stake in the area.

REDI and its managers were experienced group-home operators. They had successfully coped with and overcome neighborhood opposition elsewhere and admitted to having used "legalistic means" and lawsuits to do so. REDI anticipated some trouble in Highland Park as well: "The very issue of a group home is one that prompts and promotes a tremendous amount of community concern . . . which . . . in every incidence that I'm aware of has led to substantial opposition, . . . some type of action before a government body . . . or . . . court or the threat of suits, etc." And they believed discrimination was the reason:

> [People always say,] "This is wonderful work that you're doing but not in our neighborhood." . . . "This is great, but . . . why don't you do this someplace else, why here?" It's the same kind of arguments, unfortunately, and I have a lot of emotion on this, [as] with minorities moving into a community. "Why don't they live someplace else?" "They're not our kind." "We're a family-oriented neighborhood and these people don't fit in." It's the same kind of situation [with minorities]. People identify their own communities in a very homogeneous way and those individuals that don't fit in with the majority pattern are viewed as being different and . . . will therefore disrupt and transform the current functioning of the community or neighborhood and are therefore viewed as a threat.

REDI was correct; every resident interviewed expressed exactly these "right thing, wrong place" sentiments. The neighborhood was not unanimously opposed; some, like Anne Coomer Smith, supported community-based treatment and though that the objectors were not the majority, just "the loudest." Yet even the experienced REDI personnel, while anticipating opposition, were not prepared for the intensity they would encounter in Highland Park.

A combination of negative but typical NIMBY factors fanned the flames. First, the neighborhood was already having "considerable problems" with an existing home for the substance-dependent and mentally ill, next door to ABH, viewing it "as a threat"[19] (complaints about sanitation, inmates wandering the streets, intimidation).[20] Second, with eight group homes in a one-mile radius, Highlanders already felt like a dumping ground, and this was the last straw.[21] Third, there was "the murder" (mentioned by every resident interviewed): The nude body of a woman had been dumped in the park the year before, and the case remained unsolved. Fourth, the local city councilman lent the residents one of his aides, Shirley Schlay, who herself opposed the REDI takeover and helped organize neighbors. Fifth, the residents included more "repeat players" than we have found in other cases, people with high levels of past activism and experience in other NIMBY oppositions. Realistically, any of these five factors could have accounted for strong NIMBY reactions; together, they were deadly for the project.

REDI had been twice turned down for a permit by the Denver zoning administrator before it ever met with residents. After 1978, "group homes" were no longer allowed in residential zones such as Highland Park. The Adult Blind Home could have continued operating as a "grandfathered" nonconforming use, but REDI could not step into its shoes. On January 24, 1985, REDI (now carrying the ball with a power-of-attorney from ABH) filed an appeal to the Zoning Board of Adjustments. And four days later, in a local church, representatives met with residents for the first time. The meeting was organized by a corporate community relations specialist who lived in the neighborhood and supported REDI's work.[22] After REDI made a presentation, residents questioned staffing, parking, property values, patient-community interaction, effects on children, and density. The meeting was confrontational and reinforced stereotypes. To Richard Miles, REDI representatives were "a little too slick," drove up "in a great, big, shiny Mercedes . . . in a neighborhood with 10-year-old cars," planted "obvious ringers" for support in the audience, and made the neighbors feel "bush league." In REDI's view, the neighbors were "outraged, so wild," "panic[king] . . . envision[ing] a lot of crazy people just messing up the community,"[23] whereas REDI saw itself on a mission to serve needy clients who were "probably the most harmless neighbors that you can have."[24] After that meeting, both sides went to work. REDI waged a letter-writing campaign to city zoning authorities. Meanwhile, opponents Miles, Clark, Koza, the Tullars, and others were arguing out tactics, recruiting a neighborhood lawyer (with NIMBY experience against bars), and getting the councilman and his aide on board.

At REDI's February 20 appeal hearing, neighbors were stunned to hear the zoning administrator reverse herself and grant the permit, on the advice of the city attorney's office. Her reasoning—characterizing REDI as an "institution," which was allowable, rather than a "group home," which was not—seemed to them a semantic ploy.[25] On March 13 the five opponents appealed her reversal to the Zoning Board of Adjustments, collecting the signatures of some 65 other Highland Park residents, who were duly registered as "co-appellants."[26] The residents hired a second attorney, an experienced zoning specialist, who advised them to make "sympathy" their tactic, Miles recalls:

> [The board is] sensitive to neighborhood issues. Quite frankly, we were told one of the things they were most sensitive to was mothers with crying babies, stuff like that. So we tried all of the, I guess, "sap" tactics to try to influence them and try to act like the neighborhood was being raped by this wealthy corporation. It was a sympathy ploy, certainly.

And it was successful. The Zoning Board of Adjustments reversed the zoning administrator, ruling that REDI was a "group home" and not entitled to operate in the neighborhood.

The next month ABH and REDI filed suit,[27] claiming that the denial violated their constitutional rights and naming the city, city officials, and the five resident ringleaders. Miles was "surprised, shocked and panicked." Wavia Tullar wondered why the 65 co-appellants were not named; she thought the five were being made "scapegoats." No one else, including the targets' own attorney, was surprised. According to the zoning administrator, it is "common" in Denver for neighbors who appeal decisions to be named in zoning suits[28]—to be SLAPPed for petitioning city hall.

To this point, the suit was typical, fitting our SLAPP criteria: It was a civil action against nongovernmental individuals because of their communications to government on an issue of public concern. But this case presents an important variant: Filers felt required by state law to sue the citizens. The five residents' names were on the zoning appeal that ABH and REDI were appealing to court, and state laws (Colorado being no exception) typically require that anyone filing a court action against a government agency decision must name as defendants "all parties of record" in the proceeding being appealed. According to REDI trial attorney Mark Hannen: "We have to name those people because they are parties in interest in this matter. . . . They were the people that actively prosecuted the case before the board. . . . If we had not named them, our suit might have been . . . dismissed for not having [all the] required parties."

This "indispensable parties" requirement is based on a legitimate policy of providing notice and an opportunity to be heard to those who have established their interest in a government proceeding. It means, however, that citizens taking part in such proceedings can unknowingly expose themselves to the bigger and usually more expensive risk of court involvement. So ingrained is this concept that even the targets' own attorneys thought REDI's suit against their clients was "proper."[29] Thus, a law designed to protect petitioning citizens' interests can have exactly the opposite effect. It can also provide an effective excuse or camouflage for filers whose motives are simply retaliatory. It would be more rational, a more efficient use of court resources, and more protective of citizen participation for state legislatures to substitute a simple requirement of notice of suit and leave it up to the citizens whether to intervene in the court case or not.

In this case, it is true, the targets were simply named; none of the usual allegations of misconduct were made against them, nor was any intimidating monetary relief asked of them. But filers' motives are seldom as clear-cut as the "indispensable parties" provision implies: If that was the filers' concern in this instance, it is difficult to understand why they did *not* name the 65 co-appellants, who, having registered their names and interest and having testified publicly, were just as "indispensable." The filers knew this; their attorney bluntly stated that the five were named because "they took the leadership role" against his client. Certainly the five were not consoled by the "indispensable parties" rationale. Miles felt just as singled-out and exposed as a target in a clearly retaliatory SLAPP: "My question to [our attorney] was, 'Why just the five of us? What happened to the other 65?' . . . They just didn't want to name all of these people, I guess, and wind up with something like 70 people pooling their resources. That might've been an entirely different ball game."

Still, the apparent absence of a personal vendetta may have contributed to another atypical aspect of the case: Targets quickly adjusted to being sued and decided to stay in the case and fight. "They were worried at first," said the councilman's aide, "but then . . . they still thought they were right and they were doing what was best for the neighborhood. They just became more involved in dealing with the suit."[30] A few weeks after the filing, Miles seemed clearly unintimidated and even enjoying the fight.[31] Another reason these targets did not opt out, he felt, was that they did not trust the city to defend the case, not only because the city had flip-flopped on the permit but because the city attorney now defending the permit denial was the same one who had originally recommended that it be granted. Targets even asked the court (unsuccessfully) to disqualify the city's lawyer for conflict of interest.

Nevertheless, in the words of the country western song, targets found that "hangin' in" also left them "hangin' out and hangin' on" as the strain of SLAPP defense began to tell. Miles conceded:

> I spent the better part of a year working on this thing. I would go to my studio and spend almost all day long on the telephone . . . begging for money, talking to attorneys, talking to [other neighborhood groups], applying for money there. You name it . . . it was typing letters. You can see the thickness of my file. It was just a horrendous time. My wife was constantly saying, "Just quit." I knew that if I quit . . . pretty soon others would, and we would wind up with REDI winning.

Money was a big problem. Target attorney Gil Goldstein cut his fees in half, but his services still cost over $6,000.[32] The targets poured several hundred dollars each into the coffers, but pledges were hard to collect, and other neighborhood groups gave disappointingly little support. Eventually, the targets resorted to yard sales.

Atypically for SLAPPs, both sides avoided the media: REDI because it did not want to inflame this or future situations; the targets because they feared REDI could "hire a publicist . . . and we would get beaten to a pulp in the papers," according to Miles. Not wanting to hurt the neighborhood's reputation[33] or lower their own property values[34] was additional reason for keeping the media out.

Less than six months after the SLAPP was filed, with the judge's preliminary ruling that REDI was indeed an impermissible "group home," the case was for all intents and purposes over, though the final resolution took another 15 months and a three-day trial. Neither ABH nor REDI felt they could support an empty building during "years" of appeals, according to their lawyer, Robert Hoghaug, so when a Denver couple, Al and Janet Sleeth, offered to buy the building for the same price and convert it into a retirement home for senior citizens, ABH readily agreed. The Sleeths carefully laid their groundwork. They spent six months "literally [going] house to house" and attending "quite a few neighborhood meetings" to convince people that they were not a front for REDI and that their clients would not be mentally ill.[35] It may have been overkill; most of the targets were ready by then to throw in the towel, including the ringleader, Miles:

> [Mr. Sleeth] wound up calling [all of us] before he bought the building, before he even applied for the zoning permit . . . and said, "Look, this is what I want to do. Do you have any problem with this? I would like you to come over and take a look at the facility and walk through." And they actually had a Saturday morning meeting for us. . . . Had he known how beat down we were there would have been no problem. He could have waltzed right in and run a brothel there if he wanted to.

Also, the neighbors felt that a home for seniors did not present the same threats as a home for the mentally ill, and "we couldn't be absolute jerks about it."[36] The "Heather Grove Retirement Home" opened in May 1987, and once again the old building "is vibrant with life."[37]

Life has not gone out of the targets, either. Richard Miles is "soured on community organizations," "angry" at filers and city zoning officials, but

> I wouldn't say to somebody, "Don't get involved." I've become more involved in things to a certain extent. This has been an affirmation that the system has its aberrations but it works. It may be painful at times and I'll be a little leery at times. . . . If something like this crops up again, I'm going to see if I can get somebody else to shoulder the brunt of the work.

Likewise, the Tullars still "would probably fight anything that was coming in our neighborhood" for which it was not zoned. Why the minimal discouragement in these targets? Five factors stand out: They did not face a demand for money damages; they voluntarily decided to stay in the lawsuit; they had substantial support from the government they petitioned; they had confidence in their lawyers; and they won both in court and in the real world. Although these factors do occur in other SLAPPs we have studied, it is extremely rare to find them all together.

In this case it was the filers themselves who were chilled. REDI's representatives admit that the outcome forced them to avoid large, visible group homes and to disperse their clients in less obvious apartments and smaller units. They are bitter about the case and the neighbors' ability to thwart what they viewed as better care for the mentally ill. Yet ironically, by the 1990s big group homes had become a thing of the past; the dominant policy in housing the mentally or emotionally ill is to integrate them into the community and avoid large facilities.

The city councilman's assistant, Susan Schlay, provided a retrospective containing some real insights on NIMBY SLAPPs:

> [REDI] should have just realized that the neighbors were against them. I don't think they should have carried it this far [to sue]. . . . City Council . . . almost has to go along with the neighborhood. . . . [Developers] have got to work out some sort of situation where it is going to be acceptable and be part of the neighborhood, or it is going to fail. This goes for liquor stores, restaurants, halfway houses, almost anything.
>
> Neighbors, citizens, are getting more active. They are very protective of their neighborhoods. . . . Maybe [this is because] they feel helpless on the national scene . . . and they want to accomplish something and they can do that in their neighborhood. . . . The neighborhoods are very, very active. You've got to listen to them.

Racism and Housing

NIMBYism is, in part, a rejection of "minorities," as the REDI representative aptly noted. Race and ethnic prejudice can stimulate fears and catapult a facility into the "objectionable" category, just as mental health issues do. Three typical minority-housing SLAPPs show just how large a factor race can be.

Racial bias was clear to the court in a 1978 dispute over a proposed 156-unit, low-income apartment complex in Greenville County, South Carolina.[38] Residents lobbied county officials, "rais[ing] questions about the desirability of housing minority and low-income residents in the . . . neighborhood."[39] Agreeing, the county tried to "freeze" building permits, but the developer got a court order overturning the freeze; then the residents intervened and appealed, tying the permit up for another 16 months until the state supreme court found for the developer. It was too late; the low-income developer's plans had fallen through "due to the pall cast over the project" by targets' litigation, and he had to sell out at a loss. Despite all this, the federal courts threw out his subsequent $300,000 SLAPP charging three resident ringleaders with race discrimination. "Even overtly biased citizens who write letters, speak up at public meetings, or even express their prejudices in private meetings with public officials" are protected by the right to petition, the court ruled.[40]

Discrimination was blatant in an often cited New York SLAPP, *Weiss v. Willow Tree Civic Ass'n.*[41] Ramapo, New York, neighbors blocked Hasidic Jews from building a housing development for their congregation in the community. Members of the Willow Tree Civic Association, mostly non-Hasidic Jews, testified at public hearings, filed state complaints, instituted a lawsuit against the town, and publicized their campaign against "the peculiar way of life of 'these people.'"[42] In 1978, their housing application denied, the Hasidic Jews sued the civic association and 37 of its members for civil rights discrimination. The federal court, despite its lack of sympathy for targets' bigotry, speedily dismissed the SLAPP, creating another strong precedent for avoiding the "fact quagmire":

> The protection of the First Amendment does not depend on "motivation"; it depends on the nature of defendants' conduct. Defendants' activities . . . fall squarely under the protection of the First Amendment's guarantees of citizens' rights "peaceably to assemble and to petition the Government for a redress of grievances."[43]

"The petitioning is protected however unpalatable the ideas or whatever the underlying motive" if the goal is "to band together for the advancement of beliefs and ideas."[44] Even "groundless" lawsuits and complaints "hardly amount to grave [enough] abuse" to destroy the right.[45] And, underscoring exactly what is wrong with SLAPPs as a form of dispute transformation, the court pointed out: "Indeed, [filers] do not allege that they were prevented from responding to [targets'] charges . . . [or] denied access to the [government] Board which heard and considered their applications."[46] The First Amendment the court concluded, "protects 'attempts to influence the passage or enforcement of laws,' no matter how harmful their incidental impact on third parties may be."[47]

"One telephone call" from a white resident triggered a 1984 Chicago SLAPP. The resident's telephoned threat of litigation caused the state housing authority to drop a black, low-income-housing developer from the state's bond sale, cutting off his financing.[48] The developer filed a $1,015,000 suit against the white resident, alleging wrongful interference with business and bias against integration. The situation grayed considerably when the white target countered that he was a supporter of racial integration and a member of a multiracial community organization of Hispanics, blacks, and whites; their objection was economics, not race: "Logan Square has become . . . 'oversaturated' with subsidized low income housing . . . [and] needs new middle income housing . . . [because] if the middle class leaves, only the poor will be left behind, and what is now an integrated neighborhood will be so no longer."[49] An early motion to dismiss was denied, but after hearing the filer's evidence at trial, the judge stopped the proceedings and directed a verdict for the target, which the appeals court affirmed. The target thus won in court—but the filer won in the real world, building the low-income housing in Logan Square with city, instead of state, funding (the target's SLAPPback is discussed in Chapter 9).

Apparently anyone can file race-discrimination SLAPPs. In 1995 self-described "Irish-Catholics" sued the tiny village of Briarcliff Manor, New York, individuals, and a residents' group for $750,000,000 for alleged discrimination and civil rights violations against "persons of Irish heritage and the Irish race"—because the residents had opposed plaintiffs' development of a 58-acre Irish cultural and athletic facility in their town.[50]

Bar-the-Bars and Disband-the-Discos Cases

The neighborhood bar may be the stuff of fond memories and television reruns, but bars and other so-called "entertainment centers" are fought fiercely by many neighborhoods and have generated more NIMBY SLAPPs than any other LULU we have found. Owners of restaurants,[51] discos,[52] poker clubs,[53] video arcades,[54] and flea markets[55] have all sued neighbors and neighborhood groups for reporting their violations or opposing their licenses and renewals. A pair of opposite-result cases illustrates the range.

Residents of the upscale Tacoma neighborhood in Washington, D.C., were appalled to find out that a defunct bar in their midst was about to reopen under new management. Plan Takoma, Inc., a neighborhood group experienced in zoning fights, denounced the buyers in a leaflet as "a shady group of bar owners who operate a number of topless/bottomless 'GO-GO' dancer bars in D.C., which are the hangouts of motorcycle gangs and toughs."[56] The leaflet was clearly part of an effort to persuade the local liquor licensing board to deny the new license. Plan Takoma and seven of its officers were promptly sued by the new owners for $40,000,000 for libel on the basis of the one word "shady." Arnold & Porter, a national law firm, immediately won a motion to dismiss, later affirmed, because the target's leafleting was fully protected by the Petition Clause. The filers' license was denied.

Exactly the opposite was happening in nearby Baltimore. In 1980 the Northeast Community Organization (NECO) launched a similar campaign against renewal of a liquor license for the Locker Room bar, circulating a leaflet and newsletter to government officials, the community, and the media alleging "underaged drinking," "drug trafficking," "vandalism," "harassment of senior citizens," and "littering and rat infestation."[57] The bar owner sued them the next month for $1,000,000 for libel.[58] Significantly, the complaint admitted outright that targets "have spoken and written . . . to public officials, and have solicited signatures for petitions" to close the bar. Targets were at first thrilled to find that their insurance covered them. But after nearly four years in court the insurance company settled, paying the filer a reported $30,000 to avoid further expense and trial in the case.[59] A NECO participant who was not sued reports:

> The litigation exacted quite a toll from the community organization. Some of the more timid members . . . began to shy away from controversial activities. . . . One of the individual [targets] suffered extreme emotional distress and was under a physician's care because of it. [Another target] moved out of town to get a "fresh start." He was a professional organizer."[60]

In a way, however, the neighbors won in the real world: The bar was sold to a new owner, and according to NECO it now operates innocuously as "Uncle Harry's Tavern."

An interesting aspect of liquor licensing and zoning cases is that the laws frequently require the licensing board to consider "the wishes of the persons residing or owning property in the neighborhood."[61] One could not ask for a clearer call for citizens to exercise their right to petition. Yet having made citizen input mandatory, many local governments in the cases studied did little or nothing to protect complying residents who got SLAPPed. In a healthy exception, Denver officials castigated an attorney who sent letters to neighborhood groups warning that they were open to a lawsuit for opposing his client, whose tavern license renewal had been denied by the city.[62] The lawyer's "insulting, intimidating and offensive letter," according to the recipients, "ignores the fact that citizens have a [constitutional] right to petition the government."[63] Susan Duncan, director of Denver's Excise and License Department, agreed: "I was angered when I saw this letter. I grant or deny [bar] renewals based on the needs and desires of the neighborhood. If you intimidate people and keep them from exercising that very important right to petition, you're destroying the very thing that makes the city work."[64] It remains to be seen whether other government officials will, in their own enlightened self-interest, take a supportive stand for neighbors and against SLAPPs, or watch their public participation and public confidence "destroy[ed]."

The Most Objectionable LULUs

Tier 3 projects, according to the DYG study, are those wholly unacceptable to one-third or more of individuals queried. Widespread SLAPPs in this category illustrate citizen opposition to such normal industrial facilities as radio towers and quarries, as well as to the more exotic, toxics-tainted waste-to-energy plants and hazardous waste dumps. Interestingly, although these LULUs may be opposed more strongly by more people, we found comparable fierceness of disputes and likelihood of SLAPPs throughout all three tiers.

Recycling and Burning

The disposition of waste materials is a frequent source of NIMBY activism and consequent SLAPPs, whether the problem is recycling manure or burning used medical supplies. For example, Robert and Joan Vardaman live in one of the most beautiful parts of the country, unincorporated Broward County, Florida, outside Fort Lauderdale. Unfortunately, their next door neighbor is an "organic waste recycling landfill." The Vardamans and other area residents complained repeatedly to state and local code enforcement agencies about "flies, rats, dust and the smell of horse dung."[65] They stirred up more than they bargained for. Organic Recycling Company's president, Jeffrey Wolf, who lives in New York, said that the "constant complaining" made his life "miserable,"[66] and that he was cited for violations "only because county officials want to appease the incessant Vardaman."[67] So, his company sued the couple in February 1992, charging them with having a "personal agenda and vendetta" against Organic and engaging in "a systematic campaign of harassment, annoyance, threatening, slandering, libeling, harming, insulting or otherwise interfering or disturbing the peace, tranquillity and business operations of [Organic's] place of business."[68] Wolf admitted to the press that "his goal was to silence Vardaman."[69]

Commendably, the state attorney general's office conducted a survey of Floridians involved in SLAPPs, including the Vardamans, and its findings have made it an active supporter of legislative solutions (see Chapter 10). The *Miami Herald* summed it up best:

> Even if Vardaman is driving Wolf silly, her access to government is a basic right that ought to be nearly immune to such tactics [as SLAPPs]. But corporate lawyers,

who use lawsuits like fill dirt to bury citizen opposition, tend to forget some of the little niceties of democratic government. A new state law might be a perfect reminder.[70]

In Missouri a classic toxics LULU, a medical waste incineration plant, polarized neighbors, galvanized a state legislature, and provoked SLAPPs and SLAPPbacks. Medical waste has been generated as long as there have been doctors, hospitals, and nursing homes. Until quite recently, most was simply burned on the premises, but new federal and state laws now strictly limit disposal of these "red bag" wastes, creating a new industry made up of commercial disposal companies. One of these, DeCom Medical Waste Systems, Inc., a Canadian company, experienced extreme NIMBY difficulties wherever it tried to locate its "traveling incinerator," leaving behind "a trail of lawsuits, incomplete information and angry citizens."[71]

In 1987 the tiny town of Bunker (population 600) in the Missouri Ozarks must have looked to DeCom like the last place for NIMBYism: It had one of the highest unemployment rates in the state, politicians eager to keep the community alive economically, and a mayor who would agree to be president of DeCom's Missouri subsidiary and supply a site on his own property. But DeCom immediately had problems. Soon after it began operating, it was discovered not to have the necessary state permit; its incinerator-supplier sued to be relieved of liability; local residents got a court order closing the unlicensed plant; and the state department of natural resources scheduled hearings on its permit.[72]

Jacqueline Sommer Alexander, a 28-year-old high school English teacher in nearby Viburnum, let DeCom have it in a lengthy letter to the editor, urging her neighbors to come testify at the upcoming state permit hearings:

> Residents gathered nightly to watch the incinerator spout out smoke, flames (nearly ten to fifteen feet high) and smell the repugnant odor. . . . Thirty-three residents have signed affidavits . . . that they experienced headaches, nose bleeds, and other health problems which experts say are caused by hydrochloric acid gas emissions. . . . [Another resident] is being tested and treated for Legionnaire's Disease. . . . [A deputy sheriff reports that his car] was covered with ash fall-out from the facility. . . . DeCom . . . is gaining a reputation . . . as a money-hungry company with little regard for the public health, safety or the environment.[73]

Earlier that same week hospital worker Linda J. Tanner of nearby Black, Missouri, had written to a reporter on a newspaper in South Carolina, similarly criticizing DeCom and asking for information on its activities there.

In Missouri the state hearing was packed with 200 people, most of whom opposed the incinerator.[74] DeCom did not get its permit. The next month it SLAPPed the two letter writers with separate $1,000,000 federal court libel suits.[75] DeCom then engaged in some Petition Clause activity of its own, which backfired. It sent a letter to the governor, state attorney general, and each state senator suggesting that Alexander and Tanner were "unbalanced fanatics" and guilty of "outright, scurrilous lies"; it set out the company's version of the facts and stated that DeCom was the "victim of some sort of unscrupulous campaign, orchestrated by whom or for what exact reason we are not sure, but we certainly have our suspicions."[76] It followed up the letter by making $300 "campaign contributions" to members of the state legislative committee that was considering a bill to regulate infectious waste disposal.

DeCom's political moves, far from helping its cause, brought on an immediate public outcry and devastated its support base. State representatives termed the $300 checks "tacky, ill-timed, and clumsy."[77] One legislator called the company's suits against the two women "blackmail by an arrogant outsider."[78] The major St. Louis newspaper buried DeCom with bad publicity. First a sarcastic editorial criticized the SLAPPs:

> In most cases, a company that believes it is the victim of an unfair or inaccurate attack responds by writing a letter of rebuttal. Filing a libel suit against a school teacher of modest means is a lot more effective, however. Vocal opposition is likely to evaporate as critics contemplate the cost of hiring a lawyer. . . . Few libel suits against letter writers succeed in producing damage payments for the plaintiff, but they can certainly have a chilling effect on debate. And those who seek to shut off debate usually have a reason for doing so.[79]

Three days later the newspaper ran a large editorial cartoon of a man (labeled "DeCom") burning a letter to the editor (held by a woman) with a blowtorch (labeled "$1 Million Libel Suit"). The caption read: "After All, We Are In The Incinerator Business."[80] The next month an editorial accused DeCom of a "crude and heavy-handed" attempt at "buying influence," and a cartoon showed its smokestacks showering the state capitol with money and smoke.[81] National media picked up the story and gave the SLAPP national notoriety.[82] Then the Missouri legislature passed a comprehensive infectious waste disposal law with language designed to make sure DeCom's facility never operated again.[83] By the end of 1988 the company had voluntarily dismissed both SLAPPs—but its tribulations were not over. In January 1989 a St. Louis attorney, Richard Witzel, filed SLAPPbacks for the two women, accusing DeCom of libel, abuse of process, malicious prosecution, and intentional infliction of emotional distress. And in 1989 a St. Louis jury awarded Linda Tanner the largest SLAPP-back recovery to date, ordering DeCom to pay her a total of $86,500,000 (see Chapter 9).

Down and Dirty in the Oil Patch

What locals call "the environmental awakening of Plaquemines Parish"[84] began in 1987 with a 67-year-old retired schoolteacher leading the charge. Just south of New Orleans, Plaquemines is the last part of the United States through which the Mississippi rolls before entering the Gulf of Mexico. Louisiana, with a reputation for pollution problems,[85] has over 22,000 oilfield pits full of used drilling fluids and other wastes waiting for disposal, and Plaquemines Parish has nearly 10 percent of the state's total pits.[86]

"The matriarch of Plaquemines' fledgling environmental movement,"[87] Ann Williams knows her parish and the oil industry well. When she heard that Delta Environmental Services, Inc., had applied for state and local permits to build a disposal and recycling plant for "nonhazardous" oilield wastes seven miles upstream, she swung into action. Though legally classified as "nonhazardous," such wastes can contain heavy metals and other potentially harmful substances, according to experts.[88] Williams immediate concern was a NIMBY one: her community's drinking water, which is taken from the Mississippi.[89] She wrote letters to her parish government opposing the permit, testified at hearings, circulated leaflets encouraging others to testify, worked the media, and even filed a lawsuit against the parish council for approving the permit without public notice. The grandmotherly Williams can make a hearing come alive like the best revival preacher:

WILLIAMS: Please listen to me, friends and neighbors. Do we want the waste from the rest of Louisiana seven miles above our water intake?
VOICES IN THE AUDIENCE: No, no, no.
WILLIAMS: Do we want the waste of the world seven miles above our water intake?
VOICES IN THE AUDIENCE: No, no, no.
WILLIAMS: Do we want to be the cesspool of the world?
VOICES IN THE AUDIENCE: No, no.
WILLIAMS: Do we folks?
VOICES IN THE AUDIENCE: No, no. We don't want it.
WILLIAMS: I hope that the [state] Department of Conservation feels the same way. Louisiana already has 35 percent of the oilfield waste of the United States and Plaquemines Parish has probably more than the rest of the world. I'm asking [the state], please don't dump any more waste in our drinking water. Thank you."[90]

At first she was successful: On March 26, 1987, the parish council narrowly denied Delta a permit in a five-to-four vote. Then Delta turned on its own lobbying campaign. On October 12 it received its state permit, and on February 11, 1988, without public notice, the council quietly reversed itself and granted the local permit. "Then all hell broke loose," the newspaper reported.[91] Angry citizens flooded the next council meeting with 1,500 names on petitions,[92] and the parish president vetoed the permit, orating that the democratic process had been "annihilated, assassinated, obliterated, eliminated and decimated."[93] Delta filed an unsuccessful lawsuit against parish officials to overturn the veto,[94] but since only government bodies and officials were sued, it was not a SLAPP. Ann Williams countered with her own lawsuit, a nonmonetary challenge against parish officials contesting their right to override the veto.[95] Delta's president, J. Stuart Ellis Jr., felt politically stymied: "My permit was put in the hands of a bunch of freshman legislators, and they've been batting me around like a baseball. We have lost total sight of the project itself. I've become the victim of a political struggle."[96] His company spent four more months lobbying to get back on council's agenda, to no avail.[97]

Frustrated, Delta filed two more lawsuits on August 19, 1988: a $2,000,000 federal court suit against county officials for denying its permit,[98] and a $2,000,000 state court SLAPP against Ann Williams and a local newspaper for defamation and conspiracy.[99] The "defamation" and "conspiracy" consisted of two of Williams's letters to parish council members and a handbill to citizens, all urging government denial of the permit and a moratorium on dumping.[100] Delta was acutely aware that the words she used constituted political communication:

> This false and defamatory material has been circulated, distributed, delivered, and / or disseminated by defendants for the announced purpose, and with the specific intent, of causing the Plaquemines Parish Council to deny, disapprove, or refuse to approve Delta's application for a permit.[101]

Nevertheless, Ellis justified the SLAPP:

> I've readjusted my strategy over and over, and I've come to the unfortunate conclusion that these suits are the only way to go. . . . After all the legal brouhaha settles and people realize Delta isn't the environmental monster it's painted as, I honestly feel I'll be able to do business in Plaquemines Parish.[102]

But local reaction dashed his hopes. Parish President Luke Petrovich spoke for many: "They've had four hearings now, and they've been denied each time. I'd say they've had more opportunities than the average citizen."[103]

A national organization devoted to aiding grassroots groups on toxics problems—the Citizen's Clearinghouse for Hazardous Wastes (CCHW), headquartered in Arlington, Virginia—came to Williams's aid. Lois Marie Gibbs, its executive director, had this to say:

> Here stands Ann Williams, a good citizen, a retired school teacher and a valued member of her community. She's under assault by an international chemical waste dumper. Her only offense was to act on her First Amendment rights to free speech, rights held sacred by every American.
>
> I know how she feels. I, too, had to make the choice she made to speak out against injustice when my family and I discovered we lived next to the now famous Love Canal in Niagara Falls, N.Y. I could have remained silent, as so many others did, but I cared about my home, family and community and took the chance to stand up for my rights. For this, I took insult and injury from the chemical polluters who dumped at Love Canal, and still do. However, I was lucky—Occidental Petroleum chose not to do what Delta Chemical has done and attempt to intimidate me into silence through the tactic of a harassment law suit.
>
> Let us be clear about what is happening here in Plaquemines Parish. There is no other motivation on the part of Delta other than to try to scare Ann into silence and to prompt the members and supporters of [her group to] stop their opposition to their plan to dump toxics in their community. Does Delta seriously expect to win $2 million in damages from a senior citizen, payable from her teacher's pension? No way. This is nothing less than a dirty and unAmerican tactic by a company that has been foiled in its dirty business. . . .
>
> I know Ann stands strong and proud, determined to exercise her Constitutional rights. She won't be cowed into submission.[104]

But even the strong and proud wither under SLAPPs. Delta's case against the parish was thrown out by the federal court in six months, but its SLAPP against Williams survived, lying dormant and undismissed seven years later. Delta has lost its legal battles, lost its real-world campaign for a permit, but kept its suit pending against Ann Williams and left her in limbo, wondering whether her next statement or action will cause Delta to rekindle that costly attack.

The Spreading Spectrum and the Solution

That NIMBY fights against objectionable facilities go on across the country is evidenced by the emergence of groups such as Lois Gibbs's CCHW, which are assisting or monitoring scores of similar community battles against such projects. We have found SLAPPs filed over incinerators,[105] oil recycling facilities,[106] waste-water treatment,[107] asphalt plants,[108] landfills and dumps,[109] a garbage truck parking lot,[110] factories,[111] a bus company[112] radio towers,[113] quarries,[114] shopping malls,[115] adult bookstores,[116]—and the list goes on. Clearly, the array of facilities that can trigger a NIMBY reaction and then a SLAPP is virtually endless. The LULUs range from projects that affect community aesthetics to those that implicate life-style to those that actually threaten human health. All three are strong community motivators.

The cases also show how easily a NIMBY opposition campaign can bring on a SLAPP—usually when the citizens are experiencing the most success, suggesting that court action is a relatively desperate strategy of project promoters who feel themselves losing out to the NIMBY syndrome. But as in SLAPPs of other types, victories in court do not necessarily mean victories in reality. Targets handily won dismissal in virtually all these cases but often became unwilling to participate further in public issues, despite their court victory—whereas some (though not all) filers got what they really wanted, despite their technical loss in court.

The solution to NIMBY SLAPPs rests squarely on the government body being petitioned: a zoning board, building inspector, liquor license agency, health department, or other public body can actively discourage the filing of such suits in disputes under its jurisdiction. Denver's liquor licensing authorities and others have illustrated both the why and the how, as shown earlier in the chapter (see also Chapter 10). It is simply enlightened self-interest for government agencies to take this stand, since SLAPPs deny them the citizen input, information, support base, and credibility without which they cannot carry out their missions.

7 Rights SLAPPS

Turning Against Consumers', Workers', Women's . . . and Your Rights

The Attorney General [intervenes in this lawsuit] to protect the rights of concerned consumers to file complaints concerning deceptive trade practices with this and any other public agency, officer or representative. . . . It is in the public's best interest for its citizens to register their grievances. . . . The Attorney General . . . [is] concern[ed] that consumers exercising their rights will be silenced by lawsuits alleging libel and slander.

Texas Attorney General,
in State of Texas Petition in Intervention,
Westlawn Cemetery Corp. v. Forston, No. B850394
(Dist. Ct., Orange County, Tex.,
filed July 30, 1985)

No country on earth protects the "rights" of its citizens as does ours. Every American almost instinctively says, "I have my rights," "I know my rights," "I insist on my rights." From the Constitution down to the smallest village ordinance, from the great freedoms of the First Amendment down to a parking meter ticket, our laws spell out individual freedoms, rights, guarantees, and securities against unjust treatment from government or our fellow citizens. Those laws guarantee us rights in hundreds of categories—as citizens, voters, consumers, workers, employers, women, children, parents, property owners, travelers, retirees, arrestees, disableds, students, contracting parties, entrepreneurs, victims, and more. Those same laws encourage us to assert, demand, and defend our rights when they are abused. The list of rights is far from perfect and far from perfectly distributed, but even the disadvantaged, disenfranchised, and discriminated against have the right to object and to seek to change their lot. This concept of human rights is one of the great strengths of America and a source of our pride as a people.

SLAPPs endanger those rights. What is the value of having a right when, if you assert it, you can be sued for millions of dollars? What is the value of a protected right if it is not protected from retaliatory litigation? Throughout the cases we can call "consumer SLAPPs," "employment SLAPPs," "women's rights SLAPPs," and the like runs a common thread: Individuals believe themselves to have certain legal rights; they feel that those rights are being violated by someone else; they complain about the violation through appropriate government channels; and they are then SLAPPed for money damages by the violator. These are the "rights" SLAPPs, a breathtaking collection of lawsuits against ordinary people who stood up for their rights.

The Caveat Emptor SLAPP

Caveat emptor—let the buyer beware!—has been a byword for the seamy side of commerce since ancient Romans coined the phrase. Today's consumers face something even more daunting than a bad deal or a faulty product: Those who complain can find themselves facing a multimillion-dollar lawsuit.

Ralph Nader galvanized the "consumer movement" in the 1970s and is the role model for thousands of Americans who now speak out on behalf of consumer interests.[1] Some are professional consumer advocates in government or in public interest groups; many are expert repeat players focused on a single area; even more are "one-shotters," individuals who, finding themselves swept up by the injustice of their own consumer problem, decide to take a stand.[2]

Who among us has not been rankled by a bad purchase, defective product, shoddy service, or shortchanging—and thought about complaining? On the other hand, what businessperson has not been stung by unjust criticism, excessive expectations, buyers' remorse, or budding Ralph Naders—and thought about striking back? American commerce is a perfect breeding ground for SLAPPs. It produces grievances, which government "consumer protection" agencies encourage the public to report, which threatens commercial interests, which then seek a "more friendly" forum. Filers see courts as less buyer-oriented than consumer protection agencies and therefore the better forum.

A "Household" Word

Dissatisfied tenants, purchasers of houses, and persons who contract for home improvements often seek government intervention, only to find themselves the targets of SLAPPs filed by the offending home developers, real estate companies, landlords, and contractors. Landlords very commonly sue their tenants and tenant organizations simply for filing complaints with city and state housing and health officials about rent overcharging,[3] unsanitary conditions,[4] defective properties,[5] and other management problems.[6] Home improvement contractors sue dissatisfied customers for reporting unsatisfactory work to appropriate state licensing boards.[7] Condo management companies sue unit owners who complain to state authorities about fiscal and management irregularities.[8] Recreational communities sue lot purchasers for complaining to federal and state housing and consumer agencies.[9] Retirement communities sue their purchasers into silence.[10]

A truly horrendous example is the case of a young Vancouver, Washington, housewife who helped the state recover over $350,000 in unpaid taxes from her housing developer, only to be SLAPPed by the company and have the ungrateful state turn its back when she needed its help. In 1984 it was a dream come true for Brenda Hill—20 years old and pregnant with the second of three children—and her husband Gary, a warehouse worker, when they finally found a four-bedroom house they could afford on their slender income. The seller, Robert John Real Estate Co., an Oregon firm, offered the $78,000 house for only $2,000 down and low monthly payments. "It all happened so fast. It was unreal, like a dream," she recalls.[11]

But the dream became a nightmare three years later when the Hills tried to get a loan on the house and could find no record that they owned it. Robert John Real Estate had not paid the state excise tax on the sale and had not recorded their purchase contract. The Hills were told that some $1,400 in taxes and penalties would have to be paid before they could be recorded as the owners and get their loan,[12] and if they did not pay up, they could lose the house.[13] Brenda Hill contacted the Robert John company but got no satisfaction,[14] so she called her state government. Interested, the real estate tax coordinator wrote back on June 17, 1987, asking for "the names, addresses and telephone numbers of other people in your situation."[15] With that official urging, Hill went door to door in the subdivision, searched county records, and showed the state hundreds of thousands of dollars in taxes on some 300 homes, unpaid by Robert John.[16]

Within a month, Robert John hit the young couple with a one-two punch. First, it filed foreclosure proceedings; in financial straits at the time, the Hills had missed a monthly house payment and were two days late with another.[17] Second, it filed a defamation SLAPP for $100,000 and an injunction against the couple.[18] Brenda remembers the moment vividly:

At about 8:30 P.M., Gary and I were sitting down to have dinner when the doorbell rang. The lady [process server] at the door inquired about our names, then handed us the papers and said, "You have been served." I was upset and crying . . . the [court] appearance date [was] the next day. Gary had to call in to work early the next morning, and we had to get someone to watch the kids. That is the court appearance that resulted in the gag order.[19]

Just before a big neighborhood meeting on the problem next day, Robert John's attorneys got Superior Court Judge Robert Harris to sign an incredible gag order, barring the Hills from making "any reckless . . . statements of alleged fact" concerning the real estate company.[20] The Hills' attorney, the first of several who would represent and then abandon the financially strapped couple, did not object.[21] The legal maneuver worked: The Hills were terrified into silence.

Yet they were in the right. On the basis of Brenda Hill's information, the state of Washington soon collected an estimated $351,000 in back taxes from Robert John[22] and ordered the company to stop selling other people's property and to cease using unlicensed brokers.[23] Warren Ashmann, then president of Robert John, took it personally: "Do you have any idea how much effort she put into destroying our reputation, our credit, our whole business? She did it, and now we're going to get every last nickel she has."[24] She "ruined our reputation," and "we will sue her till we are insolvent," the Beverly Hills lawyer-developer vowed.[25] In a letter to homeowners in its subdivisions, the company not only blamed Brenda Hill for its financial liquidation but implied that she was the reason her neighbors had "lost their homes or had their credit damaged."[26] A backlash of neighborhood pressure mounted against the Hills, their homeowners' insurance was canceled,[27] and they had to file for bankruptcy to protect their home.

The young couple was devastated, particularly Brenda: "I don't sleep or eat. I cry. I'm a total reck [*sic*] and sometimes I don't want to wake up any more. My life emotionally and everything else is a wreck!"[28] Their marriage nearly broke up.[29] She found herself seeing a psychologist, was hospitalized for stress, and was given "anti-depressants and sleeping pills for the first time in my life."[30] Moreover, instead of helping, the state of Washington turned its back on the Hills. They got no further support from the now paid-up tax authorities, no intervention in the SLAPP from the attorney general's office or its consumer protection staff, and nothing but sympathy and "no comment" from a much-publicized meeting with Governor Booth Gardner.[31] "I never figured that, when things started going wrong, I'd be left out in the cold. I feel betrayed by those people [in the state government]," she recalls.[32]

But finally, the tide began to turn. When gutsy Brenda Hill and her three children picketed on the state capitol steps, the media jumped on the story with extensive pro-Hill, anti–Robert John, and anti-state coverage. State Senator Phil Talmadge, a Seattle Democrat, took up her cause: "We afford whistle-blowers in state government considerable protection from retribution. We may want to think about a similar kind of protection for people who, in good faith, make a report to government about a company they think is breaking the law."[33] An opposition candidate for attorney general used the situation in his campaign, bringing Brenda into a press conference and accusing the incumbent of failing to protect the Hills.[34] Tacoma attorney Howard L. Graham took up their case and on October 19, 1988, filed a class action SLAPPback on behalf of the Hills and "300 other home owners," charging Robert John and Ashman with unfair and deceptive trade practices, defamation, intimidation, emotional distress, and violation of the Hills' right to petition.[35]

Then, in 1989, freshman state legislator Holly Myers, a Vancouver Democrat, introduced the "Washington Whistleblowers Bill"—also known as "the Brenda Hill Bill"—which flatly makes "immune" from lawsuits any person who in good faith reports a violation of law, and allows those sued to recover attorneys' fees and court costs from filers. Brenda Hill was the star witness at the hearings on the bill, where she broke into tears:

> I cried through some of my testimony[;] as wrong as it is I have at times become very suicidal. At first I had no intention of being quite as open during my testimony but it was important to me that they [the senators] saw beyond the statistics in front of them and saw a real statstic [*sic*] in front of them. Me.[36]

The hitherto silent governor and attorney general now jumped on the bandwagon, and the bill sped through both houses unanimously.[37] Three years later, in November 1992, Brenda Hill was persuaded to accept a confidential settlement and dismiss the SLAPPback. Yet, inexplicably, despite her dropping the countersuit, Robert John was allowed to keep the SLAPP alive, and the Hills had to endure a full-scale trial in March 1993. The jury found her "not guilty" of slander. Robert John did not appeal, and the SLAPP was finally over.[38]

What has it meant to Brenda Hill? Her marriage recovered, but she lost her home, and the physical and mental suffering lingers: "I'm very tired of the whole mess. I only wish that I could try to function day by day without the whole thing over my head. [At least] this new legislation means that maybe down the road someone will find the protection they need."[39] She is still "angry that I had to go through what I did,"[40] but she is grateful in some important ways:

I missed an awful lot in the years that I didn't get involved. Now when people say your vote doesn't count, I disagree with them.

I want people to understand that if they come forward it's going to cost them dearly. But I do hope my story inspires other people to believe that they can make a difference and it's worth fighting for something.[41]

Would she do it again? "It was the principle of it all that bothers me. Why is that so hard for people to understand? . . . To me the big deal is it's too darn easy to take away rites [*sic*] earned by our ancestors who I think we owe something to."[42] But should maintaining a constitutional right require this kind of personal suffering and will power?

Fighting for his rights was the farthest thing from Cliff Mortensen's mind when he and his family moved into their newly built Huntington Beach, California, home in 1977. But 13 years later he was still in court fighting the construction firm he claims did a shoddy job of building his and perhaps 100 other houses. The Mortensens' new $150,000 home leaked when it rained, ruining carpets, damaging walls, bringing insect infestations; they and their children began to have recurrent illnesses and allergies.[43] He contacted the S & S Construction Company, owned by California developer, philanthropist, and political figure Nathan Shapell. S & S blamed subcontractors and told Mortensen he was the only buyer in the subdivision who had any problems. He found, however, that other neighbors' houses were leaking too.[44] Since their collective complaints to government agencies went unanswered, in January 1979 Mortensen and some of the others filed a $280,000,000 class action against S & S and other Shapell Industries affiliates.[45]

Before the year was out, S & S had its mega-lawfirm, Gibson, Dunn & Crutcher of Los Angeles, SLAPP Mortensen and 100 Does for over $500,000 each with the standard charges of business interference, defamation, and extortion, largely because of their government complaints.[46] "We think we're a pretty reasonable group of people here and we don't like to fight with our homeowners. But there is a point beyond which you don't push us. We believe in free speech, but not slander," asserted Shapell's Vice-President Larry Faigin.[47] But Mortensen countered: "This is the builder's way of putting a muzzle on the people who spoke out. It's a strong-arm tactic to intimidate us."[48] "I thought I was a tough guy, but [the SLAPP] got my attention," he recalls.[49] Faigin responded with the very common filer distinction: "Our point with the suit is that some of [the homeowners] have gone beyond complaining and are attempting to hurt the company."[50] In other words, you have a right to free speech until it becomes effective.

The homeowners' lawsuit and the SLAPP proceeded, intertwined. Finally, S & S agreed to buy back Mortensen's home for $225,000; in 1983 the

Mortensens won a $125,000 jury verdict for their illnesses and expenses; and in 1984 the SLAPP was dismissed. A jubilant Mortensen said: "We did beat them. . . . Everything we said was true; the house was built wrong. . . . It was a long, drawn out fight, but it was worth it. . . . A lot of good came out of it. The little guy won."[51] Other owners settled out of court, and in some cases the contractor won.

Meanwhile, Mortensen's attorney had filed a multimillion-dollar SLAPback against S & S, later expanded to include its law firm.[52] The suit alleged that the contractors and their attorneys had committed malicious prosecution, abuse of process, negligent and intentional infliction of emotional distress, and conspiracy.[53] Mortensen doggedly pursued his SLAPPback with a revolving door of attorneys until in 1988 he settled on "Lawyer of the Year" John Taylor of Los Angeles. Taylor focused on the law firm and in October 1990 won a jury verdict of $80,000 against Gibson, Dunn & Crutcher for filing the SLAPP. It was a disappointingly small sum to Mortensen but a large warning for lawyers whose clients want to file SLAPPs and for those lawyers' liability insurance carriers.[54]

Other Consumer SLAPPs

Consumers get SLAPPed away from home, too. An amazing array of innocent-seeming products and services can trigger SLAPPs—from child care to baby furniture, school buses to milk, cemeteries to stocks.

In the mid-1980s, Westlawn Cemetery in McLewis, Texas, was itself in rigor mortis. Numerous consumer complaints had been filed with the state attorney general's consumer protection office, charging Westlawn and its owners with failing to maintain the cemetery, build paid-for crypts, and deliver headstones, and even with selling the same plots to more than one person.[55] Terry Forston, who had purchased a plot in Westlawn, contacted the consumer office and state legislators, organized other Westlawn plot owners, and was interviewed by the media. For this, the cemetery owners filed a $200,000 suit for slander, alleging that her complaints and the publicity caused them "a sudden and substantial loss of business."[56]

The Texas attorney general's office, which "had sufficient evidence . . . to file a deceptive trade practice lawsuit against Westlawn Cemetery,"[57] was outraged that consumers reporting violations to government might "silenced by lawsuits alleging libel and slander." Two months after the SLAPP was filed the attorney general intervened to protect all complaining consumers, and the case died.[58] Neither the owners nor trustee in bankruptcy pursued the case, and today Westlawn Cemetery and its plot owners rest easier under new management.

Reporting stock fraud to the U.S. Securities and Exchange Commission (SEC) would seem safe, given that agency's investigation and hearings procedures. But after three investors in an oil and gas development (all Chicago lawyers) reported fraud and mismanagement concerns about Havoco of America—both to the SEC and to the National Association of Security Dealers—and filed a state court suit to get their money back, Havoco responded with a $120,000,000 federal court suit for tortious interference with business.[59] The court threw the SLAPP out, ruling that SEC complaints and other actions were protected by the Petition Clause:

> The First Amendment guarantees [targets'] right to attempt to enlist the government on their side of the dispute. That this petitioning activity may have had incidentally an adverse effect on [filer's] business, even that [targets] knew this and intended such a result, has no effect on the First Amendment's protection, as long as the activity represents a genuine attempt to influence government action.[60]

Even though the investors' failed to get all their funds back,[61] they were surprisingly unchilled: "We tweaked [the filer's] tail and cost them thousands of dollars in attorneys' fees. And it cost us practically zero, since we represented ourselves as attorneys in the state court case and our insurance carrier paid [the legal fees for the SLAPP] in federal court."[62]

A delayed delivery of baby furniture triggered a 1990 consumer SLAPP and a consumer advocacy career for its victim. Karin Weber's baby furniture did not arrive as guaranteed, so she proceeded to picket the store, write letters to the county's Department of Consumer Affairs and the Better Business Bureau, and even appeared on the *Phil Donahue Show* to discuss consumer problems. The store filed a defamation SLAPP against her,[63] also naming Donahue, NBC, and other "media defendants" for "broadcasting, producing and distributing" Weber's words. The trial court dismissed and the appeals court affirmed, ending the case a year after it started, and launched Karin Weber as a consumer activist.

Bashing Consumer Advocates

Can you be sued if you are asked to testify before the United States Senate? Kenneth Wooden, a New Jersey–based freelance reporter, was. When the Senate Subcommittee on Child and Human Development held hearings in 1979 on the child-care industry, Wooden testified as an expert about his investigations of problems with government-funded child-care facilities. The owner of one such facility in Wisconsin immediately filed a $200,000 libel suit.[64] The SLAPP hung over Wooden's head for more than four years. In 1982 he persuaded the Wisconsin ACLU to take up his case;

shortly thereafter, however, the filer died and the case fizzled. Nevertheless, Wooden was left with years of legal bills, and the shadow of SLAPPs spread over his future reporting on children.

Another expert witness was sued for a total of $220,000,000 over the seemingly noncontroversial issue of "pure milk." The Alta-Dena Certified Dairy in Los Angeles is reportedly the largest producer of raw (unpasteurized) milk products in the United States, one of 15 such diaries in California alone.[65] But the U.S. Public Health Service's Center for Disease Control calls raw milk "inherently unsafe,"[66] and for years public health officials and medical organizations have accused producers of marketing products contaminated with bacteria that can cause fatal illnesses; some companies' batches have even been pulled off grocers' shelves after government testing.[67]

Dr. John C. Bolton, a charismatic, dedicated San Francisco pediatrician, has been tireless in his efforts to warn his patients and the American public of the health risks of raw milk. He has testified before legislatures, lobbied state licensing agencies, and used national television, radio talk shows, press conferences, and the lecture circuit to urge an end to the sale of unpasteurized dairy products. When the success his message was having reached Alta-Dena's owners, they SLAPPed him, the American Academy of Pediatrics, and 50 Does with not one but two defamation lawsuits—specifically for his sworn, expert testimony before the California General Assembly and the U.S. House of Representatives.[68] Simultaneously, they hit the California State Department of Health and several of its individual inspectors with a conspiracy suit for $560,000,000. Dr. Bolton's reaction: "I think these suits are intended to intimidate me and prevent me from warning the public against the health hazards of all raw milk. . . . The[se] suits won't stop me from doing my job as a physician, and they can't stifle me from warning the public about health threats."[69]

Outrage greeted the *Alta-Dena* SLAPPs. The *Los Angeles Times* editorialized that the suits "look like an effort to silence scientific criticism" and urged an alternative:

> We think that those differences can be resolved better in scientific debate than through litigation. . . . The questions raised by a reputable physician and a distinguished medical society . . . seem to us consistent with the obligation of scientists to share with the public their concerns about potential risks to health. . . . We vigorously support the need for those purchasing the products to be aware of the controversy surrounding their safety.[70]

U.S. Congressman Henry Waxman, before whose Subcommittee on Health and Environment the doctor had testified, was livid:

This particular action may be more than intimidation. It may well be a violation of a federal law designed to protect witnesses appearing before congressional committees (Section 1505 of Title 18 of the Federal Criminal Code). A suit against a scientist or any other witness for testimony presented to a congressional committee may have a chilling effect on the willingness of others to come forward to give their opinions. Efforts to intimidate witnesses before congressional committees cannot be tolerated. Such acts threaten to undermine the legislative branch's responsibility to assure that the nation's laws are properly administered. . . . In particular where consumers need to make rational health decisions, attempts to stifle the flow of information must be strongly resisted.[71]

In one of the happier SLAPP outcomes the pediatrician's motion for summary judgment was granted in 1986, and Alta-Dena paid his court costs, dropped the other SLAPP, and did not appeal. Dr. Bolton continues to crusade against raw milk, but the lawsuits have caused him, he admits, to be more "cautious" in speaking out.

Wooden and Bolton are not unique. Even a division of pharmaceutical giant Johnson & Johnson found itself the target of a SLAPP for testifying before Congress. In 1979 an executive of the firm's drug manufacturing arm, Ortho Pharmaceutical Corporation, appeared before the U.S. Senate Subcommittee on Health and Scientific Research, which was conducting hearings on fraud and abuse in the testing of new drugs on human subjects. Questioned by Senator Ted Kennedy, the Ortho executive admitted that the testing of one of its new drugs by a subcontractor, Bio/Basics International Corporation, had proved to be "worthless" and the data "not usable."[72] Bio/Basics responded with a suit against Ortho's testimony, alleging interference with contract, interference with precontractual relations, breach of fiduciary duty, and defamation.[73] In 1982 the federal court dismissed, ruling that such legislative testimony was "absolutely immune" from suit under New York law.[74]

An Uncooperative Co-op

The common consumer dissatisfaction with utilities sparked a firestorm of litigation that became one of our in-depth studies and a major illustration of consumer SLAPPs.

A visionary outcome of the Great Depression, the U.S. Rural Electrification Administration (REA) has truly brought "light to the farms of America." Its low-cost loans and supports enable rural areas that would otherwise not be served to have their own federally subsidized, customer-run electricity cooperatives. Since 1938 one of these co-ops, the Intermountain Rural Electric Association (IREA), has been serving a large nine-county area southwest of Denver. By the 1980s it had become a huge corporation whose management was perceived by many member-consumers as insulated and nonresponsive.[75] It was alleged that IREA was losing money, was paying huge salaries to executives ($125,000 a year for the general manager), had nearly doubled electric rates in one year, was giving lucrative "pro-growth" concessions to developers, had audit trouble, and had amended its bylaws to strip members of governance rights.[76] Frustrated and beleaguered, all sides turned to the courts. Between 1984 and 1986 an incredible total of 11 lawsuits and countersuits were filed: by the IREA against minority board members, customers, and state regulatory officials; by customers and employees against the IREA. Among them, not surprisingly, was a dyed-in-the-wool SLAPP.

It began when a group of dissatisfied customers calling themselves "Concerned Members of IREA" organized a petition drive to recall the board of directors and elect new leaders. In 1984, Concerned Members filed ample petitions (over 4,000 signatures), but the directors, acting as their own judges, rejected the petitions "due to lack of cause for recall."[77] Concerned Members next filed two court appeals, seeking nonmonetary rulings on whether the law required an election and public board meetings.[78] The group saw itself as battling "the demise of corporate democracy at IREA."[79] IREA's management filed a SLAPP counterclaim demanding $1,200,000 from Concerned Members and six of its individual leaders for abuse of process (filing the election suit) and libel (the violations of law alleged in the complaint).[80]

We are often asked, "If one side can sue, why can't the other sue back? Don't they both have a right to petition the courts?" This case illustrates the answer. When one side petitions a court to change a disputed government decision or outcome (such as a new board election or not), without seeking money damages from anyone, it is "tit for tat" for the other side to defend to the fullest on the substantive issues. It is most certainly *not* equivalent "petitioning," however, for that other side to add a claim for monetary damages, separate from the merits of the dispute. Such a maneuver is not an on-point response geared to resolving the dispute but a tactic designed to divert both the court's and opponents' resources away from resolving the real dispute, as well as to escalate the opposition's risks with a threat irrelevant to the issues. In short, a SLAPP counterclaim or countersuit for money, in response to a nonmonetary, governmental-action court challenge, is counter to societal problem-solving; it is designed to punish and to prevent recourse to the courts for appropriate judicial review of government action.

The SLAPP against the Concerned Members worked in precisely this way. No longer were the consumer-members on the offense; rather, avoiding the $1,200,000 damage claim became their focus. Tom Evans recalls:

"That [counterclaim] had a dampening effect. Everyone asked, 'How can I get out of this? I don't want to go ahead with [our] suits if I put my family on the line.' There is a point, you know, where community awareness and activity drop off and your family comes first."[81] Targets were fortunate to have one of the country's mega-lawfirms, Kirkland & Ellis, volunteer to handle their cases pro bono. But despite free, top-notch legal resources, the SLAPP "struck terror into [the targets]," admitted Kevin O'Brien, one of their attorneys. "They were quite upset, quite fearful. I think it probably put us on the defensive. From that point on the clients' main objective became how do we get out of this?"[82]

Doubtless, this was what the filers wanted. They had taken the Concerned Members' attacks personally; as IREA General Manager Stanley Lewandowski's put it:

> I am not a weak individual. I am probably a pretty strong individual in what I feel and what I believe. . . . I think anybody has a right to take a shot at me . . . to try to knock me out of the box. But . . . [the targets] not only wanted me removed but they wanted to make sure that I never got a job any place again."[83]

The utility's directors claimed to see the targets as self-interested liars, not "public citizens." Said one: "I don't like the word 'dissident,' but that's what they are. . . . They catch other people up, and they don't give them the true story on what they are doing and why they are doing it and what the outcome might be."[84]

Things went poorly for targets in the trial court (which is not unusual), so their attorneys, frustrated at having their dismissal motions denied, made a successful appeal to the Colorado Supreme Court.[85] The Colorado ACLU, League of Women Voters, and Common Cause requested Professor Pring to file a friend-of-the-court brief in support of dismissal.[86] A unanimous Colorado Supreme Court agreed, holding that the trial court judge had violated its previous ruling on how to handle SLAPPs (in the precedent-setting *POME* case; see Chapters 1 and 3); it remanded the case and instructed the judge to have an immediate hearing and protect Concerned Members' constitutional rights to petition.[87]

Stung, the trial judge, Winston W. Wolvington, made the following extraordinary statement in open court:

> [I]t came as kind of a shock to me . . . when I got not only the [appeal] to the Supreme Court, but papers indicating that several organizations that I have the greatest respect for, including the League of Women Voters which my wife is a prominent member of, were amicus curiae and were filing briefs which I considered belligerent . . . about my extraordinary misconduct in this case. . . . All I could

do is wait for my reversal, which I knew was coming, because I hadn't done what you have to do in these cases.[88]

He grudgingly granted dismissal, but not without giving targets' a slap of his own by ruling that one of their purposes—even if not the primary one—was "to harass" IREA.[89]

Once more the targets had "won" in court, but in another very common scenario filers were able to drag the litigation on by appealing through the courts for two more years before finally pressuring targets into a secret settlement. Such "gag-order" settlements are not uncommon SLAPP outcomes. Filers frequently agree to drop their suit if targets will agree to three things: to drop or forgo a SLAPPback, quit their opposition campaign, and promise never to discuss the settlement. Such agreements really represent a complete victory for the filers—they could not do better in court—and targets pressured into accepting them account for most of the small but worrisome percentage of SLAPPs in which targets do not win a court dismissal. Filers alone are not to blame for the success of these settlements, however; the judicial system is to blame as well. Filers could not pressure settlement if SLAPPs were processed efficiently, and filers could not play on court inertia without the aid of trial judges reluctant to dismiss before trial and of appeals courts prone to remand cases for further trial court proceedings instead of ending them by outright reversal.

Who won *IREA* in the real world? The SLAPP filers, hands down. Board meetings did become public, but the same insiders retained control, and Stanley Lewandowski stayed general manager. The litigation cost IREA "tens of thousands of dollars," but management passed its costs on to its consumer-ratepayers,[90] and the dissidents find "no change . . . in how IREA treats members,"[91] except that it spends more time and money on public and customer relations.[92] The strongest indicator that the targets were frustrated and frightened came in their responses during interviews. All qualified their statements, were suspicious of the interviewers, were nervous about saying anything that might be published, and clearly would not take part in such a consumer campaign again. One of the originally outspoken leaders later retracted the interview and asked not to be named at all in the study. We have respected those wishes. That person is not alone.

What Rights Are Left?

There seems no rights issue, cause, or problem that does not spawn SLAPPs. Consider Carolyn McDowell's all too familiar problem. She was a professional woman trying to advance in a "man's world,"[93] a civilian employee at Warner Robins Air Force Base in Georgia, which one newspaper exposé called a place where "subtle and not-so-subtle sexism scars [the] employment picture."[94] When she reported her supervisor for sexual harassment ("He grabbed me and hugged me, and kissed me" and promised job advancement "in return for sexual favors"),[95] he struck back with a $1,500,000 SLAPP.[96] The Air Force found in McDowell's favor.[97] But the supervisor kept the case alive for almost four years—until the U.S. Equal Employment Opportunity Commission (EEOC) weighed in with a friend-of-the-court brief demanding an "absolute immunity" for complainants: "The filing of charges is essential . . . the lifeblood of [the EEO Act]. . . . Effective enforcement [can] . . . only be expected if employees [feel] free to approach officials with their grievances. . . . [The] filing process must be protected from any chilling effect."[98] Within months the judge dismissed the SLAPP and McDowell's SLAPPback. She felt she had done the right thing, but left her job and the state. The filer kept his job and told us that in retrospect he would not do anything differently.[99]

The American workplace is a labyrinth of SLAPPs, by no means all involving sexual harassment. Employees SLAPP bosses; bosses SLAPP employees; employees SLAPP employees; and labor unions SLAPP them all.

Labor leader Cesar Chávez, his union, and their election committee filed a $10,000,000 SLAPP after losing a 1976 election to reform California farm labor law.[100] They charged their successful opponents—big agribusiness corporations and their political action committees, publicists, and election committees—with violations of election laws and improper advocacy to the voters. The case was quickly dismissed and the dismissal affirmed.

An economist complained to the New York State Division of Human Rights that his employer fired him because he was Jewish. When company officials testified in their own defense before the state agency, the employee filed federal and state court SLAPPs against them for defaming him in their testimony.[101] It took seven years for the company to get all counts dismissed by the appellate courts.

Employees who argue for getting rid of their unions can be sued by the unions, as the teacher case in Chapter 4 illustrates. The National Right to Work Legal Defense Education Foundation was SLAPPed by the United Auto Workers and nine other labor unions for helping workers file government and legal challenges to deunionize their companies;[102] the filers kept the case alive for 13 years, through a maze of court machinations, before letting it quietly die.[103] A 1990 case reversed the situation: A small, non-union company SLAPPed the California Pipe and Trades Union and the AFL-CIO, alleging that the big unions intervene in government permit proceedings as a means of pressuring developers to contract only with union shops.[104]

In what may be the most ghastly antiwar protesting SLAPP we have encountered, Vietnam veteran Brian Willson and others, protesting U.S. arms shipments to Central America, staged a sit-in on train tracks entering the Concord Naval Weapons Station in California. The approaching munitions train did not stop. The other demonstrators scattered, but Willson was not so fortunate: The train severed both his legs. He later filed a standard bodily injury tort case against the train crew, but then, in a ghoulish SLAPP, the train crew counterclaimed for money damages against Willson, alleging that his protest and lawsuit had caused them "humiliation, physical pain, mental anguish and severe emotional distress."[105] Some three years later, the court dismissed the railroaders' SLAPP claims, and in 1992, on the eve of trial, Wilson received an approximate $1,000,000 settlement from the U.S. Navy.[106]

More fortunate were several hundred antiwar, antinuclear protesters arrested in 1983 at the Minneapolis headquarters of Honeywell, Inc., a major U.S. weapons manufacturer. They had to answer misdemeanor criminal trespass charges as well as a $500,000 SLAPP.[107] When a conservative, pro-business law group, North Star Legal Foundation, filed suit on behalf of taxpayers for causing "the public to incur . . . extraordinary expenses, including . . . police, . . . city attorneys, judges and courtrooms, and jail facilities."[108] But the trial judge flayed North Star's suit, saying that "no facts which could be introduced . . . would warrant the relief [filers] seek under any legal theory."[109] The appeals court affirmed.

In 1995 a new battlefield for SLAPPs is emerging, pitting First Amendment rights of free speech, petition, and religion against each other. The Church of Scientology and its members have begun filing tort and copyright lawsuits against church opponents and seizing their computer equipment, in an effort to keep opponents from disseminating information and criticism on the Internet and otherwise speaking and acting against the church.[110]

"Rights" SLAPPs, then, are typically money lawsuits heaped like fresh coals on those who have been burned once already. Courts have a duty to protect rights, especially those of political and other minorities, yet the device of SLAPPs uses those same courts as unwitting tools to deprive further those who petition or protest in defense of their rights.

To be sure, in these rights cases even more than in other SLAPP areas, trial judges quickly perceive the abusive nature of the filings and dismiss. But is even prompt dismissal enough? Or do others who should speak up and assert their rights get a message that will keep them silent and deprive them of rights we all should share? Do we not all then lose? The concluding chapters consider "cures" for the SLAPP onslaught, for the chill it can send far beyond the parties in a case, and for the threat it thereby poses to continued public involvement in our country's political life and future.

8 Judicial Cures

Managing the SLAPP

How small, of all that human hearts endure,
That part which laws or kings can cause or cure.

—Samuel Johnson, lines added to
Oliver Goldsmith, *The Traveller*

SLAPPs are an exception to Samuel Johnson' thesis. Our laws and government officials both are the cause and can be the cure for this significant part of human suffering. They provide the political and judicial mediums in which such cases spawn and flourish, but "vigorous protection" against SLAPPs is a widely recognized need,[1] and all three branches of government and the legal profession itself have the potential to contribute to the cure. The only question is whether they have the vision and the will.

Courts and judges can contribute by being on the lookout for and identifying SLAPPs; by following the U.S. Supreme Court's lead for early review and dismissal (as set out in the breakthrough 1991 case of *City of Columbia v. Omni Outdoor Advertising, Inc.*, discussed in Chapter 2); and by putting a "reverse chill" on future SLAPPs through monetary awards of attorneys' fees, litigation costs, and SLAPPback damages.

Legislatures—federal, state, and local—can contribute by passing effective anti-SLAPP laws (based on the Supreme Court's approach in *Omni*); by strengthening existing immunity or privilege laws that protect citizens in government proceedings and communications; by holding hearings that spotlight SLAPPs, increase public awareness, and discourage filings; and by making their prevention official policy for government agencies in their jurisdiction.

The executive branch—governors, attorneys general, environmental officials, licensing bodies, zoning boards, consumer protection offices, civil rights commissions, and so on—can contribute by announcing a public policy against this threat, which is cutting them off from their constituents; by adopting rules to make it clear that SLAPPs will not be tolerated in connection with their proceedings; and by supporting persons who are sued as a result of public participation, using legal intervention, friend-of-the-court briefs, and legal, financial, and moral assistance.

Finally, the legal profession can contribute to the reduction of SLAPPs by learning to "know one when they see one"; by counseling would-be filer clients against the risks (for filers and their attorneys) of bringing such suits; by advising potential target clients about the existence of this threat and how to avoid it; by representing targets and defending them effectively; and by bringing SLAPPbacks to vindicate their clients and, indeed, to help assure the future of democracy itself.

Having studied hundreds of SLAPPs and SLAPPbacks, participated directly in many, and interviewed hundreds of participants, onlookers, and legal experts, we have observed what works and what does not. The good news is that the Supreme Court's *Omni* decision has finally provided an effective "cure," but that success model will take time to permeate our legal culture. Meanwhile, the classic "failure model" recurs over and over when attorneys, clients, and judges apply the typical, apolitical "issue spotting" approach ("This is just a 'libel' question" or "just 'business interference'" or "just a 'zoning' problem") and become mired in long-running, hard-to-end cases. The conventional legal labeling approach thus plays directly into the SLAPP strategy.

We saw the need for a different approach. Rather than dealing with these cases as conventional, separate tort or other legal categories (as individual "trees," if you will), we proposed viewing them as one entire new category (focusing on the overall "forest" of public political participation) and—given their similarities in cause and effect—seeing them collectively as lawsuits claiming injury from another's Petition Clause–protected activity. The results have been dramatic: Some would-be filers and their attorneys have recognized the risks and reconsidered suing; targets and their attorneys, seeing themselves in a bigger democratic picture, take heart, succeed at dismissal, and are more inclined to countersue for this violation of their constitutional and personal rights; judges become more willing to adjudicate the cases expeditiously, recognizing that macro (political and societal) rights are at risk, not simply micro (interpersonal and monetary) ones.

This and the remaining two chapters are a synthesis of SLAPP management, outlining defensive (Chapter 8) and offensive (Chapter 9) judicial methods, and legislative and executive methods (Chapter 10). The following "SLAPPs Practice Manual" for attorneys, judges, and legislators offers all readers an "insider view" of what really happens behind the judicial curtains.

Managing SLAPPs Before They Happen

The three cardinal rules of managing SLAPPs are Detour, Dismiss, Deter: In other words, (1) avoid them before they are filed, (2) terminate them if filed, and (3) prevent future filings. Although the majority of inquiries we receive concern how to handle SLAPPs after they have been filed, the best management—not surprisingly—is to avoid or prevent them in the first place.

The Prevention Strategy

Being informed is the key to prevention. Citizens and groups taking positions on public issues need to know about the phenomenon without, however, letting this awareness discourage their activism. Fortunately, there are warning signs. The key is recognizing them in time. Our studies show that they are similar and predictable in almost all cases:

1. Local issues: SLAPPs explode most frequently over community, neighborhood, and other geographically finite disputes. They are less likely (though not impossible) on grander-scale state or national issues.
2. Bipolar disputes: The issues sparking SLAPPs tend to be sharply two-sided, without a lot of "gray" areas or "give." The situation is win/lose, go/no-go, either/or. The developer gets the zoning permit or not; the teacher keeps the job or not; the product was a fraud or not. Someone will win; someone will lose.
3. Public versus private values: One side (the potential target) normally views the issue from a public-good, nonmonetary, or value perspective. The other side (potential filer) sees it in terms of personal financial issues or private property rights.
4. Not Goliath versus David battles: Contrary to expectation, SLAPPs are more likely to be David versus David affairs. Filers are most often local operations, businesses, or individuals. They may be "big fish" in the local community or area but rarely beyond it. Large, powerful, or national players have other options, constraints, and assets and do not need the dubious SLAPP strategy to get their way. Targets, too, are most often local individuals and groups; although large, well-heeled, experienced players (the League of Women Voters, the Sierra Club) are not immune.
5. Labeling: Prospective filers commonly signal their intentions by the use of legitimizing and delegitimizing labels to characterize themselves and their opponents respectively. For themselves they speak of

"experts," "professionals," "free enterprise," "having rights," "upholding values," "protecting property interests," etc. They portray opponents as "ignorant," "self-interested," "newcomers," "troublemakers," "little old [persons] in tennis shoes," or "opportunists."

6. Forum bias: "Losers" file SLAPPs; those who see themselves as "winners" rarely do. Prospective filers have doubts about their ability to be vindicated in the public, political forum in which the dispute starts—be it a zoning board, police conduct review board, legislative committee, or law-reform lawsuit. So, ironically, it is when citizen opponents are being most successful in the political forum that they ought to be most concerned about SLAPPs, which are, above all else, dispute-transformation devices—a way for one side to switch to an alternative (judicial) forum in which they hope to have more success.
7. Likely issues: Particular public issues seem to generate the most SLAPPs. Objections to real estate development and zoning changes head the list, with criticism of public officials, public employees, and public works a close second. The environment, animal/wildlife rights, objectionable neighborhood facilities, consumer fraud, and the rights of women, minorities, and workers are the other key sparkplugs.

Of course, subtle warning signals may not be needed; outright SLAPP threats are not uncommon. In one highhanded example a school administrators' union publicly threatened to sue parents for criticizing the principal of a Nevada grade school in 1991.[2] That backfired; the local newspaper editorialized:

> This outrageous attempt to intimidate the fathers and mothers of . . . students represents a clear example of SLAPP—Strategic Lawsuits Against Public Participation. In these efforts, an organization with deep pockets brandishes the threat of legal action at critics, hoping to scare the noisemakers into silence. . . . The SLAPP approach is especially ironic in the case of the school system. One of the most common complaints from educators is that parents don't take enough interest in the education of their children. Now, when a group of parents seeks to become involved, they're told in no uncertain terms to shut up and go stand in the corner. . . . An organization representing school administrators . . . wants to stymie debate on an educational issue. Don't they teach the First Amendment anymore?[3]

In 1993 a Colorado school administrators' union did the same thing (suggesting that a de facto national practice may be developing). A Vail merchant and parent, in a three-page letter to the county board of education, expressed concern over alleged shoplifting by students in her stores, lack of school leadership, and discipline problems. (One particularly noxious practice, she wrote—called "swirlies"—involved "a couple of kids . . . [who] flush the toilet and stick the victim's head in the swirling water.") It was a hard-hitting, critical letter that laid blame at the feet of the school authorities. The school administrators' group promptly wrote back, castigating her on behalf of their beleaguered principal. Their message was clear: The principal has asked us to "look into legal action"; we "find his request with merit"; and "if any further unsubstantiated allegations come forward . . . we will move forward with his request."[4] Fortunately, the parent moved faster—straight to the ACLU of Colorado, which squelched the educators' group with a hard-hitting letter of their own for threatening to SLAPP a parent who expressed her views to the school board.

Tactical Considerations

When any of the signals—overt or covert—appear, the politically active and their lawyers must move quickly. The right move is simple, as the foregoing success stories show: Immediately work with all sides to head off the SLAPP. We call this "taking cover in the open."

As a first step, potential targets should recognize certain things (or be advised of them).

1. Rights: They have a safeguarded constitutional right to make their views known to government bodies, officials, and the public on any issue that interests or affects them.
2. Limits: The right should not be assumed to be absolute. They should take care that their campaign statements, leaflets, posters, testimony, petitions, positions, ads, or whatever are, first and foremost, *outcome oriented:* definitely seeking some government decision, action or inaction, or other result. Ideally, their statements should be as factually accurate and legally sound as possible (regardless of how much editorialization, hype, hoopla, and rhetoric they are packaged in). Even though the Constitution does not limit its protection solely to the truthful, legalistic, or pure of heart, these precautions are in targets' obvious self-interest.
3. The need for an attorney: When the opposition even suggests, let alone threatens, money-damage lawsuits in response to petitioning, the time for self-help is over. A lawyer is necessary.
4. The risk of being "chilled": Lawyers counseling the politically active about the SLAPP risk face a difficult dilemma: how to avoid becoming part of the chill themselves yet keep their clients informed. We ourselves worry whether our research and information—including this

book—could in that way do more harm than good. We conclude, on balance, that the risks of ignorance outweigh the risks of becoming discouraged. Our recommendation is to dispel the ignorance but buttress the activism. We agree with the target attorney who told us, after a particularly long, vicious SLAPP: "I guess if I were going to do it again [file a public-interest lawsuit for citizens] . . . I would take great pains to sit [the citizens] down and discuss with them the risks."[5] We point out how unlikely SLAPPs are to win in court and how easily they can be turned against filers in the real world.

Next, once potential targets are aware of the facts, they should be sure potential filers are. Opponents who even hint at filing a SLAPP should be promptly informed—by a lawyer, public official, or other credible party—that they are exposing themselves to four kinds of loss.

1. Lawsuit loss: SLAPPs are proven losers, with an overwhelming track record of failure in court.
2. Reputation loss: Even threatening a SLAPP makes them violators of citizens' constitutional and civil rights. (Many filers really are not aware that such threats and suits are wrong.)
3. Public relations loss: Strong media, community, and government backlash is predictable.
4. Financial loss: There is a high risk of judicial sanctions upon losing the SLAPP (paying targets' attorneys' fees, litigation and court costs), plus a real risk of facing a successful SLAPPback (with the potential for multimillion-dollar damages against both filers and their attorneys).

Quite surprisingly, our interviews show that many prospective filers and even their attorneys do not realize that what they are contemplating is a violation of the Constitution, a losing proposition, or a financial risk. Curing that ignorance can prevent the SLAPP.

Finally, one should not stop with informing potential filers but spread the word to other "influentials" as well.

1. Filer's attorneys: Lawyers who are asked to file a constitutional-rights-violating, groundless, frivolous, or otherwise improper lawsuit can be even more at risk than their clients. After SLAPPs are dismissed, the "falling-out-among-thieves" syndrome is common. Losing filers—faced with high legal expenses, damage or attorneys' fee awards to targets, or related business losses—often turn on their own lawyers, who may then face client refusals to pay legal fees, professional grievances,

malpractice actions, and defenses of "advice of counsel" (a.k.a. the "Nuremberg Defense": "I was told to do it" by my lawyer). Targets can be equally unforgiving: Filers' attorneys can be hit with bad press, ethical grievances, and targets' attorneys' fees. Moreover, naming the attorneys as prime defendants in multimillion-dollar SLAPPbacks is now standard practice (see Chapter 9). We have found that approaching attorneys for a prospective filer with such information frequently turns them into advocates against filing SLAPPs.

2. Government: The government agencies and officials involved should also be informed of the threat; they can then advise against a SLAPP in their own self-interest. State attorneys general, school boards, civil rights offices, and other agencies have begun to engage in proactive prevention in order to protect their own communication lines (see Chapter 10).
3. Filer's peer groups: An appeal to the filer's trade association, industry leaders, chamber of commerce, or corporate superiors may be worthwhile. Because SLAPPs are a black eye for everyone associated with filers, numerous business groups and representatives have gone on record to their members and clients recommending against such action.[6]
4. Media: Prospective targets and their attorneys should consider going public. The media—themselves frequently sued for expressing views—readily understand SLAPPs and sympathize with targets. Beyond a single news story or sound bite, threatened citizens may urge an anti-SLAPP editorial, follow-up stories, letters to the editor, and other continuing coverage. Media grilling and exposure can shrivel up the SLAPP threat quicker than any other preventive tactic.

In short, prompt informing and counseling of all involved interests may well stop a SLAPP from being filed or further threatened. Sometimes, however, information, logic, and good sense do not prevail.

Managing SLAPPs as Soon as They Happen

Once a SLAPP is filed, two things are crucial to the targets' success: first recognizing and then dealing with it for what it is, without being distracted by any "camouflage." When targets do lose in court, are forced to settle, or are bogged down in a case for years, it is almost always because they, their attorneys, or the judge failed to grasp these fundamentals.

Recall the "theory" of SLAPPs in Chapters 1 and 2. Filers (with or without knowing it) are transforming a public, political controversy into a private, legalistic one. The advantages of this transformation strategy for filers include diversion (of targets' time, funds, energies, and supporters), punishment (of successful opposition), and chilling (targets' and others' future opposition). To avoid those outcomes, targets must "retransform" the "legal" action back into a "political" one by getting the court to see that it is being used to infringe on the constitutionally protected political rights of citizens. They must remind the court that First Amendment rights normally outweigh ordinary "legal" claims of personal injury. If targets, targets' attorneys, or courts fail to recognize the case as a political one, if no retransformation occurs and the case is adjudicated as a narrow legal dispute, targets typically lose, both in the courtroom and the real world.

Recognizing a SLAPP

SLAPPs normally do not advertise themselves as such. Filers do not usually sue people for "exercising their First Amendment rights" or "petitioning the government" or "speaking out politically" (although some unsophisticated complaints actually are that blatant). Instead, to gain and maintain access to the court, filers must recast or camouflage the targets' political behavior as common personal injuries or legal violations. They need to mask the nature of the dispute and present it as personal and legal, not public and political.

Two litmus tests can determine whether a case is a SLAPP: defendants' actions, and plaintiffs' claims.

1. Defendants' actions: To begin with, exactly what activities of defendant-targets are described in the fact section of the filer's complaint? Do any of those activities involve communicating with government officials, bodies, or the electorate, or encouraging others to do so? Are government hearings, complaints, appeals, letters, reports, or filings mentioned? If so (and regardless of how many nongovernment activities are also mentioned), the case is a SLAPP. Even if no government-connected actions are mentioned, however, one must ask: Are targets politically active citizens and groups? Are they involved in speaking out for or against some issue under consideration by some level of government or the voters? If so, there is a high likelihood that a suit against them is a disguised SLAPP, regardless of the facts alleged.
2. Plaintiffs' claims: SLAPPs repeatedly use six very predictable tort or other legal categories to mask their real purpose. They are, in order of frequency, (1) defamation (libel, slander, business libel, product disparagement, and so on), (2) business torts (interference with business, with contract, with prospective economic advantage; antitrust, restraint of trade, or unfair competition), (3) conspiracy (planning and

acting together with others for any illegal purpose), (4) judicial or administrative process violations (malicious prosecution, abuse of process), (5) violation of constitutional or civil rights (denial of due process or equal protection, taking of property, discrimination), and (6) other violations (nuisance, trespass, invasion of privacy, outrageous conduct, falsifying tax-exempt status, and so on). If any of these categories are specified, suspect a SLAPP.

Three other filer tactics are further indicators:

1. Unrealistically high dollar demands: Large claims of monetary injury, out of proportion to any real harms done, are a hallmark of SLAPPs. Small claims do occur, but filings in the $100,000, $1,000,000, or even $100,000,000 range are not unusual. (In states that have a rule against specifying dollar amounts, the complaints bear the ominous phrase "damages in an amount to be determined at trial.") The key is that the dollar figures demanded are huge but typically bear no relationship to the amount of any actual damages the filer could have suffered, even if the complaint were 100 percent true.
2. "Does": The inclusion of unnamed John or Jane Doe defendants—a blank check device used only occasionally in other litigation—is frequent in SLAPPs. It is a highly effective way of creating "ripple effects" among citizens and officials who support or might support the targets' campaign.[7] We have found whole communities chilled by the inclusion of Does, fearing "they will add my name to the suit."
3. Naming individuals but not the organizations they represent: When the League of Women Voters of Beverly Hills led an election campaign to block a condo development, the $63,555,000 SLAPP was filed only against the individual leaders—the league was not named—and the same thing has happened to Sierra Club volunteers (*Maple Properties; McKeon,* Chapter 3). This "divide and conquer" technique seems designed to isolate the individuals (for greater chilling effect) and cut them off from organizational financial support, since some groups' rules or insurance may not permit them to cover a legal defense unless the group is actually named.

Given any of the foregoing indicators, targets should scrutinize the complaint with special care. In judging whether the case is really a SLAPP, search for any mention of Petition Clause–protected activity by defendants. Some complaints are embarrassingly blatant. Even if the complaint avoids mentioning protected government communications and focuses instead on seemingly nongovernmental communications such as letters to the editor, media statements, or leaflets to the community look to see whether the actions complained of are (1) part of an overall petitioning strategy or (2) too minor to support the massive dollar damages demanded; in either case, other, unmentioned activity is probably provoking the filing. The target attorney should carefully probe all target activities in the previous year that involved or affected the filer, whether mentioned in the complaint or not. If any of those activities are either direct government communications or indirectly government-connected or designed to influence others to communicate with government, the attorney should proceed on the basis that this is a bona fide SLAPP. Then the attorney can "pierce the veil" of the camouflage claims and use the Petition Clause defense.

Dealing with the Reality

Next to recognizing a SLAPP, it is most crucial to deal directly with its reality, not the window dressing in which it comes camouflaged. SLAPPs must, of necessity, be masked. To be accepted by the courts they must not press the wrong buttons (such as suing someone for "petitioning the government" or "expressing views to public officials"); they must press the ones with which a court is familiar: tort, contract, and other claims. To survive in court, they must transform the nature of the dispute from the real world of public political debate into the court world of private legalistic injuries.

Again, to defeat a SLAPP, one must do the opposite: retransform the dispute in the court's eyes. The case must be unmasked, retransformed from private and legal to public and political, so that the court will send it back to the more appropriate decisional forum. One very effective method is to focus the judge on the political forum that bred the dispute. This can be done by pointing out (1) that targets' statements or actions took place in or in relation to another government forum;[8] (2) that filer therefore already has (or has had) a remedy—the opportunity in that other, more appropriate forum to respond, repudiate, or rebut target's "objectionable" opposition on the merits;[9] and (3) that invoking the court is counterproductive because the court cannot resolve a real public dispute (the zoning approval or the teacher's competence) that is exclusively in the jurisdiction of the other political forum.[10] The SLAPP court's hands are tied because it is limited to deciding only peripheral issues (defamation, not zoning or teacher tenure). Further, the court's hands are tied to money damages, an inappropriate substitute for the real dispute resolution needed.

Many targets' attorneys we have interviewed clearly did not recognize that they were dealing with a SLAPP and considered only the masks—the camouflaging legal issues. They saw the suit as "routine," recognized the claims only as conventional ones, and defended it as they would have done in a normal personal injury case. "Too often, attorneys become so involved with defending the 'convenience heading' of the [SLAPP] lawsuit that they miss the underlying political issue," warns a leading legal trial manual.[11] In short, target attorneys are responsible for target losses more often than not. One reason is that the bulk of lawyers' training, from law school and bar exams on, programs them to "issue spot," to identify factual issues under conventional legalistic (not political) labels: for example, "That statement is factually false, malicious, and causes injury, so it constitutes 'libel.'" Another is that most lawyers' practices involve routine, nonpolitical personal injury, contract, business, and criminal cases in which one wins by focusing narrowly on the specific, technical claims and defenses. A third reason is the lawyer mystique of seeing oneself as engaged in a "profession," a "higher calling," not in "mere politics."[12] In sum, lawyers are unfortunately programmed to routinize and particularize cases, not to search out the larger issues and constitutionalize and generalize them.

Not surprisingly, since judges receive the same training, courts abet this myopia. For example, a Rhode Island judge refused to dismiss a 1993 suit filed by dump owners against a woman who had complained about them to government health and environment authorities; the judge even turned a blind eye to the state attorney general's plea that the case was a SLAPP, saying: "This is strictly a private suit. I know you're trying to give it a public flavor (but) I just can't go beyond reading your brief."[13] Some judges really do understand, as one New Jersey attorney informed us: "At oral argument, the presiding appellate judge expressed his view that this might be a 'SLAPP' suit, even before I could [speak]."[14] Not infrequently, however, both attorneys and judges became angry when asked why they were not looking at the First Amendment issues in their cases.

What can be done about this myopia? One clear answer is better information, and this study is one effort to provide it by recategorizing a group of seemingly unrelated cases under a memorable descriptive acronym. Continuing education for attorneys, SLAPP conferences, and other educational approaches are also expanding sensitivity. The media—with hundreds of articles and television and radio shows on SLAPPs—are doing a great service. Politically active clients themselves should press their attorneys to analyze their situations in Petition Clause terms. But the best answer is for attorneys to watch for the SLAPP "indicators" discussed above, particularly the political activity of defendants and the typical six plaintiffs claims.

Recruiting the Defense Attorney

One of the most daunting problems for targets can be finding an attorney. Filers rarely sue a well-heeled individual or a powerful, lawyer-laden organization. Quixotic filers who do go up against litigation powerhouses such as the Sierra Club and NOW are the exception; much more commonly, the targets are unrepresented individuals or underfunded volunteer organizations.

Securing a defense lawyer can be difficult if targets approach traditional, private practitioners of business law. These attorneys are often reluctant to take on SLAPP defenses for three primary reasons, all of which affected one unfortunate victim in a recent Georgia case:

First, SLAPP targets often do not have resources to pay full-price attorney fees, potentially thousands of dollars for a retainer, hundreds an hour, and tens of thousands for a case. As the Georgia target put it: "Keep in mind that I did not know that I was supposed to be paying for everything, and going down the tubes at a rapid rate while my attorney and the opposing attorney logged hours and played with the infinite possibilities of the state code."[15] If Abe Lincoln was right and "an attorney's only stock-in-trade is his time," many today are reluctant to give away free samples or to discount their "stock."

Second, many attorneys are uncomfortable with high-visibility "political" cases or their own lack of expertise in such cases. As the Georgia SLAPP victim summed it up:

> I have found if [attorneys] don't know about something or have not had any experience with it, they are reluctant even to get an associate to scan my pleadings—preferring to opt out and send me to someone who "knows more." Unfortunately, who would that be in [this] State . . . ? There is no case law on the books to "learn with."[16]

Third, local attorneys who take on a powerful filer may risk their popularity and future business opportunities by representing unpopular clients. Small town and rural targets seem to have the hardest time because of the relative dearth of attorneys and the tighter webs of economic and social dependency. When the Georgia target finally did get a lawyer, she felt he did not handle either her SLAPP defense or SLAPPback offense "aggressively":

> I do not know if my attorney is simply out of his league, or if I am not a politically advantageous person to be representing in the small county where he has his future based; . . . It worries me that the current judge assigned to my case is the for-

mer longtime law partner of the county attorney . . . who was in power . . . when [my] original . . . suit [against the county] was filed [triggering the SLAPP].[17]

Targets will sometimes start out being defended pro bono by a volunteer attorney who is a member of the target group. Not infrequently, these volunteers drop by the wayside when time begins to mount or court appearances loom. But there are other ways to secure a lawyer. Local chapters of the American Civil Liberties Union have aggressively defended SLAPP targets free of charge in Colorado, Rhode Island, California, Wisconsin, Connecticut, and other states, with excellent results. The ACLU exists to defend the First Amendment. SLAPPs are squarely within the First Amendment—indeed, are among its greatest threats. The ACLU chapters can call on experienced volunteer trial attorneys, eager civil liberties defenders just waiting for an opportunity like a SLAPP. And although the ACLU will not handle the monetary SLAPPback, it can assist in finding a qualified private attorney for that.

Many law firms can be persuaded to take on SLAPPs as part of their *pro bono publico* obligations to the community. Even big national firms—Arnold & Porter; Covington & Burling; Kirkland & Ellis[18]—have defended SLAPP targets as part of their pro bono services. Large or small, however, law firms must be concerned about "conflict of interest" (avoiding representations that create conflict between clients) and may define that very broadly to protect their accounts. For example, a firm with major real estate clients is unlikely to take on a SLAPP brought by a developer, even one that is not a client.

Crusading attorneys desiring to build a reputation in the civil rights field will often jump at the chance to defend a SLAPP. Others take them on and may reduce their fees because they care for the issues or people involved.[19] Some just love the limelight of a high-visibility crusade.

The target support groups that are springing up sometimes provide legal services, as do anti-SLAPP groups such as attorney Mark Goldowitz's California Anti-SLAPP Project, the Coalition Against Malicious Lawsuits (CAML) in Valley Stream, New York, Citizens Against Harassing Lawsuits (CAHL) in New York City, and the Citizens Legal Defense Fund in Suffolk County, New York (see Chapter 10). Ralph Nader has vowed to provide legal assistance to consumer advocates.[20] Groups such as Citizen's Clearinghouse for Hazardous Wastes (Chapter 6) aid targets in toxic waste disputes. The League of Women Voters, Common Cause, environmental organizations, religious groups, unions, civil rights organizations, civic lobbies, neighborhood associations, and others can provide or help recruit attorneys.

Government agencies too, recognizing that their ox is being gored by

SLAPPs, are beginning to help. State attorneys general, the U.S. Equal Employment Opportunity Commission, consumer agencies, and others have given legal support, usually through friend-of-the-court briefs (see Chapter 10). For a time, one county government even provided a Citizens Legal Defense Fund to protect residents who spoke up in county proceedings (Chapter 10).

One of the best ways to secure a top-quality defending trial lawyer, we have found, is to "package" the SLAPP with a SLAPPback. SLAPP defenses may appear unprofitable to a lawyer until they are linked with the prospect of a multimillion-dollar SLAPPback jury verdict, of which the attorney will receive a healthy percentage (see Chapter 9).

Finally, though many targets do not realize it, they may already have a paid-for lawyer through their insurance. Some homeowner, renter, umbrella, and other general liability policies actually cover some of the most frequent SLAPP claims such as defamation/libel/slander, malicious prosecution, and invasion of privacy. It pays to look and ask, and the politically active should make sure one of their policies is of this kind. Such insurance not only pays if the insured is found liable but (more important) pays for the full services of a defense attorney, as several cases in Chapter 5 illustrate. In the *Immuno* case, Shirley McGreal's insurance company paid a reported $250,000 in legal fees to defend her, then an additional $100,000 in settlement.[21] Cathy Durbin's insurance company reportedly provided free lawyers to defend her in the *Hodgins Kennel* case, and a $400,000 settlement on top of that.[22] Even in a SLAPP with only "nuisance" value—such as the *Dienes/Humane Society* case[23]—the Humane Society's insurance firm handled the defense and paid a confidential out-of-court "nuisance" settlement for the suit's quick dismissal.[24] Quite a number of targets have found the cost burden lifted off their shoulders by their insurance companies.

Being defended by an insurance company can have major drawbacks, however. The companies usually want to use lawyers of their selection (without telling insureds if they have the option of selecting their own attorney), and insurance defense lawyers typically view the company and its assets as their primary "client." Thus, they are less interested in winning a First Amendment precedent than in limiting their company's losses. If a settlement can be reached which avoids a risky trial or cuts down on legal expenses, the insurance lawyer will recommend settlement. An insured who refuses to settle and insists on vindication may simply be cut off, and target complaints of being "sold out" are not uncommon. Another drawback is that targets may have trouble getting insured afterward. Both Shirley McGreal and the farmers in the *Boswell* SLAPPback (Chapter 9) reported such problems.

Managing SLAPPs in Court

A SLAPP defense counsel has not one but two possible winning strategies. Attorneys can seek immediate dismissal or pursue lengthier summary judgment to end the case. The choice hinges on the targets. Prompt dismissal is indicated if the targets are weak, badly frightened, seriously diverted from their campaign, or hopelessly low on resources. Summary judgment is more attractive, however, if the targets have fortitude, will "go the distance," can juggle both a lawsuit and the political campaign, and have access to resources. Dismissal's prime advantage, if it succeeds, is a quick end to the chill. Summary judgment's advantage is a more compelling fact record for the dismissal, any appeals, and a successful SLAPP-back. A closer look shows the pros and cons of each.

The Dismissal Motion

The motion to dismiss, to strike, for judgment on the pleadings, or demurrer attacks the SLAPP complaint "on its face" without extended presentation of evidence. Such a motion must be filed early, generally before defendants answer the complaint, and it can cut off harassing discovery in many jurisdictions. Its strengths are low exposure, limited costs, and quick closure. Its weaknesses are that it is a discretionary motion, may be postponed interminably by the judge, is chiefly decided on the "cold" paper filings (without witnesses), is one that judges are more inclined to deny than to grant, and will not build the strongest record for a SLAPP-back. Still, if targets need a quick out, this is the door.

Without question, the chief ground for dismissal should be the Petition Clause; invoking it results in dismissal (by either the trial or the intermediate appellate court) with considerably more frequency than does any other defense (either other First Amendment or nonconstitutional grounds). Successful dismissal motions argue that the lawsuit is an unconstitutional attempt to use the courts to violate the federal and state constitutional rights of targets to petition their government for redress of grievances. The mere mention of the Petition Clause enhances judicial interest and the probability of a successful outcome. Even though the U.S. Supreme Court tells us that all First Amendment rights are created equal,[25] our experience is that the Petition Clause receives special judicial solicitude for at least three reasons. First, it is so rarely used in litigation that it is a novelty and attracts interest. Second and more important, of all the individual rights and liberties in the Constitution, the right to petition is the one most directly linked with the effectiveness and survival of our representative form of government; it is enlightened self-interest for judges (who, after all, work for the government) to protect it, and it focuses the judge not only on the harm SLAPPs do to individuals but on the harm they do to our entire government system. Third, characterizing targets' conduct as Petition Clause–protected focuses the court away from the camouflage of personal injury claims; allowing counsel and court to escape the risks and resource-intensiveness of arguing and deciding each of the (typically numerous) technical claims that filers plead and to sweep them away collectively with a constitutional broom. The result can be dramatic: In the famous *Sierra Club v. Butz* (Chapter 5) and a number of other cases,[26] a motion based on the Petition Clause resulted in dismissal of the filer's counterclaim within a few months.

Although seeking dismissal has worked in the great majority of SLAPPs, some trial courts will delay, refuse to hear, or even deny SLAPP dismissal motions as a result of what we call the six "Dismissal Dilemmas." The first Dismissal Dilemma is the "wait and see" bias. As noted earlier, judges are programmed by legal training and the system not to dismiss but to allow cases to continue to trial. Two reasons (see Chapter 2) are based on the same Petition Clause: the notions that filers have a "right to sue" (a right to petition the courts) and a "right to a trial and jury" (the right to "prove their case"). A third reason is the inherently conservative wait-and-see outlook of trial judges: When in doubt about the legitimacy of a suit, they tend to pick the "safe" course of going to full-scale trial and "a fair hearing" for all sides. Fourth is the jurisprudential notion that disputed "facts" are best resolved in full-scale trials, not on pretrial motions; thus filers' claims that facts are in dispute can trigger a judicial "wait and see" that defeats pretrial dismissal.

These institutional biases were perfectly expressed by the trial court judge in the Stevens teacher SLAPP (Chapter 4):

> The court . . . is uncomfortable with the prospect of deciding this constitutional issue based merely on the [pretrial dismissal motion] record before it. . . . The court abides by the settled principle that if it has doubts about whether to grant a motion for [dismissal], the better practice is to deny the motion and let the jury return a verdict.[27]

Of course, this "settled principle" in fact results in protecting the filer's right to sue, not the target's right not to be sued. In SLAPPs, the judge must be persuaded (1) that no action is action; (2) that no action is a victory for the filer, because it extends the chill; and (3) that no action makes the court an accessory to the chill.

There are many horror stories caused by this judicial reluctance to dismiss before trial. In the *SRW, McKeon,* and *POME* real estate SLAPPs (Chapter 3), the *Denver Water Board* politician SLAPP (Chapter 4), the *IREA* consumer SLAPP (Chapter 7), and many others, trial court judges steadfastly refused to hear, postponed decision on, or flatly denied motions to dismiss. In the *Maple Properties* condo SLAPP (Chapter 3), it took six long years of dismissal motions and multiple appeals before the trial judge could be forced to dismiss all claims.

The second Dismissal Dilemma is the "non-fatal" dismissal. There are dismissals—and there are dismissals. Success is having the court dismiss "with prejudice" (meaning the case is over), not "with leave to amend" (court jargon for "try it again, plaintiff, and better luck next time"). Judges who see the constitutional forest, not just the trees, quickly conclude that there is no way a SLAPP can be rewritten without violating targets' constitutional rights. These judges will grant full, final dismissal "with prejudice" or "without leave to amend." Then the only way for a filer to continue the case is to appeal. Many judges, however, whether conservative, uncertain, or just overworked, automatically grant filers another chance by dismissing "with leave to amend." If the "amended complaint" is dismissed too, a "second amended complaint" may follow, and so on. We have seen SLAPPs on their "fourth amended complaint": that is, the judge has given the filer a fifth try.

In routine cases without constitutional issues, it may be fair to give filers more than one chance to create a competent complaint. Where public participation in government, court abuse, and the First Amendment are clearly at stake, however, routine "leaves to amend" are dereliction of duty on the part of the judge. Fortunately, appeals courts are wise to this device and generally quick to cut it short. New York state's top court roasted a trial judge in language well worth quoting in future cases:

> The importance of summary adjudication in . . . [SLAPP] litigation cannot be overemphasized. [These] actions are notoriously expensive to defend, and, indeed, "The threat of being put to the defense of a lawsuit . . . may be as chilling to the exercise of First Amendment freedoms as fear of the outcome of the lawsuit itself." . . . To unnecessarily delay the disposition of [such an] action is not only to countenance waste and inefficiency but to enhance the value of such actions as instruments of harassment and coercion inimical to the exercise of First Amendment rights. . . .
>
> That [the trial court judge] . . . was evidently reluctant to apply the ordinary summary judgment criteria . . . is regrettable. It is disturbing that [filer] . . . succeeded in coercing . . . "substantial settlements" from all but one of the original defendants for the obvious reason that the costs of continuing to defend the action were prohibitive.[28]

The third Dismissal Dilemma is the "voluntary amendment," a close corollary to the "leave to amend." In these cases, as soon as targets file a motion to dismiss and before the judge rules, the filer submits an "amended" complaint, which attempts to cure defects pointed out by the targets' motion; at the least, it puts defendants to the time and expense of filing a revised motion to dismiss. Targets' attorneys should take care not to write a motion and brief that suggest ways in which the filer can cure the constitutional infirmities in the original complaint; they should also object strenuously to court acceptance of the "amended" complaint.

The fourth Dismissal Dilemma involves the "winner (must) take all" rule. In multi-claim SLAPP complaints (which almost all are), targets must persuade the court to dismiss all the claims; if even one survives, the case grinds on. Myopic judges may miss this point; even a judge who dismisses some claims with outrage, recognizing them as constitutional violations, may leave one or two others untouched and the SLAPP alive. *Maple Properties* (Chapter 3) is a classic example: the targets resolutely whittled down claims at every step but never quite got them all until the sixth year of the lawsuit.

We have found three situations in which this happens. First, the judge may quickly grasp that the Petition Clause is a defense to defamation/libel/slander but balk at seeing it as a defense to charges less associated with the First Amendment, such as business interference or trespass. Second, targets' lawyers may not have based the motion squarely on the Petition Clause, or placed too much emphasis on nonconstitutional, technical legal defenses (truth as a defense to defamation, lack-of-contract as a defense to contract interference, and so on). Third, a judge who takes a very narrow view of what is protected by the Petition Clause may dismiss a claim against targets' statements to government bodies but refuse to dismiss a second claim for identical statements made to the media or the public. In all cases the cure is to relate all filers' claims and all targets' actions (directly or indirectly) to the public political controversy, emphasizing for example, that statements to the media as well as statements at an official hearing were integrated parts of the targets' campaign to influence the government's decision or action.

The fifth Dismissal Dilemma, it must be said, is the biased judge. Judicial prejudice against targets can have many causes, take many forms, and be hard to detect or prove, but it was clearly at work in a number of the SLAPPs we studied. First, not all targets are "white hats," let alone members of the judge's own peer group, political party, or life-style. Second, particularly in the tightly knit communities of small-town or rural America, a judge may have professional, personal, or business links with the filer, the filer's attorney, or a government body supporting the filer (recall the judge in *Jenkins v. Smith* [Chapter 4], who was not only the filer's former law partner but the attorney who had approved the disputed permits). Or a judge may identify with majority community sentiment favorable to the filer ("This project is an economic boon to our community") and unfavorable to the targets ("They are just spoilers"). Some judges have even recommended that the citizens be sued.

The sixth and final Dismissal Dilemma is the "fact quagmire." A first-year law student quickly learns that the way to defeat a pretrial dismissal motion is to assert that "fact" issues in the case require a trial. When facts are in dispute, our legal system sees a trial as the optimum way to resolve the dispute; in theory, it is the best forum for bringing out all the evidence and counterevidence. Judges can generally decide cases before trial only if the facts are agreed to, not greatly in dispute, or not decisive. When in doubt, judges tend to think that "the better practice" is to deny the motion and let a trial decide the case. By claiming that fact issues such as "malice," "truth," "intent," "motive," and "good faith" are relevant, filers hope to defeat the dismissal motion, get on with discovery, and keep the SLAPP alive for the years necessary to get it through trial. Even if the filer has no interest in trial, the fact quagmire is still an attractive chill-prolonging tactic.

Even judges who recognize that constitutional rights are being violated frequently fall into the fact quagmire. One of many examples is the *Welter* police SLAPP (Chapter 4), in which the first judge recognized that a citizen report of police wrongdoing should indeed be protected from the chill of the policeman's SLAPP yet still denied dismissal. Why? Because the policeman argued that the citizen had lost her constitutional protection by acting out of "malice." Malice is a fact issue, and the judge ruled that a trial was required to see if it was true. In effect, the judge turned the Constitution on its head, ruling that without a trial he could not decide whether the Constitution protected the target from a trial. In the *Weisman* case (Chapter 4), a teacher SLAPPed parents for criticizing him in a petition to school authorities. The trial judge recognized the constitutional issues and dismissed all claims based on the parents' petition, yet he ruled that a trial was necessary to determine if the parents acted with "malice" in releasing an exact copy of the petition to the media. This judge saw the constitutional violation but blindly helped it continue.

To summarize, filers will oppose the motion to dismiss with three predictable arguments. First, they will argue that the case is not political or constitutional but an "ordinary" libel or business interference action or the like. This is no more than the standard dispute-transformation camouflage, and targets should counter it by urging the judge to take the "forest" view of the case. Second, filers will argue that targets were not engaged in constitutionally protected activity if they communicated to nongovernment entities (letters to the editor, handbills to neighbors, and so on), or if they trespassed, or if they were engaged in a "sham" or in blackmail. Targets should counter by arguing that all their activities were (directly or indirectly) part of an integrated campaign to influence a government result, including influencing others to influence their government; they should also urge that the burden of proof on such issues be shifted to the filer, who after all is the one relying on them.

To filers' third argument, "Facts are in dispute requiring a trial," targets should counter that the only relevant facts are those related to the Petition Clause issue and that these "constitutional facts" should not be disputable or open to dilatory discovery. They should be handled on a dismissal motion, to curtail the chill.

Since Rule 11 of the Federal Rules of Civil Procedure and state law equivalents permit judges to make one side pay the other side sanctions for "groundless-frivolous" lawsuits or procedures, a successful dismissal motion can be followed by targets' motion for sanctions (payment of their attorneys' fees, expert witness fees, court costs, and other litigation expenses). These are certainly appropriate when a SLAPP is dismissed on constitutional grounds, and a winning target attorney should consider such a motion. Some authorities, however, are so enamored with sanctions that they recommend them as the only cure for SLAPPs.[29] In fact, however, they fall far short of a cure: Courts are reluctant to grant them;[30] awards are typically low (a few thousand dollars—and well worth it to filers if it shuts up their opponents);[31] and focusing on sanctions to the exclusion of other cures potentially diverts attention from the best cure—the SLAPPback (Chapter 9).

If the trial court denies the motion to dismiss (or refuses to hold hearings or to rule on it), success lies in taking an immediate appeal. The alternatives are (1) summary judgment, (2) going to trial, or (3) settlement. Summary judgment (discussed below) may be appropriate if the dismissal denial is largely based on some fact quagmire. Going to trial should rarely, if ever, be considered, given the mounting pressures, time, expenses, and the chilling effect on targets and the community; moreover, juries have occasionally been swayed to award filers big-money damages, and an appeal of a jury's fact verdict is much more difficult than appeal of a judge's law ruling. Settlement (see below) is usually tantamount to surrender, providing filers more than any court would ever have given them.

Immediate appeal, on the other hand, is an attractive option. Appeals courts have shown a real ability to recognize SLAPPs, understand them, and reverse foot-dragging trial courts—probably because of appellate courts' traditional focus on and greater experience with constitutional issues. Some jurisdictions will allow an appeal from a dismissal denial without waiting for trial, especially if it is based on a constitutional issue; in others, a direct appeal or special writ may be made to the state supreme court on the ground that the court system itself is violating constitutional rights; the *POME* case (Chapter 3) and *IREA* case (Chapter 7) are excellent precedents. As always, the Petition Clause should be the core appeal ground; other, nonconstitutional issues should be eliminated or kept to a minimum.

In the infrequent cases where the appeals fail, targets must file an answer, engage in discovery, and try again with a motion for summary judgment. If that fails, and trial becomes unavoidable, it is generally best to request a jury, both because the judge has already indicated a "negative leaning" with the motion denials and because juries of peers should relate well to the plight of most targets and adversely to the heavy-handedness of most filers.

The Summary Judgment Motion

If targets have the fortitude and finances to do so, and favor a SLAPP-free future, they should consider "going on the attack." The attack scenario involves launching discovery against the filer in preparation for a fully supported summary judgment motion before trial. Sometimes this move is enough: In the *Friends of Animals* anti-trapping case (Chapter 5), as soon as targets launched discovery, filers promptly dismissed their SLAPPs. Usually, though, the greatest advantage of this proactive approach is getting data into the record from which to develop an airtight fact case, both for dismissal and for a subsequent SLAPPback.

Since quick-strike discovery can catch filers and their attorneys before they understand the Petition Clause dimensions of the case, targets' attorneys should immediately take the depositions of filers and their representatives and force document production. The discovery should focus on two areas of admissions—those supporting the Petition Clause summary judgment, and those supporting a future sanctions motion and SLAPPback—and should probe (1) filers' real-world plans; (2) filers' business practices, policies, political activities, and power structure; (3) filers' knowledge, views, and biases about targets; (4) the relationship of targets' political activities to filers' plans; (5) filers' (political) motivation for filing the SLAPP; (6) any "pattern and practice" of chilling activity by the filers in other contexts;[32] and (7) exactly what actual losses filers have suffered because of target's political activity. Filers often drop admissions at this stage—"There is a price to be paid" for opposing us; "Our goal was to teach them a lesson"; "We wanted to make sure no one else spoke out"—which strongly support the Petition Clause summary judgment.

Targets' attorneys should also get information into the pretrial record to show that (1) targets definitely were seeking a government decision, outcome, or result (as required by *Omni*), not just "sham" playing with the system or attempting blackmail or other impropriety; (2) their nongovernment activities (contacts with the media, nongovernment officials, and the like) were part of an overall campaign to influence government decision-making or persuade others to do so; (3) targets' political statements and activities were factually accurate; (4) their positions were based on sound legal grounds and advice of counsel; and (5) targets have suffered real losses (in dollars, time, and other resources diverted to defending the lawsuit, in support for the political campaign, in emotional stress, and so on). Establishing this record not only supports the summary judgment but can also block two common, eve-of-motion-hearing filer strategies: a voluntary dismissal of the case, or a counter summary judgment motion (with only filer-favorable facts).

Targets' counsel should do "two-track" thinking from the outset: that is, build both the case for dismissal of the SLAPP and the case for the SLAPPback, however remote or unlikely the latter may seem at this early stage. Countersuits can be based on a number of different legal theories—from malicious prosecution to civil rights to infliction of emotional distress—for which the proof elements should be captured in the SLAPP discovery.[33] Getting filers' and targets' motives, goals, methods, and injuries on record in this fashion creates the constitutional case. Ralph Wegis, one of the most experienced and successful Petition Clause attorneys, credits his wins in the *Boswell* SLAPP and SLAPPback (Chapter 9) to this approach.[34]

The summary judgment motion itself is really identical to the motion to dismiss but is supported by a more thorough fact record. The overall strategy is the same: the retransformation of the case back to its political basis. The grounds are the same: Petition Clause rights, plus any other appropriate defense. And, predictably, filers will oppose with the same three arguments as those used against the motion to dismiss (see above). Targets' counterarguments will also be the same but backed by a fuller, largely undisputable record nailed down by discovery. If summary judgment is denied, immediate appeal is again the best alternative.

Filer Tactics

Some filers are not content with just the chilling effects of a SLAPP but seek to increase those effects through the pressures of discovery. Depositions of targets and their supporters can be grueling and abusive. For example, in the *Immuno* animal protection SLAPP (Chapter 5), the filer's attorneys even tried to inquire into target Shirley McGreal's "sexual acts," a matter completely outside the issues of the case. Nonparties may be subpoenaed to spread the chill more widely throughout the community. Demands for targets' highly sensitive or secret records—membership lists, donor lists, funding sources, meeting minutes, informants' names—are not uncommon. Blocking these "fishing expeditions" can mire targets in rounds of additional research, briefs, hearings, expense, and even appeals.

Another tactic is to attack the targets' lawyers, perhaps naming them as defendants. This happened to Florida attorney Thomas Reese, when he represented 17 national, state, and local environmental, sport, and civic organizations opposing a huge Gulf Coast development next to two Florida state wetland reserves.[35] Reese admitted that he felt the pressure—"Their suit is an attempt to intimidate us and chill our participation in the administrative process"[36]—but he fought back and won dismissal; filers were castigated by the judge and paid an out-of-court settlement of $7,500 to the attorney, but they won in the real world and got their development built. The *POME* case (Chapter 3), the *Miami Trace* school-bond case (Chapter 4), and the *Gorman Towers* elderly high-rise case (Chapter 6) are other examples of target attorneys themselves becoming targets.

Lambasting the lawyers can take other forms, too. For example, in 1991 a Denver environmental and personal injury attorney, Macon Cowles, filed a class action for local residents against the only cadmium smelter in the United States located in a residential area. At a press conference he blasted the smelter owner, ASARCO:

> We are talking about toilet training transnational corporations. That's what this lawsuit is all about. We don't want our lands polluted, our waters made unsafe to drink and our air a cause of sickness and disease. Rich corporations who violate our citizens and our environment must be punished and they shall be.[37]

Thereupon, ASARCO's prestigious Denver law firm filed a formal grievance with the Colorado Supreme Court, accusing Cowles of violating the Lawyers' Code of Professional Responsibility, which forbids out-of-court statements that would interfere with fair trial (a rule rarely enforced today, particularly in public-interest cases).[38]

The Colorado ACLU took up Cowles's defense, viewing it as a SLAPP in "professional grievance" clothing; still, the specter of losing his license haunted the attorney, and fighting the grievance siphoned time away from the smelter suit. But Cowles is one of those who fights even harder under pressure, and in 1993 he won the largest jury award in an environmental case in Colorado history: a $28,100,000 verdict against ASARCO for the 567 families he represented.[39] A month later the Supreme Court Grievance Subcommittee dismissed the grievance, finding that no "grounds for discipline exist."[40] The twice-vindicated crusader admits to having had "some sleepless nights" but says the experience will not change him: "I'm going to go on doing it as I've been doing it. . . . I'm going to continue to speak truth to power until the last breath. If the right to speak the truth has gone out of the legal system, it still exists on the outside."[41]

Sometimes filers will dismiss their own SLAPPs if they have served their purpose or hit a snag. In Ann Arbor, Michigan, the Gelman Sciences factory dismissed its three-month-old suit as soon as the judge granted a restraining order prohibiting the target from posting any more "Gelman Is a Polluter" signs on its property.[42] Other filers dismiss just as the case is coming to trial or, as in the *Shell Oil* toxics SLAPP (Chapter 5), when they are threatened with a SLAPPback. Voluntary dismissals underscore the actual intent of SLAPPs: to scare off community protest, not to win an actual in-court victory. Filer dismissals leave the chill unchanged, keep the SLAPP tactic available for another day, set no protective precedent, make a SLAPPback more difficult to win, and put targets in the ironic position of having to argue against dismissal and for continuation of the lawsuit until it can be dismissed on the merits by the court.

Since settlement—not trial—is the natural outcome of American litigation (in the United States over 90 percent of all lawsuits are settled out of court), it is not surprising that SLAPP filers frequently offer to settle soon after the case is filed. Bargaining the case away may look attractive to frightened targets, but doing so can be costly. Filers usually demand three concessions to settle and dismiss. The "price" of dropping the suit is targets' agreement to (1) stop their political campaign against filers (and, frequently, publicly apologize), (2) waive their right to file a SLAPPback or motion for sanctions, and (3) submit to a "gag order" to keep the settlement details confidential. This is, of course, a complete victory for filers (better even than they could expect from a court, given the overwhelming majority of dismissals that our study found). It means that the SLAPP has succeeded in punishing past opposition, preventing future opposition, and insulating filers from retaliation—all without risking a bad court outcome, bad publicity, or a bad precedent.

There is no telling how many SLAPPs are "lost" by targets this way, but instructive examples include the *IREA* case (Chapter 7), the *Oxnard* and *Napa County* real estate cases (Chapter 3), and a number of police and public official SLAPPs (Chapter 4). Not all settlements are free, either;

some filers insist on being paid to drop the case. The payment may be a relatively small ("nuisance") amount, as in the *Dienes* case (Chapter 5), or it may be a substantial sum, as in the *Cole* case (Chapter 4) and the *Immuno* and *Hodgins Kennels* cases (Chapter 5). Still, a settlement can sometimes work to the targets' advantage. In the *Denver Water Board* case (Chapter 4) the negotiated settlement did allow filers to build their project but obligated them to apologize for filing the suit, establish a new public participation process, do studies, and pay targets' attorneys' fees.

In sum, it is important for the politically active and their attorneys to remember that SLAPPs are predictable, preventable, dismissable, and readily turned on their makers. Prediction is a function of watching for the "warning signs." Prevention is best done by "taking cover in the open," by being well informed about SLAPPs and making sure the opposition and other interests are, too. Dismissal of filed SLAPPs requires "retransforming" the private and legalistic suit back into the public and political controversy it really is; dismissals are the overwhelming norm, whether sought immediately or tactically delayed for record-building purposes. Turning a SLAPP on its makers comes about through media exposure, getting the involved government agency and other opinion molders to side with targets, seeking trial court sanctions, and filing a SLAPPback—to which we turn next.

9 Judicial Cures

Managing the SLAPPback

Slapp suits are becoming an organized and promoted strategy. They're gaining momentum. But once firms [contemplating a Slapp suit] realize that they're in for a countersuit, they'll think twice.

—Ralph Nader

What chance does a big corporation [filing a SLAPP] have against a family farmer . . . or a humongous developer against an environmentalist? The plaintiffs will have a field day [with a SLAPPback].

—Attorney defending a real estate developer in a SLAPPback

The most promising prevention and cure for the SLAPP phenomenon, we find, is what we call the "SLAPPback": a countersuit in which targets turn the tables and sue the filers for the injuries and losses caused by the SLAPP.[1]

SLAPPbacks are exercises in irony. The first irony is, as one target put it, that "the cure is a dose of the same disease." It is true that they fight fire with fire, one lawsuit with another, but each of the two stands on a quite different footing. The SLAPP, the dismissals tell us, is an abuse of the courts, a violation of constitutional rights, and an unconstitutional effort to quell public participation in government. The SLAPPback, on the other hand, is an accepted use of the courts, a vindication of constitutional rights, and an effort to hold persons accountable for the injuries they cause individuals and the body politic. A second irony is that SLAPPbacks are really conventional personal injury actions, with more similarities to a vehicle accident or medical malpractice suit than to a constitutional test case. A third irony is that SLAPPbacks "recycle" the SLAPP filers' original charges. Malicious prosecution and abuse of process head the list, followed by defamation, interference with business, conspiracy, and other familiar complaints. A final irony is that whereas SLAPPs are usually losers, SLAPPbacks tend to be winners in court. The filer's attorney quoted above is correct: plaintiffs and juries do have a "field day" in many SLAPPbacks. Jury verdicts of $5,000,000, $9,000,000, $13,000,000, and even a staggering $86,000,000 have been handed down against SLAPP filers in the 1980s and 1990s.

Those ironies are not lost on filers. As consumer-advocate Ralph Nader observes, real estate developers, polluters, public officials, and others who just a few years ago might have unthinkingly SLAPPed their opposition are now "thinking twice."[2] Even though SLAPPbacks are not a panacea,[3] the risk of having to defend against them may prove the most effective SLAPP deterrent of all.

The Birth and Growth of SLAPPbacks

McKeon: The Earliest Success

The pioneering countersuits in the *McKeon* case (Chapter 3) set the pattern for future SLAPPbacks. In 1972, Sierra Clubbers opposed McKeon Construction Company's plans to subdivide Sacramento's scenic Elliot Ranch into "ranchettes," and McKeon filed one of the more blatant SLAPPs we have seen—actually charging the targets with criticizing the project "to local government agencies." In 1977, five years and three courts later, McKeon's suit was finally dismissed. Not feeling vindicated, four of the targets sought legal advice. Bruce Kennedy and Bruce Swirehart talked with Sacramento lawyer John Poswall (see the *Leonardini* case, below); Frederick Styles and Linda Best consulted a San Francisco law firm, today's Keker & Brockett (see the *Perini* cases, below). All four got the same advice: "Countersue."

From the very first, SLAPPbacks looked like winners, and so they became "self-funding." The filers did not have to pay attorney fees, because their lawyers agreed to bring the countersuits on a contingency fee basis. Plaintiff attorneys routinely take promising personal injury cases on contingency: That is, they agree to be paid only if the case wins (generally one-third of the verdict amount), taking nothing but expenses if it loses. Needless to say, such cases have to have winning potential, for the attorney is in fact "gambling" on (or "investing" in) its winnability.

Setting a precedent without knowing it, the *McKeon* SLAPPbacks were based on malicious prosecution (using a lawsuit for improper, ulterior purposes) and abuse of process (using other court processes for improper, ulterior purposes). They accused the SLAPP filers of suing for

> the ulterior and collateral purpose of frightening and intimidating the plaintiffs and other like-minded, concerned Sacramento citizens, so that these people would cease and refrain from speaking out at public meetings, expressing positions contrary to the interests of McKeon Construction, and otherwise exercising their constitutionally protected rights.[4]

Setting yet another precedent for future SLAPPbacks, both the construction company and its lawyers were made defendants. Actual and punitive damages of "no less than $1,000,000" per plaintiff were demanded.

Oddly, McKeon Construction did not move to dismiss but instead routinely answered the complaints, denying everything. Its SLAPP lawyers, now defendants who were separately represented by lawyers of their own, took a different tack: They moved to dismiss the complaints for lack of facts, suggesting that silencing the environmentalists had been the purpose of their suit and was a proper use of the courts.[5] To no avail—the SLAPPback complaints survived. Faced with trial, McKeon and its lawyers began to talk settlement. What resulted is secret (researchers find confidential settlements a troublesome part of many SLAPPback endings), but in less than a year the SLAPPbacks were over, and a "substantial" dollar settlement (rumored to be in six figures) was paid to the four targets. The environmentalists had "won big," and others took note: SLAPP filers had just funded their opposition far into the future.

Leonardini: The First Multimillion-Dollar Verdict

A megacorporation, Shell Oil Company, has the distinction of being the first to lose a multimillion-dollar SLAPPback. In *Shell v. Leonardini* (Chapter 5), Shell sued a consumer advocate and union attorney for reporting to a state health agency that there were cancer-causing substances in a Shell product used in home plumbing. Target Ray Leonardini took the SLAPP to Sacramento trial attorney John M. Poswall; the two attorneys immediately saw the Petition Clause aspects of the case and lashed back with a dismissal motion charging constitutional rights violations. Shell first pressed its lawsuit and then, in a turnabout, voluntarily dismissed it, claiming that a codefendant's settlement was vindication. Now truly outraged, the Leonardini-Poswall team filed their SLAPPback, charging malicious prosecution to violate Leonardini's constitutional rights.

The case went to trial in 1986, and Shell lost badly. Poswall hammered away at the constitutional issues, arguing that Shell's suit had been groundless and designed to keep Leonardini from testifying to the government against its product:

> This case is not about chemicals. . . . The issues . . . are more fundamental to our society than the dangers posed to millions of Californians by toxic chemicals in their drinking water.
>
> . . . Ray Leonardini advocated that the public bodies charged with the responsibility for health and safety independently test and examine the polybutylene pipe system before exposing millions of Californians to the unknown consequences of such use. In the midst of the ongoing public debate regarding the policies that California governmental bodies should follow, the Shell Oil Company sued its most effective political opponent.[6]

Shell pursued the standard SLAPPback defense strategy, denying that its suit had anything to do with constitutional rights and portraying it instead as an ordinary, defamation action "based on Leonardini's circulation of false, incomplete, and misleading statements concerning Shell's polybutylene resin . . . result[ing] in irreparable and unquantifiable harm to Shell. . . . Shell requested injunctive relief . . . to stop the continued dissemination of false statements about its product."[7] The five-week case put Shell's product, truthfulness, mental state, and politics on trial.

Malicious prosecution, the core charge in virtually all SLAPPbacks, is not an easy charge to prove. Some courts even call it "a disfavored action," because the Petition Clause and public policy favor giving everyone open access to the courts for redress of grievances.[8] Even though no one has an absolute right to sue (one does not have a right, for example, to file an unconstitutional suit), strict proof requirements are customary to justify suing someone for suing you—state-of-mind proofs like "malice" and "lack of probable cause." Nonetheless, after both sides had presented their evidence, Judge Lloyd A. Phillips Jr. of Sacramento County Superior Court found the evidence so one-sided that he decided the issue of probable cause himself, issuing a directed verdict that Shell had no reasonable, good-faith grounds to regard its suit against Leonardini as proper.[9] The jury unanimously found that Shell had been malicious and awarded Leonardini $175,000 in actual damages for intimidation, $22,000 in attorneys' fees, and a whopping $5,000,000 in punitive damages (damages designed not to compensate victims but to punish perpetrators, and therefore based less on the magnitude of the wrong than on the perpetrator's net worth).

Shell appealed the $5,197,000 verdict, but the state appeals court upheld it in full in 1989 in a detailed 32-page opinion, the first published SLAPPback opinion of which we are aware.[10] The court clearly saw the case as one involving an attempt "to influence government"[11] in a "public debate . . . being aired before a branch of state government . . . of great public interest and concern."[12] It affirmed: "Given the constitutional constraints necessarily implicated by this political dispute, no reasonable attorney would have thought this action was tenable,"[13] and concluded that "Shell was guilty of maliciously bringing a lawsuit against plaintiff to silence and muzzle him. . . . Shell engaged in a continuous course of conduct to thwart the open governmental process of resolving conflicting claims."[14]

Shell appealed, but both the California and U.S. Supreme Courts refused to reconsider the ruling. An elated, if exhausted, John Poswall wrote us in 1990:

> On Tuesday, October 23, the Shell Oil Company delivered to this office a check in payment of the [SLAPPback] award, which check, together with interest, totaled $7,547,643.10. . . . You will note that the case was clearly presented to the United States Supreme Court as a SLAPP suit. . . . I hope . . . you will draw attention to the case . . . so that those defending SLAPP suits have . . . the encouragement to SLAPP back.[15]

Rumor has it that Poswall invested part of his contingency fee in a sailboat and christened it *Malicious Prosecution.*

Boswell: **Making SLAPPbacks Pay**

The record SLAPPback victory to date which has been upheld on appeal is an $11,100,000 jury verdict for three family farmers in the Central Valley of southern California. In 1982, it was hard to find a more notorious political issue in California than "Prop 9." The ballot proposition asked voters to approve a $5 billion package of water projects, including the controversial "Peripheral Canal."[16] The canal would be the third major diversion to take northern California water (from the Sacramento and San Joaquin Rivers) and pipe it south to slake southern California's endless thirst.

Prop 9 pitted northerners against southerners, San Francisco against Los Angeles, environmentalists against business, and—as it turned out—farmers against farmers. In the arid West, where water is a virtual object of worship, the canal struggle became (as one newspaper put it) "a religious war."[17] That war created strange bedfellows. The anti-canal forces consisted of California environmentalists in an uneasy alliance with their traditional foes, the agribusiness giants of the south. The canal supporters linked small southern farmers thirsting for more water with *their* traditional enemies: water-guzzling Los Angeles, some wildlife groups, real estate developers, and multinational oil conglomerates. Critics charged that the massive shift of water would destroy the fragile San Francisco Bay delta, kill free-running whitewater rivers, subsidize "pork," undercut water conservation, and lead to more water-wasting agriculture "in the desert." Supporters argued that the new water was vitally needed for existing farms and municipalities and for expected growth in southern California.

In the West it is said that "water flows uphill toward money," and this campaign was no exception. Lifelong Kern County farmers and community leaders Ken Wegis and Jack and Jeff Thomson, who believed that more water was vital for their Bakersfield area, were outraged to find out that two of the area's largest and richest corporate farmers—J.G. Boswell Company and Salyer Land Company—had jointly pledged $2,000,000 to defeat Prop 9 and kill the canal.[18] Boswell was reputedly the world's largest cotton producer and the largest farmland owner (nearly 200,000 acres) in the state of California, with 1981 revenues of $200,000,000; Salyer was not far behind.[19] Together, the Thomsons and Wegis farm 5,000 acres, growing cotton, alfalfa, and other crops. They and their supporters could scrape together only $8,200 for the campaign.

As the canal's popularity fell, a political consultant persuaded the Thomsons and Wegis to form a group called "Family Farmers for Proposition 9." Unknown to the trusting farmers, this was the brainchild of the statewide pro–Prop 9 campaign committee, which was run by Getty Oil, Tenneco Oil, the Los Angeles Metropolitan Water District, and other giants desperate to add a "common touch" to their sagging polls.[20] The consultant prepared a full-page newspaper ad for the farmers; they approved it, and it ran in local valley newspapers on May 10, 1982, bannered: "Who Are Boswell & Salyer? And why are they trying to cut off our water?"[21] The ad answered its own question with zingers like these: "Salyer and Boswell['s] . . . only interest is in getting cheap water for themselves, regardless of water quality or the environment"; "Salyer and Boswell have been against responsible water development in California"; "If the small farms go out of business, Boswell and Salyer will be able to totally dominate California agriculture."

Although this was mild mudslinging by California standards, Board Chairman James G. Boswell II later testified that it made him "mad as hell."[22] Political pros just scoffed, calling the ad "ineffective" and advising Boswell "to be delighted they are spending their money that way."[23] Nevertheless, four days later (and only three weeks before the election) Boswell slammed Family Farmers, Ken Wegis, and "Does 1 through 1000" with a $2,500,000 libel suit (Salyer prudently refused to join in).[24] The one word "dominate," Boswell complained, accused the company of "committing the crime of conspiring . . . to prevent competition . . . and to fix prices" (violations of the antitrust laws).

The SLAPP worked almost at once in the real world. Ken Wegis ruefully admits that as soon as it was filed, "we were, you know, like we had the plague as far as campaign contributions were concerned."[25] Boswell soon substituted the two Thomsons for two of the Does, and it sent a letter to all newspapers it thought might run the ad and threatened to include them as defendants if they published it.[26] Boswell personnel called Family Farmer contributors and used their economic clout to dry up some donations,[27] and the fear of being named one of the Does did the rest. Supporters dived for cover. The targets' insurance companies refused to cover damages, warned them not to engage in any other political debate, and cut their coverage in half.[28] The farmers dropped out of the Prop 9 campaign immediately and entirely. (What they did not know was that the SLAPP would drag on for four more years and the SLAPPback for six years beyond that.) Boswell won big in the election, too. On June 8, 1982, California voters rejected Prop 9 and the Peripheral Canal by almost two to one overall (in northern California the vote was 91.9 percent against).[29] Elated delta defenders, paraphrasing the Munchkins' cheer from *The Wizard of Oz*, sang:

> *Ding dong, the ditch is dead!*
> *The wicked ditch is dead!"*[30]

The farmers had better luck in selecting a lawyer. Target Ken Wegis's second cousin was Ralph Wegis, a prominent southern California trial lawyer in Bakersfield. Ralph Wegis would not only go on to defend them successfully and win the biggest SLAPPback victory to date but would become an expert dubbed "the Sultan of SLAPPbacks" by the media.[31] He has defended against a dozen SLAPPs, fought four SLAPPbacks, and is called for advice on as many as a dozen new cases a week.[32] The law firm also brought in John Means, a psychologist and political expert, as the litigation coordinator. This "dream team" fought the SLAPP in classic style, defending on constitutional, political, and other grounds and attacking with cross-complaints for $5,000,000 each against Boswell for abuse of process and violation of state constitutional free speech.[33]

Attorney Wegis is a firm believer in using the SLAPP to build the SLAPPback, and having resilient clients who really wanted to establish a precedent, he ruled out a quick dismissal: "[Boswell] undoubtedly thought we'd cave in. . . . [The defense] cost a lot of money . . . [but we] fought for this thing we believe in for a long time, and you don't just give up."[34] Wegis immediately launched discovery against Boswell, working to get on record the filer's business practices, its political positions, its patterns of dealing with both business and political opponents, and the personalities of the people in power.[35] Depositions, written interrogatories, requests for production of documents, and requests for admissions had to show "a pattern and practice of chilling activity" by the filer.[36] Wegis deposed the filer's management, including Board Chairman Boswell himself; although none would admit to a political-chill motive, they were made to testify about their political opposition, their anger, their desire to punish, the advice they had received against suing and their reasons for going ahead, their pressure on the farmers' supporters, and their lack of dollar damages from the targets' activities.[37]

At the same time, when the targets were deposed by Boswell attorneys or required to turn over files, Wegis made sure they filled the record with facts supporting their side. This produced proof both of positives (their political altruism; the factual and legal bases of their actions; their goal of winning the election, not harassing or libeling an opponent) and of negatives (the fear and intimidation that persuaded them to drop out of politics; their financial losses; and the impact of the SLAPP on their neighbors and supporters). Facts like these from both sides' discovery formed the proofs not only for Petition Clause–protected dismissal of the SLAPP but for the "malice," "lack of probable cause," and "bad faith" requirements of the SLAPPback. Wegis, like Leonardini's Poswall before him, had hit on the ultimate winning strategy: "two-tracking," or planning everything in the SLAPP defense to work for both the SLAPP and the SLAPPback.

For two years the two sides hammered each other with discovery and the usual skirmishes of litigation. Finally, on June 8, 1984, Trial Judge Len M. McGillivray dismissed Boswell's SLAPP, and in two more years the appeals court agreed. That threat was over; now, the SLAPPback could go into overdrive. At first it ran a rocky course. In January 1985 another trial judge, Gerald K. Davis, dismissed it, and targets had to file amended complaints three times over the next two years, adding malicious prosecution and honing the other charges. At the end the Boswell protests only resulted in better, undismissable SLAPPback complaints against itself; neither side would settle, and trial was inevitable.

For 17 days in June 1988 the parties battled in a basement courtroom in the Kern County Courthouse before Marvin E. Ferguson, a judge called out of retirement just to handle this politically charged trial. Wegis's strategy was straightforward, emphasizing the targets' constitutionally protected right to engage in advocacy on public political issues and the filer's goal to interfere with that right for its own gain. Wegis advises: "Make a home in the facts,"[38] and he did, using the one-two-three combination of testimony by targets, by other concerned citizens, and by experts to impress the jury with the individual, community, and national ramifications of SLAPPs.[39]

The selection of the jury of eight women and four men took two days (Wegis prefers a jury, believing its members are more likely to see themselves in the targets' place than a judge is). Then Wegis took nine days to put on his witnesses. He led with his most eloquent target farmer, moved to his experts, returned to the other two farmers and community observers, and closed with his targets' wives—in some of the saddest and most compelling testimony of the trial. (He did not need to call Boswell executives, since he knew the defense would have to produce them.) The targets' tough, weathered faces stared solemnly at the jury and told how the SLAPP had ruined their lives: They feared they would lose the farms their families had held for generations; they were terrified the banks would deny them loans and foreclose; their insurance companies had canceled policies, denied coverage, and pressured them to get out of politics; they had lost friends and had to drop out of political activities in which they had traditionally participated, even community volunteer service; pressure, worry, loss of sleep, shock, depression, and "severe emotional distress" had gripped them all.[40]

The experts were Professor Pring (co-author of this book) and Edmund Costantini, the latter a respected political scientist from the University of California at Davis and formerly the state of California's secretary of education. The judge quickly qualified both as experts in their fields. Pring testified about the SLAPPs phenomenon, the national study, the causes of such suits and their personal and political effects, their relation to the Petition Clause, and their general failure in court; he opined that the *Boswell* case was a SLAPP and that its purpose was to pressure opposition into silence. Costantini testified about Boswell's campaign tactics and techniques, described general norms of campaigning in California, and concluded that Boswell could not have had a reasonable good-faith belief in the merits of its libel case but was trying to stifle the opposition.

Attorney Wegis's cross-examination of Boswell's executives and closing argument were so emotional and effective that Boswell screamed foul and, in their appeal, accused him of "misconduct." The court of appeals disagreed; its description of Wegis's arguments outlines a textbook-perfect SLAPPback prosecution strategy:

> Counsel [Wegis] stated to the jury that corporations were designed for making money. He noted they could also be mindless monsters in pursuit of profit . . . out to have their way . . . [and] willing to say or do whatever it took to win, . . . [that they] considered the political campaign akin to war . . . [and were] willing to sabotage the other side's lines of supply and sources of revenue.

. . . Counsel [said] he was representing small farmers and they were fighting "a virtual giant." Counsel claimed that litigation was a familiar weapon to Boswell's executives. He argued that Boswell used the lawsuit as a political weapon against Family Farmers. He even sarcastically disparaged [Boswell's lawyer's] research because every [other] judge and court that looked at the statements [in the ad] saw them as being privileged.

. . . Counsel then argued that Boswell wanted to teach a lesson to people who had the audacity to exercise their rights as Americans. . . . He characterized Boswell as being ruthless and its executives as being the kind of people who would look at you and shut down your business and have people lose jobs and say that it really does not bother them. Boswell's lawsuit was described as a fraudulent piece of litigation.

Counsel contended that under the Constitution everyone was supposed to be equal. He asked the jury to be appreciative of Family Farmers' constitutional rights and to protect their rights of life, liberty and the pursuit of happiness. Counsel explained that to deny one the ability to exercise one's rights and to oppress them was something associated with communist countries. Counsel also described Boswell's complete disregard for the rights of citizens as a reflection of the kind of mentality that "the German leaders had in World War II."

These last three comments perhaps give the initial appearance of being the most inflammatory. However, . . . to the extent that Boswell did attempt to silence its critics to gain advantage in a political campaign through the abuse of process and by maliciously prosecuting [a lawsuit], counsel's analogies may be . . . not unfair.[41]

Damages—putting a dollar value on the loss of political rights—may be the most difficult problem in a SLAPPback. Wegis decided to let the jury decide: in his closing he took out his checkbook and asked each member of the jury to tell him how large a check he would have to write them to give up all their rights to participate in American political life from then on. How much, he asked, never again to go to a town meeting, speak your mind, argue about candidates and issues, help solve public problems, write a letter to the editor, or even vote? That, he told them, is the correct measure of "compensatory damages" for the chill of a SLAPP. The jury was out for only seven hours and came back with a unanimous verdict: Boswell's conduct was "malicious, oppressive or fraudulent" on all counts, and $1,000,000 was the amount of damage Boswell's SLAPP had inflicted on each of the farmers.[42] The next step was to determine whether "punitive damages" should be granted as well. A "puny," so called, is anything but. This is the amount of money, beyond actual damages, which a defendant may be ordered to pay in a civil suit if it has injured another "with malice." Since the amount is calculated by how much money it would take to "punish" the defendant financially, witnesses and attorneys debated Boswell's net worth for three more days. The company claimed to be worth a mere $232 million; Wegis argued that its fair market value was nearly four times that much. The jury retired for only five hours and came back with the verdict. They were split ten to two, but the majority ruled: $10,500,000 was what it would take to be "punitive" enough to Boswell's bank account.

The targets at that point had won a total verdict of $13,500,000—reputedly the largest ever in a California political case. But when Judge Ferguson became ill and could not hear Boswell's after-trial motions and objections, Judge McGillivray,—who had originally dismissed Boswell's SLAPP—was brought back in. Surprisingly, he ruled that the punitive damage award was not excessive but that the compensatory damages of $1,000,000 each was too high: he ordered the farmers to accept a cut to only $200,000 each, plus the punitives (for a total of $11,100,000), or he would order a new trial. Both sides appealed.

The appeals court upheld the SLAPPback victory, ruling that the farmers' ad "was within the scope of normal political debate and discourse" and that Boswell's SLAPP was both malicious prosecution and abuse of process.[43] It upheld the use of the experts' testimony and found ample evidence to support both the punitive and compensatory damages (at the reduced $11,100,000 level).[44] But then the appeals court did a very odd thing: It ordered its own 73-page opinion "not to be published." It is a frustrating practice of California appellate courts to write an opinion but sometimes keep it from being cited as a future legal precedent by not officially publishing the reasoning. In the *Boswell* case, speculation is that it was not published in order to keep from casting into question California's very convoluted, limiting law on malicious prosecution (discussed below).

Still, a win is a win, and on October 3, 1991, the California Supreme Court also upheld the unusually large $11,100,000 award,[45] and (technicalities aside) the nine-and-a-half-year battle was over. As so often happens, though the filer won in the political world, it was targets' game all the way in the courts, yet "to this day, that suit has chilled them from getting involved in political activity ever again," reports psychologist John Means.[46] That, Ralph Wegis confesses, is the reason he takes on SLAPPs: "This is not radical stuff [that targets do]. This is vanilla ice cream speech that is touching somebody's economic sensibilities, and [SLAPP filers] are using the litigation process as a battering ram. That [is why I] feel good about spending time on these cases."[47]

Who's Winning?

With SLAPPbacks, however, the "battering ram" points both ways. When we uncovered and tracked a total of 51 SLAPPbacks from 1974 to

1992, (the majority after 1987), we found wins outnumbering losses two to one: Former targets have won 21 SLAPPbacks and lost 10. (The majority of the remaining 20 were still pending; a few were untrackable for various reasons.) Of the 21 winners, jury verdicts were won in 6, and out-of-court settlements figured in 15. The jury verdicts ranged from an unbelievable high of $86,500,000—settled for considerably less on appeal—in *Tanner v. Decom* (Chapter 6) to a low of $80,000 in the *Mortensen* home-buyer case (Chapter 7). Other verdicts included the $11,100,000 *Boswell* case, the $9,800,000 in *Humana Inc. v. Hemmeter* (below),[48] the $5,200,000 *Leonardini* verdict, and a recent $2,650,000 award in a St. Louis developer SLAPP-back.[49] Substantial payments have been made to a number of the 15 SLAPPbackers who settled, but the majority of these are confidential, and both sides' lips are sealed along with the court records. The highest settlement known to date is $450,000 paid by an attorney for a filer in a California trailer park SLAPP;[50] others in six figures are reliably rumored or probable in the *McKeon, Tanner,* and *Perini* SLAPPs (below);[51] and settlements in the $10,000 to $100,000 range are public in four others.

What about the 10 losers?[52] In most of these cases the targets had filed SLAPPback counterclaims before the original SLAPP was over; the judge simply dismissed both sides without opinion (in "a plague on both houses" manner); and targets did not appeal. SLAPPbacks as a whole are almost evenly divided between those that are filed while the SLAPP is pending and those filed after it is dismissed, but more winners by double are filed afterward. Does this suggest not filing SLAPPbacks until the SLAPP is over? Not necessarily; Ralph Wegis won his $11,100,000 *Boswell* SLAPPback with both pending from the start, as did Morton Galane in the $9,800,000 *Humana Hospitals* case. Winning a SLAPP-SLAPPback combo may have more to do with how successful target's counsel is in getting the court to see the two suits as fundamentally different and deserving of radically different court treatment.

The Legal Grounds for SLAPPbacks

On what legal claims are SLAPPbacks based? Here, attorney ingenuity abounds: We found some 30 different grounds used. Yet one stands out as the core, indispensable claim: malicious prosecution. Only a half-dozen others figure repeatedly in the win column.

In some states, as noted earlier, *malicious prosecution* is called "a disfavored action" because of the strong constitutional policy of "open access" to all to the courts;[53] this usually means only that plaintiffs must be even more careful and persuasive in proving their case. While its definition varies somewhat from state to state, generally it requires proof of five elements: (1) the filing of a lawsuit, (2) without probable cause, (3) with malice, (4) which terminated favorably for the party or parties sued, but (5) resulted in damage or injury to them.

The first element creates no problem; the SLAPP satisfies that. Favorable termination typically means that malicious prosecution can be filed only after the SLAPP is dismissed by the court; a SLAPP filer that voluntarily dismisses its case—as Shell Oil did—may claim that there was no "favorable" termination, but the courts generally count voluntary dismissals as satisfying the fourth element.[54] The fifth element, damage or injury to targets, can be a problem because actual, out-of-pocket dollar damages are usually limited, unlike those in a physical injury case; SLAPPbacks must overcome this as any civil rights or dignitary tort does by showing the extent of political and emotional injuries done. It is the second and third elements—probable cause and malice—that can be terrors to prove, given the "catch-22" explained below.

Another charge often used in SLAPPbacks is *abuse of process,* which is similar to malicious prosecution. To distinguish them: The filing of the SLAPP is malicious prosecution, but the subsequent use of the judicial processes or filings for a purpose separate from the suit is what constitutes abuse of process. Its general proof requirements are (1) a willful use of process, (2) which is not proper, (3) for an ulterior motive or purpose. In the Boswell case, the Family Farmers argued that the company not only maliciously prosecuted the SLAPP but also broadcast it for the ulterior purpose of intimidating them, drying up their funding, and undermining their political campaign. Boswell's suggestion to newspapers, local businesses, and others that they could be drawn into its suit bolstered the willfulness and impropriety proofs. Here, the tough proof is ulterior purpose, which presents some of the same psychological catch-22s as malice and probable cause.

The next most popular claim is violation of or interference with the targets' *constitutional rights.* Ironically, though this is the core public policy objection to SLAPPs, technically it is a difficult one to win in SLAPPbacks. First, the federal constitution is not "self-executing": That is, its guarantees of free speech, right to petition, due process, and the like are not standing alone grounds for filing a damage lawsuit unless Congress has passed implementing legislation (such as the Civil Rights Acts). Pure First Amendment rights can be raised as a shield, to protect oneself from the lawsuits or actions of others, but not as a sword, to strike back and punish offenders. By contrast, some state constitutions, such as California's, *are* self-executing; a suit may be filed to enforce guaranteed rights and to seek damages for violations without special enabling legislation.[55]

Even if one can sue under a state constitution, there is another obstacle: the "state action" requirement. Since the nineteenth century the U.S. Supreme Court has maintained that such constitutional violations are actionable (through the Fifth and Fourteenth Amendments) only if the violator is a government actor or acting under government authority.[56] This so-called "state action" requirement means that most private parties cannot be sued under a constitution or under enabling legislation based on those constitutional provisions. Exceptions allow suits against private violators if they are performing a "government function" or are "governmentally involved" to a significant degree. Most state constitutions likewise limit constitutional torts; for this reason the court of appeals dismissed that claim in the *Boswell* SLAPPback, ruling that Boswell was nongovernmental and not engaged in a government function. Still, the second largest category of SLAPPs (over one-third) comprises cases in which the filer is a government entity, official, or employee (Chapter 4); for these, the charge of violation of state constitutional rights, (if self-executing) can be effective.

Federal, state, or local *civil rights statutes* and ordinances convert non-self-executing constitutional rights, such as those guaranteed by the Petition Clause, into full-fledged, litigatable causes of action. Civil rights laws typically prohibit violations of constitutional rights and authorize damage actions (including SLAPPbacks) by parties whose rights are violated. The same "state action" limitation can be a stumbling block here as well, however. Federal civil rights statutes, notably section 1983,[57] are limited to government actors and governmentally related private parties.[58] Others lack across-the-board utility because they are limited to race or other special-target discriminations.[59] In states whose civil rights statutes are less limited, making even private actors' violations actionable through a SLAPPback,[60] they can be first-consideration counts.

A tempting claim used in more than a third of the SLAPPbacks we studied is infliction of *emotional harm*—usually intentional infliction only, although a significant number of cases combined it with a backstop charge of negligent infliction. In most states, proving such a claim requires showing (1) conduct that is extreme or outrageous, (2) a causal connection between that conduct and the emotional distress, and (3) resulting severe distress, plus the usual elements of intentionality or negligence.[61] What makes this claim attractive is its "trial-ability." It permits testimony about targets' stress, anxiety, fear, political chill, and resultant injuries from the SLAPP, putting these sympathy-evoking issues squarely before the jury.

Claims found much less frequently in the SLAPPbacks studied include outrageous conduct, prima facie tort, conspiracy, and, in 1991, the first known appearance of "abuse of process—SLAPP." Still others depend on the particular facts of the case involved: defamation, unfair trade, business interference, invasion of privacy, extortion, abuse of position of public trust, impairment of administrative functions, barratry, misrepresentation, sex discrimination, gross negligence—and even assault and battery.

Are so many claims necessary? California attorney Phillip Berry, a long-time Sierra Club leader and experienced SLAPP and SLAPPback attorney, thinks not. In filing the first SLAPPback in the Sierra Club's hundred-year history, against Perini Land and Development Company, he used only the one count of malicious prosecution. Betting on one horse worked: In 18 months Perini forces paid a substantial out-of-court settlement to the club and others. Likewise, the Leonardini victory was based on a single count of malicious prosecution; nationally known Las Vegas trial attorney Morton Galane relied on abuse of process in winning a SLAPPback against Humana Hospitals; and the *Boswell* case, although it started with more charges, was upheld on appeal on just the two, malicious prosecution and abuse of process.

The "Catch-22" of Filer's Motive

In Joseph Heller's famous World War II satire, *Catch-22*, the only way to get out of the war was to be insane, but only sane people wanted out, so those wanting out were sane and could not get out. A similarly circular, seemingly no-win proof of mental state can be the biggest single problem in SLAPPbacks. Their standard counts—malicious prosecution and abuse of process—generally require proof of filer's state of mind, whether expressed as "probable cause," "malice," "ill will," "bad faith," "ulterior purpose or motive," or "conscious disregard of rights of others." Obviously, the best proof would be out of the filer's own mouth—a rare occurrence, although some filers have been so rash as to state that targets "needed to be taught a lesson," or needed to learn that "there is a price for speaking out." But if confessions are not forthcoming, what then? Law professors, legal experts, political scientists, and sociologists can testify about SLAPP cause and effect, motive, and malice, but anyone's testimony about another's state of mind (even that of a psychiatrist or psychologist) is problematic. How can this seeming catch-22—of being required to prove the unprovable—be overcome?

Actually, several different approaches do work. Courts customarily will hear the "best evidence" available, settling for an expert's circumstantial testimony on motive in the absence of better proof and counseling the jury that they may consider it but are not bound to accept it. When Boswell's own attorney "opened the door" by asking Professor Pring's opinion, the judge ruled:

[His] testimony is certainly relevant. It's the issue in the case, the motive of your client, and [targets' attorney] is bringing in an expert, a man that's made a study on the motives. I take it [Professor Pring] is going to state a study of this case and read the depositions and he's going to tell the jury what the motives of Mr. Sterling [a Boswell manager] were, apparently. . . . We do it all the time in personal injury cases. . . . He's certainly qualified if he's making a study. You found somebody making a study on the very thing that we're dealing with and he has dealt with at least 100 cases.[62]

Pring then testified:

It doesn't matter what the label is, the real effect of the case—no matter what the parties intend—is to chill citizens' future political activity, to teach people there will be a high price to pay to get involved in the future in government decision making.

. . . You, ladies and gentlemen of the jury, are doing that today. You're participating in government processes. If you thought you could be sued by the losing side in this case, you would think twice about that. So, you have many safeguards to protect you. . . . [SLAPPs] make those people and anyone else who hears about it think twice the next time about getting involved in government. . . . And if this trend continues . . . obviously an ultimate result could be a nation of people staying at home . . . not participating as citizens in their government, basically for fear of being sued."[63]

The Court of Appeals found such testimony "somewhat speculative" but upheld it:

Any objection . . . goes more to the weight of his testimony than its admissibility. Pring's testimony did focus on the very difficult to prove issue of Boswell's motive and ulterior purpose in filing the libel action. Experts have great latitude in relying on studies and even hearsay opinions of other experts. . . . To the extent that [expert testimony] could be construed as evidence of . . . motive or intent, it has bearing, it being up to the trier of fact [jury] to give weight to that evidence as it sees fit.[64]

Similarly, in the *Leonardini* toxics SLAPPback, two lawyers and a judge testified at length about the motives, mind-set, and malice of Shell Oil. The appeals court regarded that testimony as part of the malicious prosecution proof but as insufficient standing alone.[65]

In other cases, Attorney Ralph Wegis has solved the dilemma by putting on Professor Canan, an expert sociologist and co-author of this book. Her testimony was accepted by both the trial and appeals courts in

Monia v. Parnas, a real estate SLAPPback. The appeals court summed up the trial strategy:

> The trial court permitted Dr. Canan, a professor of sociology, to testify as an expert on the motivation behind, and effects of, the phenomenon of Strategic Lawsuits Against Public Participation (SLAPP suits), of which she opined the present case is an example. The trial court overruled objections to her testimony, noting that [filer] Parnas was free to challenge her qualifications and to argue [that] her opinion should be given little weight. By offering Dr. Canan's testimony on the issues of malice and damages, [target] Monia sought to establish that Parnas acted from an ulterior motive or purpose distinct from that of enforcing its right not to be defamed: that is, to affect the political process and chill the first amendment rights of its opponents. . . .
>
> Dr. Canan considered Parnas' libel action against Monia to fit the SLAPP criteria. She based this opinion on Professor Pring's review of court documents filed in the case and on her own review of deposition transcripts, newspaper articles, and statistics. . . . In Dr. Canan's opinion, Parnas's motives in bringing the libel action were (1) to retaliate against political opposition; (2) to prevent future political opposition; (3) to warn others that political opposition would be punished; and (4) to deny others their rights as citizens. She also testified that Parnas's suit revealed a lack of concern for its effects on democracy.[66]

The court of appeals ruled that "in light of Dr. Canan's scholarly background and long study of SLAPP suits," her testimony was valid, helpful, not speculative, and analogous to the well-accepted use of expert opinion to prove that an insurance company acted in bad faith in denying coverage under a policy.[67]

The Special Problem of "Special Injuries"

About a third of the states[68] throw up an extra barrier to SLAPPbacks in the form of an old English rule of law that requires malicious prosecution plaintiffs to plead and prove that they have sustained "special injuries" or "special damages," defined as those "not necessarily resulting in any and all [like] suits."[69] For example, an arrest or a seizure of one's property would qualify as "special," but lawyers' fees, court costs, emotional stress, loss of time, and so on, would not. In these states one may not be allowed to bring a malicious prosecution SLAPPback without showing that the SLAPP caused injuries different from any involved in a normal civil lawsuit. The "special injuries" rule, like California's "disfavorment" of malicious prosecution actions, is intended to prevent every suit from turning into another, ad infinitum. To that extent it has some validity, but it has been applied unthinkingly to dismiss SLAPPbacks without considering their special merits.

The solution, according to Chicago attorney and SLAPP expert David Letvin, is to recognize that SLAPPs are not normal civil litigation; therefore, the rule should not apply[70]—or, if the rule does apply, that a SLAPP's constitutional violations automatically qualify as "special injuries."[71] When Letvin filed a SLAPPback after winning dismissal in *King v. Levin,* a minority-housing SLAPP (Chapter 6), he anticipated the problem and pleaded in his complaint: "Levin sustained damages and special damages by reason of King's malicious prosecution of the [SLAPP], including loss, harm and damage to his constitutional rights . . . , emotional distress, reducing his involvement and visibility in public affairs, attorney fees, expenses and costs."[72] Three different judges considered the special damages argument on motions and agreed with Letvin that the SLAPP chill qualified, but a fourth judge mechanically applied the rule and dismissed,[73] the appeals court affirmed,[74] and in October 1995 the state supreme court refused even to hear the case.[75] Thus, Illinois judges refused to unmake their judge-made rule, an anachronism that has no place in American constitutional litigation, as the great majority of states have found.[76] So the best recourse is for the legislature to adopt an anti-SLAPP law to nullify the problem (see Chapter 10).

What Makes a SLAPPback Worth Filing?

Many factors make SLAPPbacks attractive, among them: vindication of targets, compensation for monetary and psychological losses, penalization of filers, a prophylactic chill on future SLAPPs, and a restoration of public confidence in participatory democracy. But SLAPPbacks have their costs. Many targets express reluctance to "go through it again," given the financial, emotional, time, and other stress they have just experienced with the judicial process. They may also find it difficult to persuade an attorney to take the case.

In representing defendants (as in a SLAPP), attorneys typically charge the client by the hour or by flat fee for their legal services (frequently with an advance payment as a "retainer"), regardless of whether they win or lose. In representing plaintiffs in a personal injury suit (such as a SLAPPback), however, attorneys typically do not expect to be paid a fee unless they win. If they win, they collect a so-called contingency fee (as much as 33 percent of the client's recovery); if they lose, the client pays only the out-of-pocket expenses.

Persuading an attorney to take on the risk of a contingency fee case then can boil down to a question of dollars: No one wants to invest in a stock that has either too high a risk or too low a return. Even when relatively straightforward, the SLAPP and SLAPPback can run up over $100,000 in attorney time and thousands more for discovery costs, transcripts, court fees, travel, investigations, experts, and other out-of-pocket expenses. If the case loses or settles below cost, the attorney can lose all or a significant part of that investment. Still, these are the inherent risks of contingent fee litigation. Personal injury plaintiff lawyers expect to lose a certain percentage of the cases, recouping on the big winners. That is the public policy justification for the seemingly high contingency fee. Many individuals today cannot afford to retain a lawyer on a pay-as-you-go basis, however meritorious their case or great their suffering, and contingency fees are a way to make more legal services available to all, as the potentially large recovery makes attorneys willing to risk their services for causes and clients that would otherwise go unrepresented.

Two pragmatic "dollar signs" are key factors in whether an attorney will "risk" a SLAPPback: jury generosity and filer collectibility. Every lawyer has a minimum cutoff below which it is not economical to take on a contingency fee case. In a fairly conservative-jury state such as Colorado, the prospect of a $250,000 verdict could be sufficient, but in a high-rolling verdict state such as California, some attorneys will turn down SLAPPbacks if the prospect is less than a $1,000,000. A number of factors go into estimating the jury-award prospect: how atrocious the filers' behavior and SLAPP demands have been; how sympathetic the targets and their cause appear and how reasonable their petitioning activity; whether targets hung tough and did not settle; whether the targets' defense attorneys handled the SLAPP properly and set up the SLAPPback record well; whether the filer's attorneys are likely to fight and drag out the countersuit; and, last but not least, how intimidated, devastated, and depoliticized targets (and the community) have become as a result of the original suit.

Filer collectibility depends on how solvent the SLAPP filer is. Winning a money verdict is one thing; collecting the award is another. A multimillion-dollar verdict against a small, economically marginal operator is a paper victory, as it will only drive the filer into flight or bankruptcy. Also, since the filer's net worth is the key factor on which punitive damages are based, if the filer is marginal, so too will be the punitives—which can be the major portion of the jury award in a SLAPPback. One attorney tells us his rule of thumb is to turn down a SLAPPback unless the filer has a net worth of $1,000,000 or more. This could nullify a number of SLAPPbacks, in view of our finding that the majority of SLAPPs are filed by small, local operators rather than wealthy giants such as Shell Oil. One way around the marginal-filer problem, however, is to name the filer's attorneys as codefendants, thus bringing a solvent law firm or its insurance carrier into the equation. Another is to structure the claims to mirror whatever insurance coverage the filer has, forcing the solvent insurance carrier to become the "deep pocket."

Because SLAPPbacks give SLAPP filers a dose of their own medicine, they can be the "miracle cure." They are strong medicine, admittedly, using large-dollar exposure to capture filers' attention and change their practices. As succinctly put by Vawter "Buck" Parker, head attorney for the Sierra Club Legal Defense Fund: "[SLAPPbacks] should make [filers] think twice before filing a SLAPP suit and make them realize the potential big cost to them."[77] Or, as the "Sultan of SLAPPbacks" Ralph Wegis puts it, such verdicts as the $11,100,000 in the Boswell case are "the kind of language [filers] can understand."[78]

Attorneys representing filers are getting the message, too. Dwight Merriam, a Hartford, Connecticut, lawyer who chairs the American Planning Association's *amicus curiae* committee and represents real estate developers, generally considers SLAPPs a foolish strategy because they can drag on for years and may result in an expensive SLAPPback.[79] San Jose attorney William H. Gavin III, after unsuccessfully defending a developer in a SLAPPback, has cautioned filers that "the plaintiffs will have a field day" with them in a countersuit.[80] The top lobbyist for the California Building Industry Association, Richard J. Lyon, warns its members: "This is a very glamorous media issue. It feeds the stereotype of David Versus Goliath."[81] And Don Collin, house counsel for the same building association, concludes: "It's a fairly uninformed [filer] that brings a SLAPP suit. On balance these are basically very difficult cases to win, and . . . they are an open invitation to a lawsuit."[82]

SLAPPbacks not only deter filings but encourage citizens to keep involved and give them hope, as one observer attests: "Now, Ralph Wegis ain't my second cousin, but I write easier knowing he's out there . . . wielding a legal shield against the truncheons of vengeful corporations, and his 800 number is in my Rolodex."[83] And with him "out there" are Sacramento's John Poswall, Oakland's Phil Berry, Chicago's David Letvin, St. Louis's Richard Witzel, Los Angeles's John Taylor, Las Vegas's Morton Galane, and legions of other attorneys known and unknown, sung and unsung, who are making SLAPPers pay for their attacks on citizens and the democratic process.

10 Anti-SLAPP Legislation and Other Cures

No obstacle is more chilling than the fear of personal liability. . . . The ripple effect of just one suit on the willingness of people to serve as volunteers is great. Although volunteers may seldom actually pay judgments, the fear of lawsuits, which place an individual's bank account and home at risk, has increasingly deterred volunteer activity.

—Former President George Bush

The legislature hereby declares it to be the policy of the state that the rights of citizens to participate freely in the public process must be safeguarded with great diligence. The laws . . . must provide the utmost protection for the free exercise of speech, petition and association rights, particularly . . . in a public forum with respect to issues of public concern. The . . . threat of . . . litigation . . . can be and has been used as a means of harassing, intimidating or punishing individuals, unincorporated associations, not-for-profit corporations and others who have involved themselves in public affairs.

—New York State Legislature,
adopting the 1992 "anti-SLAPP"
Citizen Participation Act

The Attorney General is interested in the dismissal of this [SLAPP] for two reasons: . . . Society as whole benefits in the long run from a free airing of grievances on the major public issues of the times . . . [and] State programs directly benefit from the freedom of citizens to petition, i.e., complain to, government. . . . There are over a hundred sections of the [state's] General Laws calling for public hearings . . . , public comment . . . , or both. . . . In short, the State has an interest . . . in the free flow of information from its citizens to the agencies responsible for protecting the public safety, health and welfare.

—Rhode Island Attorney General Jeffrey B. Pine (1993)

Finally, an issue on which Republicans and Democrats, conservatives and liberals, presidents and legislators, attorneys general and local government lawyers can all agree: SLAPPs are real; they chill citizen participation, volunteerism, and public service; they threaten the functioning of government; and they must be stopped. Fortunately, in addition to the judicial cures discussed in the last two chapters, both the legislative and executive branches of government have substantial power to counteract and prevent these lawsuits. This chapter examines what these other two branches can do and are doing to deter SLAPPs and provides a "Model SLAPP Act" based on those accomplishments.

The Legislative Cure: "Anti-SLAPP Laws"

The former president,[1] the New York legislature, and Rhode Island's attorney general are correct: Volunteers and public interest groups must be "safeguarded with diligence" from the threat of SLAPPs if we hope to continue a tradition of public involvement and service in America. For the "utmost protection," both Republican and Democratic leaders are turning to bipartisan legislation—"anti-SLAPP" laws.[2] These acts are desirable both at the federal level and in every state, just as we have civil rights and anti-discrimination laws at both levels. Even in jurisdictions with tough judicial precedents such as Colorado's *POME* case (Chapters 1 and 3), enacting them into statutory law will give them the added power of state legislative policy.

Nine states—California, Delaware, Massachusetts, Minnesota, Nebraska, Nevada, New York, Rhode Island, and Washington—have adopted modern, "active" anti-SLAPP statutes in the 1990s, and a number of others—including Florida, Georgia, New Jersey, Pennsylvania, Tennessee, Texas, and the territory of Guam—are considering them.

The legislative drafting task is straightforward. If public participation in government is to be effectively protected, the law must pass three tests.

1. Communications: It must cover all public advocacy and communications to government, whether direct or indirect and whether in the form of testimony, letters, reports of crime, peaceful demonstrations, or petitions.
2. Forums: It must cover all government bodies and agents, whether federal, state, or local, and whether legislative, executive, judicial, or the electorate.
3. Prevention and cure: It must set out an effective early review for filed SLAPPs, shifting the burden of proof to the filer and, in so doing, serving a clear warning against the future filing of such suits.

Given the ease of meeting these tests, we predict that laws against SLAPPs will eventually be as commonplace as the laws protecting Americans' other civil rights.

Federal and State Approaches

First, why not a federal law? The U.S. Congress has the power under the Constitution to create national standards in this area, as it has done in other human welfare areas (civil rights, public health, worker safety, and so on). A federal bill similar to the model state bill presented below would be a great step forward, given the very uneven results we found from state to state. But states will still need their own anti-SLAPP laws—to protect their citizens in the absence of a U.S. law and, even when a federal law goes on the books, to guide the special circumstances of that state and its courts.

Some limited anti-SLAPP legislation already exists at the federal level, such as the laws criminalizing intimidation of witnesses in federal courts,[3] protecting those testifying before Congress,[4] and shielding "whistleblowers."[5] So far, however, the prevailing mood has been "let the states do it"; Congress even introduced legislation a few years ago "to encourage the States to enact legislation" in this area.[6] States have gotten that message and are taking the lead. Now, with SLAPPs being brought in federal courts, triggered by federal government programs, and filed by federal officials or employees, it is time for congressional action as well.

Many states, even those without specific anti-SLAPP laws, provide some safeguards in the form of statutes or judge-made case precedents that grant a "privilege" from being sued or otherwise "immunize" communications in some government contexts. Over 40 states protect witnesses in judicial proceedings, and about half the states protect legislative and executive branch testimony.[7] Although these "passive" laws announce that the protection exists, however, they do nothing "active" to implement it, such as providing substantive rules and procedural safeguards; nor do they deal with SLAPPs as a constitutional issue. Still, some of these privilege-immunity protections can be fairly helpful to targets and attorneys. A 1981 Oklahoma statute provides:

> A privileged publication or communication is one made: . . . In any legislative or judicial proceeding or any other proceeding authorized by law; . . . or anything said in the course thereof, and any and all expressions of opinion in regard thereto, and criticisms thereon, and any and all criticisms upon the official acts of any and all public officers, except where [it] . . . falsely imputes crime. . . . "No [such] publication . . . shall be punishable as libel.[8]

This Oklahoma law obviously fails test 1 by preventing "libel" SLAPPs only; it does not cover all the other typical camouflage claims such as business torts, conspiracy, civil rights, abuse of process, and malicious prosecution. It does better on test 2; it appears to cover most government bodies and representatives—but does "proceedings" mean there must be some formal process under way before citizens are protected? This typical privilege-immunity law's biggest failure, though, is that it flatly flunks test 3; by not establishing an effective court review process for SLAPPs, it fails to prevent or cure them effectively.

Are we being too critical? Isn't this kind of law enough? Let's see how it worked in a typical case (from Chapter 4). A Tulsa policeman caught a homeowner watering his lawn in apparent violation of an emergency water rationing ban. They had words. The homeowner filed an official complaint against the officer; the policeman filed a defamation SLAPP, and—on the basis of this Oklahoma law—the trial court granted the homeowner summary judgment (affirmed on appeal), holding that the law provided the target with an "absolute privilege."[9] A success story? That SLAPP was filed and kept alive in court for nearly five years! That is a failure-model law in action, and privilege-immunity laws (without more) all work this way.

California's previous privilege-immunity law reads much like Oklahoma's[10] but, as if to emphasize its impotence, is immediately followed by a shocking provision actually authorizing and encouraging police SLAPPs against citizens who report police misconduct: Citizens lose their immunity if their complaint is "knowingly false or malicious"—easy facts for police to allege but hard facts for citizens to rebut without a full-scale trial.[11] And California is not the only state to adopt SLAPP-promoting laws. A current example is the "Veggie Libel" laws now being promoted in state legislatures around the country; agribusiness interests, frightened by the Alar scare and other criticism of agrichemically treated products, are pushing bills to make "disparagement" of agricultural products actionable as "libel," most recently in Ohio in October 1995.[12] Even without this schizophrenia, current federal and state privilege-immunity statutes do not adequately safeguard citizens.

Washington's "Brenda Hill Bill"

Credit for the first modern anti-SLAPP law goes to the state of Washington, where the *Brenda Hill* case (Chapter 7) galvanized the state legislature into action. In 1987, when Hill found she might lose her home because her subdivision developer had not paid its taxes, she reported the company to state officials, who eventually collected some $351,000 in back taxes. The outraged developer swore it would "sue her till we are insolvent," and its SLAPP was not tossed out of court until 1993. Outraged at the company's action, freshman state legislator Holly Myers introduced "the Brenda Hill Bill" in 1989, and it passed unanimously on a wave of anti-SLAPP media.[13] The legislative purpose shows how closely it was tailored to fit Hill's case:

> Information provided by citizens concerning potential wrongdoing is vital to effective law enforcement and the efficient operation of government. The legislature finds that the threat of civil action for damages can act as a deterrent to citizens who wish to report information to federal, state, or local agencies. The costs of defending against such suits can be severely burdensome. The purpose of [this act] is to protect individuals who make good-faith reports to appropriate governmental bodies.[14]

The law provides the following specific protection:

> A person who in good faith communicates a complaint or information to any agency of federal, state, or local government regarding any matter reasonably of concern to that agency shall be immune from civil liability on claims based upon the communication to the agency.[15]

That language passes test 1 reasonably well, covering most types of government communications that trigger SLAPPs.[16] It appears to pass test 2 as well, assuming that Washington courts interpret "agency" in the broad sense of "any government body" and do not limit it to "executive branch agencies" alone.[17] It fails test 3 badly, however, by not setting forth clear rules for an early dismissal review (instead of the murky "good faith" requirement).[18]

These defects were glaringly apparent in the first test case of the law. In 1991 a developer sued a homeowner for complaining to county officials that the filer's subdivision was flooding onto his property. When the homeowner moved for summary judgment, a very peculiar thing happened: The trial judge granted him summary judgment under the preexisting common law (case law) immunity but refused to grant it under the new statute, finding that the homeowner had not proved he acted in "good faith," as the statute language requires.[19] Fortunately, the appeals court reversed and, in the process, smoothed out some of the statute's rough edges: it limited "good faith" to lack of "actual malice,"[20] shifted the burden of proof to the filer (a very important point), and put filers under a strict "clear and convincing" evidence standard (equally crucial).[21] If these judicial glosses hold, the Brenda Hill Bill will pass the tests of an effective anti-SLAPP law, but it would be prudent for the legislature to amend the statute to preserve their intent, given the propensity of trial judges to resist dismissal.

Our recommendation against a "good faith" requirement may seem odd. At first blush, no one wants to protect "bad faith" petitioning—but our Constitution does. As the U.S. Supreme Court ruled in *Omni* in 1991, the only petitioning that is not protected is that which does not seek an actual government decision, result, or outcome (see Chapter 2). Whether the communications are "unreasonable," in "bad faith," or otherwise stem from "bad motives," the Supreme Court says, is irrelevant. The Constitution protects advocacy to government, regardless of content or motive, so long as it is designed to have some effect on government decision-making.

Nevada's anti-SLAPP law, adopted in 1993,[22] copies the Washington approach and so inherits its problems but does provide a broader description of the government: Petition is protected if made "to a legislator, officer or employee of this state or of a political subdivision, or . . . of the Federal Government."[23] Though Washington and Nevada courts will doubtless construe "agency" broadly, it is never a mistake to be concrete. New York's law is a giant step in that direction.

New York and "the Citizen Participation Act"

It was eight years in the making, but in 1992 New York overwhelmingly adopted its anti-SLAPP law, "the Citizen Participation Act."[24] The bill originally introduced in 1985 by Assemblyman Robert A. Gaffney and Senator Kenneth Lavalle ran into heavy opposition, principally from the New York State Builders Association and other real estate interests, according to Rudy Stegemoeller, environmental counsel to the New York Assembly and a key adviser on the bill.[25] When it was first introduced, one state senator fumed:

> Under . . . this bill the neighbors can go out and say practically anything they want relative to this [real estate] development in trying to stop it for whatever reasons they might have; fear of what it might do to the neighborhood, or whatever it might do to the environment . . . . This is a rotten bill. This is a very bad bill.[26]

The builders never let up, but their support slowly collapsed. By the time Senator John Marchi and Assemblyman I. William Bianchi introduced the 1991 bills that would ultimately become law, they had the support of Governor Mario Cuomo and his administration (with the State Consumer Protection Board leading the charge), Attorney General Robert Abrams, numerous civic, consumer, and environmental organizations, and SLAPP targets and anti-

SLAPP groups such as the Coalition Against Malicious Lawsuits (directed by Lisa Stellis Mackey, herself the victim of a developer SLAPP).[27]

By 1992 the builders were reduced to self-pity:

> We recognize and do not condone lawsuits brought by permit applicants for the sole purpose of stifling criticism by an individual, a civic or an environmental group. But, the subject bill would have a chilling effect upon a builder's legitimate right to bring an action for . . . slander or libel. . . .
>
> Often the project proponent is an isolated individual surrounded by a hoard [*sic*] of opponents. A hearing can rapidly degenerate into a builder bashing sessions with few holds barred. Project opposition leaders turn out and stir up crowds with circulars and phone networking designed to paint the blackest picture of a project and its sponsor. When truth is left behind . . . real and often lasting damage can be done to the permit applicant.[28]

Legislators were not impressed with this claim of a "legitimate right" to sue project opponents; moreover, in the assessment of one experienced observer, they saw the courts as part of the problem: "The problem has been perceived as sufficiently serious to warrant the enactment of legislation . . . because New York State courts, by and large, did not act with sufficient alacrity and firmness to discourage SLAPP suits."[29] In 1991 the bill passed the Democrat controlled state assembly 134 to 1 but died in the Republican senate. Victory came the next year, however, when it passed the assembly (this time unanimously) and made it out of committee in the senate, to be greeted by an overwhelming 53 to 5 vote on the floor.

Because most of the pro-bill testimony came from victims of real estate developer SLAPPs, the "Citizen Participation Act" has a narrower focus than Washington's and Nevada's laws. The New York version limits itself to SLAPPs filed by "public applicants or permittees"—that is, only those filers who have "applied for or obtained a permit, zoning change, lease, license, certificate or other entitlement for use or permission to act from any government body" or persons affiliated with them—and similarly limits targets to those who "report on, comment on, rule on, challenge or oppose such application or permission."[30] This means it covers only about half of all SLAPPs (see the Appendix), and may cover even less. In 1995, the first judicial interpretation of the New York law took a very narrow view of this legislative definition, ruling that the law does not cover citizen petitioning three years after an application process, even if the applicant was acting illegally without a permit![31]

Still, the law is a leader in providing procedural safeguards. It requires that a dismissal or summary judgment motion be given a quick hearing ("preference"),[32] shifts the burden of proof to the filer ("party responding to the motion"),[33] and places a fairly heavy burden (a strict scrutiny standard) on the filer's proof by requiring dismissal "unless the [SLAPP filer] demonstrates that the [SLAPP] has a substantial basis in law or is supported by a substantial argument for an extension, modification or reversal of existing law."[34] Even if the case is not dismissed under this standard, the filer may not recover monetary damages from the target without proving "by clear and convincing evidence" that target's petitioning was done with actual malice ("knowledge of its falsity or with reckless disregard of whether it was false").[35]

The law provides for reimbursement of targets' costs and their attorneys' fees[36] and permits targets to countersue for compensatory[37] and even punitive damages.[38] This is a solid reform. As discussed in Chapter 9, most SLAPPbacks have been based on a charge of malicious prosecution with all its catch-22 proof problems. Now, to win a SLAPPback in New York, plaintiffs need prove only that filer (1) lacked "substantial basis" for suing (which should be clearer than lack of "probable cause") and (2) had the "purpose of harassing, intimidating" (which should be less convoluted than the "malice" requirement). On the down side, punitive damages may be harder to win under this law, as they require proof that "harassing, intimidating" was the filer's *sole* purpose, and human motivation is seldom so singular and uncomplex that a filer cannot conjure up a second or third purpose to avoid punitives.

The New York law is a commendable step forward in procedures but is not without its compromises and limitations. Even supporters such as Mark Chertok, who represented targets in the *Mianus Gorge* SLAPP (Chapter 5), see it as "only a partial answer."[39] As noted above, it fails test 1 by not safeguarding all Petition Clause–protected activity, since it applies only to SLAPPs filed by "public applicants or permittees." The legislators were obviously reacting to the large number of New York SLAPPs filed by developers seeking zoning or building permits and companies seeking operating or pollution permits, and these, granted, are two of the largest categories. But left largely untouched by this law are those filed by government agencies and officials, by landlords against tenants, companies against consumers, employers against employees, police against citizens, and others. On the plus side, the law stands up well on test 2, being commendably inclusive of government entities,[40] and on test 3, providing as it does an effective early review and a clear warning against the filing of SLAPPs.

Two other states have adopted the New York anti-SLAPP law virtually word for word: Delaware in 1992[41] and Nebraska in 1994.[42] Still, Ralph Stein, professor of constitutional law at Pace University School of Law, calls the New York approach "not as great as it should be," as it does not completely prevent the filing of SLAPPs.[43] And Attorney Chertok reminds us that statutes do not enforce themselves: "The challenge [will be] to educate the judges and practicing bar [to] recognize SLAPPs."[44] The California approach meets more of those challenges.

California—Third Time's the Charm

It took the California legislature three tries to put an anti-SLAPP law on the books. Twice, in 1990 and 1991, it adopted bills by huge legislative majorities, only to have them vetoed by two different governors. But by 1992 the anti-SLAPP tide had washed that final resistance away.

The law's champion was powerful Senator Bill Lockyer, chair of the California Senate Judiciary Committee and a Democrat from Hayward, across the bay from San Francisco. Assisted by his staff counsel, Gene Wong, Lockyer became an expert on the issue after hearing of the Alan LaPointe case (Chapter 4). The main opposition throughout was the California Building Industry Association (counterpart to the builders' group that opposed the New York law). Lockyer's first bill in 1990[45] took a very controversial approach, prohibiting the filing of any lawsuit affecting someone's "first amendment right of petition or free speech" without an advance court ruling of "substantial probability" that the filer could win. Such "pre-filing screens" are anathema to those who like to sue, and the builders and one bar group[46] protested, proposing instead that the state adopt the more limited Washington state Brenda Hill Bill. Lockyer declined, and despite the opposition his bill easily passed both houses. But the opponents had the one vote that counted: In September 1990 the lame duck Republican governor, George Deukmejian, vetoed the bill. Citing existing law providing sanctions for "frivolous lawsuits," the governor said, "I do not believe the bill is necessary to protect citizen involvement in public issues."[47] Lockyer lashed back, calling it "outrageous" that Deukmejian would approve "the exact same protections for doctors, churches, and non-profit organizations" but not for "ordinary citizens who are sued by well-heeled special interests."[48]

In 1991 the senator made two tactical shifts. He dropped his requirement for pre-filing approval and tacked the new bill on to a popular one limiting liability for officers and directors of nonprofit organizations.[49] The revised bill made SLAPPs subject to a post-filing "motion to strike," with the burden of proof shifted to the filer to show "a substantial probability" that it would win. The bill passed all three tests. It covered the full range of advocacy protected by both the federal and state constitutions (California's being construed more broadly), covered all of government, set up the most effective post-filing review yet developed, and sent a clear warning against SLAPPs. Its legislative finding is also significant:

The Legislature finds and declares that there has been a disturbing increase in lawsuits brought primarily to chill the valid exercise of the constitutional rights of freedom of speech and petition for the redress of grievances. The Legislature finds and declares that it is in the public interest to encourage continued participation in matters of public significance, and that this participation should not be chilled through abuse of the judicial process.

Opponents were not assuaged. This time they objected to the "substantial probability" test, which they saw (rightly) as a tough proof for filers and asserted (wrongly) to be an "unconstitutional . . . violation of the right to trial by jury."[50] As the builders continued their heavyweight opposition, however, even the conservative *San Diego Union* took them to task in an editorial:

[Developers' rights to sue] must be balanced against the Constitution's guarantee of freedom of expression. The right to speak out and to petition government are central to democratic values. Gov. Wilson should protect them by signing Lockyer's bill into law.[51]

Widespread public and media support gathered behind the bill: Over two dozen civic, government, and professional groups (including the California Newspaper Publishers Association, the Planning and Conservation League, ACLU, Bar Association of San Francisco, California Association of Professional Liability Insurers, and the Cities of San Francisco, Los Angeles, and San Diego) and some 18 newspaper editorials (including those in the major Los Angeles and San Francisco papers) came out in its favor. The bill swept through the Senate unanimously and the Assembly by a near two-to-one majority.

But again, the opponents had the one vote that counted: that of the newly elected Republican governor, Pete Wilson. Undeterred by the lopsided public support, he vetoed the bill on October 14, 1991, having bought the builders' objections to the "substantial probability" test: "[The bill] enacts legal hurdles against filing so-called SLAPP lawsuits. . . . I am convinced that the pleading hurdles, specifically, the evidence test . . . are higher than for deterrents for other malicious lawsuits."[52] Again, Lockyer was incensed, terming the veto "ironic" because Wilson supported efforts to limit tort liability, and the "substantial probability" test was already on the books for punitive damages against doctors and religious organizations.[53] The editorial outcry against the governor was withering: "Pete Wilson [has] dealt a blow to free expression";[54] "A SLAPP in the face to the ideals of vigorous debate in public policy";[55] "We hope the governor shows better judgment next time."[56]

Bloody but unbowed, Lockyer reintroduced the identical bill in 1992.[57] Later that year he made an important concession, changing "substantial probability" to "probability" in an effort to persuade the governor to sign (a concession that would have serious repercussions in the years ahead). Once again the bill passed both houses overwhelmingly; once again the builders' association pulled out all the stops and "lobbied Wilson hard,"[58] its fear tactics including claims that the anti-SLAPP bill would be used by government employees, unions, and teachers to sue others.[59] This time, however, with Governor Cuomo's ink barely dry on the New York anti-SLAPP law, Governor Wilson followed suit. In "a defeat for developers and the California Building Industry Association,"[60] he signed the California bill into law on September 16, 1992,[61] saying: "It is our right as Americans to hold and express differing opinions about key public issues. This legislation will give courts new powers to throw out frivolous lawsuits whose only intent is to cut off public debate and stifle free speech."[62] Senator Bill Lockyer summed up three years of hard work in three words: "I am happy."[63] It made other states happy as well. Rhode Island in 1993 and Massachusetts in 1994 adopted anti-SLAPP laws based on the California model.

But the happiness did not last. In its first year and a half (January 1993–September 1994), special motions to strike based on the new law were filed in at least 49 cases in California; targets won some 18 of these and were dismissed but lost at least 22, demonstrating trial court confusion about the law.[64] The key problem is the "probability" standard of proof required to defeat the motion to strike. Courts have read this as a very easy standard of proof for filers, not requiring the judge to weigh the evidence at the motion stage but meaning only a prima facie showing of facts which, if provable at trial, would support a judgment for the filer.[65] This interpretation is wrong, according to Mark Goldowitz, an Oakland attorney and director of the California Anti-SLAPP Project:

> The legislative history makes clear that opponents as well as supporters of section 425.16 [the California anti-SLAPP law] understood "probability" to have its normal and usual meaning: that to defeat a special motion to strike, a plaintiff must establish it is more likely than not to prevail [if there is a trial]. Further, to rule on the motion, the trial court must weigh the evidence presented by both sides. This result is compelled from the legislative history of the statute and from fundamental principles of statutory construction, such as the plain meaning rule.
>
> This tougher and more effective standard is constitutional because it gives important protections to the fundamental federal and state constitutional rights of petition and speech. When these rights conflict with the state constitutional right to a jury trial, the Legislature has the authority to strike a reasonable balance between them. . . .

> Section 425.16 strikes a reasonable balance. . . . There is no constitutional right to a jury trial of a lawsuit that violates the First Amendment.[66]

He is correct. Legislatures do have the power to balance conflicting constitutional rights and frequently have done so (see Chapter 2). If the California courts fail to interpret SLAPP review as strictly as Goldowitz urges, then the law will be ineffective in eliminating a number of SLAPPs that should be dismissed; if that proves to be the case, the legislature will have no choice but to amend the law to clarify its intent.[67]

New Hampshire's anti-SLAPP legislation—a copy of California's—fell victim to this exact problem in 1994. When legislators referred their bill to their state supreme court for an advisory ruling, despite that court's "profound concern with abuse of the judicial system by lawsuits designed to intimidate citizens and exact a price for participation in the democratic process,"[68] it advised that the bill was unconstitutional. The sole reason was that requiring dismissal unless the plaintiff can show a "probability" of prevailing at trial violates a plaintiff's "right to have all factual issues resolved by a jury."[69] The opinion is based on a very expansive view of New Hampshire's constitutional right to trial by jury (which "shall be held sacred");[70] it largely ignores the fact that pretrial motions routinely adjudicate fact-laden cases and that there is "no serious doubt about [such motions'] constitutionality."[71] Most important, even if it is necessary for a judge to resolve some fact issues, it is appropriate and constitutional for legislatures to weigh the two competing constitutional rights (the right to petition versus the right to a jury) and strike a balance in favor of protecting the First Amendment right, as Attorney Goldowitz states.

The Massachusetts and Rhode Island Laws

The "probability" standard focuses attention on the merits (or lack of them) of the filer's SLAPP instead of focusing on the merits (or lack of them) of the target's petitioning. In their different ways, both the 1994 Massachusetts and 1995 Rhode Island anti-SLAPP laws avoid this problem by using the more appropriate, latter focus.[72] The Massachusetts law, also adopted over a governor's veto, like California's, appropriately shifts the burden of proof on the motion to the lawsuit filer. But instead of requiring the filer to show a "probability" of prevailing at trial, the law adopts the *POME* case approach (Chapter 3): For the suit to survive, filer must show that target's petitioning "was devoid of any reasonable factual support or any arguable basis in law" and "caused actual injury" to filer.[73]

Rhode Island's 1995 law was also adopted over a veto, thanks to strong leadership from the Office of Attorney General Jeffrey B. Pine. It is weaker procedurally than the Massachusetts law, in not shifting the burden of proof to the filer. But it is stronger substantively, because its definition of the immunity avoids the problematic *POME* tests in favor of a combination of both of the more protective *Omni* and *PRE* tests (see Chapter 2); the governor vetoed because he felt the two tests together created "unreasonable and unworkable standards of proof," and we have used just the simpler *Omni* test in our model bill for that reason.[74]

The Massachusetts and Rhode Island approaches put the focus where it should be: on the petitioning. While they have problems avoided by our model bill, if the Massachusetts courts are successful (as the Colorado courts have largely been under *POME*) in not letting their substantive tests open up a "fact quagmire" and the Rhode Island courts use streamlined procedures, the laws should be effective and not suffer the dismissal dilemmas experienced in California.

Minnesota—The Best Law Yet

Leave it to Minnesota, with its great populist history, to adopt the first anti-SLAPP law based on the U.S. Supreme Court's *Omni* decision. It did not start that way. As first introduced in 1992, the "Citizen Participation Bill" was based on the *POME* tests, like the Massachusetts law.[75] Though classed as "noncontroversial" by the legislature, it was tabled that year because of developer objections, according to John Gryzbek, an experienced St. Paul SLAPP attorney and a lobbyist for 27 environmental and justice groups supporting the bill.[76]

In 1993 the legislators reconsidered the bill in light of *Omni* and our model bill (below). That became their preferred approach: *POME* was out, *Omni* was in. Coalition building, legislative hearings, and favorable editorials and other media grounded the bill well: "People were flat-out outraged" about SLAPPs, said Gryzbek.[77] But the bill was held up again; even though there were no major groups in opposition, petititioning or demonstrating in general became taboo political topics during Operation Rescue's anti-abortion campaign that year.[78] Once those concerns dissipated, success came quickly: A law patterned "fairly closely" on the model bill[79] passed handily the following year and was signed by the governor on May 5, 1994.[80] Substantively, in the broad, straightforward strokes of the *Omni* case it immunizes "lawful conduct or speech that is genuinely aimed in whole or in part at procuring favorable government action."[81] It defines "Public Participation" with those same words[82] and defines "Government" broadly.[83] It sets up effective procedures by making any judicial claim that "materially relates to an act . . . that involves public participation" subject to a motion to dismiss,[84] suspending discovery, shifting the burden of proof to the filer, allowing the relevant governmental body or state attorney general to intervene,[85] and providing for attorneys' fees and costs as well as SLAPPback damages.[86] In the crucial section it requires the trial court to dismiss "unless . . . [the SLAPP filer] has produced clear and convincing evidence that the acts of the [target] are not immunized."[87]

Minnesota has achieved a breakthrough in effectiveness. Although there may be some difficulties with words like "genuinely," "materially," and "lawful,"[88] there is great improvement over the fact quagmire language of previous laws. It means the only issue on the motion is whether the filer can prove that the petitioning was not aimed at producing government action.

A Model Anti-SLAPP Bill

Among the organizations sponsoring anti-SLAPP bills elsewhere are state ACLUs, environmental groups, homeowners' associations, legal reform organizations, and the state chapters of the American Trial Lawyers Association (TLA).[89] Representatives of these and other groups, interested legislators, and lawyers have consulted with the University of Denver Political Litigation Project. Is it possible to craft an ideal or "model" bill to counteract SLAPPs? Definitely yes. Our recommendation melds the most effective elements of the U.S. Supreme Court's *Omni* decision, the federal Model State Volunteer Service bill, and the California, New York, and Minnesota approaches.[90] The result is presented here, followed by section-by-section explanations.

A BILL

1 SECTION 1. SHORT TITLE.
2 This Act may be cited as the "Citizen Participation in Government Act of
3 199__."
4
5 SECTION 2. LEGISLATIVE FINDINGS AND DECLARATION OF PUR-
6 POSES.
7 (a) FINDINGS. The Legislature finds and declares that
8 (1) the framers of our Constitutions, recognizing citizen participation
9 in government as an inalienable right essential to the survival of democracy,
10 secured its protection through the right to petition the government for re-
11 dress of grievances in the First Amendment to the U.S. Constitution and Sec-
12 tion ___ of the Constitution of this State;
13 (2) the communications, information, opinions, reports, testimony,
14 claims, and arguments provided by citizens to their government are essen-

tial to wise government decisions and public policy, the public health, safety, and welfare, effective law enforcement, the efficient operation of government programs, the credibility and trust afforded government, and the continuation of America's republican form of government through representative democracy;

(3) civil lawsuits and counterclaims, often claiming millions of dollars, have been and are being filed against thousands of citizens, businesses, and organizationss based on their valid exercise of their right to petition, including seeking relief, influencing action, informing, communicating, and otherwise participating with government bodies, officials, or employees or the electorate;

(4) such lawsuits, called "Strategic Lawsuits Against Public Participation" or "SLAPPs," are typically dismissed as unconstitutional, but often not before the defendants are put to great expense, harassment, and interruption of their productive activities;

(5) the number of SLAPPs has increased significantly over the past 30 years;

(6) SLAPPs are an abuse of the judicial process; they are used to censor, chill, intimidate, or punish citizens, businesses, and organizations for involving themselves in public affairs, and controlling SLAPPs will make a major contribution to lawsuit reform;

(7) the threat of financial liability, litigation costs, destruction of one's business, loss of one's home, and other personal losses from groundless lawsuits seriously affects government, commerce, and individual rights by significantly diminishing public participation in government, in public issues, and in voluntary service;

(8) while courts have recognized and discouraged SLAPPs, protection of these important rights has not been uniform or comprehensive;

(9) while some citizen communications to government inevitably will be incorrect, unsound, self-interested, or not in good faith, it is essential in our democracy that the constitutional rights of citizens to participate fully in the process of government be uniformly, consistently and comprehensively protected and encouraged.

(b) PURPOSES. The purpose of this Act are

(1) to protect and encourage citizen participation in government to the maximum extent permitted by law;

(2) to create a more equitable balance between the rights of persons to file lawsuits and to trial by jury and the rights of persons to petition, speak out, associate, and otherwise participate in their governments;

(3) to support the operations of and assure the continuation of representative government in America, including the protection and regulation

of public health, safety, and welfare by protecting public participation in government programs, public policy decisions, and other actions;

(4) to establish a balanced, uniform, comprehensive process for speedy adjudication of SLAPPs as a major contribution to lawsuit reform;

(5) to provide for attorney fees, costs, and damages for persons whose citizen participation rights have been violated by the filing of a SLAPP against them.

SECTION 3. IMMUNITY.

Acts in furtherance of the constitutional right to petition, including seeking relief, influencing action, informing, communicating, and otherwise participating in the processes of government, shall be immune from civil liability, regardless of intent or purpose, except where not aimed at procuring any governmental or electoral action, result, or outcome.

SECTION 4. APPLICABILITY.

This Act applies to any motion to dispose of a claim in a judicial proceeding on the grounds that the claim is based on, relates to, or is in response to any act of the moving party in furtherance of the moving party's rights as described in Section 3.

SECTION 5. REQUIRED PROCEDURES.

On the filing of any motion as described in Section 4

(a) the motion shall be treated as one for summary judgment:

(1) the trial court shall use a time period appropriate to preferred or expedited motions; and

(2) the moving party shall have a right of expedited appeal from a trial court order denying such a motion or from a trial court failure to rule on such a motion in expedited fashion;

(b) discovery shall be suspended, pending decision on the motion and appeals;

(c) the responding party shall have the burden of proof, of going forward with the evidence, and of persuasion on the motion;

(d) the court shall make its determination based upon the facts contained in the pleadings and affidavits filed;

(e) the court shall grant the motion and dismiss the judicial claim, unless the responding party has produced clear and convincing evidence that the acts of the moving party are not immunized from liability by Section 3;

(f) any government body to which the moving party's acts were directed or the Attorney General may intervene to defend or otherwise support the moving party in the SLAPP;

(g) the court shall award a moving party who is dismissed, without regard to any limits under state law:

(1) costs of litigation (including reasonable attorney and expert witness fees) incurred in connection with the motion; and

(2) such additional sanctions upon the responding party, its attorneys, or law firms as it determines will be sufficient to deter repetition of such conduct and comparable conduct by others similarly situated;

(h) a person damaged or injured by reason of a claim filed in violation of their rights under Section 3 may seek relief in the form of a claim for actual or compensatory damages, as well as punitive damages, attorney fees, and costs, from the person or persons responsible.

SECTION 6. DEFINITIONS.

As used in this Act

(a) "government" includes a branch, department, agency, instrumentality, official, employee, agent, or other person acting under color of law of the United States, a state, or subdivision of a state or other public authority, including the electorate;

(b) "state" includes the District of Columbia, the Commonwealth of Puerto Rico, and each territory and possession of the United States;

(c) "person" includes any individual, corporation, association, organization, partnership, two or more persons having a joint or common interest, or other legal entity;

(d) "judicial claim" or "claim" includes any lawsuit, cause of action, claim, cross-claim, counterclaim, or other judicial pleading or filing requesting relief;

(e) "motion" includes any motion to dismiss, for summary judgment, for judgment on the pleadings, to strike, demurrer, or any other judicial pleading filed to dispose of a judicial claim;

(f) "moving party" means any person on whose behalf the motion described in Section 4 is filed seeking dismissal of the judicial claim; and

(g) "responding party" means any person against whom the motion described in Section 4 is filed.

SECTION 7. GENERAL PROVISIONS.

(a) RELATIONSHIP TO OTHER LAWS. Nothing in this Act shall limit or preclude any rights the moving party may have under any other constitutional, statutory, case or common law, or rule provisions.

(b) RULE OF CONSTRUCTION. This Act shall be construed liberally to effectuate its purposes and intent fully.

(c) SEVERALABILITY OF PROVISIONS. If any provision of this Act or the application of any provision of this Act to any person or circumstance

1 is held invalid, the application of such provision to other persons or cir-
2 cumstances and the remainder of this Act shall not be affected thereby.
3 (d) EFFECTIVE DATE. This Act shall take effect immediately.

The following comments explain the purposes of the various sections of the model act:

Section 1: The Act can have any title deemed relevant, but this variation on the New York and Minnesota titles, says it all.

Section 2: Legislative findings and purposes are not an absolute requirement in most states, but California and New York used them to good effect. These present the supporting arguments for the law's need and should materially assist court interpretation of the legislative intent.

Section 3: The "heart" of the Act, this section describes the substantive immunity provided for legitimate citizen participation in government (petitioning). It spells out the acts or communications covered with the maximum constitutional breadth under the U.S. Supreme Court ruling in the *Omni* case. Minnesota adopted a similar provision.

Section 4: As specified here, the Act's application or operation is triggered by targets' filing of a motion to dismiss or otherwise dispose of a SLAPP. New York, California, Minnesota, and others use this approach.

Section 5: These subsections spell out the procedural safeguards essential to make the review process effective. The procedures to be followed on a SLAPP dismissal motion are automatically making it a final summary judgment motion,[91] requiring it to be heard quickly, providing for appeal if a decision is delayed or denied, suspending discovery, shifting the burden of proof to the SLAPP filer, applying the heightened scrutiny of "clear and convincing evidence," and authorizing the involved government body or the state attorney general to participate. Minnesota's law uses these provisions, and New York and California have similar ones. Subsection (g) provides for mandatory awards of targets' costs of litigation (attorneys' fee and other court expenses) as well as sanctions against the filer and its attorneys (as a deterrence to future SLAPPs).[92] Subsection (h) provides specific authorization for SLAPPbacks; existing state laws governing malicious prosecution and abuse of process will work, but express authorization enhances their effectiveness in court by making it clear that they are state legislative policy in the case of SLAPPs. This section can also be expanded to deal with a given state's problems under existing malicious prosecution and abuse of process laws, such as expert testimony on "probable cause," "special damages" requirements, excessive proof hurdles for "punitive damages," and the like (see Chapter 9).

Section 6: These definitions of key words are those that Minnesota uses.

Section 7: Miscellaneous desirable provisions are offered here.

Executive Branch Contributions

Citizen contact with executive branch agencies, officials, and employees is the most frequent generator of SLAPPs, the study found. As the Rhode Island attorney general's brief quoted at the start of this chapter indicates, SLAPPs threaten the executive branch by stifling "the free flow of information" to its agencies and cutting them off from the very people and missions for which they are "responsible."[93] Paradoxically, executive branch agencies, officials, and employees are among those most likely to file SLAPPs. These points give the third branch of government the strongest interest of all in preventing and controlling such suits. Failing, they will be cut off from essential citizen information, support, and trust. School boards, license bureaus, zoning bodies, housing authorities, development commissions, environmental agencies, consumer protection boards, attorneys general, civil rights commissions, even the Environmental Protection Agency, Equal Employment Opportunity Commission, Federal Deposit Insurance Corporation, and Internal Revenue Service—all these and more have been swept up in SLAPPs and their missions, credibility, and effectiveness threatened as a result.

Government officials who recognize these hazards have already taken the lead in discouraging SLAPPs. Attorneys general, the top legal officers of their states, have been particularly notable in fighting SLAPPs: speaking out against them, lobbying for legislation, filing friend-of-the-court briefs, and even intervening to defend targets. Robert Abrams, while New York attorney general, was an exemplary advocate against SLAPPs. He frequently spoke on the topic, published a very thoughtful article,[94] lobbied for the New York anti-SLAPP law, and authorized his staff to file interventions supporting targets. Nancy Stearns, at the time the New York AG's key SLAPP expert, explains:

> Many of our laws are set up to encourage citizen participation. If suits discourage that participation then government loses out, because citizen involvement brings up issues that government officials aren't aware of, or haven't thought of, or may just have missed. From the government perspective, that [citizen] participation is crucial.[95]

The attorneys general of Washington,[96] California,[97] Texas,[98] Rhode Island,[99] and Florida[100] have also intervened in SLAPPs in their states. Yet doing so is not always easy. In 1993, when an obvious defamation SLAPP was filed by local dump owners against a woman who wrote to the Rhode Island Department of Environmental Management complaining about the pollution of groundwater, Superior Court Judge Vincent A. Ragosta refused to recognize the case as a SLAPP or to let the attorney general's office argue in court on a motion to dismiss it: "I think the attorney general is taking a more active role in this case than it should be taking. This is strictly a private suit. I know you're trying to give it a public flavor."[101] One hopes this judge will eventually see the forest as well as the trees.

Other federal, state, and local agencies have not left it all to the attorney general. School boards,[102] liquor licensing authorities,[103] and consumer agencies,[104] among others, have intervened in SLAPPs, warned applicants against them, and lobbied for protective legislation. They have used every forum available, including speeches, press conferences, interviews, articles, one-on-one counseling, lobbying, lawsuit interventions, testimony, and legal assistance.[105]

Clearly, legislatures, attorneys general, and government agencies at all levels have a crucial role in counteracting the SLAPP phenomenon. Although judge-made law may sometimes serve as a solution (as in the *POME* case), trusting to the gamble of litigation outcomes is a risk worthy of Las Vegas. States do better not to gamble on individual cases to make law, but to move ahead progressively with anti-SLAPP legislation, allowing all sides to be heard and establishing clear-cut policy. The states' top law enforcers, the attorneys general, and government agencies that need citizen input in order to accomplish their missions also have a win-win role in preventing and curing SLAPPs.

They have everything to gain, and everything to lose—their constituents.

Appendix

The SLAPPs Study Methods and Findings: A Conflict Between Democracy and Capitalism

THE STUDY METHODOLOGY

The Political Litigation Project instituted at the University of Denver in 1984 is an interdisciplinary research and education initiative of the Department of Sociology and the College of Law. The project's pioneering study of SLAPPs—"Strategic Lawsuits Against Public Participation" in government—also began in 1984. SLAPPs are defined for our study by four objective criteria: They (1) involve communications made to influence a government action or outcome, (2) which result in civil lawsuits (complaints, counterclaims, or cross-claims) (3) filed against nongovernmental individuals or groups (4) on a substantive issue of some public interest or social significance. A full, annotated discussion of these study criteria and their rationales is contained in Chapter 1.[1]

When we examined previous research on government-petitioning behavior,[2] we found none analyzing lawsuits that attack such constitutionally protected political action. Studies of the use of power generally to suppress political participation are not uncommon,[3] the investigation of the political damage done by Senator Joseph McCarthy being a case in point.[4] Extensive research has been done as well on lawsuits threatening free speech and free press,[5] but the right to petition was surprisingly unexplored. Studies of political repression had simply not examined the use of lawsuits as an instrument of political power.[6]

In breaking this new ground, we consciously sought to integrate micro-sociolegal questions about the experience of participants in these disputes with macro-sociopolitical questions about their consequences for political participation in a democracy. The theoretical underpinnings of the study come from legal scholarship on the constitutional protection of political speech,[7] the sociology of community conflict and democratic decision-making,[8] empirical studies of political participation in America,[9] and sociolegal disputing studies.[10]

Our study of this cross-institutional disputing phenomenon has proceeded in three phases, integrating different methodological approaches and measurement techniques. Phases I and II were supported by the Hughes Research and Development Fund and the University of Denver; Phase III, by the National Science Foundation (NSF grant SES 87-14495) and the university. The Political Litigation Project has produced numerous scholarly and professional articles covering the overall study plan[11] and the individual phases I,[12] II,[13] and III.[14]

Phase I: The Legal "Statics"

The first phase involved quantitative statistical description of SLAPPs as a legal phenomenon: their origins, parties, processes, and outcomes. Our first hurdle was one common to all researchers of litigation in the United States: It is impossible to collect a complete universe of trial court phenomena. Like the Iowa Libel Study Project[15] and other trial researchers, we cannot ever know with precision how many of these suits have been filed and whether they are increasing or decreasing, because of imprecise cataloguing, inadequate reporting, and a lack of centralized recording.[16] Technically, given these collection barriers, no study of trial litigation can be statistically representative, because the whole set from which to sample cannot be discovered. Nevertheless, the hundreds of SLAPPs we have studied provide a body of data sufficiently comprehensive and diverse to permit us to understand the landscape of the problem and know its contours with a high level of confidence.

We obtained an initial set of 100 SLAPP cases from four sources: (1) computerized and keyword searches of case reporter systems and legal literature; (2) referrals from attorneys, parties, and journalists in response to our publications, conferences, and educational outreach; (3) a mail survey of 975 public interest and political groups across the country; and (4) a random sample of six trial courts' computerized case-filing systems for the year 1983. We studied the key legal documents,[17] personal papers and correspondence, transcripts, and media accounts, coding information on precipitating events, parties, issues, legal claims, defenses, court processing, and outcomes.[18] From these documentary records, forming the "legal statics database," we developed a quantifiable picture of basic characteristics and patterns (see "The Study Findings," below). Additionally, we compared the social, political, and economic conditions of the counties in which the 100 cases occurred with those in all 3,137 counties in the United States.[19] We subsequently added another 141 cases to the database (now $N = 241$) and verified that the SLAPP characteristics remained virtually unchanged, substantiating our confidence in the data's representativeness. Virtually all SLAPPs found were filed after 1958, most after 1970, and they occurred in every state and the District of Columbia.

Phase II: The Case Studies

As a complement to the documentary analysis, we conducted qualitative case studies on 11 cases, selected to represent the range of issues, types of communities, and participant diversity apparent in the first set of 100 cases. We performed in-depth interviews (one to five hours each) with 93 participants and observers in the 11 SLAPPS, then analyzed verbatim transcripts of the interviews.

In this qualitative component the emphasis was on the social psychology of the encounters and interactions. We structured the interview protocol on the "Naming, Blaming, Claiming" framework of Felstiner, Abel, and Sarat[20] and incorporated the work of Coates and Penrod[21] to explore attribution, equity, and frustration as social-psychological factors affecting the emergence, development, and resolution of disputes.

Phase III: The National Survey

The third phase was a nationwide survey on SLAPPs to determine the motives of participants, to test the "chill" hypothesis empirically, and to explore the larger question of the effect of SLAPPs on legal and political institutions in America. For each of the 241 cases then in the database we attempted to administer both lengthy telephone interviews and follow-up mail questionnaires to four types of respondents:

1. Filers, the parties who filed the SLAPPs;[22]
2. Targets, the parties who communicated with government and were then sued;
3. Ripple Effects, any persons or entities (typically identified to us by targets) who (1) had communicated similar views to the government or had otherwise visibly supported targets and (2) for whatever reason were not named as defendants in the SLAPP but (3) were aware of the SLAPP filing;
4. Untouchables, a comparison/control group of (1) comparably/contemporaneously politically active citizens/entities in the area, (2) nominated by targets and (3) confirmed (later) as having no knowledge of SLAPPs specifically or conceptually. Our hypothesis, later validated, was that these "SLAPP-naives," untested by firsthand experience with SLAPPs and therefore assuming themselves to be "untouchable," would not be chilled politically and would therefore present a distinct comparison group with the targets.

We were successful in reaching 268 respondents in 123 of the 241 SLAPPs.[23] Our respondents included 104 Targets, 51 Filers, 55 Ripple Effects, and 58 Untouchables.

To measure the effect of SLAPPs, we presented respondents with a random sample of five "vignettes" or descriptions of a hypothetical public dispute. These were constructed through a chance process, so that by randomly varying their internal construction and their assignment to respondents, they would provide separate treatment conditions. For example, a vignette might cast the respondent as a Fortune 500 company, a small business, a citizens' group, or an individual; the issue in conflict could be about property, authority, or values (categories we found significant in the actual cases); the petitioning behavior could vary from signing a petition to appearing at a public hearing to joining a lawsuit. Here is a typical example:

> KEYSTONE INC. (a small business) and CATHY JOHNSON (an individual) have been opponents over KEYSTONE'S proposal to REZONE RURAL LAND IN ORDER TO DEVELOP A SHOPPING CENTER. Cathy has a CIVIC interest in the outcome of the proposal. Cathy was asked to SIGN A PETITION opposing the proposal.
>
> *How likely would you be to advise Cathy to sign the petition? Score from 1 (very unlikely) to 10 (very likely).*

A factorial survey method,[24] involving regression analysis, was used to estimate the weights of vignette characteristics on respondents' choice to advise or not to advise political participation. This enabled us to see what factors, if any, affected political involvement and, for the first time, to validate the "chill" hypothesis scientifically.

The motives of Filers and Targets were explored through 13 motive statements representing various reasons for entering public disputes, as recorded in our earlier interviews: for example, "I was exercising my right to decide how to use my own property"; "I saw it as my civic responsibility." Respondents were asked to rate on a five-point scale the influence of each motivating statement for their involvement in the dispute. A factor analysis of the coded motive items revealed two underlying factors: civic and economic. Two ideologic factors were also explored: the effect of conservative political views and the sense of opponents' legitimate status as a disputant. Six nonideologic factors were investigated—disputants' gender, age, education, income, litigation experience, and level of political participation—and a statistical test for significant differences was performed.

THE STUDY FINDINGS

The study found that SLAPPs are filed by one side of a public, political dispute to punish or prevent opposing points of view. The typical SLAPP involves citizens or groups whose political communications to a government official, body, or the electorate threaten the economic interests of another party. The suits are an attempt to "privatize" public debate: a unilateral initiative by one side to transform a public, political dispute into a private, legalistic adjudication, shifting both forum and issues to disadvantage the opposition. To accomplish this cross-institutional transformation, filers must claim that the citizens' constitutionally protected political acts or communications injured them; to do this, they must transform protected petitioning into traditional judicially cognizable torts and other injuries. Thus, citizens may involve themselves in a municipal zoning dispute, only to find that "city hall" has become "courtroom," and "zoning" has become "defamation" or "interference with business."

SLAPPs differ from conventional litigation in three important ways. First, they are not typical countermoves in the transformation of legal disputes, where litigation represents little more than a new but predictable stage in an ongoing conflict;[25] instead, they turn the tables on speakers in a political forum, forcing them into a different and unanticipated judicial forum where they are cast in the role of the defendant. Second, the SLAPP typically does not seek to solve the original issue in dispute; its filing alters "the name of the game" (to a garden-variety claim of a legal violation), and as a consequence the court typically can resolve only the camouflage claim (defamation), not the original dispute (zoning). Third, as tactics to drain the resources, commitment, and vocabulary of political debate, SLAPPs are a creative means for ideologically warring against egalitarian principles of citizen participation; their unusually inflated stakes ($100,000 to $100,000,000 claims are common), attorney expense, time demands, and psychological pressure create a "chilling" effect that constitutes a fundamental threat to continued citizen involvement in public affairs and thus to our entire concept of a participatory democracy.

What Triggers SLAPPs?

The Triggering Actions

The political actions that trigger SLAPPs, according to our 241 cases, span the entire spectrum of citizen involvement in modern American government. Only a small minority of cases (3 percent) involve actually circulating or signing a "petition" but enough do to make even this mildest, most traditional of citizen rights a risk. More frequently, SLAPPs are provoked by participation at public hearings (47 percent), filing public interest litigation (20 percent), reporting violations of law (18 percent), and lodging formal government protest-appeals (8 percent). Peaceful demonstrations and legal boycotts also trigger SLAPPs but less frequently (3 percent).

Targets' actions are a mix of those aiming to change the status quo and those aiming to preserve it. In the great majority of cases (75 percent), targets are advocating change, whether reporting violations of law, urging closure of a noxious enterprise, or advocating new laws. In one-third of the cases they are opposing change: for example, acting to prevent real estate developments, destruction of natural areas, or tax increases. (Statistics adding to greater than 100 percent indicate that multiple actions were coded.)

The Issues

The "fighting issues" provoking SLAPPs run the gamut of today's important public interest and community concerns. Naturally there are some overlaps, as some conflicts are about more than one issue, but urban-suburban real estate developments, zoning, and land use questions (including NIMBY conflicts) generate the most (38 percent of the cases), with criticism of public officials and public employees a close second (30 percent). Protection of the environment, natural areas, and animal rights are also significant contributors (16 percent), as are civil/human rights (13 percent) and consumer protection (20 percent).[26]

Government Forums

No government level or branch is safe from SLAPPs. Citizen contacts with federal, state, and local governments trigger these lawsuits, although contact with local government is most vulnerable. Contacts with all three branches and the electorate result in SLAPPs, with the executive branch agencies being most represented (50 percent), judicial (24 percent) and legislative (23 percent) correspondingly less, and the electorate least (6 percent).

The Locations

Comparing the social, political, and economic conditions of the counties in which SLAPPs arise with all 3,137 U.S. counties produces interesting insights. SLAPP locations are more urban, more densely populated, and wealthier and have slightly more mobile populations than the average for the rest of the country.

The Patterns

The most common pattern of disputants/issues/forums is the simplest: One party approaches government about a matter affecting some other party, and the latter sues. This configuration occurs in 76 percent of the cases. Rick Webb's complaint to USEPA about a coal company's pollution is one such example (*Webb v. Fury* in Chapter 5).

In the second most frequent pattern (17 percent), two parties concurrently invoke the same government body but seek different (usually opposite) actions. An example is Medema Homes and Betty Johnson both petitioning the city council, one to grant and the other to block approval of a new housing development (*Warembourg v. Louisville* in Chapter 1).

A third, more complex pattern appears less frequently (3 percent): One party petitions one government body while another invokes a different body. Typically, this happens when one government agency acts favorably to a potential filer (e.g., the zoning board grants a permit) and citizens invoke a second government body such as the planning board to overturn the first agency's decision.

Finally, the study discloses a fourth pattern: Demonstrations or secondary boycotts trigger SLAPPs. In these, the government body being petitioned is one or more steps removed from the citizens' acts/communications. A picket line or sit-in at a nuclear power plant to protest federal government nuclear policies is an example of the demonstration model (*San Luis Obispo County v. The Abalone Alliance* in Chapter 4). Citizens urging others not to shop or hold conventions in a given jurisdiction until the local government adopts civil rights laws or endorses the Equal Rights Amendment are classic boycotts (*NAACP v. Claiborne Hardware Co.* in Chapter 2, and *State of Missouri v. National Organization for Women* in Chapter 4).

Who Are the Targets?

Spreading the Chill

Although many cases (one-third of the 241) are filed against a single target, the average is five targets per case, not counting the thousands of people implicated under the intimidating category of "Doe" defendants (some 1,100 named targets were sued in the 241 cases, with "Does" included as defendants in 10 percent). "Doe" defendants are scarcely this common in conventional litigation, being reserved for those cases where filer's attorney cannot identify at the outset all parties responsible; they are the equivalent of a blank check, a space to be filled in when the real person's name is discovered. Their use in SLAPPs appears to come from a different motivation: the desire not to identify all known opponents but rather to spread the chill to all target supporters and even to those thinking of becoming supporters. Anecdotal evidence confirms that this *in terrorem* effect works, making "Does" a device worrisomely similar to the devastating "fellow traveler" charge of the McCarthy era.

Individuals and Organizations

Overwhelmingly (90 percent of the 241 cases), SLAPP filings are aimed at one or more individuals. Typically, these are not "political pros" or "professional agitators." Although some are "experienced" in public or political activity prior to the dispute that breeds the SLAPP, the majority are "first-timers" or "one-shotters," not regularly involved in political action but spurred to engage in it for the first time by filers' pre-lawsuit actions.

Of the individuals sued, 67 percent are classifiable as "concerned citizens"; 15 percent represent organizations as volunteers; 16 percent report acting on their own economic (e.g., property) or employment interests, and the remaining few on family matters (typically as parents). Even when individuals specifically act as representatives of an organization (for example, the League of Women Voters officers in the *Maple Properties* condo SLAPP, Chapter 3), they are still likely to be sued individually; in a number of cases, presumably to keep group resources out and isolate the individuals, the organization is not even named as a co-defendant.

Among organizations named are public interest groups (16 percent of the cases), mutual benefit associations (12 percent), business concerns (14 percent), and service organizations (2 percent). Nearly half (47 percent) are public interest groups (environmental, animal-protection, civil rights groups) or civic organizations (neighborhood associations, good-government groups such as the League of Women Voters); 7 percent are labor unions/organizations and 8 percent political groups; and a surprising 38 percent of the targets report association with industry, business, and professional groups, suggesting that economically vested interests are at risk for some targets.

SLAPPs are rarely aimed at national "big shots." Overwhelmingly (87 percent), targets are local individuals and groups working on local issues, without broad state or national ties.

Across the Political Spectrum

Targets, we discovered, represent all shades of political views, from radical to liberal to centrist to conservative to ultra-right-wing. SLAPPs are by no means, as many suppose, just a tool of the political and economic right against the left. Although liberal causes frequently do create targets (environmentalism, civil rights, and so on), many moderate causes do so as well (League of Women Voters, neighborhood, and consumer issues), as do conservative and ultraconservative causes (fundamentalist religion, anti-Semitism, even the Ku Klux Klan).

That discovery leads to a significant finding: SLAPPs are not simply cases of unsympathetic "black hats" suing sympathetic "white hats," again as many appear to think. Although the majority of targets tend to be "do-gooders," working for public benefit as opposed to their own profit and espousing at least arguably sympathetic causes, a significant minority are out for obvious self-gain or blatant revenge (see the hypothetical case in Chapter 1). Some of the latter advance views that a substantial number of people would oppose or find offensive: right-wing religious parents criticizing a liberal teacher-of-the-year; criminals using police-brutality complaints to gain plea-bargain leverage; townspeople trying to keep a retirement home for Hasidic Jews or low-income/minority housing out of their communities. In a number of SLAPPs, we find our immediate sympathies lying not with the targets but with the filers (especially teachers suing their critics). Does this mean one should sympathize with the SLAPP as well? Our constitutional system says not. Using lawsuits to punish political expression is just another form of censorship. The destructive effects on the parties, the issues, the political and judicial arenas, the hopes for airing and solving the dispute, and the future of citizen political involvement require as much constitutional protection for minority as for majority views (see Chapter 2).

Who Are the Filers?

Filers have a different profile, but with many surprising similarities to targets.

Individuals and Organizations

There are individual filers (63 percent of the cases), but multiparty business concerns are also heavily represented (44 percent). Also found as filers are government bodies, as distinct from government officers or employees (7 percent), mutual benefit organizations (3 percent), and public interest organizations (1 percent). Of the organizations filing SLAPPs, 93 percent report being associated with industry, business, labor, or professional groups.

Economic Stake

Unlike most targets, the great majority of filers are acting to protect their own economic interest. They are typically prompted by perceived threats to their land ownership, development plans, business operations, contract expectations, profits, or employment. Criticism of the way filers operate their businesses, opposition to their attempts to get government permits/licenses/approvals, or adverse influence on their future positions in official, professional, or employment settings are the issues typically at stake.

Government SLAPPs

A staggering 20 percent of all SLAPPs are filed by government agencies, officials, or employees because they do not like the petitioning message they are receiving from their own taxpayers, voters, citizens. Of these government SLAPPs, most are filed by entities and individuals at the local government level, far less by those at the state level, and almost never at the federal level.

Power Balance

Like targets, filers are predominantly local individuals and entities. Clearly wrong is the view of most SLAPPs as "Goliath versus David" contests, of big corporations suing the little guy. These are present but rare; SLAPP filers are overwhelmingly local Davids suing local Davids, even though they may be bigger frogs in their local pond. The numbers suggest that nationwide, larger and more powerful entities have less need for this particular empowerment tactic.

Nevertheless, all four possible power balances or patterns are represented in the cases: (1) "David versus David," the small-scale conflict between two local, comparably unpowerful individuals (the tennis court problem in *Bell v. Mazza* in Chapter 3); (2) "Goliath versus David," the conflict in which a powerful filer (Medema Homes, Chapter 1) sues local, far-less-powerful individuals; (3) "Goliath versus Goliath," the SLAPPs that pit one big, powerful, litigation-experienced party against another (Chapter 4's *State of Missouri v. National Organization for Women*); (4) "David versus Goliath," the rare case of a small, local filer suing a titan (*Sierra Club v. Butz* in Chapter 5, in which the local logging firm sued the powerful environmental group).

Case Characteristics

Alleged Injury

To access the courthouse, filers must name some judicially recognizable injury. They cannot legally sue persons for "exercising their right to petition" or "participating in the political process too effectively" (although a surprising number of complaints are this naive). Instead, filers must transform the offending political behavior into legalistic tort injury and other illegality claims to mask the political nature of the dispute and make it judicially acceptable.

Six legal claims are the trademarks of SLAPPs: (1) defamation (libel, slander, business libel, and so on); (2) business torts (interference with contract or business or economic advantage/expectation, antitrust, restraint of trade, unfair competition); (3) process violations (malicious prosecution, judicial or administrative abuse of process); (4) conspiracy; (5) constitutional and civil rights violations; and (6) other violations of law (nuisance, emotional harms, trespass, attacks on tax exemption, and so on). While defamation is the most frequently used (53 percent), business torts (33 percent), process violations (19 percent), conspiracy (18 percent), and constitutional/civil rights (17 percent) are also favorite candidates. SLAPPs characteristically use multiple claims; "shotgun pleading" of two or more charges is the norm. The public issue in dispute (urban development, environment, neighborhood, consumer, etc.) did not significantly influence the choice of claim. This lack of relationship between the political and the legal aspects underscores our conclusion that the lawsuit claims are arbitrary dispute-transformation camouflage.

Preferred Courts

State courts are the choice of filers (75 percent); the balance of cases are filed in the federal courts. That the preponderance of SLAPPs go to state or county courts is further evidence of their local nature.

Relief Requested

Astronomical money-damage claims, out of all proportion to the realistic damages a filer could have suffered, are typical of SLAPPs. In 54 percent of the cases, damages were specified, ranging from $10,000 to $100,000,000 and averaging $9.1 million. Clearly, the high price tag is part of the calculated chilling effect. In states that bar these dollar demands from complaints no numeric figure was given, merely a phrase such as "damages to be proved at trial." This blank-check approach, however, appears no less intimidating to targets.

Injunctions (whether labeled "temporary restraining order," "preliminary injunction," or "gag order"), significantly, are requested in only a minority of the complaints. Even more telling, filers rarely push after the filing for the injunctions to be granted—possibly because an injunction would require an early judicial hearing, putting the continuation of the SLAPP at risk. Clearly, the SLAPP tactic does not need the extra power of an injunction to stop the opposition.

Target Victories

SLAPPs, as lawsuits go, are "losers": the vast majority are ultimately dismissed by the courts, and in the remainder the targets (or their insurance companies) give up and enter into a settlement to get the case dismissed. Only a very small number of SLAPPs proceed to trial and result in a judgment for filers that is upheld on appeal, but these aberrational losses can result in very large verdicts or settlements (such as the record $835,000 reportedly collected by filers in *Hodgins v. Durbin,* Chapter 5).

Targets win dismissals at the very first trial court appearance in approximately two-thirds of the cases, and when trial court dismissal is denied or delayed, appeals courts typically reverse and dismiss (as the *POME* case, in Chapters 1 and 3, illustrates).

The particular characteristics of the political disputes and subsequent lawsuits seem to have little influence on the outcomes. Targets are likely to win a legal victory regardless of the branch or level of government petitioned, the nature of their petitioning activities and communications, or the substantive basis of the dispute. Likewise, factors such as court level, number of claims, amount of damages demanded, or time elapsed between filing and disposition make no statistically significant difference. No particular characteristics stand out as significant factors in the few target losses.

The one factor that does make a significant difference is the Petition Clause (raised as a defense in the majority of the cases); its invocation typically results in a ruling for targets. Indeed, raising the Petition Clause defense almost doubles targets' chances of winning. Its clear-cut political message (even more than ordinary free speech or nonconstitutional defenses) enables the targets to "retransform" the legalistic dispute back into the political dispute, in the court's mind.

These victory statistics paint a rather more rosy picture than exists in reality, however. Though SLAPPs are losers, like the Wagnerian heroine, they can take a long time to die. Less than one-third (31 percent) of the cases were over "quickly" (appreciating court delay, 1 to 18 months was our "quick" category). More than one-quarter (28 percent) took 1.5 to 3 years, and an amazing 41 percent dragged on from 3 to 13 years. The average was 40 months.

Worse, there appears to be no correlation between victory in court and victory in the real world. Although filers routinely lose in court, SLAPPs frequently enable them to win the victory they really want in the political dispute. It is more difficult to "measure" real-world victories than court ones: for example, that filers get the permit does not mean targets do not get the concessions they wanted; that the teacher keeps her job does not mean her career is not impaired. Still, though targets sometimes win in both forums, there is a very clear pattern of filers losing in court only to achieve all their aims in the real world. In those cases the SLAPPs are sacrificial goats, tactical moves to assist out-of-court aims rather than to win in-court coups.

The Chilling Effect of SLAPPs

Conventional scholarship argues that participation in politics builds a commitment to democratic values and enhances public involvement.[27] Our findings are the opposite. SLAPPs very effectively teach even the most politically active not to participate, not to speak out, not to take a stand. Indeed, SLAPPs encourage the active to return to the vast ranks of uninvolved and apathetic Americans, further decreasing the already small percentage of citizens who take part in the political life of our country.[28]

The factorial surveys of the "vignette" responses prove scientifically for the first time that SLAPP litigation typically "chills" victims' willingness to participate politically in the future. The SLAPP-experienced respondents (Filers, Targets, and Ripple Effects) overwhelmingly respond by discouraging others from future participation, thus confirming their own chill. Those with no experience or knowledge of SLAPPs (Untouchables) are significantly less cautious and more optimistic about political involvement, putting few conditions on the decision to participate. The sole difference is that they are unaware of the risk of these lawsuits.

SLAPP exposure or awareness make a difference. Other factors may or may not. Opponents: For the SLAPP veterans, most opponent types are chilling (especially the Fortune 500 company); opponent types make no difference to Untouchables' willingness to jump into the fray. Involvements: Types of political involvement makes a significant difference to the veterans, for whom petitioning and testifying are clearly more positive than litigation; for the Untouchables there is no significant difference in approval based on type of involvement. Issues: The type of political issue makes a difference for both the SLAPP-savvy and the SLAPP-naive; land use issues are strong approval motivators, professional criticism the weakest.

That those experienced with SLAPPs become less likely to encourage others to get involved in community controversies demonstrates the chilling effectiveness and potential of these suits. Targets see the procedural safeguards and rationality of the judicial system not as protection but as tools of power and suppression, to be avoided at almost all costs in the future. That such a high percentage of individuals among SLAPP Targets and Ripple Effects would not continue their campaign or take part in a new one and would discourage others from speaking out highlights the antidemocratic nature of SLAPPs.

SLAPPs are proven, effective tools for eliminating many persons from public political participation and constraining those that do survive. Since American political ideology assumes both the openness of the political system and the representative accountability of government, this chill points to the need to reinforce and reaffirm constitutional protections.

A Profile of Capitalism versus Democracy

Finally, we wanted to answer two overriding questions:

1. How do these SLAPPs disputants explain their motives for becoming involved in public disputes and for resorting to lawsuits to stifle opposition?

2. What do these motives reveal about the relationship between political and legal institutions in America and the tension between those two coexisting cultural values in the United States—democracy and capitalism?

The national survey information suggests that ideologic motives prompt both filers and targets, making SLAPPs the quintessential example of the modern social conflict between politics / democracy and economics / capitalism.[29]

Filers: The Economic Motive

Economic values—protection of property and business interests—are the most common motives for filers. In declaring that filing a SLAPP was part of the ideologic right to pursue economic gain, filers appear typical of the American ethos as described by McClosky and Zaller: "Even under the changed conditions of the industrial age, most Americans continue to adhere to the traditional conception of property as the bulwark of individual freedom and the source of economic well-being."[30] Our study suggests that filers typically assume their property interests to be of higher value than the political concerns expressed by their opponents. Filers say to us: "They have nothing to lose, like I do!" or "I'm just protecting my property; they were out to ruin me!" Filers express concern over protecting reputation and honor, and a need to strike back at those they see as attacking them. If blocked from achieving their economic aims in the political arena, through "normal channels," frustrated filers resort to the judicial arena to change their luck. Filers score positively on the economic motive factors and negatively on the civic. They defend the values and practices of a capitalist economy as reasonable, legitimate, "American." They dismiss their opponents' participation in the political process as unwarranted interference with economic freedom, growth, betterment.

Two other ideologic perceptions motivate filers: political conservatism and opponent delegitimizing. On a conservative-liberal index, filers view themselves as significantly more conservative politically than targets do. Filers are also substantially more likely than targets to justify their actions by attacking their opponents' legitimacy: "They don't know what they're talking about"; "They don't have the expertise we do"; "They are meddling troublemakers" or "rabble rousers," "a bunch of ignorant housewives" or "environmental extremists."

A comparison of filers with targets on nonideologic factors—gender, age, education, income, litigation experience, and level of political participation—surprisingly produces no statistically significant differences on average. The typical filer *or* target is a male college graduate in his forties with an annual household income of $40,000–60,000 per year. That the average income of filers and targets is not significantly different dispels easy explanations of SLAPPs as "Rich Capitalists versus Poor Reformers." The homogeneity of background also underscores the significant role that ideology alone plays in distinguishing the motives of the two sides.

Targets: The Civic Motive

In contrast to filers, targets claim to be motivated by civic or political principles. They see themselves as demonstrating a sense of responsibility to their neighborhood, to others, or to justice in opposing actions that they perceive as socially, politically, economically, or environmentally unjust, damaging, or illegal. By exercising their political right to speak out, targets become highly visible, but many are dismayed when taken to court: "I didn't think they could do this to me!"; "All I did was express an opinion!" Targets score positively on civic motive factors and negatively on economic.

Targets tend, on average, to classify themselves as substantially more liberal politically than filers. They are less likely to malign their opponents' legitimacy. On nonideologic characteristics, as noted above, they are substantially the same as filers.

The Larger Issues

We were not surprised to find that motives for involvement in these public disputes are substantially different for filers and targets. Both our quantitative statistical studies and qualitative interviewing had led us to expect filers to be more economically motivated and politically conservative, and targets to be more civically motivated and politically liberal. We had not, however, anticipated the degree of homogeneity of the disputants' backgrounds or the similarity of their political participation levels.

These findings lead to a central one: The conflict between democracy and capitalism is being fought out between filers and targets as they move back and forth between political and judicial arenas. As McClosky and Zaller have found among the general public,[31] some people are firmly attached to the value of democracy, while others adhere to the values of capitalism. Filers and targets initially act out this conflict in the political arena, but when civic-motivated opponents block economic interests, those attached to capitalist values seek to turn the tables by filing a lawsuit. Although Americans overwhelmingly support, in the abstract, the equal participation of all citizens in matters of public governance,[32] filers' attitudes are conceptually similar to political intolerance: a "willingness to restrict a disliked group's democratic rights based on the content of one's views."[33] Indeed, lack of principled support for democratic values is an important source of intolerance.[34]

By filing the SLAPP, economic interests express their intolerance for and seek to stifle the expressions and views of other citizens, effectively denying the equality of citizenship so fundamental to informed political decision-making. SLAPP filers justify solving political disputes nonpolitically on the basis of righteous economic self-interest coupled with intolerance for conflicting civic-minded participation. This is an ideologic argument for economic interests as the superior voice in determining public policy. Significantly, this ideology of the supremacy of property rights is being espoused in SLAPPs at a time when conservative legal and other scholars are urging reexamination of the traditional constitutional balancing of rights of citizenship versus rights of property.[35]

The conflict between political and economic freedoms, between democracy and capitalism, is "a definitive feature of American life that . . . shapes the nation's politics";[36] it is "the modern social conflict."[37] Both freedoms are essential, but some see the drive for economic prosperity as taking precedence over the democratic rights of citizens.[38] SLAPPs demonstrate how the larger "modern social conflict" between democratic and capitalist ideologies is played out in political disputes that are transformed into judicial actions. Rather than a legitimate means of conflict resolution, SLAPPs are a use of litigation to promote and enforce one view of economic values, a form of ideological power that is both a reflection of intolerance and a means of undemocratic dominance.

Notes

Preface

1. *Note, Counterclaim and Countersuit Harassment of Private Environmental Plaintiffs: The Problem, Its Implications, and Proposed Solutions,* 74 MICHIGAN LAW REVIEW 106 (1975).

2. WILLIAM SHAKESPEARE, KING HENRY IV, PART I, act 4, sc. 1.

Chapter 1

1. New York Times Co. v. Sullivan, 376 U.S. 254, 270 (1964).

2. Articles and other publications of our University of Denver Political Litigation Project (the SLAPPs Study) include Pring & Canan, *SLAPPs: An Overview of the Practice,* in SLAPPS: STRATEGIC LAWSUITS AGAINST PUBLIC PARTICIPATION IN GOVERNMENT at 1 (ALI-ABA Course of Study Materials 1994); Pring, Canan, & Thomas-McGuirk, *SLAPPs: A New Crisis and Opportunity for the Government Attorney,* 9 NATIONAL ASS'N OF ATTORNEYS GENERAL, NATIONAL ENVIRONMENTAL ENFORCEMENT JOURNAL 3 (Apr. 1994, Part I) and 3 (May 1994, Part II); Canan, Hennessy, & Pring, *The Chilling Effect of SLAPPs: Legal Risk and Attitudes Toward Political Involvement,* 6 RESEARCH IN POLITICAL SOCIOLOGY 347 (1993); Pring & Canan, *Podium: Striking Back at the Dreaded SLAPP,* NATIONAL LAW JOURNAL, Oct. 12, 1992, at 13; Pring & Canan, *"Strategic Lawsuits Against Public Participation" ("SLAPPs"): An Introduction for Bench, Bar, and Bystanders,* 12 UNIVERSITY OF BRIDGEPORT LAW REVIEW 937 (1992); Canan, *SLAPPs: Democratic Rights and Professional Risks,* ASA FOOTNOTES 4 (Aug. 1992); Canan, Kretzmann, Hennessy & Pring, *Using Law Ideologically: The Conflict Between Economic and Political Liberty,* 8 JOURNAL OF LAW AND POLITICS 539 (1992); Canan, Satterfield, Larson, & Kretzmann, *Political Claims, Legal Derailment, and the Context of Disputes,* 24 LAW & SOCIETY REVIEW 923 (1990); Canan, Pring & Ryan, *Images of Citizen Opponents: The Politics of Denying Equal Citizenship Rights* (paper presented at Law & Soc'y Ass'n Ann. Mtg. 1990); Pring, *"SLAPPs": Strategic Lawsuits Against Public Participation,* 7 PACE ENVIRONMENTAL LAW REVIEW 3 (1989); Canan, *The SLAPP from a Sociological Perspective, id.* at 23 (1989); Canan & Pring, *Strategic Lawsuits Against Public Participation,* 35 SOCIAL PROBLEMS 506 (1988); Canan & Pring, *Studying Strategic Lawsuits Against Public Participation: Mixing Quantitative and Qualitative Approaches,* 22 LAW & SOCIETY REVIEW 385 (1988); Pring, *Intimidation Suits Against Citizens: A Risk for Public Policy Advocates,* NATIONAL LAW JOURNAL, July 22, 1985, at 16; Pring, *Retaliation Lawsuits Against Citizen-Group Opponents: "Risky Business" for the Real Estate Developer,* 3D ANNUAL REAL ESTATE SYMPOSIUM 71 (Colo. Bar Ass'n 1985); Pring & Cohen, *"Intimidation Lawsuits" Against Citizen Advocates: New Colorado Supreme Court Decision Strengthens Public's First Amendment Protections,* 33 TRIAL TALK 3 (Colo. Trial Lawyers Ass'n, April 1984).

3. *E.g.,* McDonald v. Smith, 472 U.S. 479 (1985); and see Immuno, A.G. v. Moor-Jankowski, 537 N.Y.S.2d 129, *aff'd,* 74 N.Y.2d 548, 549 N.E.2d 129 (letter to editor).

4. *E.g.,* Gorman Towers, Inc. v. Bogoslavsky, 626 F.2d 607 (8th Cir. 1980); Weiss v. Willow Tree Civic Ass'n, 467 F. Supp. 803 (S.D.N.Y. 1979).

5. *E.g.*, Webb v. Fury, 282 S.E.2d 28 (W. Va. 1981); U.S. v. Environmental Waste Control, Inc., No. 5800055 (N.D. Ind., counterclaim May 31, 1988).

6. *E.g.*, Weissman v. Mogol, 118 Misc.2d 911, 462 N.Y.S.2d 383 (Sup. Ct. 1983); Martin v. Kearney, 51 Cal. App. 3d 309, 124 Cal. Rptr. 281 (1975).

7. *E.g.*, Leonardini v. Shell Oil Co., 216 Cal. App. 3d 547, 264 Cal. Rptr. 883 (1989), *cert. denied,* 111 S.Ct. 293 (1990); Story v. Shelter Bay Co., 52 Wash. App. 334, 760 P.2d 368 (1988).

8. *E.g.*, Lange v. Nature Conservancy, Inc., 24 Wash. App. 416, 601 P.2d 963 (1979).

9. *E.g.*, City of Long Beach v. Bozek, 31 Cal.3d 527, 645 P.2d 137 (1982)(en banc), *vacated and remanded,* 459 U.S. 1095, *aff'd on indep. state const. grounds,* 33 Cal.3d 727, 661 P.2d 1072 (1983) (police misconduct); Patane v. Griffin, 164 A.D.2d 192, 562 N.Y.S.2d 1005 (1990) (county supervisor).

10. *E.g.*, San Luis Obispo County v. Abalone Alliance, 178 Cal. App. 3d 848, 223 Cal. Rptr. 846 (1986) (demonstration); North Star Legal Foundation v. Honeywell Project, 355 N.W.2d 186 (Minn. Ct. App. 1984) (demonstration); NAACP v. Claiborne Hardware Co., 458 U.S. 886 (1982) (boycott); Missouri v. Nat'l Organization for Women, Inc., 620 F.2d 1301 (8th Cir. 1980), *cert. denied,* 449 U.S. 842 (1980) (boycott).

11. *E.g.*, Dreske v. Wooden, No. 79CV1046 (Cir. Ct. Waukesha County, Wis., vol. dism. June 16, 1983); Perlman, *Alta Dena Sues Its Critics for $780,000,000,* SAN FRANCISCO CHRONICLE, June 22, 1985.

12. *E.g.*, Streif v. Bovinette, 88 Ill. App. 3d 1079, 411 N.E.2d 341 (1980); Smith v. Silvey, 149 Cal. App. 3d 400, 197 Cal. Rptr. 15 (1983).

13. *E.g.*, Sierra Club v. Butz, 349 F. Supp. 934 (N.D. Cal. 1972); Protect Our Mountain Environment v. District Court, 677 P.2d 1361 (Colo. 1984)(en banc).

14. *E.g.*, Eastern R.R. President's Conference v. Noerr Motor Freight, 365 U.S. 127 (1961); City of Columbia v. Omni Outdoor Advertising, Inc., 111 S.Ct. 1344 (1991).

15. *E.g.*, Okun v. Superior Court, 29 Cal.3d 442, 629 P.2d 1369, *cert. denied,* 454 U.S. 1099 (1981), *on remand sub nom.* Maple Properties v. Harris, 158 Cal. App.3d 997, 205 Cal. Rptr. 532 (1984), *cert. denied,* 470 U.S. 1054 (1985); Chavez v. Citizens for a Fair Farm Labor Law, 84 Cal. App. 3d 77, 148 Cal. Rptr. 278 (1978).

16. *E.g.*, Pronger v. O'Dell, 127 Wis. 2d 292, 379 N.W.2d 330 (App. Ct. 1985); Carter v. Reehling, No. 25112 (Super. Ct., Houston County, Ga., dismissed June 15, 1986).

17. *E.g.*, Botos v. Los Angeles County Bar Ass'n, 151 Cal. App. 3d 1083, 199 Cal. Rptr. 236 (1984).

18. *E.g.*, Westfield Partners, Ltd. v. Hogan, 740 F. Supp. 523 (N.D. Ill. 1990); Monia v. Parnas Corp., 227 Cal. App. 3d 1349, 278 Cal. Rptr. 426 (1991), *review denied but opinion decertified,* Cal. Sup. Ct. (July 11, 1991).

19. The exceptions are the two fine law review articles (which nevertheless treat the phenomenon as a single-constituency problem) cited last in note 21, below.

20. There are now over 20 recently reported federal and state court opinions using the word "SLAPP": Lafayette Morehouse Inc. v. The Chronicle Pub. Co., 1995 Westlaw 475679 (Cal. Ct. App., Aug. 9, 1995); Levin v. King, 648 N.E. 2d 1108, 1109 (Ill. App. 1995); Dixon v. Super. Ct., 30 Cal. App. 4th 733, 36 Cal. Rptr. 2d 687, 690 (Ct. App. 1994), *review denied* (Cal. 1995); College Hospital Inc. v. Superior Court, 34 Cal. Rptr. 2d 898, 903 (Cal. 1994); Wilcox v. Super. Ct., 33 Cal. Rptr. 2d 446, 448–55 (Ct. App. 1994), *review denied* (Cal. 1994); Allan and Allan Arts Ltd. v. Rosenblum, 615 N.Y.S.2d 410, 415 (App. Div. 1994); Opinion of the Justices (SLAPP Suit Procedure), 641 A.2d 1012 (N.H. 1994); Hillside Assocs. v. Stravato, 642 A.2d 664, 667 (R.I. 1994); People for the Ethical Treatment of Animals v. Berosini, 867 P.2d 1121, 1127 n. 7 (Nev. Sup. Ct. 1994); Entertainment Partners Group, Inc. v. Davis, 603 N.Y.S.2d 439, 440 (App. Div. 1993); Edmondson and Gallagher v. Alban Towers Tenants Ass'n, 829 F. Supp

420, 427 (D.D.C. 1993); Computer Assocs. Int'l Inc. v. American Fundware Inc., 831 F. Supp. 1516, 1522 n. 3 (D. Colo. 1993); Hotel St. George Assocs. v. Morgenstern, 819 F. Supp. 310, 319 n. 8, 323 (S.D.N.Y. 1993); Florida Fern Growers Ass'n v. Concerned Citizens of Putnam County, 616 So.2d 562, 570 (Fla. Dist. Ct. App. 1993); Hull v. Rossi, 13 Cal. App. 4th 1763, 1766, 17 Cal. Rptr. 2d 457, 459 (1993); 600 West 115th St. Corp. v. Von Gutfeld, 80 N.Y.2d 130, 138 n. 1, 589 N.Y.S.2d 825 (1992); Gordon v. Marrone, 155 Misc.2d 726, 590 N.Y.S.2d 727, 735–40 (Sup. Ct. 1992), *aff'd*, 616 N.Y.S.2d 98 (App. Div. 1994); McGill v. Parker, 582 N.Y.S.2d 91, 111 (App. Div. 1992); Petrochem Insulation, Inc. v. Northern California and Northern Nevada Pipe Trades Council, 1992 Westlaw 131162, at 1, 11 (N.D. Cal. 1992); Monia v. Parnas Corp., 278 Cal. Rptr. 426, 435–36 (Ct. App. 1991), *review denied*, Cal. Sup. Ct. (1991) (ordered not to be officially published); Live Oak Publishing Co. v. Cohagan, 234 Cal. App. 3d 1277, 286 Cal. Rptr. 198 (1991); Westfield Partners, Ltd. v. Hogan, 740 F. Supp. 523, 525 (N.D. Ill. 1990).

21. In addition to our own, over 30 additional professional and scholarly articles have now been written on "SLAPPs": Chertok, *The Real Estate Development SLAPP*, in SLAPPS: STRATEGIC LAWSUITS AGAINST PUBLIC PARTICIPATION IN GOVERNMENT at 35 (ALI-ABA Course of Study Materials 1994); Berry, *The "Environmental" SLAPP, id.* at 61; Bethke, *Cole v. Lehmann: Practical Reflections on a Teacher Slander Suit Against Parents, id.* at 85; Chertok, *Sanctions as a SLAPP Deterrent: How Effective Are They? id.* at 117; Chapman, *LaPointe v. West Contra Costa Sanitary District: A Successful First Amendment "SLAPPback" Brought Under 42 U.S.C. 1983, id.* at 155; Stearns, *SLAPPs: A Government Perspective, id.* at 185; Goldowitz, *Study Outline Regarding [SLAPPs] Legislative Developments, id.* at 195; Cohen, *Should Lawyers Be Disciplined or Sanctioned for Bringing SLAPP Suits, id.* at 253; Shiffrin, *A Half a Cheer for SLAPPs, id.* at 274 (suppl.); Harper, *Note, Attorneys as State Actors: A State Action Model and Argument for Holding SLAPP-Plaintiffs' Attorneys Liable Under 42 U.S.C. 1983*, 21 HASTINGS CONSTITUTIONAL LAW QUARTERLY 405 (1994); *Note, The Empire State SLAPPs Back: New York's Legislative Response to SLAPP Suits*, 17 VERMONT LAW REVIEW 925 (1993); Abell, *Comment, Exercise of Constitutional Privileges: Deterring Abuse of the First Amendment—"Strategic Lawsuits Against Public Participation,"* 47 SOUTHERN METHODIST UNIVERSITY LAW REVIEW 95 (1993); Barker, *Common-Law and Statutory Solutions to the Problem of SLAPPs*, 26 LOYOLA OF LOS ANGELES LAW REVIEW 395 (1993); Merriam & Benson, *Identifying and Beating a Strategic Lawsuit Against Public Participation*, 1993 DUKE ENVIRONMENTAL LAW & POLICY FORUM 17; Ericson-Siegel, *Silencing SLAPPs: An Examination of Proposed Legislative Remedies and a "Solution" for Florida*, 20 FLORIDA STATE UNIVERSITY LAW REVIEW 487 (1992); Rubin, *Are SLAPP Suits Unethical?* 12 ENVIRONMENTAL LAW SECTION JOURNAL 29 (Feb. 1992) (publication of the New York State Bar Association); Waldman, *SLAPP Suits: Weaknesses in First Amendment Law and in the Courts' Responses to Frivolous Litigation*, 39 UCLA LAW REVIEW 979 (1992); Costantini & Nash, *SLAPP/SLAPPback: The Misuse of Libel Law for Political Purposes and a Countersuit Response*, 7 JOURNAL OF LAW & POLITICS 417 (1991); Cosentino, *Comment, Strategic Lawsuits Against Public Participation: An Analysis of the Solutions*, 27 CALIFORNIA WESTERN LAW REVIEW 399 (1991); McEvoy, *"The Big Chill": Business Use of the Tort of Defamation to Discourage the Exercise of First Amendment Rights*, 17 HASTINGS CONSTITUTIONAL LAW QUARTERLY 503 (1990); Barry, *When Protesters Become "Racketeers": RICO Runs Afoul of the First Amendment*, 64 ST. JOHN'S LAW REVIEW 899 (1990); Reed, *Can I Be Sued? The Retaliatory Lawsuit*, 26 IDAHO LAW REVIEW 249 (1990); Abrams, *Strategic Lawsuits Against Public Participation (SLAPP)*, 7 PACE ENVIRONMENTAL LAW REVIEW 33 (1989); Stein, *SLAPP Suits: A Slap at the First Amendment, id.* at 45 (1989); Brooks, *Les Mains Sales: The Ethical and Political Implications of SLAPP Suits, id.* at 61 (1989); Schnapper, *"Libelous" Petitions for Redress of Grievances—Bad Historiography Makes Worse Law*, 74 IOWA LAW REVIEW 303 (1989); Sive, *Countersuits, Delay, Intimidation Caused by Public Interest*

Suits, NATIONAL LAW JOURNAL, June 19, 1989, at 26; Brecher, *The Public Interest and Intimidation Suits: A New Approach,* 28 SANTA CLARA LAW REVIEW 105 (1988); *Political Intimidation Suits: SLAPP Defendant Slaps Back,* 4 CIVIL TRIAL MANUAL (BNA) 459 (Oct. 19, 1988); Zauzmer, *Note, The Misapplication of the Noerr-Pennington Doctrine in Non-Antitrust Right to Petition Cases,* 36 STANFORD LAW REVIEW 1243 (1984); McGrath, *Suing the Citizen: Should a Developer Strike Back?* in COLORADO CLE LAND USE CONFERENCE (Denver, Sept. 7, 1984); Jacobs, *Protecting the First Amendment Right to Petition: Immunity for Defendants in Defamation Actions Through the Application of the Noerr-Pennington Doctrine,* 31 AMERICAN UNIVERSITY LAW REVIEW 147 (1981); *Note, Counterclaim and Countersuit Harassment of Private Environmental Plaintiffs: The Problem, Its Implications, and Proposed Solutions,* 74 MICHIGAN LAW REVIEW 106 (1975); Sandifer & Smith, *The Tort Suit for Damages: The New Threat to Civil Rights Organizations,* 41 BROOKLYN LAW REVIEW 559 (1975).

22. A sample of the extensive popular press on SLAPPs: Ziegler, *Anti-SLAPP Law a Valid Defense in Libel Cases,* LOS ANGELES DAILY JOURNAL, Aug. 11, 1995, at 1; Askari, *Suing to Silence Opposition Is Latest Tool of Big Business,* DETROIT FREE PRESS, Jan. 3, 1995, at 1A; Ayer, *Citizens Slapped for Speaking Out,* ROCKY MOUNTAIN NEWS, Oct. 5, 1994, at 42A; *Editorial: Slap Down SLAPPs,* PROVIDENCE [R.I.] JOURNAL-BULLETIN, Sept. 11, 1994; McMorris, *Ruling Protects Citizens' Public Speech,* WALL STREET JOURNAL, Aug. 17, 1994, at B6; Speart, *When Citizens SLAPP Back!* NATIONAL WILDLIFE, June/July 1994, at 12; Springston, *If You Speak Out in Public, the Target May SLAPP You,* RICHMOND TIMES-DISPATCH, June 5, 1994, at C2; Lhotka, *Jury Rewards Pair Who Got SLAPPed,* ST. LOUIS POST-DISPATCH, Apr. 24, 1994, at 1A; Ferdinand, *SLAPP-ed Into Silence,* MIAMI HERALD, May 25, 1992, at 1A; Blum, *SLAPP Suits Continue in High Gear,* NATIONAL LAW JOURNAL, May 18, 1992, at 3; Carroll, *Lawsuits as Weapons,* BOSTON SUNDAY GLOBE, May 10, 1992, at A1; Wolfson, *Countersuit over Freeway Site Seen as Move to Silence Foes,* LOUISVILLE COURIER-JOURNAL, Jan. 26, 1992, at 1; *Open Debate "SLAPPs" Shut,* ATLANTA CONSTITUTION, Dec. 3, 1991; Clavin, *The High Price of High Ideals,* WOMAN'S DAY, Sept. 24, 1991, at 44; *SLAPP Happy,* PLAYBOY, Aug. 1991, at 52; Keaton, *Farmers Fight Off the New Valley Land Rush,* SAN FRANCISCO DAILY JOURNAL, Aug. 6, 1991, at 1; *Debate: Curb Lawsuits That Attack Free Speech,* USA TODAY, May 6, 1991; Hager, *Tide Turns for Targets of SLAPP Lawsuits,* LOS ANGELES TIMES, May 3, 1991, at A-3; Bishop, *New Tool of Developers and Others Quells Private Opposition to Projects,* NEW YORK TIMES, Apr. 26, 1991, at B-9; Melvin, *Developer's Suit Is Ruled Retaliatory,* NEW YORK TIMES, April 14, 1991, at 12WC-6; Boyle, *Activists at Risk of Being SLAPPed,* SPORTS ILLUSTRATED, Mar. 25, 1991, at 6; Coates, *Lawsuits Aim to Silence Public,* CHICAGO TRIBUNE, Mar. 24, 1991, at 1; Rice, *SLAPP Happy: Developers Weigh Lawsuits' Wisdom,* REAL ESTATE JOURNAL, Jan. 31, 1991; Turque, *SLAPPing the Opposition: How Developers and Officials Fight Their Critics,* NEWSWEEK, Mar. 5, 1990, at 22; Marcus, *Law: Intimidation Lawsuits Creep up on Critics,* WALL STREET JOURNAL, Feb. 21, 1990; Pell, *SLAPPed Silly,* CALIFORNIA LAWYER, Feb. 1990, at 24; Stiak, *Stand Up and Be Sued,* SIERRA, Nov./Dec. 1989, at 28; *Political Intimidation Suits: SLAPP Defendant Slaps Back,* 4 CIVIL TRIAL MANUAL (BNA) 459 (Oct. 19, 1989); Pell, *The SLAPPs Are Back,* CALIFORNIA, Sept. 1989, at 18; Zweig, *A SLAPP in the Face,* FORBES, May 29, 1989, at 106; Pell, *The High Cost of Speaking Out,* CALIFORNIA, Nov. 1988, at 88; Holzberg, *Defamation Suits "Chill" Activists,* NATIONAL LAW JOURNAL, July 25, 1988, at 3; Wiemer, *Developers Use the Law to Stifle Opposition,* NEWSDAY, May 29, 1988, Sec. 10 (Ideas) at 10; Gest, *A Chilling Flurry of Lawsuits,* U.S. NEWS & WORLD REPORT, May 23, 1988, at 64; Hentoff, *You Don't Need a Press Card to Be Sued for Libel,* WASHINGTON POST, July 19, 1986, at A-23; Anderson & Spear, *Legal System Abused to Stifle Critics,* WASHINGTON POST, Mar. 20, 1986, at 23; Anderson & Spear, *First Amendment Rights Expensive,* WASHINGTON POST, Mar 21, 1986, at 23.

23. *L.A. Law ("Armand's Hammer")* (CBS, Nov. 8, 1990). There has been more serious TV

coverage of SLAPPs on *The MacNeil-Lehrer News Hour* (PBS, Feb. 19, 1990); *CBS Evening News (with Dan Rather)* (CBS, Apr. 20, 1990); *20/20 (with Barbara Walters)* (ABC, May 25, 1990); *World Monitor News* (Discovery Cable, May 10, 1991); *NBC Nightly News (with Tom Brokaw)* (NBC, May 13, 1991).

24. *E.g.*, Harris v. Huntington, 2 Tyler 129 (Vt. 1802); and discussion in Chapter 2.

25. Study Interview with Betty Johnson (Apr. 29, 1986). "Study Interview" quotes are from the Phase II in-depth interviews (see the Appendix); throughout the book they are individually cited on first appearance but not subsequently when the source is obvious from the text.

26. Complaint, Warembourg v. Louisville, No. 83-CV-1232–2 (Dist. Ct., Boulder County, Colo., filed 1982).

27. Opinion, *id.* (Jan. 4, 1983).

28. Protect Our Mountain Environment v. Bd. of County Commissioners of Jefferson County, No. 78CV1783 (Dist. Ct., Jefferson County, Colo., filed Sept. 12, 1978).

29. Lockport Corporation v. Protect Our Mountain Environment, No. 81CV973 (Dist. Ct., Jefferson County, Colo., filed Apr. 1, 1981).

30. Gougis, *SLAPPed with a Lawsuit? West Covina Residents to Face BKK in Court,* SAN GABRIEL VALLEY [CAL.] TRIBUNE, May 3, 1995, at A1.

31. Durham v. Brock, No. CJ-95-15 (Dist. Ct., Creek County, Okla., filed Feb. 15, 1995); Fricker, *Oklahoma Libel Case Puts Tort Reform Movement on Trial,* NATIONAL LAW JOURNAL, Mar. 13, 1995, at A11.

32. Hickox, *Critics of City Hall Slapped with Suits,* ORANGE COUNTY REGISTER, Apr. 7, 1995, at 1.

33. Phillips May Corp. v. Herold, No. CC94050833-B (County Ct., Dallas County, Tex., filed 1994).

34. Dixon v. Super. Ct., note 20 above.

35. Central Transportation, Inc. v. Stephens, No. 1978–2083 & 1978–2475 (Ct. C.P., Cambria County, Pa.) (dismissed 1979).

36. Hometown Properties, Inc. v. Fleming, No. WC-91–0154 (Super. Ct., Washington County, R.I., filed Dec. 1992).

37. Florida Affordable Housing, Inc. v. Taxpayers Action Group of Collier County, Inc., No. 91–3571-CA-01 (Cir. Ct., Collier County, Fla., filed Oct. 23, 1991).

38. Welu v. Tiedeman, No. 91–1711 (Dist. Ct., Dallas County, Iowa) (filed Apr. 22, 1991; dism. July 17, 1991).

39. SRW Associates v. Bellport Beach Property Owners, No. 24211/84 (Sup. Ct., Suffolk County, N.Y., filed Oct. 26, 1984).

40. Ross Investment Corp. v. The Northeast Community Org., No. 80122 812/22500 (Super. Ct., Baltimore County, Md., dismissed per stipulation Mar. 27, 1984).

41. Maple Properties v. Harris, No. C299570 (Super. Ct., Los Angeles County, Cal., Apr. 24, 1980), *rev'd and remanded sub. nom.*, Okun v. Superior Court, 29 Cal.3d 442, 629 P.2d 1369, 175 Cal. Rptr. 157 (1981), *cert. denied,* 454 U.S. 1099 (1981), *dism. on remand* (Super. Ct., Los Angeles County, Cal. 1984), *aff'd,* 158 Cal. App. 3d 997, 205 Cal. Rptr. 532 (1984), *cert denied,* 105 S.Ct. 1758 (1985).

42. Sierra Club v. Butz, 349 F.Supp. 934 (N.D. Cal., Oct. 17, 1972).

43. Cole v. Lehman, No. 85CV2187 (Dist. Ct., Adams County, Colo., filed Sept. 1985).

44. Carter v. Reehling, No. 25112 (Super. Ct., Houston County, Ga., summary judgment 1986).

45. San Luis Obispo County v. Abalone Alliance, No. 55664 (Super. Ct., San Luis Obispo County, Cal., filed Nov. 25, 1981), *aff'd,* 178 Cal. App. 3d 848, 223 Cal. Rptr. 846 (1986).

46. Bass v. Rohr, No. 1103642 (Cir. Ct., Anne Arundel County, Md., Mar. 28, 1983), *aff'd,* 57 Md. App. 609, 471 A.2d 752 (1984), *cert. granted,* 300 Md. 88, 475 A.2d 1200 (1984), *cert. dism. as improvidently granted,* 301 Md. 641, 484 A.2d 275 (1984).

47. Goldberg, *SLAPPs Surge North: Canadian Activists Under Attack,* THE NEW CATALYST, Winter 1992/93, at 1; *Legal Threat to Free Speech,* GREENPEACE AUSTRALIA at 5 (1994); Pope, *Turning the Tables: Charged with Libel, Pair of Activists Puts McDonald's on the Grill,* WALL STREET JOURNAL, July 18, 1995, at 1; *Singapore Concedes MPs Use Law to Ruin Opponents,* TIMES OF LONDON, Jan. 10, 1995.

48. *See* Whitney v. California, 274 U.S. 357, 375–76 (1926) (Brandeis, J., concurring); G. DANEKE, ED., PUBLIC INVOLVEMENT AND SOCIAL IMPACT ASSESSMENT (1983); H. ZEIGLER, THE IRONY OF DEMOCRACY, 2d ed. (1972); C. PATEMAN, PARTICIPATION AND DEMOCRATIC THEORY (1970); P. BACHRACH, THE THEORIES OF DEMOCRATIC ELITISM (1967); A. MEIKLEJOHN, FREE SPEECH AND ITS RELATION TO SELF GOVERNMENT (1948); Aron, *Citizen Participation at Government Expense,* 39 PUBLIC ADMINISTRATION REVIEW 477 (1979); Schuck, *Public Interest Groups and the Policy Process,* 37 PUBLIC ADMINISTRATION REVIEW 132 (1977); Cramton, *The Why, Where and How of Broadened Public Participation in the Administrative Process,* 60 GEORGETOWN LAW JOURNAL 525 (1972).

Political participation levels are already low in the United States. Political involvement, other than voting, is confined to approximately 10 percent of the adult population and is correlated with income, occupational prestige, and education. *See* L. MILBRAITH, POLITICAL PARTICIPATION: HOW AND WHY PEOPLE GET INVOLVED IN POLITICS (1965); R. WOLFINGER & S. ROSENSTONE, WHO VOTES? (1980); S. VERBA & N. NIE, POLITICAL PARTICIPATION IN AMERICA (1976). Further, even voting levels are lower in the United States than in any other industrialized, multiparty democracy where voting is voluntary. *See* C. TAYLOR & D. JODICE, WORLD HANDBOOK OF POLITICAL AND SOCIAL INDICATORS (1983). Since SLAPPs most directly affect the small percentage of active participants in the political process, they decrease participation levels even further, we found.

49. A few commentators have suggested that the secondary criteria are too narrow, either without understanding them or without offering cogent alternatives. *See* Cosentino, note 21 above, at 400–401; Harper, *id.* at 407; Brooks, *id.* at 66. Everyone, it seems, wants to stretch the definition of "SLAPPs" to fit a particular case or cause.

50. Typically, in those counterclaims the plaintiffs (targets) have filed a non-SLAPP lawsuit against the government, challenging a government decision or outcome (core petitioning; see Chapter 2), but opposition interests (filers) who support the government decision then file a SLAPP counterclaim or cross-claim against the plaintiffs (targets) alleging that filers are injured by targets' government-challenge lawsuit. A typical example is *Sierra Club v. Butz* (Chapter 5), in which the club filed a nonmonetary lawsuit against the U.S. government seeking court reversal of the government's decision to allow logging in a wilderness; the logging company intervened as a defendant in support of the government and then filed a SLAPP counterclaim for money damages against the Sierra Club.

51. Gordon v. Marrone, 155 Misc. 2d 726, 736, 590 N.Y.S.2d 649, 656 (1992).

52. 819 F. Supp. 310 (S.D.N.Y. 1993).

Chapter 2

1. D. Smith, The Right to Petition for Redress of Grievances: Constitutional Development and Interpretations (1971) (unpublished dissertation, Texas Tech University); Smith, *"Shall Make No Law Abridging . . . ": An Analysis of the Neglected, But Nearly Absolute, Right of Petition,* 54 CINCINNATI LAW REVIEW 1153 (1986); Higginson, *A Short History of the Right to Petition Government for the Redress of Grievances,* 96 YALE LAW JOURNAL 142 (1986); Hodgkiss,

Petitioning and the Empowerment Theory of Practice, 96 YALE LAW JOURNAL 569 (1987); Zauzmer, *Note, The Misapplication of the Noerr-Pennington Doctrine to Non-antitrust Right to Petition Cases*, 36 STANFORD LAW REVIEW 1243 (1984).

2. L. NADER & H. TODD, EDS., THE DISPUTING PROCESS—LAW IN TEN SOCIETIES at 1 (1978).

3. McDonald v. Smith, 472 U.S. 479, 489 (1985) (Brennan, J., concurring).

4. It has been traced as far back as the tenth-century "Andover Code" of Edgar the Peaceful; *see* Smith Dissertation, note 1 above, at 12–13, 45.

5. C. STEPHENSON & F. MARCHAM, EDS., SOURCES OF ENGLISH CONSTITUTIONAL HISTORY at 125 (2d ed. 1972).

6. E. DUMBAULD, THE BILL OF RIGHTS AND WHAT IT MEANS TODAY at 168 (1979).

7. B. SCHWARTZ, THE BILL OF RIGHTS: A DOCUMENTARY HISTORY at 198 (1971).

8. *Id.* at 254.

9. *Id.* at 383. It also played a key role in the abolition of slavery in the nineteenth century. A. KELLY & W. HARBISON, THE AMERICAN CONSTITUTION: ITS ORIGINS AND DEVELOPMENT 357–58 (4th ed. 1970).

10. Smith Dissertation, note 1 above, at 2–3.

11. Zauzmer, note 1 above, at 1244.

12. LIBRARY OF CONGRESS, THE CONSTITUTION OF THE UNITED STATES OF AMERICA: ANALYSIS AND INTERPRETATION, S. DOC. NO. 96–16, 99th Cong., 1st Sess. 1141–45 (1982).

13. NAACP v. Claiborne Hardware Co., 458 U.S. 886 (1982); Missouri v. Nat'l Organization for Women, Inc., 620 F.2d 1301 (8th Cir. 1980), *cert. denied*, 449 U.S. 842 (1980); McDonald v. Smith, 472 U.S. 479, 488 n. 2 (1985) (Brennan, J., concurring).

14. Griffin v. Thomas, 929 F.2d 1210, 1214 (7th Cir. 1991).

15. Mine Workers v. Illinois Bar Ass'n, 389 U.S. 217, 222 (1967).

16. De Jonge v. Oregon, 299 U.S. 353, 364 (1937).

17. McDonald v. Smith, 472 U.S. 479, 483 (1985).

18. U.S. v. Cruikshank, 92 U.S. 542, 552 (1875).

19. Article 21 (1) of the Universal Declaration of Human Rights, U.N. General Assembly Resolution 217, 3 GAOR, U.N. Doc. 1/77/7 (1948).

20. For example, state constitutional petition clauses, federal and state privilege or immunity statutes, citizen-suit statutes, open meeting laws, administrative procedure codes, freedom of information and public records acts, civil rights statutes, and court decisions. *See*, Feller, *Private Enforcement of Federal Anti-Pollution Laws Through Citizen Suits: A Model*, 60 DENVER LAW JOURNAL 553 (1983); DiMento, *Citizen Environmental Litigation and the Administrative Process*, 1977 DUKE LAW JOURNAL 409; *Public Participation in Regulatory Agency Proceedings: Hearing Before the Senate Committee on Governmental Affairs*, in III STUDY ON FEDERAL REGULATION PURSUANT TO S. RES. 71, 95th Cong., 1st Sess. 1 (1977); P. SCHUCK, SUING GOVERNMENT: CITIZEN REMEDIES FOR OFFICIAL WRONGS (1983); G. DANEKE, ED., PUBLIC INVOLVEMENT AND SOCIAL IMPACT ASSESSMENT (1983); H. ZEIGLER, THE IRONY OF DEMOCRACY (2d ed. 1972); C. PATEMAN, PARTICIPATION AND DEMOCRATIC THEORY (1970); P. BACHRACH, THE THEORIES OF DEMOCRATIC ELITISM (1967); A. MEIKLEJOHN, FREE SPEECH AND ITS RELATION TO SELF GOVERNMENT (1948); Aron, *Citizen Participation at Government Expense*, 39 PUBLIC ADMINISTRATION REVIEW 477 (1979); Schuck, *Public Interest Groups and the Policy Process*, 37 PUBLIC ADMINISTRATION REVIEW 132 (1977); Cramton, *The Why, Where and How of Broadened Public Participation in the Administrative Process*, 60 GEORGETOWN LAW JOURNAL 525 (1972).

21. Protect Our Mountain Environment, Inc. v. District Court, 677 P.2d 1361, 1364 (Colo. 1984) ("POME" case).

22. See discussion of *Omni* later this chapter.

23. Abrams v. U.S, 250 U.S. 616, 630 (1919) (Holmes, J., dissenting).

24. Whitney v. California, 274 U.S. 357, 375–76 (1927) (Brandeis, J., concurring).

25. Bill Johnson's Restaurants v. NLRB, 461 U.S. 731, 740–41 (1983). After all that hand-wringing, the Court ruled that lawsuit could continue (see discussion of *Bill Johnson* later in this chapter).

26. 2 Tyler 129 (Vt. 1802).

27. *Id.* at 140–41, 146.

28. *E.g.*, Gray v. Pentland, 2 Serg. & R. 23 (Penn. 1815) (citizen sued for deposition to governor charging a government official with "frequent intoxication" and being "unfit to perform the duties of his office with dignity and propriety"); White v. Nicholls, 3 How. 266 (U.S. 1845) (seven citizens sued for writing to U.S. president complaining of malfeasance by a U.S. customs collector); Larkin v. Noonan, 19 Wis. 93 (1865) (citizens sued for reporting to governor that the Milwaukee County sheriff made "several attempts to cheat and defraud the county"). For a modern version of the same "seditious libel" ethos, *see* Garrison v. Louisiana, 379 U.S. 64 (1964)(overturning district attorney's conviction for criminal defamation for criticizing eight judges at a press conference).

29. Webb v. Fury, 282 S.E.2d 28, 43 (W.Va. 1981).

30. *See* authorities, note 20 above.

31. The only in-depth analysis is Smith Dissertation, note 1 above; see also other authorities, *id.* (Blackstone's sarcastic comment on the inverse ratio between the importance of a right and the amount of legal writing about it comes to mind.)

32. Even constitutional law textbooks give it little or no treatment, concentrating First Amendment coverage typically on speech, press, and religion issues. For example, R. ROTUNDA, MODERN CONSTITUTIONAL LAW: CASES AND NOTES at 881 (4th ed. 1993), devotes one paragraph to it and does not even index the term separately. Like any workers, law professors and lawyers are no better than their tools.

33. Its first U.S. Supreme Court test case did not come for 85 years: U.S. v. Cruikshank, 92 U.S. 542 (1875), and the Court has handled less than two dozen cases mentioning it since.

34. Smith Dissertation, note 1 above, at 151.

35. For an excellent argument for "absolute" protection, see Logan, *Tort Law and the Central Meaning of the First Amendment*, 51 UNIVERSITY OF PITTSBURGH LAW REVIEW 493 (1990).

36. McDonald v. Smith, note 17 above.

37. Eastern R.R. Presidents Conference v. Noerr Motor Freight, Inc., 365 U.S. 127 (1961); United Mine Workers of America v. Pennington, 381 U.S. 657 (1965); California Motor Transport Co. v. Trucking Unlimited, 404 U.S. 508 (1972).

38. POME, note 21 above.

39. 499 U.S. 365, 111 S.Ct. 1344, 113 L.Ed.2d 382 (1991).

40. The *Noerr-Pennington* cases, note 37 above.

41. Bill Johnson's Restaurants v. NLRB, note 25 above.

42. McDonald v. Smith, note 17 above.

43. Some of the best-handled examples being federal court decisions such as *Sierra Club v. Butz* (Chapter 5); *Stevens v. Tillman* (Chapter 4); *Adams County v. Shroyer* (Chapter 4); *Gorman Towers v. Bogoslavsky* (Chapter 6); and state cases like Colorado's *POME* (Chapters 1 and 3); Maryland's *Minor v. Novotny* (Chapter 4); California's *Martin v. Kearney* (Chapter 4); West Virginia's *Webb v. Fury* (Chapter 5); New York's *Immuno* (Chapter 5); New York's *Weiss v. Willow Tree* (Chapter 6).

44. Bill Johnson's Restaurant v. NLRB, note 25 above, at 734.

45. *Id.* at 733.

46. *Id.* at 737.

47. *Id.* at 740–41.

48. Freedman, *Mixed Motives,* LEGAL TIMES, Oct. 17, 1994.

49. *Bill Johnson's,* note 25 above, at 745.

50. *Id.* at 748–49.

51. *Id.* at 744.

52. *Id.* at 748.

53. *Id.* at 741.

54. *Id.*

55. *Id.* at 742.

56. *Id.* at 743.

57. *Id.* (footnote omitted).

58. Complaint Exhs. A & B, in Joint Appendix in the U.S. Supreme Court at 9 & 15, McDonald v. Smith.

59. *Id.*

60. 472 U.S. 479 (1985). (For a compelling argument that the Court was wrong on both law and history in denying an absolute immunity for petitioning, *see* Schnapper, *"Libelous" Petitions for Redress of Grievances—Bad Historiography Makes Worse Law,* 74 IOWA LAW REVIEW 303 (1989).)

61. *Id.* at 483.

62. 376 U.S. 254 (1964).

63. For criticisms of how poorly *New York Times v. Sullivan* works in practice, *see* Smolla, *Let the Author Beware: The Rejuvenation of the American Law of Libel,* 132 UNIVERSITY OF PENNSYLVANIA LAW REVIEW 1, 14 (1983); Logan, *Tort Law and the Central Meaning of the First Amendment,* 51 UNIVERSITY OF PITTSBURGH LAW REVIEW 493 (1990).

64. Shiffrin, *A Half a Cheer for SLAPPs,* in SLAPPS: STRATEGIC LAWSUITS AGAINST PUBLIC PARTICIPATION IN GOVERNMENT at 274 (ms. pp. 7–8) (1994).

65. 349 F. Supp. 934, 938 (N.D. Cal. 1972).

66. *E.g.,* Webb v. Fury, 282 S.E.2d 28, 40 (W. Va. 1981); accord Westfield Partners, Inc. v. Hogan, 740 F. Supp. 523 (N.D. Ill. 1990) (relying on the *Noerr-Pennington* cases); Waldman, *SLAPP Suits: Weaknesses in First Amendment Law and in the Courts' Responses to Frivolous Litigation,* 39 UCLA LAW REVIEW 979, 1022–25 (1992).

67. We have found four different "avoidance techniques" used by lower courts: (1) treating *McDonald* as limited to the *federal* Constitution, and announcing that the *state* constitution is more protective (*e.g.,* Webb v. Fury, 282 S.E.2d 28 (W. Va. 1991)); Dixon v. Super. Ct., 30 Cal. App. 4th 733, 36 Cal. Rptr. 2d 687 (Ct. App. 1994); (2) treating *McDonald* as a *constitutional* interpretation, and applying more protective *state* statutes that do not allow malice exceptions (*e.g.,* Miner v. Novotny, 60 Md. App. 124, 481 A.2d 508, 511–13 (1984), *aff'd* 304 Md. 164 (1985)); (3) creating a very strict, narrow definition of malice which is easy to avoid on pretrial motion (*e.g.,* Stevens v. Tillman, 855 F.2d 394, 403, 405 (7th Cir. 1988); Nodar v. Galbreath, 462 So.2d 803 (Fla. 1984)); (4) shifting the burden of proof of malice to the filer (*e.g.,* Martin v. Kearney, 51 Cal. App. 3d 309, 124 Cal. Rptr. 281 (1975)). *See* Waldman, note 66 above, at 997 *et seq.*

68. 365 U.S. 127 (1961).

69. *Id.* at 139–40.

70. *Id.* at 145.

71. *Id.* at 144.

72. 381 U.S. 657 (1965).

73. *Id.* at 670.

74. 404 U.S. 508 (1972).

75. *Id.* at 512.

76. 458 U.S. 886 (1982).

77. *Id.* at 911–12, 914, 916, 933.

78. 499 U.S. 365, 111 S. Ct. 1344 (1991).

79. *Id.* at 367.

80. *Id.*

81. *Id.* at 368.

82. *Id.* at 381.

83. Justice Scalia's "established record of favoring reputation values over first amendment values" makes some suspect that he would not expand *Omni* to cover citizen petitioning-defamation cases like *McDonald* (Shiffrin, note 64 above, at 9). But, how could even Justice Scalia justify having a different, let alone *more protective,* government-petitioning standard for monopoly business than for individual citizens?

84. See dissenters' opinion, 499 U.S. at 398. The bigger issue, over which the justices part company, is whether there should be a conspiracy exception to the so-called *Parker* doctrine, which generally immunizes anticompetitive acts done by state government or local governments under state authority. The majority holds no, even a conspiracy between a monopoly business and its local government allies does not lose the latter their *Parker* protection, to which the dissenters objected.

85. *Id.* at 380 (emphasis added).

86. *Id.* at 366, 380.

87. *Id.* at 380.

88. *Id.*

89. *Id.*

90. Reaffirmation and refinement of *Omni*'s "outcome-process" test continues. Professional Real Estate Investors, Inc. v. Columbia Pictures Industries, Inc., 113 S. Ct. 1920 (1993), refines *Omni* into a "two-tiered process" when the petitioning complained of is litigation—that is, when someone files a lawsuit, and the other side countersues, claiming that the first suit was a "sham." *PRE* sets out a two-part, sequential, conjunctive standard for dismissal of the countersuit SLAPP. First, the familiar "objective" test: the SLAPP filer must prove that the target's petitioning litigation was "objectively baseless" ("no reasonable litigant could realistically expect success on the merits"). If there is any objective basis for suit, it is categorically protected petitioning, and the SLAPP is dismissed. Even if the suit fails the objective test and is found to be baseless, however, a second, subjective test must be met: the SLAPP filer must prove that the baseless litigation was "'an attempt to interfere' . . . through the 'use [of] the governmental process—as opposed to the outcome of the process—as an anticompetitive weapon.' "*Id.* at 1928.

It remains to be seen whether the Court will continue to apply this somewhat cumbersome two-tier test (three concurring justices seem skeptical) or extend it to petitioning other than judicial (such as executive and legislative testimony or lobbying); *PRE*'s discussion of *Omni* makes that appear unlikely. Regardless, few SLAPPs will get past the first or "objective" test and move on to the potential "fact quagmire" of the "subjective" test.

91. [Rhode Island] Attorney General's Memorandum as Intervenor in Support of the Constitutionality of a Statute at 40 *et seq.*, in Hometown Properties v. Fleming, No. WC-91–0154 (Super. Ct., Washington County, R.I., filed Feb. 23, 1994); in 1995 Rhode Island amended its anti-SLAPP law to add the *PRE* tests (see Chapter 10).

92. *E.g.*, Shiffrin, note 64 above, at 274, suppl. p. 9 *et seq.*; Zauzmer, note 1 above, at 1258. Shiffrin sees *Omni* as "an important antitrust case—not much more." But that is because he holds the self-described "romantic" view that the First Amendment's central purpose is to

protect the "dissenter" in society—not, more broadly, all citizens and the entire political process, as we (and Holmes and Brandeis and the U.S. Supreme Court) see it. Accordingly, he sees the targets in *Omni* and the other *Noerr-Pennington* cases as "monopoly business[es]" not "citizen activists" deserving of protection from "progressives." We disagree. Our fundamental belief (and happily the majoritarian view) is that the First Amendment's protections must extend to everyone, regardless of whether they or their messages are objectionable. To limit First Amendment protection to those we like is subjective, and ultimately more dangerous to progressives the next time they find themselves in the minority. Shiffrin is also concerned that *Omni* may not really be classed as a constitutional law decision, because Justice Scalia treads so lightly on that point—("perhaps in derogation of the Constitution"). 111 S. Ct. at 1353. Treading lightly, however, is also symptomatic of first steps with new doctrine.

The 1984 Zauzmer student note has simply been outmoded by the U.S. Supreme Court's own stated views in *Claiborne Hardware* or *PRE ("Whether applying Noerr as an antitrust doctrine or invoking it in other contexts."* 113 S. Ct. at 1927; emphasis added). The note's views have been expressly rejected for this reason. Computer Assocs. Int'l, Inc. v. American Fundware, Inc., 831 F. Supp. 1516, 1522 (D. Colo. 1993).

93. Westfield Partners, Ltd. v. Hogan, 740 F. Supp. 523, 526 (N.D. Ill. 1990) (citing cases); *accord* Computer Assocs. Int'l, Inc. v. American Fundware, Inc., note 92 above, 831 F. Supp. at 1522 (citing cases); Edmondson and Gallagher v. Alban Towers Tenants Ass'n, 829 F. Supp. 420, 426 (D.D.C. 1993).

94. Computer Associates, note 92 above, 831 F. Supp. at 1522.

95. *Id.* at 1522–23 (citations omitted).

96. [Rhode Island] Attorney General's Memorandum, note 91 above.

Chapter 3

1. Bocella, *Expensive Free Speech, Developers Suing Civic Activists,* NEWSDAY, Mar. 14, 1988, at 1.

2. Chertok, *The Real Estate Development SLAPP,* in SLAPPS: STRATEGIC LAWSUITS AGAINST PUBLIC PARTICIPATION IN GOVERNMENT at 37–38 (ALI-ABA Course of Study Materials 1994).

3. No. 24211/84 (Sup. Ct., Suffolk County, N.Y., filed Oct. 26, 1984); 129 A.D.2d 328, 517 N.Y.S.2d 741 (dismissed July 13, 1987); Chertok, note 2 above, at 40–45.

4. Public Hearing Transcript (Oct. 3, 1984), Exh. E to the Record on Appeal before the N.Y. Sup. Ct., App. Div., 2d Dept. at 31, 32.

5. *Id.* at 37.

6. Note 3 above.

7. Shaman, *Libel Suits: Protection or Intimidation,* NEW YORK TIMES, Nov. 1, 1987, at 12 R.L.I.

8. Press, *A New Kind of Hush Money,* NEWSWEEK, June 3, 1985.

9. Note 7 above.

10. Transcript, note 4 above.

11. Verified Answer and Counterclaim ¶ 28.

12. Note 7 above.

13. *Id.*

14. Cambridge Associates v. Inland Vale Farm Co., No. 1625/83 (Sup. Ct., Westchester County, N.Y., all but one claim dismissed June 15, 1984), *aff'd as modified,* 116 A.D.2d 684. 497 N.Y.S.2d 751 (1986); see Chertok, note 2 above, at 38–40.

15. Oceanside Enterprises, Inc. v. Capobianco, No. 84–10335 (Sup. Ct., Suffolk County, N.Y., dismissed in part Jan. 23, 1987), *aff'd,* 146 A.D.2d 685, 537 N.Y.S.2d 190 (1989).

16. Terra Homes v. Blake, No. 1563188 (Sup. Ct., Nassau County, N.Y., filed Aug. 17, 1987).

17. 64th Street "400" Block Ass'n v. City of New York, No. 7788/87 (Sup. Ct., Kings County, N.Y., counterclaim filed June 8, 1987).

18. Esposito v. Citizens for the Preservation of Windsor Terrace, No. 12163/87 (Sup. Ct., Kings County, N.Y., dismissed July 14, 1987).

19. Lukashok v. Concerned Residents of North Salem, No. 5301/88 (Sup. Ct., Westchester County, N.Y., dismissed July 8, 1988).

20. Sutton Area Community, Inc. v. City of New York, No. 8478–88 (Sup. Ct., New York County, N.Y., voluntarily dismissed 1988).

21. Liverzani v. Jorling, No. 90–7332 (S.D.N.Y., filed Nov. 15, 1990; summary judgment June 18, 1991).

22. Gordon v. Marrone, 573 N.Y.S.2d 105, 109 (Sup. Ct., dismissed Mar. 1991); 590 N.Y.S.2d 649 (Sup. Ct. 1992)(award of attorneys fees); *aff'd* 616 N.Y.S.2d 98 (App. Div. 1994); *appeal denied* Motion No. 1358 (Ct. Aps. 1975); see Chertok, note 2 above, at 45–53 (Chertok was the target's attorney in the case).

23. McKeon Construction v. Kennedy, No. 221454 (Super. Ct., Sacramento County, Cal., demurrer sustained Apr. 24, 1977), *aff'd,* 3 Civil No. 14673 (Cal. Ct. Aps., 3d App. Dist. 1977).

24. Letter from Bruce Kennedy to co-author, Professor Pring (Oct. 7, 1985).

25. Appellant's Opening Brief to the Court of Appeals at 7 (Oct. 7, 1974).

26. Swinehart v. McKeon Construction Co., No. 270792 (Super. Ct., Sacramento County, Cal., filed May 17, 1978); Styles v. McKeon Construction Co., No. 270793 (Super. Ct., Sacramento County, Cal., filed May 17, 1978).

27. Complaint, Styles v. McKeon Construction Co., *id.* ¶ 9.

28. Maple Properties v. Harris, No. C299570 (Super. Ct., Los Angeles County, Cal., Apr. 24, 1980), *rev'd and remanded sub. nom.* Okun v. Superior Court, 29 Cal. 3d 442, 629 P.2d 1369, 175 Cal. Rptr. 157 (1981), *cert. denied,* 454 U.S. 1099 (1981), *dism. on remand* (Super. Ct., Los Angeles County, Cal., 1984), *aff'd,* 158 Cal. App. 3d 997, 205 Cal. Rptr. 532 (1984), *cert. denied,* 105 S.Ct. 1758 (1985).

29. *Voters Pamphlet: Argument Against Proposition B,* attached as Exh. A to First Amended Complaint, *id.*

30. "Open Letter to Mayor Tilem," published in BEVERLY HILLS COURIER, EXH. C to First Amended Complaint, *id.*

31. *Id.*

32. Complaint, *id.*

33. Pell, *Lawsuits That Chill Local Politics,* CALIFORNIA LAWYER, Feb. 1984, at 42; Pell, *Libel as a Political Weapon,* THE NATION, June 6, 1981, at 699.

34. Pell, *Libel,* note 33 above.

35. See quotation at end of this chapter, Okun v. Superior Court, 29 Cal. 3d at 461, 629 P.2d at 1381 (Mosk, J., concurring).

36. Waldman, *SLAPP Suits: Weaknesses in First Amendment Law and in the Courts' Responses to Frivolous Litigation,* 39 UCLA LAW REVIEW 979, 1016–18 (1992).

37. Oxnard Shores Oceanfront Lot Owners Ass'n v. City of Oxnard, No. 84–3016 RG (GX) (Cent. Dist. Ct., Cal., filed Apr. 27, 1984). A beachfront property-owners' association and members filed two $40,000,000-plus federal court SLAPPs against a beach preservation group, its officers, and local government officials for petitioning the city and suing the State Coastal Commission not to approve filers' 122-home development on the beach. A 1992 settlement provided public access to half the beach and an end to the suits.

38. Concerned Citizens to Save the Wilcox v. Santa Barbara Capital, No. 167248 (Super. Ct., Santa Barbara County, Cal., dismissed 1988). Developers of an elderly housing project

on the coast outside Santa Barbara were willing to be bought out by the city, but when the $10,000,000-plus bond issue failed, they blamed local preservationists and SLAPPed them. Within a year, the parties agreed to let the high rise be built, in return for the developers dropping the SLAPP, providing public beach access, and paying targets $7,500 for attorneys' fees.

39. Burbank Hill Properties, Inc. v. Baecker, No. BCO14741 (Super. Ct., Los Angeles County, Cal., dismissed July 1991). Burbank may have trouble keeping its wetlands: the president of a neighborhood group there was SLAPPed for complaining to government agencies about a development that would affect wetlands; the trial court dismissed the suit in 1991, but the developer appealed.

40. H. R. Kaufman v. Fidelity Federal Savings and Loan Ass'n, No. 27935 (Super. Ct., San Bernadino County, Cal., summary judgment for defendant 1982), *aff'd*, 140 Cal. App. 3d 913, 189 Cal. Rptr. 818 (1983). A big savings and loan in Blue Jay Village filed a SLAPP as part of an apparent campaign to block a smaller competitor's county building permit.

41. Reed v. Sierra Club (Chapter 5).

42. Maher v. Toddei, No. 48452 (Super. Ct., Napa County, Cal., dismissed per stipulation, 1986). "Sour grapes" over Napa County's pro-growth 1982 general plan led residents to challenge it (and subsequent development applications) in court, only to be SLAPPed by developers. After nearly two years in trial court and the county's adoption of an improved general plan, targets gave up their opposition to the subdivision, and the SLAPP was dismissed.

43. Parnas Corp. v. Pierce Canyon Homeowners Ass'n, No. 450512 (Super. Ct., Santa Clara County, Cal., filed May 19, 1980). The development company filed this $40,150,000 SLAPP against homeowner and civic groups, individuals, and "Does" involved in a successful election for a building moratorium on the scenic hillsides framing Saratoga, a suburb of San Jose. Some thirty months later the trial court dismissed the case "for failure to prosecute." Co-author Penelope Canan testified as an expert witness in the subsequent SLAPP-back, and the homeowners' president won a $260,000 jury verdict against Parnas and its lawyers, later affirmed on appeal. Monia v. Parnas Corp., 278 Cal. Rptr. 426 (Ct. App. 1991); *review denied and opinion ordered not to be officially published, id.* (Cal. S. Ct. 1991).

44. Study Interview with Nancy Snow, former City Council member, Wheat Ridge, Colo. (May 6, 1986). As indicated in Chapter 1, quotations from these interviews are individually cited on first appearance but not subsequently when the source is obvious from the text. Throughout the book, quotes not otherwise identified are taken from the Phase II interviews.

45. Einarsen v. Sang, No. 83-CV-2092 (Dist. Ct., Jefferson County, Colo., dismissed Dec. 2, 1983).

46. Interviews with Jerry Walp (May 6, 1986) and John Mahoffer (Apr. 22, 1986).

47. Interview with Scott Albertson (Apr. 24, 1986).

48. Interview with Wanda Sang, Wheat Ridge City Clerk (May 6, 1986).

49. Walp and Snow Interviews, notes 46 and 44 above; interview with Vesper Vaseen (Apr. 23, 1986).

50. Interview with Terre Lee Ruston (Apr. 24, 1986).

51. Chertok, note 2 above, at 54.

52. *Id.* at 37.

53. Lockport Corporation v. Protect Our Mountain Environment, No. 81CV973 (Dist. Ct., Jefferson County, Colo., filed Apr. 1, 1981).

54. Protect Our Mountain Environment v. District Court, 677 P.2d 1361, 1364, 1368–69 (Colo. 1984).

55. *Noble Meadow Drive Top Story of '94,* CANYON COURIER (Evergreen, Colo.), Dec. 28, 1994, at 1A; DiBattista, *Officials: Wal-Mart Should Be Open by End of Year, id.,* July 19, 1995, at 4A.

56. *Editorial, Open-Space Purchase Can Preserve Clear Creek Canyon,* DENVER POST, May 27, 1995; Garnaas, *Jeffco Moves to Save Canyon,* DENVER POST, Oct. 14, 1994; Hernandez, *Future Clears for 2 Landmarks,* ROCKY MOUNTAIN NEWS, Nov. 16, 1994; *Foes Hope to Crush Gravel Quarry Proposal,* HIGH COUNTRY NEWS, June 18, 1990, at 5.

57. Okun v. Superior Court, 29 Cal. 3d 442, 461, 175 Cal. Rptr. 157, 629 P.2d 1369, 1381 (Mosk, J., concurring in part and dissenting in part).

Chapter 4

1. Study Interview with Lora Fellin (Aug. 23, 1988).

2. Letter from Lora Fellin to Police Captain Joseph Kalivoda (Jan. 4, 1979).

3. Study Interview with William Welter (Aug. 23, 1988).

4. Letter from Frank T. Crivello Sr., First Assistant District Attorney, to Lora Fellin (Feb. 13, 1979).

5. Welter v. Fellin, No. 539–519 (Cir. Ct., Milwaukee County, Wis., filed Dec. 1980).

6. Study Interview with Robert Lerner (Aug. 1988).

7. Study Interview with Bill Kruger (Aug. 1988).

8. Study Interview with Ken Murray (Aug. 1988).

9. Grilli v. Reinartz, No. 634251 (Super. Ct., Santa Clara County, Cal., settled prior to trial 1989).

10. Villa v. Cole, 4 Cal. App. 4th 1327, 1331, 6 Cal. Rptr. 2d 644 (1992).

11. Defendant's Answer and Counterclaim at 3 (filed Feb. 1988), Jones v. Wurm, No. 88–134-33 (Dist. Ct., Hennepin County, Minn., case filed Jan. 21, 1988).

12. Complaint, *id.*

13. Letter from B. Stephen Miller III to co-author, Professor Pring (July 24, 1985), at 1.

14. Mayes v. Holloway, No. CV 181–3627CC (Cir. Ct., St. Charles County, Mo., filed Oct. 15, 1981).

15. Miller, note 13 above.

16. Flynn v. Chamberlain, No. 66069 (Com. Pleas Ct., Cuyahoga County, Ohio) (dismissed 1986).

17. Anderson v. McCabe, No. 80–637 (Super. Ct., Kent County, R.I., dismissed per stipulation March 17, 1981).

18. Moriarty v. Lippe (Com. Pleas Ct., Fairfield County, Conn.) (filed 1966), *rev'd in part and remanded in part,* 162 Conn. 371, 294 A.2d 326, 329 (1972).

19. *Id.*

20. Berkey v. Delia, 413 A.2d 170, 172 (Md. 1980).

21. Berkey v. Delia, No. 65-573 (Cir. Ct., Prince George's County, Md., summary judgment for defendant 1978), *rev'd and remanded,* 41 Md. App. 47, 395 A.2d 1189 (1978), *aff'd and remanded,* 287 Md. 302, 413 A.2d 170 (1980).

22. White v. Basnett, No. 61860 (Dist. Ct., Tulsa County, Okla., summary judgment for defendant 1981), *aff'd,* 700 P.2d 666 (Okla. App. 1985).

23. Strong v. Byers, No. 85-CP-10–1515 (Com. Pleas Ct., Charleston County, S.C., voluntarily dismissed Mar. 20, 1986).

24. Williams v. Yacknin, No. 22333 (Super. Ct., Wyoming County, N.Y. 1984).

25. Catalfamo v. The Florida Clearinghouse on Criminal Justice, No. CI-80–12156, (Cir. Ct., Orange County, Fla., directed verdict for defendants Oct. 12, 1983).

26. *Opinion, State Attacks a Watchdog for Justice,* ST. PETERSBURG TIMES, Oct. 8, 1983, at 18.

27. Cushman v. Day, No. A7805–07992 (Cir. Ct., Multnomah County, Ore., demurrer to second amended complaint sustained 1977), *rev'd and remanded,* 43 Or. App. 123, 602 P.2d 327 (1979), *on remand,* (voluntary dismissal and settlement 1982); Cushman v. Edgar, No. 7805–07990 (Cir. Ct., Multnomah County, Ore.) (demurrer to third amended complaint sustained 1979), *aff'd in part, rev'd in part and remanded,* 44 Or. App. 297, 605 P.2d 1210 (1980), *on remand* (dismissed per stipulation March 9, 1981).

28. Roche v. Egan (Super. Ct., Cumberland County, Me. 1977), *rev'd and remanded,* 433 A.2d 757 (Me. 1981) (settled on remand).

29. Miner v. Novotny, No. 12340/21/341 (Cir. Ct., Harford County, Md., dismissed 1983), *aff'd,* 60 Md. App. 124, 481 A.2d 508 (1984), *aff'd,* 304 Md. 164, 498 A.2d 269 (1985).

30. 481 A.2d at 511–13 (citations omitted).

31. California Civil Code § 47.5.

32. City of Long Beach v. Bozek, No. 32–50-47 (Super. Ct., Orange County, Cal., dismissed 1982), *aff'd,* 31 Cal.3d 527, 645 P.2d 137, 183 Cal. Rptr. 86 (1982), *vacated and remanded,* 459 U.S. 1095 (1983), *aff'd,* 33 Cal.3d 727, 661 P.2d 1072, 190 Cal. Rptr. 918 (1983).

33. 183 Cal. Rptr. at 87–93.

34. Telephone interview with Alan J. Azzara (June 1, 1989).

35. Granelli, *Police Sue to Silence Detractors,* NATIONAL LAW JOURNAL, June 9, 1980, at 16.

36. Friendly, *Public Figures and the Law on Libel,* NEW YORK TIMES, Nov. 10, 1982.

37. E. PELL, THE BIG CHILL at 184–88 (1984).

38. Granelli, note 35 above, at 3.

39. *Id.* at 16.

40. *Id.*

41. Spicer v. City of Dearborn, No. 83–306-939-CZ (Cir. Ct., Wayne County, Mich. 1985), *on removal,* No. 83–306-939-CZ (Dist. Ct., 19th Judicial Dist, Mich., dismissed Oct. 31, 1985). The SLAPP countercomplaint appears on letterhead of the city's Office of Corporation Counsel.

42. *E.g.,* Maryland Court of Appeals, 304 Md. 146, 498 A.2d 269, 274–75 (1985).

43. Bethke, *Cole v. Lehmann: Practical Reflections on a Teacher Slander Suit Against Parents,* in SLAPPs: STRATEGIC LAWSUITS AGAINST PUBLIC PARTICIPATION IN GOVERNMENT at 85 (ALI-ABA Course of Study Materials 1994).

44. Letter from William Martel to Milo R. White, Principal of Pioneer High School at 1 (Nov. 13, 1980), Exh. A to Complaint in Swenson-Davis v. Martel, No. 81–22048 N.Z. (Cir. Ct., Washtenaw County, Mich., summary judgment for defendant 1982), *aff'd,* 135 Mich. App. 632, 354 N.W.2d 288 (1984) (leave to appeal denied).

45. Brief of Plaintiff in Opposition to Motion of Ann Arbor School Dist. to Intervene at 1, *id.*

46. Brief of Defendant in Support of Sum. Jgmt. at 3, *id.*

47. Martel letter, note 44 above, at 2.

48. *Id.*

49. Fair Treatment Policy Hearing Jgmt; attached as Exh. C to Brief of Defendant in Support of Sum. Jgmt.

50. Plaintiff's Answer in Opposition to Ann Arbor School District's Motion to Intervene at 2.

51. Swenson-Davis v. Martel, note 44 above.

52. *Id.*

53. Motion of the School Dist. of the City of Ann Arbor to Intervene as a Party Defendant at ¶ 1.

54. Affidavit of Dr. Harry Howard, Superintendent of Ann Arbor School Dist, at ¶ 5.

55. 354 N.W.2d at 292 (citations omitted).

56. Nodar v. Galbreath, No. 8012287 (Cir. Ct., Broward County, Fla., jury verdict for plaintiff 1982), *aff'd*, 429 So. 2d 715 (Fla. Dist. Ct. App. 1983), *rev'd*, 462 So. 2d 803 (Fla. 1984).

57. "Transcript from Tape—Broward County School Board Meeting of May 15, 1980" at 1, Exh. A to Complaint, *id.*

58. *Id.* at 2.

59. Note 56 above.

60. Weissman v. Mogol, 118 Misc. 2d 911, 462 N.Y.S.2d 383 (Sup. Ct. Spec. Term, Nassau County, N.Y., partial summary judgment 1983).

61. 462 N.Y.S.2d at 387 (citation omitted).

62. Martin v. Kearney, No. 44647 (Super. Ct., Los Angeles County, Cal., dismissed 1975), *aff'd*, 51 Cal. App. 3d 309, 124 Cal. Rptr. 281 (1975).

63. One startling example is two separate votes of the U.S. Congress in 1868: In the first Congress overwhelmingly passed the Fourteenth Amendment, whose "Equal Protection" clause would be the basis for desegregating our schools in the twentieth century; in the second vote the same Congress set up a racially segregated public school system for the nation's capital. The D.C. public schools were still segregated (by federal government action) at the time of *Brown v. Board of Education;* see Bolling v. Sharpe, 347 U.S. 497 (1954), ordering them desegregated on the same day as *Brown.*

64. 163 U.S. 537 (1896).

65. 347 U.S. 483 (1954).

66. Stevens v. Tillman, 855 F.2d 394, 395 (7th Cir. 1988).

67. *Id.*

68. Stevens v. Tillman, 568 F. Supp. 289 (N.D. Ill.) (motion to dismiss denied 1983), 661 F. Supp. 702 (N.D. Ill., 1986), *aff'd*, 855 F.2d 394 (7th Cir. 1988).

69. 661 F. Supp. at 706–07.

70. 855 F.2d at 402.

71. *Id.* at 403.

72. *Id.* at 405.

73. Camiolo v. Fottler, No. 61576 (Super. Ct., Suffolk County, Mass., attachment order granted plaintiff 1983), *on removal*, No. 83–1637-G (D. Mass., summary judgment granted defendants 1984).

74. Letter to Roger Beattie, Superintendent (Feb. 24, 1983), Exh. A to Complaint, *id.*

75. For a thoughtful analysis from the filer's attorney's point of view, see Bethke, note 43 above.

76. Study Interview with Arlene Lehmann (July 6, 1988).

77. Bethke, note 43 above, at 88.

78. *Id.*

79. *Id.*

80. Study Interview with Bill Jack (June 23, 1988).

81. Bethke, note 43 above, at 89, 90.

82. DENVER POST, Sept. 5, 1985, at 3A.

83. Bethke, note 43 above, at 90–91.

84. *Id.* at 89.

85. Tinsley, *Adams Sets Rules on Teaching Controversial Subjects*, ROCKY MOUNTAIN NEWS, Oct. 22, 1985, at 32.

86. Bethke, note 43 above, at 89.

87. *Id.* at 91.

88. *Id.* at 93.

89. Connick v. Meyers, 461 U.S. 138 (1983), had just shocked the education establishment by holding that public employees could be fired even for truthful statements, if those statements did not rise to the level of a "public concern." This made many teachers feel that "if we, as teachers, can't express ourselves freely, why should we have to put up with outrageous complaints by parents?" Bethke, note 43 above, at 92.

90. Bethke, note 43 above, at 91–92.

91. Cole v. Lehman, No. 85CV2187 (Dist. Ct., Adams County, Colo., filed Sept. 1985).

92. Study Interview with Jan Cole (June 16, 1988).

93. Bethke, note 43 above, at 89–90.

94. Study Interview with William Bethke (June 29, 1988); *see also* Bethke, note 43 above, at 89 *et seq.*

95. Study Interview with Marlene Gresh (June 22, 1988).

96. Study Interview with Harold Hagan (June 28, 1988).

97. Bethke, note 43 above, at 95 *et seq.*

98. *Id.* at 95, 103. Before trial Bethke offered to settle the case without payment by the parents if they would publish an apology to the effect that "they had been misunderstood and had never accused Ms. Cole of the satanism and the like," but the parents refused. *Id.* at 95.

99. Study Interview with Sandy Montoya (June 20, 1988).

100. Bethke, note 43 above, at 95 *et seq.*

101. *Id.* at 96.

102. *Id.* at 93.

103. Stachura v. Truszkowski, Nos. 82–1575, 83–1344 & 83–1345 (U.S. Dist. Ct., E.D. Mich. 1983), *aff'd*, 763 F.2d 211 (6th Cir. 1985).

104. 763 F.2d at 213.

105. The Riverside Publishing Company, Inc. v. Bay Area Family Association, No. H 92–1527 (U.S. Dist. Ct., S.D.Tex., filed May 1992).

106. *Free Thought Imperiled, Panel of Experts Warns,* DENVER POST, Nov. 2, 1989, at 5A.

107. Culver, *Secular Humanism Foes Plan Rally,* DENVER POST, Sept. 16, 1989; *Editorial, Phony Reports of School Censorship Belittle Parental Role,* ROCKY MOUNTAIN NEWS, Sept. 1, 1989, at 64.

108. Covarrubias, *State Hit over Censorship Bids,* ROCKY MOUNTAIN NEWS, Aug. 30, 1989, at 26.

109. Culver, note 107 above.

110. *Id.*

111. Central Transportation, Inc. v. Stephens, Nos. 1978–2083 (Com. Pleas Ct., Cambria County, Pa., filed May 26, 1978; dismissed 1979).

112. Draft Brief of American Civil Liberties Union as Amicus Curiae in Support of Defendants at 1–2, *id.* (undated 1978).

113. Complaint at ¶ 6.

114. Unpublished Opinion and Order at 4 (original emphasis).

115. *Id.* at 5.

116. Board of Educ. of the Miami Trace School Dist. v. Marting, 7 Ohio Misc. 64, 217 N.E.2d 712 (Com. Pleas Ct., Madison County, dismissed 1966).

117. Roach v. The Rest of the Prairie, No. 70578-E (Dist. Ct., Potter County, Tex., voluntarily dismissed 1988).

118. Educational Ass'n of Worchester, Inc. v. Gustafson, No. 83–26769 (Super. Ct., Worchester County, Mass., voluntarily dismissed 1988).

119. *Letter to the Editor: Unions Impose "Tyranny" Over Teachers,* WORCHESTER [MASS.] EVENING GAZETTE, Oct. 5, 1983.

120. Jenkins v. Smith, No. 86–00269 (Com. Pleas Ct., Montgomery County, Pa., voluntarily dismissed May 19, 1988).

121. Hannagan, *Towamencin Admits Wrong,* THE REPORTER, Oct. 1985.

122. Shaw, *Montco Suit Alleges Slander During Meeting,* PHILADELPHIA INQUIRER, Jan 18, 1986.

123. *Id.*

124. *Id.*

125. Answer at 2.

126. Scicchitano, *Politician Drops Suit Against Citizen,* PHILADELPHIA INQUIRER, Sept. 26, 1987.

127. Gailey, *Jenkins Withdraws Civil Suit,* NORRISTOWN TIMES HERALD, Oct. 23, 1987.

128. Gibbons, *Towamencin Resident Sues Township Solicitor, id.,* Oct. 20, 1987.

129. *Id.*

130. Complaint at 4, Smith v. Jenkins, No. 87–6485 (E.D. Pa. filed Oct. 13, 1987).

131. Beard v. Vogt, No. 91–02-B6205CV (Dist. Ct., Brewster County, Tex., filed Feb. 4, 1991).

132. *Id.* (voluntarily dismissed Apr. 1, 1991).

133. Hawk v. Cooke, No. 77–569 (Com. Pleas Ct., Butler County, Pa., dismissed Oct. 16, 1979).

134. Cooper, *Slippery Rock Council Studies Pool Agreement,* ALLIED NEWS, May 10, 1977, at 2.

135. Corner v. Aversa, No. 2420/79 (Sup. Ct., Orange County, N.Y., summary judgment 1980), *aff'd,* No. 2420/79 (N.Y. App. Div. 1982).

136. Complaint at 12 (reprint of letter from Vincent Aversa to J. Garvey, Town Supervisor, Apr. 17, 1978).

137. Patane v. Griffin, 164 A.D.2d 192, 562 N.Y.S.2d 1005 (1990).

138. Vuyanich v. Locke, No. 433 (Com. Pleas Ct., Allegheny County, Pa., dismissed per stipulation Jan. 1983).

139. Defendant's Answer, New Matter and Counterclaim, *id.*

140. Cuddy, *N. Versailles Dissenter Wins $10,000 Settlement,* PITTSBURGH PRESS, April 21, 1983.

141. Bradley v. Computer Sciences Corp., No. 78–1893 (U.S. Dist. Ct., E.D. Va., directed verdict for defendant Oct. 18, 1978), *aff'd* 643 F.2d 1029 (4th Cir. 1981).

142. Letter from R. A. Horne to Chairman of N.H. Advisory Comm'n on Health and Welfare, appended to Complaint, Barry v. Horne, No. 967 (Sup. Ct., Hillsborough County, N.H., filed Mar. 14, 1974; jury verdict for defendant, Apr. 1978).

143. Keohane v. Lloyd (Dist. Ct., El Paso County, Colo., judgment on the pleadings 1992); Stewart v. Keohane (Colo. Ct. Aps. 1993); J. Sanko, *Court Upholds $20,000 Award in Defamation of Former Judge,* ROCKY MOUNTAIN NEWS, Apr. 9, 1993.

144. Botos v. Los Angeles County Bar Ass'n, No. C429207 (Super. Ct., Los Angeles County, Cal. dismissed 1983), *aff'd,* 151 Cal. App. 3d 1083, 199 Cal. Rptr. (1984).

145. No. 77W306 (U.S. Dist. Ct., D. Colo. filed Mar. 28, 1977).

146. 42 U.S.C. § 4321 *et seq.*

147. Complaint, note 145 above.

148. Study Interview with Alan Merson (Aug. 10, 1988).

149. Study Interview with Larry Reno (July 29, 1988).

150. Study Interview with Jack Ross (Aug. 4, 1988).

151. Study Interview with Edward Reutz (Aug. 9, 1988).

152. Settlement Agreement at unnumbered page 10 (Feb. 14, 1979).

153. Third Amendment to Complaint.

154. Fourth Amendment to Complaint.

155. As attorney for one of the target groups, co-author Professor Pring defended several at the deposition stage.

156. Study Interview with John Bermingham (July 28, 1988).

157. Study Interview with Robert Weaver (Aug. 1, 1988).

158. Note 152 above.

159. Brown, *Judge Refuses to Back Accord in Foothills Suits,* ROCKY MOUNTAIN NEWS, Feb. 1979.

160. City of Colorado Springs v. Bd. of County Comm'rs of Eagle County, No. 88-CV-142 (Dist. Ct., Eagle County, Colo., filed Mar. 16, 1988).

161. 1994 Westlaw 667741 (Colo. App. Nov. 17, 1994), rehearing denied (Colo. App. Dec. 15, 1994), cert. denied, No. 94SC765 (Colo. S.Ct. June 5, 1995).

162. San Joaquin Hills Transportation Corridor Agency v. The Laguna Greenbelt, Inc., CV 92–4156-LHM (U.S. Dist. Ct., S.D. Cal., dismissed Oct. 1992); Seager, *Agency's Alleged SLAPP Action Against Activists Thrown Out,* SAN FRANCISCO DAILY JOURNAL, Oct. 20, 1992.

163. LaPointe v. West Contra Costa Sanitary Dist., No. 295995 (Super Ct., Contra Costa County, Cal., filed May 2, 1988); see Chapman, *LaPointe v. West Contra Costa Sanitary District: A Successful First Amendment "SLAPPback" Brought Under 42 U.S.C. § 1983,* in SLAPPS: STRATEGIC LAWSUITS AGAINST PUBLIC PARTICIPATION IN GOVERNMENT at 155 (ALI-ABA Course of Study Materials 1994).

164. *E.g.,* Beaver, *Hidden Agenda Lurks in Burn Plant Suit,* WEST COUNTY TIMES, Mar. 1, 1988; *Burn Plant Stinks,* THE TRIBUNE, Mar. 7, 1988; Schutz, *State Will Support Taxpayer's Battle Against Sanitary District,* THE TRIBUNE, Apr. 15, 1988.

165. Greenwich Citizens Comm., Inc. v. Warren and Washington Counties, No. 9260C (Sup. Ct., Washington County, N.Y., filed Feb. 28, 1989).

166. E.g., Zweig, *A SLAPP in the Face,* FORBES, May 29, 1989; *Suing Citizens,* SUNDAY TIMES UNION (Albany, N.Y.), Apr. 23, 1989.

167. Board of County Comm'rs of Adams County v. Shroyer, No. 87CV0975 (Dist. Ct., Adams County, Colo., filed May 8, 1987), *removed,* 662 F. Supp 1542 (D. Colo. 1987) (motion to dismiss granted).

168. California Dept. of Fish and Game v. Mountain Lion Preservation Foundation, No. 501627 (Super. Ct., Sacramento County, Cal., dismissed 1988); Parker, *Trophy Hunt for Lions Is in Cold Blood,* INDEX-TRIBUNE, Mar. 1988; *Jumping the Gun,* LOS ANGELES TIMES, Apr. 17, 1988; *Editorial, State Lawsuit over Lion Hunt,* MARIN INDEPENDENT JOURNAL, Apr. 19, 1988.

169. *Cougar Attacks May Lead to Renewed Hunting in California,* NEW YORK TIMES, Oct. 18, 1995, at A12.

170. Missouri v. National Org. for Women, Inc., 620 F.2d 1301 (8th Cir. 1980), *cert. denied,* 449 U.S. 842 (1980).

171. NOW v. Ashcroft, No. 81–4094-CV-C-W (U.S. Dist. Ct., W.D. Mo. 1981).

172. San Luis Obispo County v. Abalone Alliance, No. 55664 (Super. Ct., San Luis Obispo County, Cal., filed Nov. 25, 1981; summary judgment 1985), *aff'd,* 178 Cal. App. 3d 848, 223 Cal. Rptr. 846 (1986); Anderson v. Abalone Alliance, No. 55664 (Super. Ct., San Luis Obispo County, Cal., filed Aug. 17, 1984; summary judgment for defendants Jan. 22, 1986).

173. Professor Pring filed a friend-of-the-court brief urging dismissal on behalf of the Bar Association of San Francisco, the League of Women Voters, and the Sierra Club.

Chapter 5

1. R. CARSON, SILENT SPRING (1962).

2. *See* COUNCIL ON ENVIRONMENTAL QUALITY, ENVIRONMENTAL QUALITY—1979: THE TENTH ANNUAL REPORT 1 *et seq.* (1980); for an excellent bibliography on the environmental movement's "seeds" or "roots," see PLATER, ABRAMS & GOLDFARB, ENVIRONMENTAL LAW AND POLICY: NATURE, LAW, AND SOCIETY at "Reference" pages 16–23 (1992).

3. 42 U.S.C. § 4321 *et seq.*

4. *Note, Counterclaim and Countersuit Harassment of Private Environmental Plaintiffs: The Problem, Its Implications, and Proposed Solutions,* 74 MICHIGAN LAW REVIEW 106 (1975).

5. *Id.* at 106. Public participation laws and opportunities are discussed in Chapter 2.

6. Comment, note 4 above; T. HOBAN & R. BROOKS, GREEN JUSTICE: THE ENVIRONMENT AND THE COURTS (1987).

7. J. SAX, DEFENDING THE ENVIRONMENT 63 (1970); Feller, DiMento, and related articles from Chapter 2.

8. *See* Berry, *The "Environmental" SLAPP,* in SLAPPS: STRATEGIC LAWSUITS AGAINST PUBLIC PARTICIPATION IN GOVERNMENT at 61 (ALI-ABA Course of Study Materials 1994). For other elements of the backlash, see D. DAY, THE ENVIRONMENTAL WARS: REPORTS FROM THE FRONT LINES (1989). We distinguish environmental issues from the NIMBY issues of Chapter 6—although they are very closely related—by classing as "environmental" those having impact beyond a single neighborhood or community.

9. Pring and Miller, *Wilderness and Natural Area Preservation in the United States: A Survey of National Laws,* in PROCEEDINGS OF THE SINO-AMERICAN CONFERENCE ON ENVIRONMENTAL LAW (U.Colo. Law Sch. 1989).

10. The Wilderness Act of 1964, 16 U.S.C. § 1131 *et seq.*

11. 349 F. Supp. 934 (N.D. Cal. 1972).

12. *Id.*

13. Cross-complaint ¶ 6.

14. Plaintiff Sierra Club's Memorandum in Support of Motion to Dismiss Counterclaim (F.R.C.P. 12(b)(6)) at 3 (July 18, 1972).

15. *Id.* at 4, 6. The Santa Barbara oil spill had occurred only two years before, and the SST ("supersonic transport" plane) was still the topic of great environmental resistance.

16. 349 F. Supp. at 936.

17. *Id.* at 936, 937.

18. Golden Bear Forest Products, Inc. v. Sierra Club, No. 195749 (Super. Ct., San Bernadino County, Cal., demurrer overruled, Oct. 8, 1981), *writ of mandate denied sub. nom.* Sierra Club v. Superior Court (Ct. Apps., 4th App. Dist.), *dismissed on remand for want of prosecution.* After a grueling five years in court, the $11,000,000 SLAPP was dismissed "for lack of prosecution" by the filer—and small wonder, for by then the timber was cut.

19. City of Angoon v. Hodel, No. A83–234 Civ. (U.S. Dist. Ct., D. Alaska., dismissed Jan. 5, 1987); *aff'd,* 836 F.2d 1245 (9th Cir. 1988). For excellent, if highly pro-environmental, background, see *The Tongass National Forest: Under Seige,* INNER VOICE (a publication of the Ass'n of U.S. Forest Service Employees for Environmental Ethics, Eugene, Ore.), Winter 1990.

20. Answer and Counterclaim of Arizona River Runners, Inc. at 5, 6 (July 6, 1978), Grand Canyon Nat'l Park v. Stitt, No. Civ.-77–722-PHX-WEC (U.S. Dist. Ct., D. Ariz.). The U.S. District Court promptly dismissed the SLAPP counterclaim (Sept. 26, 1978), and the Sierra Club went on to win a more environmental plan for the river.

21. Ass'n to Save the Savage Rapids Dam and Lake, Inc. v. Natural Resources Council of Oregon, No. C14–6111-CD (U.S. Dist. Ct., D. Ore., filed Mar. 16, 1994).

22. Sierra Club v. Hodel, 848 F.2d 1068 (10th Cir. 1988). The federal trial and appeals courts made short work of the SLAPP, but they let the road construction go ahead.

23. SBP Corp. v. Sierra Club, No. 94-11903 (Dist. Ct., El Paso County, Tex., filed Nov. 2, 1994).

24. Small, but for grand principles: The hotel was in the protected "coastal zone," and the club used it as a test case to beef up the Coastal Commission's environmental review process; the court of appeals finally dismissed the Sierra Club on technical grounds. Reed v. Sierra Club, No. 810836 (Super. Ct., San Francisco County, Cal., dismissal denied 1984), *vacated sub nom.*, Sierra Club v. Superior Court, 168 Cal. App. 3d 1138, 214 Cal. Rptr. 740 (1985).

25. The novel that inspired the eco-guerrilla movement is E. ABBEY, THE MONKEY WRENCH GANG (1975). Modern assessments of the movement include R. SCARCE, ECO-WARRIORS: UNDERSTANDING THE RADICAL ENVIRONMENTAL MOVEMENT (1990); D. HELVARG, THE WAR AGAINST THE GREENS: THE "WISE-USE" MOVEMENT, THE NEW RIGHT, AND ANTI-ENVIRONMENTAL VIOLENCE (1994).

26. Willamette Industries, Inc. v. Cathedral Forest Action Group, No. 84–1039 (Cir. Ct., Linn County, Ore., Dec. 5, 1985).

27. The Petition Clause provides the same protection to peaceful demonstrations, picketing, and boycotts designed to influence government action as it does the more conventional forms of lobbying. McDonald v. Smith, 472 U.S. 479, 488–90 (1985) (Brennan, J., concurring).

28. Walti v. Willamette Industries, Inc., No. A8512–07799 (Cir. Ct., Multnomah County, Ore., filed Dec. 12, 1985).

29. Quoted in Cockburn, *Beat the Devil*, THE NATION, July 16–23, 1990, at 79.

30. THE LAND TRUST ALLIANCE, STARTING A LAND TRUST: A GUIDE TO FORMING A LAND CONSERVATION ORGANIZATION (1990); MONTANA LAND RELIANCE, ed., PRIVATE OPTIONS: TOOLS AND CONCEPTS FOR LAND CONSERVATION (1982).

31. Lange v. The Nature Conservancy, Inc., 24 Wash. App. 416, 601 P.2d 963 (1979).

32. Lake Minnewaska Mountain Houses v. Lehman, No. 88-CV-0685 (U.S. Dist. Ct., N.D.N.Y., filed June 20, 1988).

33. Dively v. City of Pacific Grove, No. 90201 (Super. Ct., Monterey County, Cal., filed May 4, 1990).

34. Jenkins, *Contempt Bid in Jeffco Board Jail Campaign Refused*, DENVER POST, Mar. 10, 1981.

35. Baker v. Bray, No. 76-M-277 (U.S. Dist. Ct., D. Colo., partial temporary restraining order granted, Oct. 20 1980).

36. Brief of Appellants at 7, Appeal Nos. 80–2237, 81–1371 (10th Cir., June 5, 1981).

37. *E.g.*, the Clean Air Act, 42 U.S.C. § 7604; the Clean Water Act, 33 U.S.C. § 1365; the Resource Conservation and Recovery Act, 42 U.S.C. § 6972.

38. Helvarg, note 25 above.

39. 282 S.E.2d 28 (W. Va. 1981).

40. Franklin, *Coal Mining Company Sues Its Environmentalist Critics*, NEW YORK TIMES, Aug. 11, 1980, at A16.

41. Letter from Rick Webb to Jack Schramm, Regional Administrator, U.S. Environmental Protection Agency, Region III, at 1 (Oct. 12, 1979).

42. Franklin, note 40 above.

43. 282 S.E.2d 28 (W. Va. 1981).

44. Hodel, *Coal Firm's Libel Suit Ploy to Halt Protest, Group Says*, CHARLESTON [W. VA.] SUNDAY GAZETTE-MAIL, Sept. 21, 1980, at 1B.

45. Franklin, note 40 above.

46. *Id.*

47. Hodel, note 44 above.

48. 282 S.E.2d at 33–34 (citations omitted).

49. *Id.* at 37: "West Virginia's constitutional provisions respecting the right to petition

warrant that we give even greater room for activities alleged to be protected by the right. Our constitution not only expressly guarantees the right to petition under . . . article III, section 16, but article III, section 2 provides: 'All power is vested in, and consequently derived from the people. Magistrates are their trustees and servants and at all times amenable to them.' Moreover, article III, section 3 reserves to the people an 'inalienable and indefeasible right to reform, alter or abolish [the government]. . . . ' Thus, while the United States Constitution guarantees to the people the right to petition all branches of government, the West Virginia Constitution also gives the people the right to 'reform, alter or abolish' it."

50. *Id.* at 46.

51. *Pollution Wars: A Lawsuit that Turns Tables,* TIME, Aug. 25, 1980, at 44.

52. For example, in 1987 a Tennessee coal company sued local environmentalists for $350,000 for the legally authorized and encouraged activities of filing federal and state government hearing requests, complaints, and inspection demands and for testifying at government hearings against the coal mine; the SLAPP was dismissed. Ferguson v. Save Our Cumberland Mountains, No. 906 (Cir. Ct., Bledsoe County, Tenn., filed Oct. 1987). A yoga religious retreat in Michigan, accused of polluting a river, sued the state and environmentalists, claiming that the latter "actively interfered with the [government's] decision making process" by testifying against it; the following year, the ashram caved in, paid its state fines, cleaned up, and dismissed the SLAPP. Golden Lotus, Inc. v. Michigan Dept. of Natural Resources, No. 68–2802-AA (Cir. Ct., Ostego County, Mich.) (filed Sept. 18, 1984).

53. J. EGGEN, TOXIC TORTS IN A NUTSHELL (1995) is a good starting reference.

54. *Id.;* ENVIRONMENTAL DEFENSE FUND, MALIGNANT NEGLECT (1979); Meyer, *The Environmental Fate of Toxic Wastes, the Certainty of Harm, Toxic Torts, and Toxic Regulation,* 19 ENVIRONMENTAL LAW 321 (1988); DeBoskey, *Non-Ionizing Radiation: Hidden Hazards,* TRIAL, Aug. 1990, at 32.

55. Shell Oil Co. v. Leonardini, Civ. S. 81–523 (LKK) (U.S. Dist. Ct., E.D. Cal., dismissed May 10, 1982).

56. United States v. Environmental Waste Control, Inc., No. 5800055 (U.S. Dist. Ct., N.D. Ind., counterclaim filed May 31, 1988).

57. Maine Yankee Atomic Power Co. v. Maine Nuclear Referendum Committee, No. CV-82–487 (Super. Ct., Kennebec County, Me., summary judgment for defendants Jan. 18, 1983).

58. Zak, *Courts Still Lax on Animal Abuse,* ROCKY MOUNTAIN NEWS, July 12, 1990.

59. O'Connell, *Animal-Rights Activists Caught in Own Trap,* ROCKY MOUNTAIN NEWS, Aug. 7, 1991, at 53.

60. *See* SCARCE, note 25 above; Editorial, *What Humans Owe to Animals,* THE ECONOMIST, Aug. 19, 1995, at 11.

61. *See* D. DAY, THE ENVIRONMENTAL WARS (1989), for an extreme view of the "assassins and martyrs" of the animal-protection "wars."

62. Harrowe, *Getting It Straight,* FUR AGE WEEKLY, Feb. 10, 1986.

63. *"Fur-Free Friday"—No News Is Good News,* in FUR IS FOR LIFE—CONFIDENTIAL LETTER I:9 (newsletter of the Fur Retailers Information Council), Dec. 1987.

64. Searle v. Johnson, No. 7915 (Dist. Ct., Uintah County, Utah, filed Feb. 14, 1976), *rev'd and remanded,* 646 P.2d 682 (Utah 1982), *on remand* (summary judgment order), *aff'd,* 709 P.2d 328 (Utah 1985).

65. 646 P.2d at 683.

66. *Id.*

67. Third Amended Complaint ¶ 14, ¶ 15.

68. 646 P.2d at 689.

69. Adler, *Boston Aquarium Countersues Activists,* WALL STREET JOURNAL, Sept. 18, 1991,

at B6. For a positive view of aquariums, see Smith, *A New Wave of Aquariums Brings the Ocean Ashore*, SMITHSONIAN, Dec. 1994, at 50.

70. Adler, note 69 above.

71. Telephone interview with Don Vincent, Chief Financial Officer of The New England Aquarium (June 20, 1995).

72. Dienes v. Assoc. Newspapers, Inc. (Cir. Ct., Wayne County, Mich.) (one target granted summary judgment, June 10, 1983; others dismissed on vol. settlement, 1988), *aff'd*, 358 N.W.2d 562, 137 Mich. App. 272 (1984).

73. *Id.* at 564 (quoting TV news interview).

74. Telephone Interview with Sienna La Rene, house counsel for the Humane Society (June 6, 1989); per the court order the amount of the settlement was not disclosed by any parties or representatives.

75. *Id.*

76. Friends of Animals, Inc. v. Connecticut Trappers Ass'n, Inc., No. H-81-183 (U.S. Dist. Ct., D. Conn., filed Mar. 17, 1981); No. H-81–242 (U.S. Dist. Ct., D. Conn., filed Mar. 20, 1981).

77. *Id.*, complaint at 2, in H-81–242 (Mar. 20, 1981).

78. *Id.* at 3.

79. Connecticut Trappers Ass'n, Inc. v. Friends of Animals, No. H-82–302 (U.S. Dist. Ct., D. Conn., filed Mar. 22, 1982).

80. *Press Release Issued by Agreement of the Parties* (in Connecticut Trappers case), Dec. 1985.

81. Oregonians Against Trapping v. Martin, No. A8012–06768 (Cir. Ct., Multnomah County, Ore., dismissed Dec. 1982).

82. Defendants' Trial Memorandum at 1 (Nov. 1982).

83. Second Amended Complaint, ¶ III (Nov. 9, 1982).

84. Hentoff, *A Very Expensive Letter to the Editor*, VILLAGE VOICE, Feb. 13, 1990.

85. Lewis, *Abusing the Law*, NEW YORK TIMES, May 10, 1991, at A31.

86. Deposition of Shirley McGreal at 342 (1985); Lewis, note 85 above.

87. Letter from Shirley McGreal to author, Professor Pring (Jan. 12, 1987).

88. Hentoff, *The Quicksands of Libel*, WASHINGTON POST, Apr. 1, 1989; Lewis, note 85 above.

89. Order, No. 23545/84 (Sup. Ct., New York County, N.Y., Aug. 6, 1987).

90. Immuno A.G. v. Moor-Jankowski, 145 App. Div. 2d 114, 537 N.Y.S.2d 129, 134, 137, 138 (1989).

91. 537 N.Y.S.2d at 141, 146, 147.

92. *Id.* at 147.

93. 74 N.Y.2d 548, 555, 556, 558, 560, 561 (1989).

94. International Primate Protection League, NEWSLETTER 16:1 (Mar. 1989).

95. Lewis, note 85 above.

96. Hodgins Kennels v. Durbin, 429 N.W.2d 189, 191 (Mich. App. 1988).

97. Second Amended Complaint ¶ 13, Hodgins Kennels, Inc. v. Durbin, No. 81 112 149 CZ (Cir. Ct., Wayne County, Mich., filed Oct. 1982).

98. Blight, *Letter to the Editor*, LIVINGSTON COUNTY PRESS, Sept. 10, 1980.

99. *Id.*

100. *Id.*

101. Hodgins Kennels, Inc. v. Durbin, No. 81 112 149 CZ (Cir. Ct., Wayne County, Mich. 1982), *rev'd and remanded*, 429 N.W.2d 189 (Mich. App. 1988).

102. Second Amended Complaint at ¶ 29–42.

103. Letter from Mary Lou Durbin at 3 (Oct. 1985).

104. Pfaff, *Shattered Lives: Fight for Strays Costs Dearly,* DETROIT NEWS, Jan. 22, 1980, at 5A.

105. *Id.*

106. *Id.*

107. *Id.*

108. *Id.*

109. Hodgins v. Times-Herald Co., No. 0–83-14–456 CZ (Cir. Ct., St. Clair County, Mich., default judgment against target Jan. 6, 1986), *aff'd,* 169 Mich. App. 245, 425 N.W.2d 522 (1988).

110. Form letter from Nancy L. Kahn (Mar. 16, 1988).

111. Form letter from Murdaugh Stuart Madden, Vice-President and General Counsel, Humane Society of the United States (Sept. 1, 1988).

112. Pfaff, note 104 above.

113. *Id.*

Chapter 6

1. Crim, *The NIMBY Syndrome in the 1990s: Where Do You Go After Getting to "NO"?* BNA ENVIRONMENT REPORTER, CURRENT DEVELOPMENTS 132 (May 4, 1990); Mank, *The Two-Headed Dragon of Siting and Cleaning Up Hazardous Waste Dumps: Can Economic Incentives or Mediation Slay the Monster?* 19 BOSTON COLLEGE ENVIRONMENTAL AFFAIRS LAW REVIEW 239 (1991); Greenberger, *Nuclear Waste and the NIMBY Syndrome,* 128 PUBLIC UTILITY FORTNIGHTLY (Nov. 1, 1991); Walters, *Finding Sites for Unsavory Facilities Is Harder Than Ever,* LOS ANGELES DAILY JOURNAL, Mar. 18, 1991.

2. DYG, INC., PUBLIC ATTITUDES TOWARD SITING RESIDENCES FOR PEOPLE WITH CHRONIC MENTAL ILLNESS (study conducted for the Robert Wood Johnson Foundation, June 19, 1990); for permission to reference this work, we are grateful to Madelyn Hochstein and DYG, Inc., Elmsford, N.Y., and Miles Shore of the Robert Wood Johnson Foundation. *See also* Canan, *Environmental Disputes in Changing Urban Political Economies: A Dynamic Research Approach,* in 12 STUDIES IN LAW, POLITICS AND SOCIETY 287–308 (eds. A. Sarat & S. Silbey 1992).

3. Allen v. Bolton, No. 583974–0 (Super. Ct., Alameda County, Cal., filed Apr. 11, 1984).

4. Bell v. Mazza, 394 Mass. 176, 474 N.E.2d 1111 (1985).

5. 474 N.E.2d at 1113.

6. Complaint ¶ 27(b), Bell v. Mazza, No. 139356 (Sup. Ct., Norfolk County, Mass., filed Mar. 29, 1983).

7. 474 N.E.2d at 1116.

8. County of Butte v. Bach, 172 Cal. App. 3d 848, 218 Cal. Rptr. 613 (1985).

9. *E.g.,* Cantwell v. Connecticutt, 310 U.S. 296 (1940); West Virginia State Bd. of Educ. v. Barnette, 319 U.S. 624 (1943); Thomas v. Review Bd., 450 U.S. 707 (1981); Wooley v. Maynard, 430 U.S. 705 (1977).

10. Parker Congregation of Jehovah's Witnesses v. Douglas County, No. 87-CV-653 (Dist. Ct., Douglas County, Colo., targets voluntarily dismissed Dec. 22, 1987).

11. 626 F.2d 607 (8th Cir. 1980).

12. *Id.* at 615.

13. *Id.* at 611.

14. *Id.* at 615.

15. Salsich, *Group Homes, Shelters, and Congregate Housing: Deinstitutionalization Policies and the NIMBY Syndrome,* 21 REAL PROPERTY, PROBATE AND TRUST JOURNAL 413, 416–17 (1986).

16. Study Interview with a REDI representative (July 6, 1988), who agreed to be interviewed only if not identified by name. The representative was the key decision-maker on the

filer side, attracted much of the enmity of the neighbors, and continues to work for housing for the mentally ill in Denver.

17. Study Interview with Richard Miles (June 3, 1988).

18. Study Interview with Anne Coomer Smith (June 20, 1988).

19. *Id.*

20. Miles, note 17 above.

21. Study Interview with Wavia Tullar (June 7, 1988).

22. Smith, interview, note 18 above.

23. Study Interview with Robert Hoghaug, REDI attorney (June 29, 1988).

24. Study Interview with Mark Hannen, REDI trial attorney (July 11, 1988).

25. The zoning administrator crossed "group home" off the application and substituted "institution," even though the board's definition of the former expressly included mental illness facilities, and the latter did not.

26. Hearing Transcript, Board of Adjustment, at 42 (Apr. 9, 1985); Affidavit of Ronald R. Kuhn, Acting Technical Secretary, Board of Adjustment (Sept. 19, 1985).

27. Adult Blind Home, Inc. v. Board of Adjustment, No. 85CV5385 (Dist. Ct., Denver City/County, Colo., filed May 7, 1985).

28. Study Interview with Dorothy Nepa, city and county zoning administrator (June 1, 1988).

29. Study Interview with Gil Goldstein, targets' trial attorney (June 28, 1988).

30. Study Interview with Shirley Schlay, city council aide (July 12, 1988).

31. Telephone interview with Richard Miles (June 10, 1985).

32. *Id.* Filers' legal fees ran slightly over $8,000, according to their attorney, Robert Hoghaug.

33. Study Interview with Don Koza (July 8, 1988).

34. Miles, interview, note 17 above.

35. Romano, *Building Controversy Quietly Ends,* ROCKY MOUNTAIN NEWS, July 27, 1987.

36. *Id.*

37. *Id.*

38. Scott v. Greenville County (U.S. Dist. Ct., D. S.C., summary judgment for defendants 1982), *aff'd in part, rev'd in part and remanded,* 716 F.2d 1409 (4th Cir. 1983).

39. *Id.* at 1412.

40. *Id.* at 1424.

41. 467 F. Supp. 803 (S.D.N.Y. 1979).

42. *Id.* at 807.

43. *Id.* at 817.

44. *Id.* at 818 (footnote omitted).

45. *Id.*

46. *Id.*

47. *Id.* (footnote omitted).

48. Complaint ¶ 15, King v. Levin, No. 84 L 11047 (Cir. Ct., Cook County, Ill., filed 1984; directed verdict for target 1987); *aff'd,* 184 Ill. App. 3d 557, 540 N.E.2d 492 (1989).

49. Letter from Paul Levin to Patricia Flider, [State] Housing Development Officer (Apr. 9, 1984), Exh. 3 to Plaintiff's Memorandum in Opposition to Defendant's Motion for Summary Judgment (Apr. 6, 1987).

50. Complaint, The Tara Circle, Inc. v. Bifano, No. 95 Civ.—(U.S. Dist. Ct., S. Dist. N.Y., filed Aug. 17, 1995), at 1, 2, 19–20.

51. Phillips v. Trello, No. 72–622 (U.S. Dist. Ct., W.D. Pa., dismissed for failure to prosecute 1979); Matossian v. Fahmie, No. 44033 (Super. Ct., Alameda County, Cal., dismissed 1978), *aff'd,* 101 Cal. App. 3d 128, 161 Cal. Rptr. 532 (1980).

52. Aknin v. Phillips, 404 F. Supp. 1150 (S.D.N.Y. 1975), *aff'd*, 538 F.2d 307 (2d Cir. 1976).

53. Blank v. Kirwan, No. 32012 (Super. Ct., Los Angeles County, Cal., dismissed 1982), *aff'd in part, rev'd in part*, 160 Cal. App. 3d 23, 206 Cal. Rptr. 308 (1984), *aff'd*, 39 Cal. 3d 311, 216 Cal. Rptr. 718, 703 P.2d 58 (1985).

54. Markowitz v. Fisher, No. 83–314-545-CZ (Cir. Ct., Wayne County, Mich., dismissed per stipulation 1983).

55. Ford v. Interstate Racing Ass'n., No. 87CV92 (Dist. Ct., Adams County, Colo., motion to dismiss denied 1987), *petition for relief denied*, No. 87SA209 (Colo. Sup. Ct. 1987), *on remand to trial ct.* (motion for preliminary injunction denied and settled).

56. Exh. A to Defendants' Motion to Dismiss the Complaint (June 15, 1982), Myers v. Plan Takoma, Inc., No. CA 3758–82 (Super. Ct., Dist. of Columbia, filed 1982).

57. Exh. 1 to Complaint, Ross Investment Corp. v. The Northeast Community Organization, No. 80122812/22500 (Super. Ct., Baltimore County, Md., filed May 1, 1980).

58. *Id.*

59. Letter from Mark J. Adams at 1 (July 17, 1985).

60. *Id.*

61. *E.g.*, D.C. CODE ANN. 25–115(a)(6) (1991).

62. Gottlieb, *Liquor-License Renewal Hearings on Shaky Ground, Lawyer Claims*, DENVER POST, July 30, 1989.

63. *Id.*

64. *Id.*

65. Leinwand, *Organic Dump Roils Pines Neighborhood*, MIAMI HERALD, Mar. 4, 1992, at 1BR.

66. Grimm, *Suits Camouflage Brute Intimidation*, MIAMI HERALD, Aug. 16, 1992.

67. *Id.*

68. Complaint, Organic Recycling System, Inc. v. Vardaman, No. 92–03585 (Cir. Ct., Broward County, Fla., filed Feb. 6, 1992).

69. Grimm, note 66 above.

70. *Id.*

71. Ross, *"Not In My Back Yard" Reaction Greets Traveling Incinerator*, THE STATE (Columbia, S.C.), Sept. 4, 1988. For a detailed report on this case—including *the first comic strip about SLAPPs*—see, Speart, *When Citizens SLAPP Back!* NATIONAL WILDLIFE, June/July 1994, at 12.

72. *Id.*

73. Sommer, *Letter to the Editor—Public Hearing to Decide Fate of Bunker Resources*, QUAD COUNTY STAR (Viburnum, Mo.), Oct. 27, 1987.

74. Ganey, *Woman Who Wrote To Paper About Incinerator Is Sued for Libel*, ST. LOUIS POST-DISPATCH, Feb. 1, 1988.

75. DeCom Medical Waste Systems, Inc. v. Tanner, No. 87–0219C (U.S. Dist. Ct., E.D. Mo., filed Dec. 2, 1987); DeCom Medical Waste Systems, Inc. v. Alexander, No. 87–2282-C-3 (U.S. Dist. Ct., E.D. Mo., filed Dec. 15, 1987).

76. Letter from Gail Gandy, President, DeCom Medical Waste Systems, Inc. (Feb. 9, 1988).

77. Ganey, *Incinerator Firm's Gifts Irk Legislators*, ST. LOUIS POST-DISPATCH, Mar. 16, 1988.

78. *Senators Berate Disposal Firm over Libel Suit, id.*, Feb. 2, 1988.

79. *Choking Off Debate, id.*, Feb. 3, 1988.

80. Englehardt, Editorial Cartoon, *id.*, Feb. 5, 1988.

81. *Editorial, Caught Playing the Game;* and Englehardt, Editorial Cartoon, *id.*, Mar. 17, 1988.

82. *E.g.*, Gest, *A Chilling Flurry of Lawsuits*, U.S. NEWS & WORLD REPORT, May 23, 1988.

83. Ross, note 71 above.

84. Perlstein, *Environmental Concern Stirs Plaquemines,* NEW ORLEANS TIMES-PICAYUNE, Mar. 26, 1987.

85. Nauth, *La. Ranks Among Worst in U.S. Pollution Study, id.,* Feb. 24, 1988.

86. *Empire Meeting Airs Waste Problems,* WATCHMAN (Plaquemines, La.), Mar. 3, 1987.

87. Perlstein, *Permit for Myrtle Grove Plant Brings About a Legal Brouhaha,* NEW ORLEANS TIMES-PICAYUNE, May 10, 1988.

88. *Empire,* note 86 above.

89. *Williams to Address Parish Council on Proposed Plaquemines Waste Dump,* WATCHMAN (Plaquemines, La.), Jan. 20, 1987.

90. Transcript, Public Hearings of Office of Conservation, Louisiana Department of Natural Resources, at Buras, La. (Apr. 17, 1987).

91. Perlstein, note 87 above.

92. Perlstein, *Permit Provokes Protest,* NEW ORLEANS TIMES-PICAYUNE, Mar. 11, 1988.

93. Perlstein, *Oilfield Waste Disposal Idea Has New Twist, id.,* Mar. 20, 1988.

94. Delta Environmental Services, Inc. v. LaFrance, No. 31–611 (25th Jud. Dist. Ct., Plaquemines Parish, La., filed Apr. 25, 1988; order denying relief May 13, 1988).

95. Perlstein, note 87 above.

96. *Id.*

97. See Complaint ¶ 22–27, Delta Environmental Service, Inc. v. Plaquemines Parish Government, No. 88–3678 (U.S. Dist. Ct., E.D. La., filed Aug. 19, 1988).

98. *Id.*

99. Delta Environmental Services, Inc. v. Williams, No. 368–029 (24th Jud. Dist. Ct., Jefferson Parish, La., filed Aug. 19, 1988).

100. Complaint ¶ 5, *id.*

101. *Id.* ¶ 6.

102. Perlstein, *Company Files Suit in Battle over Waste Treatment Plant,* NEW ORLEANS TIMES-PICAYUNE, Aug. 27, 1988.

103. *Id.*

104. Statement by Lois Marie Gibbs, Executive Director, CCHW (Oct. 6, 1988).

105. *E.g.,* the politico SLAPPs by Warren and Washington Counties in New York, and the sewer district suit against Alan La Pointe in California (Chapter 4).

106. Nichols, *Firms SLAPPing Down Critics,* DALLAS MORNING NEWS, May 5, 1991, at 45A.

107. *Id.*

108. C. S. McCrossan, Inc. v. Poucher, No. 9116554 (Dist. Ct., Hennepin County, Minn., filed 1991); *dism. aff'd,* No. C5–92-369 (Minn. Ct. Aps. 1992).

109. Sechan Limestone Industries, Inc. v. Slippery Rock Creek Clean Water, Inc., No. 84–488 (Com. Pleas Ct., Butler County, Pa., filed 1984); Landfill Assocs. Inc. v. Town of Hamden, No. N82–610 (U.S. Dist. Ct., D. Conn., dismissed per stipulation 1983).

110. Gregg v. Murden Cove Preservation Ass'n, No. 82–2-00380–0 (Super. Ct., Kitsap County, Wash., dismissed 1983).

111. Gelman Sciences, Inc. v. Gibson, No. 88–35 482 CZ (Cir. Ct., Washtenau County, Mich., voluntarily dismissed 1988). Ironically, the factory manufactures pollution control equipment.

112. Streif v. Bovinette, No. 79-CH-20 (Cir. Ct., St. Clair County, Ill., injunction order Feb. 23, 1979), *rev'd,* 88 Ill. App. 3d 1079, 411 N.E.2d 341 (1980).

113. Milner v. Baran, No. 87CV89 (Dist. Ct., Clear Creek County, Colo., counterclaim filed Dec. 9, 1987).

114. Miller and Son Paving, Inc. v. Wrightstown Twsp. Civic Ass'n, 443 F. Supp. 1268 (E.D. Pa. 1978), *aff'd mem.,* 595 F.2d 1213 (3d Cir.), *cert. denied,* 444 U.S. 843 (1979).

115. Maryland Wyatt, Inc. v. Perpetual-Springhill Associates, No. 92 CV 0930 (Cir. Ct., Wicomico County, Md., filed 1992).

116. Moonlite Reader v. Town of Salem, No. 91-E-463 (Sup. Ct., Rockingham County, N.H., filed Sept. 12, 1991; target dismissed Oct. 4, 1991).

Chapter 7

1. C. McCarry, Citizen Nader (1972); R. de Toledano, Hit and Run: The Rise—and Fall?—of Ralph Nader (1975); A. Best, When Consumers Complain (1981); P. Asch, Consumer Safety Regulation: Putting a Price on Life and Limb (1988); Y. Rosmarin, Sales of Goods and Services (1989).

2. See Galanter, *Why the "Haves" Come Out Ahead: Speculations on the Limits of Legal Change,* 9 Law & Society Review 95 (1974).

3. Park Knoll Associates v. Schmidt, No. 20040/80 (Sup. Ct. Westchester County, N.Y., targets' third motion to dismiss denied Sept. 30, 1981), *rev'd,* 89 App. Div. 2d 164 (1982), *rev'd,* 59 N.Y.2d 205, 451 N.E.2d 182, 464 N.Y.S.2d 424 (1983), *modified on remand,* 472 N.Y.S.2d 19 (Sup. Ct. 1984), (finally mooted only by the death of the target).

4. Smith v. Silvey, No. C392008 (Super. Ct., Los Angeles County, Cal., injunction granted against target Jan. 4, 1982), *rev'd,* 149 Cal. App. 3d 400, 197 Cal. Rptr. 15 (1983) (a leading California case pro-target).

5. Edelstein v. Friedlander, No. 21537/87, (Sup. Ct., Kings County, N.Y., filed June 8, 1987). Targets founded New York City anti-SLAPP organization, "Citizens Against Harassing Lawsuits." *Tenant Group Organized to Fight Landlord Suits,* Manhattan Lawyer, Sept. 19, 1988.

6. Klorman v. Schleissner (Sup. Ct., New York County, N.Y., filed Apr. 14, 1982; followed by pretrial settlement); Demers v. Meuret (Cir. Ct., Jefferson County, Ore., dismissed 1972), *rev'd and remanded,* 512 P.2d 1348 (Ore. 1973) (airplane owner sued for telling city that its airport operator was a "terrible, mean, demented old man . . . [who] might come out and chop our airplanes up with an axe").

7. Bass v. Rohr, No. 1103642 (Cir. Ct., Anne Arundel County, Md., directed verdict for target Mar. 28, 1983), *aff'd,* 57 Md. App. 609, 471 A.2d 752 (1984), *cert. dism.* 301 Md. 641, 484 A.2d 275 (1984).

8. Summit Ridge, Inc. v. McKenny, No. 88CV191 (Dist. Ct., Summit County, Colo., targets' motion to dismiss denied Jan. 10, 1989; Colo. Sup. Ct. appeal dismissed June 23, 1989, and case voluntarily dismissed on confidential settlement agreement Mar. 15, 1990).

9. Story v. Shelter Bay Co., No. 84–2-02501–8 (Super. Ct., King County, Wash., judgment for filers Jan. 23, 1986), *vacated and remanded,* 52 Wash. App. 334, 760 P.2d 368 (1988); dismissed per agreement Sept. 21, 1988, with neither side paying damages).

10. Even a developer who, under oath, would not deny selling thousands "worthless, arid wasteland" in Colorado, still SLAPPed purchasers to stop them from organizing and bringing a fraud lawsuit against it. Great Western Cities, Inc. v. Binstein, 476 F. Supp. 827 (N.D. Ill. 1979), *aff'd mem.,* 614 F.2d 775 (7th Cir. 1979).

11. Hatch, *Dream Home Is Couple's Nightmare,* Seattle Times, Apr. 1988.

12. Werner, *Real Estate Company Sues Homeowner After She Tells State About Back Taxes,* Seattle Post-Intelligencer, Mar. 10, 1988, at A10.

13. Gilbert, *Residents, State Seek Tax Solution,* The Oregonian, July 11, 1987.

14. Werner, note 12 above.

15. *Id.*

16. *Id.*

17. *Id.*

18. Robert John Real Estate Co. v. Hill, No. 872016963 (Super. Ct., Clark County, Wash., filed July 14, 1987); Werner, note 12 above.

19. Tape-recorded message from Brenda Hill to authors (undated, 1988).

20. Temporary Restraining Order and Order to Show Cause (July 15, 1987). One of the strongest First Amendment rules is the rule against "prior restraints" on free speech, of which this court injunction is an unfortunate example. The leading case is Near v. Minnesota, 283 U.S. 697 (1931); a number of commentaries on prior restraints are cited in LOCKHART ET AL., CONSTITUTIONAL LAW: CASES—COMMENTS—QUESTIONS 869–95 (7th ed. 1991).

21. Gilbert, *Couple Told to Avoid "Reckless" Statements*, THE OREGONIAN, July 16, 1987; Stewart, *Vancouver Woman Receives Little Hope at Gardner Meeting*, *id.*, Apr. 1988, at B4.

22. Werner, *Whistleblower Meets Gardner but Expects Little Help With Legal Fight*, SEATTLE POST-INTELLIGENCER, Apr. 29, 1988, at B1; First Amended Complaint, Hill v. Robert Johns Real Estate Co., No. 88-2-02828-5 (Super Ct., Clark County, Wash., filed Oct. 26, 1988). In its defense, the company said that delaying paying the taxes was a "business decision," since there were only monetary, not criminal, penalties for late payment. Gilbert, *Clark County Firm Focus of Tax Payment Inquiry*, THE OREGONIAN, July 10, 1987.

23. Gilbert, note 21 above.

24. Hatch, note 11 above.

25. Werner, note 12 above.

26. Letter from Gerald L. Rome, President (Ashmann's successor), Robert John Real Estate Co., to "Dear Homeowner" at 1 (Mar. 28, 1988).

27. Cancellation Notice from Ron Winters, Underwriting Department, Mutual of Enumclaw Ins. Co. to Gary R. & Brenda S. Hill (Dec. 21, 1987).

28. Letter from Brenda Hill to authors (Aug. 12, 1988).

29. Hatch, note 11 above.

30. Werner, note 22 above.

31. *Id.* at B1; Stewart, note 21 above.

32. Hatch, note 11 above, at D2.

33. Werner, note 12 above.

34. *Woman Sues Real-Estate Company; She and Erxleben Chide Eikenberry*, SEATTLE TIMES, Oct. 1988.

35. Complaint, Hill v. Robert Johns Real Estate Co., No. 88-2-02828-5 (Super. Ct., Clark County, Wash., filed Oct. 19, 1988).

36. Letter from Brenda Hill to authors (undated, received Nov. 1988).

37. Wash. Rev. Code § 4.24.500–520 (Supp. 1990); *"Whistle-Blower" Bill Approved*, VANCOUVER COLUMBIAN, Mar. 4, 1989; *Whistleblower Gets Protection and Also the Governor's Pen*, SEATTLE TIMES, May 6, 1989.

38. *Jury Finds Woman Not Guilty of Slander*, THE OREGONIAN, Mar. 13, 1993.

39. Letter from Brenda Hill to authors (May 9, 1989).

40. Werner, *Tip-Off Changed Her life: Echoes Still Haunt a Whistle-Blower*, SEATTLE POST-INTELLIGENCER, Mar. 7, 1989, at B2.

41. *Id.*

42. Letter from Brenda Hill to authors (Feb. 29, 1993).

43. Neville and Marble, *Complaints Flood In—Neighbors Ankle-Deep in Home Problems*, HUNTINGTON BEACH [CAL.] INDEPENDENT, Feb. 15, 1979, at 1.

44. *Id.*

45. Mortensen v. S & S Construction Co., No. 30-58-07 (Super. Ct., Orange County, Cal., filed Jan. 22, 1979).

46. S & S Construction Co., Inc. v. Mortensen, No. 320157 (Super. Ct., Orange County, Cal., filed Sept. 12, 1979).

47. Neville, *S & S Sues 100 Homeowners,* HUNTINGTON BEACH [CAL.] INDEPENDENT, Sept. 23, 1979.

48. Marble, *Leaky-Homes Protesters Face Suit,* COSTA MESA [CAL.] DAILY PILOT, Oct. 4, 1979, at A8.

49. Telephone Interview with Cliff Mortensen (June 2, 1989).

50. Marble, note 48 above.

51. *"Leaky" House Wins HB Family $125,000,* HUNTINGTON BEACH [CAL.] INDEPENDENT, Dec. 14, 1983.

52. Mortensen v. S & S Construction Co., Inc., No. 466126 (Super. Ct., Orange County, Cal., filed Mar. 1982).

53. Complaint at ¶ 29, id.

54. A "limits of liability" $450,000 settlement paid in 1994 by a filer's attorney in a trailer-park SLAPPback (Chapter 9) illustrates further that lawyers are liable for this chilling tactic.

55. [Texas Attorney General's] Petition in Intervention at 1 and Plaintiffs' Original Petition at ¶ V, Westlawn Cemetery Corp. v. Forston, No. B850394 (Dist. Ct., Orange County, Tex., case filed July 30, 1985); *Attorney General's Office Intervenes in Slander Suit,* ORANGE [TEX.] LEADER, Aug. 7, 1985, at 2A.

56. Complaint ¶ III, Westlawn Cemetery Corp. v. Forston. They were indeed in bankruptcy; *see* ORANGE LEADER article, note 55 above.

57. [Texas Attorney General's] Petition in Intervention, note 55 above, at 2. *id.*

58. *Id.*

59. Havoco of America, Ltd. v. Hollobow, No. 79C5261 (U.S. Dist. Ct., N.D. Ill., filed 1979; summary judgment for targets Oct. 8, 1981), *aff'd* (and trial court opinion reprinted in full), 702 F.2d 643 (7th Cir. 1983).

60. 702 F.2d at 650.

61. Telephone Interview with Lawrence Taslitz, target (June 5, 1989).

62. *Id.*

63. Behr v. Weber, 172 A.D.2d 441, 568 N.Y.S.2d 948 (App. Div. 1991).

64. Dreske v. Wooden, No. 79CV1046 (Cir. Ct., Waukesha County, Wis., voluntarily dismissed June 16, 1983).

65. Perlman, *Alta-Dena Dairy Sues Its Critics for $780,000,000,* SAN FRANCISCO CHRONICLE, June 22, 1985.

66. Letter from William H. Foege, M.D., Assistant U.S. Surgeon General, to John C. Bolten, M.D. (May 27, 1983).

67. Perlman, note 65 above.

68. Stueve v. Bolton, No. EAC49085 (Super. Ct., Los Angeles County, Cal., filed Oct. 9, 1984), *transferred as* No. 122679 (Super. Ct., Marin County, Cal.); Alta-Dena Certified Dairy v. Bolton, No. 122863 (Super. Ct., Marin County, Cal., filed May 3, 1985).

69. Perlman, note 65 above.

70. *Editorial, Raw Milk and Safety,* LOS ANGELES TIMES, June 3, 1985.

71. Waxman, *Letter to the Editor, Raw Milk and Safety, id.,* June 13, 1985.

72. Bio/Basics Int'l Corp. v. Ortho Pharmaceutical Corp., 545 F. Supp. 1106, 1109 (S.D.N.Y. 1982).

73. *Id.*

74. *Id.*

75. Complaint, Concerned Members of Intermountain Rural Electric Ass'n v. McCutchen, No. 84CV1632 (Dist. Ct., Jefferson County, Colo., filed June 25, 1984).

76. *Id.; Irate Woodland Park Group Plans Ouster of Electrical Co-op's Chief,* GAZETTE TELE-

GRAPH (Colorado Springs, Colo.), Apr. 12, 1983; *IREA List Keeps Tab on Friends, id.*, Oct. 6, 1983; *IREA Executive Fired After Making Comment, id.*, Dec. 10, 1983; *Angry Customers Plan IREA Recall, id.*, Jan. 11, 1984; *IREA Concedes Wrongdoing, Seeks Dismissal of Charges, id.*, Jan. 14, 1984; *IREA Recall Gains Signatures, id.*, Jan. 17, 1984; *Questionable Loans by IREA to Be Target of Special Audit, id.*, Mar. 17, 1984; *IREA By-Law Changes Aimed at Stifling Dissent, Critics Say, id.*, Mar. 22, 1984; *IREA Aide: Board Bows to Manager, id.*, Apr. 1, 1984; *IREA Foul-Ups Costly, Ex-Supervisor Says, id.*, Apr. 8, 1984.

77. Complaint, ¶ 20, note 75 above; *IREA Directors Cite Technicality, Reject Petitions*, GAZETTE TELEGRAPH, May 31, 1984.

78. Note 75 above (election); Concerned Members of Intermountain Rural Electric Ass'n v. Intermountain Rural Electric Ass'n, No. 84CV214 (Dist. Ct., Douglas County, Colo., filed July 26, 1984) (public meetings).

79. Complaint ¶ 10, note 75 above.

80. Answer and Counterclaim, note 75 above (filed Sept. 12, 1984).

81. Study Interview with Tom Evans (1988).

82. Study Interview with Kevin O'Brien, target's attorney (1988).

83. Study Interview with Stanley Lewandowski (1988).

84. Study Interview with Herman McCutchen (1988).

85. Petition for Relief in the Nature of Prohibition and Request for Stay, No. 85SA244 (Colo. Sup. Ct., filed July 15, 1985).

86. Brief Amici Curiae in Support of Petitioners, *id.* (filed July 16, 1985).

87. Concerned Members of Intermountain Rural Electric Association v. District Court, 713 P.2d 923 (Colo. 1986).

88. Reporter's Partial Transcript at 4–5, No. 84CV1632 (July 17, 1986).

89. *Id.* at 5–6.

90. *District Court Blasts IREA Recall Leaders*, IREA WATTS & VOLTS, Sept. 1986, at 2 (member newsletter).

91. Evans interview, note 81 above.

92. *Id.*; Lewandowski interview, note 83 above.

93. Buchsbaum, *Base Remains a Man's World on Job, Pay Scales*, MACON [GA.] TELEGRAPH AND NEWS, Jan. 20, 1985, at A-1.

94. Buchsbaum, *Subtle and Not-So-Subtle Sexism Scars Base Employment Picture*, MACON [GA.] TELEGRAPH AND NEWS, Jan. 20, 1985, at A-1; Buchsbaum, *Base Remains a Man's World on Job, Pay Scales, id.*

95. Air Force Civilian Appellate Review Agency, Report of Investigation, Equal Employment Opportunity Complaint of Carolyn McDowell (Docket No. E-81–052, Nov. 22, 1980), at 2, 4.

96. Carter v. Reehling, No. 25112 (Super. Ct., Houston County, Ga., dismissed June 15, 1986).

97. Letter Decision of Karen R. Keesling, Director, Equal Employment Opportunity, Department of the Air Force (June 23, 1982).

98. Brief of the United States Equal Employment Opportunity Commission as Amicus Curiae at 5 (Mar. 25, 1986).

99. Study Interview with Lester Carter (Dec. 18, 1988).

100. Chavez v. Citizens for a Fair Farm Labor Law, No. 178281 (Super. Ct., Los Angeles County, Cal., dismissed Mar. 1, 1977), *aff'd*, 84 Cal. App. 3d 77, 148 Cal. Rptr. 278 (1978).

101. Silver v. Mohasco Corp., No. 77-CV-472 (Sup. Ct., Spec. Term, Saratoga County, N.Y., majority of claims dismissed 1978), *aff'd*, 94 A.D.2d 820, 462 N.Y.S.2d 917 (1983), *aff'd*, 62 N.Y.2d 741, 465 N.E.2d 361, 476 N.Y.S.2d 822 (1984); Silver v. Mohasco Corp., 497 F. Supp.

1 (N.D.N.Y., Oct. 17, 1978), *rev'd,* 602 F.2d 1083 (2d Cir. 1979), *cert. granted,* 444 U.S. 990 (1979), rev'd, 447 U.S. 807 (1980), *on remand,* 103 F.R.D. 614 (N.D.N.Y. 1984).

102. International Union, UAW v. National Right to Work Legal Defense and Education Foundation, Inc., 433 F. Supp. 474 (D.D.C. 1977), *aff'd in part, vacated in part and remanded,* 590 F.2d 1139 (D.C. Cir. 1978), *on remand summary judgment granted targets,* 584 F. Supp. 1219 (D.D.C. 1984).

103. Letter from Bruce N. Cameron, NRWLDEF staff attorney (June 25, 1986).

104. Petrochem Insulation, Inc. v. Northern California and Northern Nevada Pipe Trades Council, No. C 90 36281 (U.S. Dist. Ct., N.D. Cal., filed Dec. 21, 1990).

105. Counterclaim by Defendant Ralph Dawson, at 29, Willson v. Cagle, No. C88–0328 (U.S. Dist. Ct., N.D. Cal., filed Mar. 30, 1988).

106. Telephone interview with Thomas Steel, Willson's attorney (June 27, 1995).

107. North Star Legal Foundation v. Honeywell Project, No. 836955 (Dist. Ct., Hennepin County, Minn., dismissed Mar. 8, 1984), *aff'd,* 355 N.W.2d 186 (Minn. App. 1984), *petition for review denied,* No. C8–84-725 (Minn. 1985).

108. Complaint at ¶ 24, *id.*

109. Memorandum Opinion at 1 (Mar. 8, 1984), *id.*

110. Fong, *Scientologists Deleted Data Before Returning Computers,* ROCKY MOUNTAIN NEWS, Sept 26, 1995; Lane, *Items Return a Sin, Scientologist Says,* DENVER POST, Oct. 3, 1995; Cult Awareness Network, News Release, *Non-profit Forced to Bankruptcy While Seeking Reversal of Civil Case* (Oct. 19, 1995) ($1,087,500 jury verdict against CAN and other defendants).

Chapter 8

1. *E.g.,* Westfield Partners, Ltd. v. Hogan, 740 F. Supp. 523, 524–27 (N.D. Ill. 1990).

2. *Editorial, No, Not That Kind of Parental Involvement,* LAS VEGAS [NEV.] REVIEW-JOURNAL, Dec. 20, 1991.

3. *Id.*

4. Letter from Richard A. Weber, Ph.D., Executive Director, Colorado Association of School Executives, to Ms. Nicole Hoffmann-Ewing (April 6, 1993).

5. Study Interview with Kevin O'Brien, target attorney (*IREA* case, Chapter 7).

6. *See* Hager, *Tide Turns for Targets of SLAPP Lawsuits,* LOS ANGELES TIMES, May 3, 1991, at A-3 (building industry and developer representatives); Simon, *Nader Suits Up to Strike Back Against "SLAPPs,"* WALL STREET JOURNAL, July 9, 1991, at B1 (corporate); Enos, *SLAPPing Back,* PLANNING, June 1991, at 17; Keaton, *Farmers Fight Off the New Valley Land Rush,* DAILY JOURNAL (Los Angeles), Aug. 6, 1991, at 8.

7. Examples include the 1,000 "Does" listed in *Maple Properties* (Chapter 3), the 490 in *La Pointe* (Chapter 4), and the 100 in *Mortensen* and 50 in *Alta Dena* (Chapter 7).

8. Where the "other government forum" is a law-reform lawsuit filed by targets and the SLAPP comes as a counterclaim filed in that same suit, the logic still holds. Even though the same court is being invoked, the two cases are not equal. Targets have filed a public-interest lawsuit, not for personal monetary damages or gain, but to achieve a government outcome: to get the court to render or reverse a government policy or decision. Filer's counterclaim, quite the opposite, seeks to counter that by transforming the underlying policy issue into a claim for nonsolutionary, private monetary gain. The court should not be allowed to pass this off with the notion that "if you can sue them, they can sue you." That blurs the clear-cut difference between judicial review of government action and a mere private, monetary lawsuit.

9. The force of this argument is apparent in a number of the cases. The federal court ruled in dismissing *Willow Tree* (Chapter 6): "Indeed, [filers] do not allege that they were pre-

vented from responding to [targets'] charges . . . [or] denied access to the [government] Board which heard and considered their applications." 467 F. Supp. at 818. A state court judge held, in dismissing the school bus company's SLAPP against safety-conscious Pennsylvania parents: "Urging an investigation [by school authorities], in which the government may independently evaluate and redress the claims, is precisely the kind of exercise which the First Amendment is designed to protect." Opinion and Order at 5, Central Transportation, Inc. v. Stephens (Chapter 4).

10. Or, if the SLAPP is filed as a counterclaim to a nonmonetary, government-decision-challenging lawsuit brought by targets, the two judicial issues are separate, and their resolutions, unrelated.

11. *Political Intimidation Suits: SLAPP Defendant Slaps Back,* 4 CIVIL TRIAL MANUAL (BNA) 459, 461 (Oct. 19, 1988).

12. Most indicative of this attorney conceit is the U.S. Supreme Court's very precise use of the word "judicial" to describe what transpires in courts and "political" to describe what transpires in the legislative and executive branches. Gilligan v. Morgan, 413 U.S. 1 (1973); Powell v. McCormack, 395 U.S. 486 (1969); Baker v. Carr, 369 U.S. 186 (1962).

13. Heffner, *Dump Owner's Lawsuit Against Riled Neighbor Is Permitted by Court,* PROVIDENCE [R.I.] JOURNAL-BULLETIN, Apr. 20, 1993.

14. Letter from William T. Sutphin to authors (Apr. 21, 1993).

15. Letter to co-author, Professor Pring (July 23, 1991) (authors' decision to retain anonymity).

16. *Id.*

17. *Id.*

18. The *Plan Tacoma* bar SLAPP (Chapter 6), the *Missouri v. NOW* women's rights / politician SLAPP (Chapters 4 and 7), and the *IREA* consumer SLAPP (Chapter 7), respectively.

19. But even reduced fees can be costly: $6,000 in the Adult Blind Home case, (Chapter 4) and in the tens of thousands for the protracted *Maple Properties* case (Chapter 2).

20. Simon, *Nader Suits Up to Strike Back Against "Slapps,"* WALL STREET JOURNAL, July 9, 1991, at B1.

21. Hentoff, *The Quicksands of Libel,* WASHINGTON POST, Apr. 1, 1989.

22. *Id.;* DETROIT NEWS, Jan. 22, 1980.

23. DETROIT NEWS, note 22 above.

24. Telephone interview with Sienna La Rene, target attorney (June 6, 1989); per the court order, the amount of the settlement was not disclosed by any parties or representatives.

25. McDonald v. Smith, 105 S.Ct. 2787, 2789 (1985) ("The right to petition is cut from the same cloth as the other guarantees of that Amendment").

26. German Towers, Inc. v. Bogoslavsky, 626 F.2d 607 (8th Cir. 1980); Missouri v. National Org. for Women, Inc., 620 F.2d 1301 (8th Cir. 1980), *cert. denied,* 449 U.S. 842 (1980); Stern v. United States Gypsum, Inc., 547 F.2d 1329 (7th Cir. 1977), *cert. denied,* 434 U.S. 975 (1977); Weiss v. Willow Tree Civic Ass'n, 467 F. Supp. 803 (S.D.N.Y. 1979); Wilmorite, Inc. v. Eagan Real Estate, Inc., 454 F. Supp. 1124 (N.D.N.Y. 1977), *aff'd mem.,* 578 F.2d 1372 (2d Cir. 1978), *cert. denied,* 439 U.S. 983 (1978); Smith v. Silvey, 149 Cal. App. 3d 400, 197 Cal. Rptr. 15 (1983); City of Long Beach v. Bozek, 31 Cal.3d 527, 645 P.2d 137, 183 Cal. Rptr. 86 (1982) (en banc), *vacated & remanded,* 459 U.S. 1095, *aff'd on indep. state const. grounds,* 33 Cal.3d 727, 661 P.2d 1072, 190 Cal. Rptr. 918 (1983); Protect Our Mountain Env't v. District Court, 677 P.2d 1361 (Colo. 1984) (en banc); Myers v. Plan Takoma, Inc., 472 A.2d 44 (D.C. 1983); Miner v. Novotny, 60 Md. App. 124, 481 A.2d 508 (1984); Searle v. Johnson, 709 P.2d 328 (Utah 1985); Webb v. Fury, 282 S.E.2d 28 (W.Va. 1981).

27. 661 F. Supp. at 706–7.

28. Immuno A.G. v. Moor-Jankowski, 145 App. Div. 2d 114, 537 N.Y.S.2d 129, 134, 137, 138 (1989).

29. Sive, *Countersuits, Delay, Intimidation Caused by Public Interest Suits,* NATIONAL LAW JOURNAL, June 19, 1989, at 27.

30. See empirical studies reviewed in Gibbins, *Sanction Power: Revisions of Rule 11 Are Urged,* NATIONAL LAW JOURNAL, July 29, 1991, at 21; Tobias, *Environmental Litigation and Rule 11,* 33 WILLIAM & MARY LAW REVIEW 429 (1992).

31. $20,000 is the highest award we have found in the SLAPPs studied to date. Moreover, some state equivalents of FRCP 11 have ceilings, as does, for example, New York's, 22 N.Y.C.R.R. Part 130–1 ($10,000 maximum); in a very thoughtful opinion this ceiling has been analyzed and criticized as inappropriate in SLAPPs, in Gordon v. Marrone, 155 Misc.2d 726, 590 N.Y.S.2d 649 (Super. Ct., Westchester County, N.Y., Apr. 13, 1992).

32. For example, in the *Boswell* case (Chapter 9), none of the filer's representatives would admit to a political-chill intent, but target attorney Ralph Wegis got a company official to admit that Boswell threatened to cancel contracts with businesses that supported targets.

33. For example, malicious prosecution typically has four proof elements: (1) filing of a lawsuit, (2) without probable cause, (3) with malice, and (4) with favorable termination for party sued. Filer's admissions on each of these points should be sought in the SLAPP discovery record.

34. CIVIL TRIAL MANUAL (BNA), note 11 above, at 462.

35. Cape Cave Corp. v. Reese, No. 85–001005CAEOF (Cir. Ct., Charlotte County, Fla., dismissed Apr. 14 and July 28, 1986).

36. Tobin, *Judge Weighs Lawsuit's Impact on Rights of Free Speech,* CHARLOTTE [FLA.] NEWS-PRESS, Apr. 8, 1986.

37. McGrath, *The Big Chill: Attorney Macon Cowles Has Made a Habit of Speaking Out Against the Powerful—Now They'd Like to Put Him on Ice,* WESTWORD (Denver, Colo.), Mar. 11–17, 1992, at 12.

38. *Id.* at 16–18.

39. H. Pankratz, *High Court Won't Discipline Lawyer: Talk About ASARCO Spurred Complaint,* DENVER POST, Apr. 28, 1993, at 2B; P. Sleeth, *Globeville Families Win $28 Million; ASARCO to Appeal Award,* DENVER POST, April 24, 1993, at B1.

40. Pankratz, note 39 above.

41. *Id.* at 18.

42. Gelman Sciences, Inc. v. Gibson, No. 88–35 482 CZ (Cir. Ct., Washtenaw County, Mich., voluntarily dismissed 1988).

Chapter 9

1. *Political Intimidation Suits: SLAPP Defendant Slaps Back,* 4 CIVIL TRIAL MANUAL (BNA) 459 (Oct. 19, 1988); Pell, *The SLAPPs Are Back,* CALIFORNIA, Sept. 1989, at 18; Ziegler, *The Sierra Club SLAPPS Back,* SAN FRANCISCO DAILY JOURNAL, Dec. 10, 1990, at 2; Stiak, *SLAPPed by a Corporate Lawsuit? SLAPP Back,* HARROWSMITH COUNTRY LIFE, Nov./Dec. 1991, at 22, 23; *Enos, SLAPPing Back,* PLANNING, June 1991, at 16.

2. Quoted in Simon, *Nader Suits Up to Strike Back Against "Slapps,"* WALL STREET JOURNAL, July 9, 1991, at B4.

3. They may not make victims whole, can be costly, are difficult to prove, and conceivably might discourage some legitimate political lawsuits. See Costantini & Nash, *SLAPP/SLAPPback: The Misuse of Libel Law for Political Purposes and a Countersuit Response,* 7 JOURNAL OF LAW & POLITICS 417, 477–79 (1991).

4. Complaint for Malicious Prosecution and Abuse of Process at 6, Styles v. McKeon Construction, No. 270793 (Super. Ct., Sacramento County, Cal., filed Dec. 1977).

5. Defendants' Memorandum of Points and Authorities in Support of Defendants' Demurrer at 11–12, id.

6. Respondent's Brief at 1, Leonardini v. Shell Oil Co., No. C 000619 (Cal. Ct. App. filed Nov. 4, 1987).

7. Appellant's Opening Brief at 1, *id.* (May 27, 1987).

8. Leonardini v. Shell Oil Co., 216 Cal. App. 3d 547, 566, 264 Cal. Rptr. 883, 894 (1989).

9. Galante, *Malicious Prosecution Claimed: "Intimidated" Lawyer Wins $5.2M,* NATIONAL LAW JOURNAL, May 12, 1986.

10. *Leonardini,* note 8 above, at 547.

11. *Id.* at 576.

12. *Id.* at 578.

13. *Id.* at 580.

14. *Id.*

15. Letter from John M. Poswall to co-author, Professor Pring (Oct. 23, 1990). His successful U.S. Supreme Court brief in Opposition to Petition for Writ of Certiorari does indeed, in the first sentence and to our knowledge for the first time, brief a case to the U.S. Supreme Court as "a SLAPP suit."

16. See Barnes and Cline, *Peripheral Canal: Critics Claim It Can, and Will, Kill the Delta,* SAN FRANCISCO EXAMINER, Feb. 21, 1982, at 1; Western Water Education Foundation, *Layperson's Guide to the Peripheral Canal* (Sept. 1979).

17. Soble, *Anti-Canal Fervor Viewed as "Almost Like Religious War,"* LOS ANGELES TIMES, June 3, 1982, at 3.

18. Baker, *Canal's Major Farm Foes: Salyer and Boswell Unite to Defeat Proposition 9,* FRESNO BEE, June 7, 1982, at A1. For an in-depth analysis of the *Boswell* SLAPP and SLAPPback, whose lead author was the key political scientist expert witness in the SLAPPback, see Costantini & Nash, note 3 above, at 417.

19. Baker, note 18 above; Costantini & Nash; note 3 above; [Defendants'] Memorandum of Points and Authorities in Support of Summary Judgment at 7 (Mar. 23, 1984), J.G. Boswell Co. v. Family Farmers for Proposition 9, No. 179027 (Super. Ct., Kern County, Cal., complaint filed May 14, 1982).

20. Memorandum, *id.,* at 4–5, 11 *et seq.*

21. Exhibit A to Complaint, *id.* (May 14, 1982).

22. Campbell, *Farmers' Litigation over Ads Brings Bitter Harvest,* BAKERSFIELD CALIFORNIAN, Feb. 24, 1985.

23. *Id.*

24. Note 19 above.

25. *Id.*

26. Opinion of the Court at 7, Wegis v. J.G. Boswell Company, No. F011230 (5th App. Dist., Cal.) (June 14, 1991).

27. *Economic Clout Can Reach a Long Way,* BAKERSFIELD CALIFORNIAN, Feb. 24, 1985.

28. *Id.* at 11; Trihey, *2 Kern Farms Tackle Boswell on Rights Issue, id.,* June 16, 1988, at B1.

29. Nolte and Goode, *Experts Amazed by Huge Vote Against Canal,* SAN FRANCISCO CHRONICLE, June 10, 1982.

30. *Id.*

31. Stiak, note 1 above, at 23.

32. Keaton, *SLAPP Bar Calls Work a Crusade,* LOS ANGELES DAILY JOURNAL, Aug. 6, 1991.

33. Third Amended Cross-complaint, Thompson v. J.G. Boswell Co., No. 179027 (Super. Ct., Kern County, Cal., filed Nov. 17, 1986); this amended cross-complaint added malicious prosecution to the other two charges.

34. Campbell, note 22 above.

35. CIVIL TRIAL MANUAL (BNA), note 1 above, at 462–63.

36. *Id.*

37. *Id.* at 463; *Economic Clout,* note 27 above.

38. CIVIL TRIAL MANUAL, note 1 above, at 463.

39. *Id.*

40. Opinion, note 26 above, at 10–12, 49–52; see also Costantini & Nash, note 3 above, at 468–70.

41. Opinion, note 26 above, at 62–64.

42. *Id.* at 12.

43. *Id.* The appeals court did strike from the judgment the violation of California's state constitutional right of free speech, reasoning that it could be violated only by a government or quasi-government entity (a "state action" requirement), which Boswell was not.

44. *Id.* at 68.

45. Hager, *Milestone Award Upheld by Court,* LOS ANGELES TIMES, Oct. 4, 1991, at A3.

46. *Id.* at A31.

47. Keaton, note 32 above.

48. Humana Inc. v. Hemmeter, No. A274231 (Dist. Ct., Clark County, Nev., filed Dec. 18, 1991). Humana, one of the nation's largest hospital chains, SLAPPed one of its own doctors for advocating cost containment legislation before state legislative bodies and agencies. Professor Canan, coauthor of this book, testified as an expert witness in Dr. Hemmeter's SLAPPback.

49. Lhotka, *Jury Rewards Pair Who Got SLAAPed* [sic], ST. LOUIS POST-DISPATCH, Apr. 24, 1994, at 1. This was St. Louis attorney Richard Witzel's third successful SLAPPback.

50. Endeman, Lincoln, Turek & Heater v. Jagiello, No. 651436 (Super. Ct., San Diego County, Cal., Apr. 1994); *Verdicts & Settlements,* LOS ANGELES DAILY JOURNAL, Aug. 5, 1994 ($450,000 was the policy limit on the attorney's insurance); Woodring, *Park Owner's Attorney Is Successfully Sued for Alleged SLAPP Tactics,* THE CALIFORNIAN, June 1994, at 2.

51. Berry, *The "Environmental" SLAPP,* in SLAPPS: STRATEGIC LAWSUITS AGAINST PUBLIC PARTICIPATION IN GOVERNMENT at 61 (ALI-ABA Course of Study Materials 1994); Ziegler, note 1 above, at 2.

52. On "How Not to Be SLAPPed-Back," see Bethke, *Cole v. Lehmann: Practical Reflections on a Teacher Slander Suit Against Parents,* in SLAPPS: STRATEGIC LAWSUITS AGAINST PUBLIC PARTICIPATION IN GOVERNMENT at 101–4 (ALI-ABA Course of Study Materials 1994).

53. Leonardini v. Shell Oil Co., 216 Cal. App. 3d 547, 566–67, 264 Cal. Rptr. 883, 894 (1989).

54. *Id.*, 216 Cal. App. 3d at 583.

55. Fenton v. Groveland Community Services Dist., 135 Cal. App. 797, 804–5 (1982).

56. LOCKHART, KAMISAR, CHOPER & SHIFFRIN, CONSTITUTIONAL LAW: CASES—COMMENTS—QUESTIONS 1473–1535 (7th ed. 1991).

57. 42 U.S.C. § 1983.

58. LOCKHART ET AL., note 56 above.

59. *E.g.*, 42 U.S.C. § 1981.

60. 15 Am. Jur. 2d *Civil Rights* Sec. 102 (1976).

61. PROSSER, WADE & SCHWARTZ, CASES AND MATERIALS ON TORTS (1988).

62. Trial transcript at 1445–46.

63. *Id.* at 1448–49, 1454.

64. Unpublished opinion at 67–68. California law, however, makes a fine distinction between malice and probable cause. It treats the former as a fact issue for the jury on which experts may testify, the latter as a legal issue for the judge on which, ironically, legal experts may *not* testify. This byzantine hair-splitting is the result of California's extreme disfavor-

ment of malicious prosecution lawsuits and may not be a factor in more lenient states. Sheldon Appel Co. v. Albert & Oliker, 47 Cal.3d 863 (1989).

65. Leonardini v. Shell Oil Co., 216 Cal. App. 3d 547, 582 (1989).

66. Opinion at 16–18, Monia v. Parnas Corp., No. HOO6155 (Ct. App., Santa Clara County, Cal., Feb. 25, 1991; ordered not published).

67. *Id.* at 19–22.

68. Among states enforcing the rule are Illinois, Michigan, New York, Ohio, Rhode Island, Kentucky, and Virginia. Pennsylvania has rejected it through legislation: Pa. C. Stats. § 8351–54; McGee v. Feege, 535 A.2d 1020 (Pa. 1987).

69. See *Note, Groundless Litigation and the Malicious Prosecution Debate: A Historical Analysis,* 88 YALE LAW JOURNAL 1218 (1979); Pool, *Malicious Prosecution in Illinois: Wrong Without a Remedy,* 69 ILLINOIS BAR JOURNAL 754 (1981); *Comment, Torts/Malicious Prosecution,* 69 ILLINOIS BAR JOURNAL 376 (1981); R.J.R. Services, Inc. v. Aetna Casualty & Surety Co., 895 F.2d 279 (7th Cir. 1989).

70. Norin v. Scheldt Manufacturing Co., 297 Ill. 521, 527, 130 N.E. 791, 793 (1921), for example, says the English rule "should not be extended beyond ordinary civil suits, to embrace those suits which are themselves unusual in their effect upon the defendant."

71. Though no case has yet ruled on this, there are healthy parallels. Shedd v. Patterson, 302 Ill. 355, 134 N.E., 705 (1922), held that "harassment" (there, multiple lawsuits) canceled the rule; Alswang v. Clayborn, 40 Ill. App. 3d 147, 351 N.E.2d, 289 (1976), ruled that "a deprivation of liberty" would qualify; and Bank of Lyons v. Schultz, 78 Ill.2d 235, 399 N.E.2d, 1286 (1980), decided a preliminary injunction was sufficient.

72. Complaint ¶ 28–29, Levin v. King, No. 89 L 16240 (Cir. Ct., Cook County, Ill., filed Nov. 9, 1989).

73. *Id.,* dismissed June 14, 1994; see [Appeal] Brief of Plaintiff-Appellant at 5–9 (Oct. 13, 1994).

74. *Id.,* 648 N.E.2d 1108 (Ill. App. 1995).

75. *Id.,* petition for leave to appeal denied, No. 79054 (Ill. S. Ct. Oct. 4, 1995).

76. Criticisms of the rule abound: *e.g.,* Crawford v. Euclid Nat'l Bank, 19 Ohio St. 3d 135, 483 N.E.2d 1168, 1172–74 (1985) (dissent of Celebrezze, C.J.); Friedman v. Dozorc, 412 Mich. 1, 312 N.W.2d 585 (1981) (dissent); authorities, note 69 above. The Pennsylvania legislature's recent elimination of the rule is a positive sign, note 68 above.

77. Ziegler, note 1 above.

78. Stiak, note 1 above, at 23.

79. Enos, note 1 above, at 17.

80. Hager, *Tide Turns for Targets of SLAPP Lawsuits,* LOS ANGELES TIMES, May 3, 1991, at A31.

81. *Id.*

82. Keaton, *Farmers Fight Off the New Valley Land Rush,* LOS ANGELES DAILY JOURNAL, Aug. 6, 1991, at 8.

83. Stiak, note 1 above.

Chapter 10

1. President Bush was urging states to adopt the 1991 "Model State Volunteer Service Act." *See* Williams, *Protecting Volunteers from Liability,* CHRONICLE OF PHILANTHROPY, Jan. 15, 1991, at 34.

2. Additional resources on "anti-SLAPP laws" include Goldowitz, *Study Outline Regarding Legislative Developments,* in SLAPPS: STRATEGIC LAWSUITS AGAINST PUBLIC PARTICIPATION IN GOVERNMENT at 195 (ALI-ABA Course of Study Materials 1994); Ericson-Siegel, *Silencing SLAPPs: An Examination of Proposed Legislative Remedies and a "Solution" for Florida,* 20 FLORIDA STATE UNIVERSITY LAW REVIEW 487 (1992).

3. 42 U.S.C. § 1985(2).

4. 18 U.S.C. § 1505; for a SLAPP application, see text, Chapter 7, at note 71.

5. Whistleblower Protection Act of 1989, 5 U.S.C. § 1201, *et. seq*. "Whistleblowers" who report government malfeasance or mismanagment are close cousins to SLAPP targets; both are advocating views to government, but the retaliation against the typical whistleblower comes in the form of employment sanctions (firing, demotion, unpleasant transfers, on-job harassment, etc.) rather than a lawsuit.

6. H.R. 5196, 99th Cong., 2d Sess. (July 18, 1986).

7. See 50 AM. JUR. 2D, Libel and Slander § 192 *et seq.;* 12 A.L.R. 1247 (1921); 54 A.L.R. 2d 1298 (1957) (*see* Later Case Service).

8. 12 OKLA. STATS. ANN. § 1443.1.

9. 700 P.2d 666 (Okla. Ct. Aps. 1985).

10. CAL. CIV. CODE § 47(b); *see also* other subsections of the California Civil Code for additional SLAPP-type protections.

11. *Id.* § 47.5.

12. Ohio Am. H.B. No. 352 (1995) even has the state government's support. Letter from Fred L. Daily, Director, Ohio Dept. of Agriculture to Sandy Buchanan, Executive Director, Citizen Action (July 21, 1995). Colorado passed a clone in 1994; COLO. REV. STATS. § 35-31-101. *See* Cohen, *"Veggie Hate Laws" Appear Rotten to the Core,* ROCKY MOUNTAIN NEWS, Nov. 10, 1995, at 63A; Coates, *Veggie Libel Bill Called Part of Chilling Trend,* DENVER POST, Mar. 25, 1991, at 1A.

13. WASH. REV. CODE § 4.24.500–.520.

14. *Id.* § 4.24.500.

15. *Id.* § 4.24.510. It also provides attorneys' fees and costs to the target (*id.*) and authorizes the agency (or the state attorney general) to intervene and defend against the SLAPP (§ 4.24.520).

16. The first version of the bill limited the protection to "reports of violation" of laws, which clearly would have failed to cover a substantial number of SLAPPs.

17. The Washington courts appear to have done that. The first appellate court interpretation of the new law states that communications with an agency includes "communications to a public officer" of the agency. Gilman v. MacDonald, 875 P.2d 697, 700 (Wash. App. 1994).

18. *See* the "fact quagmire" discussion in Chapter 8.

19. Gilman v. MacDonald, note 17 above, 875 P.2d at 699. The judge's ruling appeared to be designed to cut the homeowner off from the costs and attorney's fees provided by the statute but not by the common law immunity.

20. The trial judge had placed "good faith" under a plain negligence standard, which many careless petitioners could fail to meet. The appeals court's actual malice test is more restrictive of the circumstances in which good faith can be negated and hence more protective of petitioners, although it creates its own (if lesser) "fact quagmire" (Chapters 2 and 8).

21. Note 17 above, 875 P.2d at 699–700.

22. NEV. REV. STATS. § 41.640–70.

23. *Id.* § 41.650.

24. Senate Bill 5441 (May 13, 1991) and Assembly Bill 4299 (Feb. 27, 1991), now codified at N.Y. CIV. RTS. LAW § 70-a, 76-a, and N.Y. CIV. PRAC. RULES 3211(g) and 3212(h) (effective Jan. 1, 1993).

25. For a history of the bill's early tribulations, see McEvoy, *"The Big Chill": Business Use of the Tort of Defamation to Discourage the Exercise of First Amendment Rights,* 17 HASTINGS CONSTITUTIONAL LAW QUARTERLY 503 (1990).

26. *Id.* at 529, 528.

27. Schemo, *Silencing the Opposition Gets Harder,* NEW YORK TIMES (Metro), July 2, 1992; Topping, *Slapping Down SLAPP Suits,* NEWSDAY, July 1, 1992, at 6.

28. New York State Builders Association, Inc., Memorandum in Opposition [to A. 4299 and S. 5441] at 1 (1992).

29. Chertok, *The Real Estate Development SLAPP,* in SLAPPS: STRATEGIC LAWSUITS AGAINST PUBLIC PARTICIPATION IN GOVERNMENT at 37–38 (ALI-ABA Course of Study Materials 1994).

30. N.Y. CIV. RTS. LAW § 76-a(1)(a)-(b).

31. Harfenes v. The Sea Gate Association, No. 103809/94 (Sup. Ct., New York County, N.Y., opinion Aug. 10, 1995). In 1990 the Sea Gate community on Coney Island applied to the state for permission to place fill on their shoreline. The state agency denied the application; the community proceeded to fill anyway, was caught, fined substantially, and forced to remove the fill. Some residents, disgruntled at the fines and costs incurred, filed suit in 1993 to shift the expense burden to the waste haulers and sought to delay a U.S. government cleanup loan to the community. Their community then SLAPPed them for monetary damages. *Id.* at 2–4. The residents' SLAPPback was rejected by the trial judge, who ruled the New York anti-SLAPP law did not apply because their 1993 suit was too late to relate to the 1990 state application and the loan application was not a license or permit application. *Id.* at 7–8. It remains to be seen whether more progressive New York appeals courts will likewise "construe . . . narrowly" this broadly remedial law. *Id.* at 8.

32. N.Y. CIV. PRAC. RULES 3211(g), 3212(h).

33. *Id.*

34. *Id.* The "clear and convincing" standard of the Minnesota law and the model bill is stricter and preferable. Drafting this standard is a key problem, as the California cases demonstrate.

35. N.Y. CIV. RTS. LAW § 76-a(2).

36. Id. § 70-a(1)(a). Proof is required that the SLAPP was filed "without a substantial basis in fact and law and could not be supported by a substantial argument for the extension, modification or reversal of existing law," which may prove a "fact quagmire" for parties seeking these sanctions.

37. *Id.* at (b). Here the proof requirement gets stiffer: Targets must show that the SLAPP filer sued "for the purpose of harassing, intimidating, punishing or otherwise maliciously inhibiting the free exercise of speech, petition or association rights," another potential fact quagmire.

38. *Id.* at (c). Here the proof gets stiffer yet, now requiring the target to show that the filer's "sole purpose" was "harassing, intimidating," and so on. Given the multiple motives of SLAPP filers, this would seem a virtually impossible proof requirement for targets to meet, since it is easy for filers to conjure up "other purposes" after the fact.

39. Gordon, *Anti-SLAPP Suit Measure Gets Positive Review,* PATENT TRADER (Bedford, N.Y.), July 9, 1992; Chertok, note 29 above, at 35.

40. With the notable exception that one must read into it communications to the electorate during an issue election.

41. DEL. STATS., tit. 10, § 8136–38.

42. NEB. REV. STATS. § 25–21,241–46.

43. Wogan, *Anti-SLAPP Legislation Is Passed,* LEWISBORO [N.Y.] LEDGER, July 16, 1992.

44. Gordon, note 39 above.

45. S.B. 2313 (Feb. 27, 1990).

46. The opposition of the Administration of Justice Committee of the California State Bar Association would soon be undercut, by its own colleagues. In 1991 the parent State Bar Association stated that it did not endorse its committee's opposition to the bill. Letter from Larry Doyle, Director, Office of Governmental Affairs, State Bar of California, to The Honorable Bill Lockyer (July 8, 1991). And in 1992 another bar group not only came out in full

support of the Lockyer bill but also publicly castigated its sister committee for underestimating the "seriousness of the problem," having "no authority" for claiming the bill was unconstitutional, and proposing amendments that "are entirely too weak, put too great a burden on the defendant, and will not protect the exercise of First Amendment rights as effectively as the [bill's] current language." Memorandum from the Executive Committee, Legal Services Section, State Bar of California, to the State Bar Board Committee on the Administration of Justice at 4, 5, 6 (Jan. 23, 1992).

47. *Deukmejian Vetoes Limits on SLAPP Suits,* SAN FRANCISCO DAILY JOURNAL, Sept. 27, 1990, at 8. (On sanctions—costs and attorneys' fees—as no cure for SLAPPs, see text, Chapter 8, at notes 29–31.)

48. *Id.*

49. S.B. 341 (Feb. 11, 1991).

50. Memorandum to Larry Doyle, Director, Office of Governmental Affairs, State Bar of California, from Committee on Administration of Justice, State Bar of California at 1 (June 14, 1991); but see note 46 above.

51. *Editorial, Let Them Speak,* SAN DIEGO UNION, Oct. 2, 1991.

52. Letter from Governor Pete Wilson to Members of the California Senate (Oct. 14, 1991).

53. Dresslar, *Veto of SLAPP Limits Legislation Ensures Demise of a Favored Bill,* LOS ANGELES DAILY JOURNAL, Oct. 16, 1991.

54. *Free Speech Harmed by Veto of SLAPP Limits,* REDDING [CAL.] RECORD SEARCHLIGHT, Oct. 24, 1991.

55. *Slapping Down SLAPPs,* BAKERSFIELD CALIFORNIAN, Oct. 22, 1991.

56. *Editorial, Free Speech and Women Both Lost,* THE ARGUS (Fremont, Cal.), Oct. 21, 1991.

57. S.B. 1264 (Jan. 6, 1992).

58. Dresslar, *Governor Signs Measure to Curb "SLAPP Suits,"* SAN FRANCISCO DAILY JOURNAL, Sept. 18, 1992.

59. Letter from Don Collin, General Counsel, and Richard Lyon, Legislative Advocate, California Building Industry Association, to the Honorable Pete Wilson, Governor (Sept. 11, 1992).

60. Dresslar, note 58 above.

61. CAL. CODE OF CIV. PROC. § 425.16.

62. Dresslar, note 58 above.

63. *Id.* Lockyer was more expressive in a letter to the authors two weeks later (Sept. 21, 1992): "I am writing to thank you both personally for your invaluable assistance . . . to secure the enactment of California Senate Bill 1264. . . . Professor Canan's testimony . . . and Professor Pring's letter to Governor Wilson were, I believe, very effective in convincing the California Legislature and the Governor of the existence of SLAPP suits in California and their serious interference with a person's exercise of constitutional free speech and petition rights.

"Your article . . . was instrumental in bringing to public attention the problem of civil lawsuits being used to stifle political expressions. It also provided empirical data, critical for our public policy discussions."

64. Goldowitz, *The Practitioner: Recent Appellate Case Upholds California's Anti-SLAPP Law,* LOS ANGELES DAILY JOURNAL, Sept. 27, 1994.

65. The first appellate court interpretation of the law suggests this, albeit in dictum—not necessary to the decision—which lowers its importance. Wilcox v. Superior Court, 27 Cal. App. 4th 809, 828, 33 Cal. Rptr. 2d 446, 454–55 (1994). See other cases discussed in Goldowitz, note 64 above.

66. Goldowitz, note 64 above.

67. Either by returning to the "substantial probability" test of the 1992 bill or, preferably, by using the "clear and convincing" test of our model legislation (below).

68. Opinion of the Justices (Slapp Suit Procedure), 138 N.H. 445, 451, 641 A.2d 1012, 1015 (N.H. 1994).

69. *Id.*, 138 N.H. 449–51, 641 A.2d 1014–15.

70. *Id.*, 138 N.H. 450, 641 A.2d 1014.

71. 10 CYCLOPEDIA OF FEDERAL PROCEDURE § 35.19.10 at 239 (3d ed. 1991) (summary judgment); 5 MOORE'S FEDERAL PRACTICE ¶ 38.36 (2d ed.) (motions to dismiss); 6 *id.* ¶ 56.06 (summary judgment).

72. H.B. 1520 (passed over veto Dec. 29, 1994), now codified at MASS. GEN. LAWS ch. 231, § 59H; S.B. 95-S-675, Substitute A (passed over veto Aug. 4, 1995), now codified at R.I. GEN. LAWS § § 9-33-2 and -3.

73. Sandy Pooler, staff counsel for the Massachusetts House, reports: "The glue that held this effort together was a consistent intellectual rationale for an anti-SLAPP bill, particularly for the insights that you provided into the Petitioning Clause and into an objective test for differentiating sham from protected petitioning" (letter to co-author, Professor Pring, Jan. 4, 1995). And it seems to have reduced the number of SLAPPs, according to counsel there. Cohen, *Is SLAPP Law Foiling Legitimate Lawsuits?* MASSACHUSETTS LAWYERS WEEKLY, Sept. 25, 1995, at 1.

74. Letter from Governor Lincoln Almond to The Honorable, The Senate (July 3, 1995). The 1995 law replaces a 1993 version that was so weak it proved unworkable in practice, according to Michael Rubin, Rhode Island Assistant Attorney General and Environmental Advocate, and the AG's SLAPP expert. Poon, *Anti-SLAPP Law Fails to Protect Dump's Critic from Defamation Suit*, PROVIDENCE [R.I.] JOURNAL-BULLETIN, Aug. 5, 1994.

75. Letter from John Grzybek to co-author, Professor Pring (Mar. 2, 1992), with unnumbered draft bill attached (dismiss unless petitioning is devoid of factual support or basis in law, and primary purpose is to harass, with adverse effect on filer).

76. Telephone Interview with John Gryzbek (Mar. 10, 1992).

77. Telephone Interview with John Gryzbek (May 10, 1994). Minnesota Public Interest Research Group and the Audubon Society were among the key supporters, holding forums and meetings on SLAPPs and organizing testimony.

78. Letter from John Grzybek to Professor Pring (Sept. 3, 1993).

79. Gryzbek, note 77 above.

80. Minnesota Citizens Participation Act of 1994, Chap. 566, S.F. No. 584, codified at MINN. STATS. § 554.01–05 (effective on and after May 6, 1994).

81. § 554.03. This is strong language, considering that there is a move against expanding immunities in Minnesota. Gryzbek, note 77 above.

82. § 554.01(6).

83. § 554.01(2).

84. § 554.02(1).

85. § 554.02(2).

86. § 554.04.

87. § 554.02(2)(3). The Senate wanted the weaker "preponderance of the evidence" standard, but the House's stricter "clear and convincing" standard won out. Strict scrutiny should apply in cases where constitutional rights of this magnitude are involved.

88. The only other potential obstacle to effectiveness is the seemingly gratuitous language suggesting that the immunity can be lost if the petitioning "constitutes a tort or violation of a person's constitutional rights." Since all SLAPPs allege exactly that and since *Omni* makes it clear that petitioning to procure government action is *not* a tort or violation of rights,

it will be up to the Minnesota courts to assure that that language does not defeat the intent of the law.

89. The plaintiff-oriented TLAs, normally averse to litigation-limiting laws, are a natural constituency for anti-SLAPP legislation, given their proactive, lawsuit-filing clients. Marina Corodemus, a leader of the New Jersey TLA, can testify to this: "We started seeing civic-minded people getting big-gunned out of their right to protest. . . . These [clients of mine] were Mom-and-Pop people who just wanted to have the law enforced in a company town, being intimidated by the threat of a lawsuit. Some of them wanted to pull out of the group, fearing they would lose their homes or their jobs." Lucas, *Using the Courts to Quiet Critics,* NEW JERSEY LAW JOURNAL, Dec. 27, 1990, at 3, 18.

90. Warning: Because legal terms and their interpretations can vary greatly from state to state, those seeking to use this model should assure that these terms are consistent with and operate effectively under the existing law of their own states.

91. The U.S. Supreme Court has said that a "heightened pleading standard" (detailed proof) may not be imposed on a plaintiff in a pretrial motion to dismiss based on a municipality's immunity in § 1983 Civil Rights Act cases. Leatherman v. Tarrant County Narcotics Intelligence and Coordination Unit, 113 S. Ct. 1160 (1993). However, that decision expressly allowed a heightened pleading standard on summary judgment, left open whether it would be allowed on motions to dismiss brought by individual officials, and did not address basing it on Rule 7(a) of the Federal Rules of Civil Procedure. For these reasons, heightened pleading standards have "survive[d]" *Leatherman.* Schultea v. Wood, 47 F.3d 1427 (5th Cir. 1995) (en banc).

92. Provisions for attorney fees and sanctions are common in federal and state law (notably Rule 11 of the Federal Rules of Civil Procedure). They are generally permissive and infrequently awarded in SLAPPs, we found (Chapter 9), hence this model act makes them mandatory, a change recently proposed for Federal Rule 11. See H.R. 988, 104th Cong., 1st Sess. (1995). Also, some states have arbitrary low ceilings on such awards (for example, New York has a $10,000 maximum on attorney fees), so this subsection makes such artificial limits inapplicable to SLAPPs.

93. Memorandum as Amicus Curiae in Support of Attorney General's Motion for Leave to Appear in Support of Fleming's Motion to Dismiss at 4–5, Hometown Properties, Inc. v. Fleming, C.A. No. WC-91–0154 (Super. Ct., Washington County, R.I., filed Mar. 2, 1993).

94. Abrams, *Strategic Lawsuits Against Public Participation (SLAPP),* 7 PACE ENVIRONMENTAL LAW REVIEW 33 (1989).

95. SAN FRANCISCO EXAMINER, June 23, 1991; Stearns, *SLAPPs: A Government Perspective,* in SLAPPS: STRATEGIC LAWSUITS AGAINST PUBLIC PARTICIPATION IN GOVERNMENT at 185 (ALI-ABA Course of Study Materials 1994).

96. Story v. Shelter Bay Co., 52 Wash. App. 334, 760 P.2d 368 (1988).

97. La Pointe v. West Contra Costa Sanitary Dist., No. 295995 (Super Ct., Contra Costa County, Cal., filed May 25, 1988).

98. Westlawn Cemetery v. Forston, No. B-850,394 (Dist. Ct., Orange County, Tex., filed May 24, 1985).

99. *Pine: Go with the Flow,* PROVIDENCE [R.I.] PHOENIX, Mar. 11, 1993; NATIONAL ASS'N OF ATTORNEYS GENERAL, NATIONAL ENVIRONMENTAL ENFORCEMENT JOURNAL 24 (Apr. 1993).

100. *Editorial, SLAPP Back, People,* MIAMI HERALD, May 29, 1992 at 14A: "[Florida Attorney General Robert] Butterworth's involvement is commendable." Butterworth's office conducted a study of Florida SLAPPs from 1989 to 1992. From 140 questionnaires mailed, he learned that 18 respondents had been SLAPPed and 11 more threatened with SLAPPs; 30 others refused to give any details for fear of another lawsuit. See Ericson-Siegel, *Silencing*

SLAPPs: An Examination of Proposed Legislative Remedies and a "Solution" for Florida, 20 FLORIDA STATE UNIVERSITY LAW REVIEW 487, 516–17 (1992).

101. S. Heffner, *Dump Owner's Lawsuit Against Riled Neighbor Is Permitted by Court,* PROVIDENCE [R.I.] JOURNAL-BULLETIN, Apr. 20, 1993.

102. For example, the Ann Arbor, Mich., school board intervened very forcefully on behalf of a parent sued by one of its teachers. Swenson-Davis v. Martel (Chapter 4).

103. Susan Duncan, director of the Division of Excise and Licenses for the City and County of Denver, castigated a tavern owner's attorney for threatening the filing of a SLAPP against two neighborhood groups: "I was angered when I saw his letter. I grant or deny [liquor license] renewals based on the needs and desires of the neighborhood. If you intimidate people and keep them from exercising that very important right to petition, you're destroying the very thing that makes the city work." Gottlieb, *Liquor-License Renewal Hearings on Shaky Ground, Lawyer Claims,* DENVER POST, July 30, 1989, at 4B.

104. Richard M. Kessel, executive director of the New York State Consumer Protection Board, led the state's lobbying efforts for the New York anti-SLAPP law and works with civic groups to protect consumers from SLAPPs. *See Kessel & Civic Groups Launch Campaign for SLAPP Suit Protections* (News Release, Mar. 24, 1992).

105. One county even experimented with direct financial support for targets. In 1985, Suffolk County, New York, made a precedent-setting move of creating a "Legal Defense Fund" for county residents who were sued because of their participation in county proceedings such as zoning. NEW YORK TIMES (LONG ISLAND WEEKLY), Nov. 18, 1987, at 1. Before any funds were disbursed, however, a new administration was elected, and the experiment suffocated for lack of funding, according to one of its originators.

Appendix

1. Previously published articles (cited in the notes particularly to Chapter 1) may be referred to for more extensive detail, as can the study data archived at the Inter-University Consortium for Political and Social Research at the University of Michigan, Ann Arbor, Michigan.

2. *E.g.,* Blake et al., *Social Forces in Petition-Signing,* 37 SOUTHWESTERN SOCIAL SCIENCE QUARTERLY 385 (1956); Helson et al., *Petition-Signing as Adjustment to Situational and Personal Factors,* 48 JOURNAL OF SOCIAL PSYCHOLOGY 3 (1958); NEIMAN & GOTTDIENER, *Qualifying Initiatives: A Heuristic Use of Data to Commend an Unexplored Stage of Direct Democracy,* 1 SOCIAL SCIENCE JOURNAL 99 (1985); Pierce & Lovrich, *Survey Measurement of Political Participation: Selective Effects of Recall in Petition Signing,* 63 SOCIAL SCIENCE QUARTERLY 164 (1982); Oegama & Klandermans, *Why Social Movement Sympathizers Don't Participate: Erosion and Nonconversion of Support,* AMERICAN SOCIOLOGICAL REVIEW (1994).

3. *E.g.,* J. GAVENTA, POWER AND POWERLESSNESS: QUIESCENCE AND REBELLION IN AN APPALACHIAN VALLEY (1980); J. GREENSTONE, PUBLIC VALUES AND PRIVATE POWER IN AMERICAN POLITICS (1982); Salamon & Van Evera, *Fear, Apathy and Discrimination: A Test of Three Explanations of Political Participation,* 67 AMERICAN POLITICAL SCIENCE REVIEW 1288 (1973); E. WOLF, PEASANT WARS OF THE TWENTIETH CENTURY (1969).

4. A. THEOHARIS, SEEDS OF REPRESSION: HARRY S. TRUMAN AND THE ORIGINS OF MCCARTHYISM (1971).

5. *E.g.,* the University of Iowa Libel Study, R. BEZANSON ET AL., LIBEL LAW AND THE PRESS: MYTH AND REALITY (1987).

6. The extensive literature on "disputing" is typically confined to formal disputes and their legal outcomes, seldom explicitly linking disputes to political conflict. See Bruer, The Environment of Public Interest Group Litigation, paper presented at the Law & Society Ass'n Annual Meeting, 1986; Zemans, *Legal Mobilization: The Neglected Role of the Law in the Political*

System, 77 AMERICAN POLITICAL SCIENCE REVIEW 690 (1983). The political implications of participating in legal battles have been considered. See Abel, *The Contradictions of Informal Justice,* in THE POLITICS OF INFORMAL JUSTICE 267 (ed. R. Abel, 1982); Harrington, *The Politics of Participation and Non-participation in Dispute Processes,* 6 LAW & POLICY 203 (1984). But no scientific investigation of the relationship between lawsuits and political participation had been conducted.

7. See the sources cited in Chapter 2.

8. Bachrach & Baratz, *Two Faces of Power,* 56 AMERICAN POLITICAL SCIENCE REVIEW 947 (1962); Bachrach & Baratz, *Decisions and NonDecisions: An Analytic Framework,* 57 AMERICAN POLITICAL SCIENCE REVIEW 632 (1963); J. COLEMAN, COMMUNITY CONFLICT (1957); J. GAVENTA, note 3 above; S. LUKES, POWER: A RADICAL VIEW (1979); J. HABERMAS, LEGITIMATION CRISIS (1975).

9. *E.g.,* Jennings & Niemi, *Continuity and Change in Political Orientations: A Longitudinal Study of Two Generations,* 69 AMERICAN POLITICAL SCIENCE REVIEW 1316 (1975); S. VERBA & N. NIE, PARTICIPATION IN AMERICA (1972).

10. Felstiner, Abel & Sarat, *The Emergence and Transformation of Disputes: Naming, Blaming, Claiming . . . ,* 15 LAW & SOCIETY REVIEW 631 (1981); Mather & Yngvesson, *Language, Audience, and the Transformation of Disputes, id.* at 775 (1980–81); Coates & Penrod, *Social Psychology and the Emergence of Disputes, id.* at 655 (1980–81).

11. On the overall Study plan: Canan & Pring, *Studying Strategic Lawsuits Against Public Participation: Mixing Quantitative and Qualitative Approaches,* 22 LAW & SOCIETY REVIEW 385 (1988).

12. On Phase I of the Study: Canan & Pring, *Strategic Lawsuits Against Public Participation,* 35 SOCIAL PROBLEMS 506 (1988); Pring & Canan, *"Strategic Lawsuits Against Public Participation" ("SLAPPs"): An Introduction for Bench, Bar, and Bystanders,* 12 UNIVERSITY OF BRIDGEPORT LAW REVIEW 937 (1992); Canan, *The SLAPP from a Sociological Perspective,* 7 PACE ENVIRONMENTAL LAW REVIEW 23 (1989); Pring, *"SLAPPs": Strategic Lawsuits Against Public Participation, id.* at 3 (1989).

13. On Phase II of the Study: Canan, Satterfield, Larson & Kretzmann, *Political Claims, Legal Derailment, and the Context of Disputes,* 24 LAW & SOCIETY REVIEW 923 (1990); and articles in notes 12, 14.

14. On Phase III of the Study: Canan, Hennessy & Pring, *The Chilling Effect of SLAPPs: Legal Risk and Attitudes Toward Political Involvement,* 6 RESEARCH IN POLITICAL SOCIOLOGY 347 (1993) (documenting the chilling effect of SLAPPs on targets); Canan, Kretzmann, Hennessy & Pring, *Using Law Ideologically: The Conflict Between Economic and Political Liberty,* 8 JOURNAL OF LAW & POLICY 539 (1992) (analyzing SLAPP parties' characteristics and motives); Canan, Pring & Ryan, Images of Citizen Opponents: The Politics of Denying Equal Citizenship Rights, paper presented at the Law & Society Ass'n Annual Meeting, Berkeley, Cal. (1990) (examining role of characterizations of SLAPP opponents in denial of political rights).

15. See discussion in R. BEZANSON ET AL., note 5 above, at 237–47.

16. First, official court reports (print or computer) cover only a very small amount of the actual litigation, chiefly confined as they are to appellate decisions. Few states report even a fraction of their trial court final decisions (California and New York being exceptions); almost none reports judges' rulings on dismissal or summary judgment motions; and none reports the vast mass of cases (more than 90 percent) that are "settled" by the parties before a judicial decision (see L. ROSS, SETTLED OUT OF COURT (1979)), often "confidential" agreements that further shut off access to parties and records. Second, few SLAPPs result in officially reported decisions, and those that do may not be representative. Third, even the most sophisticated trial court tracking or cataloguing systems are designed for "case manage-

ment," so their records do not lend themselves to substantive research. Fourth, SLAPPs are by their nature "camouflaged": they are not labeled by filers or catalogued by courts as "Petition Clause–violating lawsuits" or "political dispute lawsuits" but masked under a welter of conventional claims such as "defamation," "business interference," or "conspiracy."

17. Complaint, answer, motions/briefs for dismissal, summary judgment, or demurrer, and trial and appellate court rulings, if any.

18. A detailed nine-page code sheet was designed to permit computer entry of the data.

19. U.S. Bureau of the Census data for 1980 were utilized.

20. Felstiner, Abel & Sarat, note 10 above.

21. Coates and Penrod, *id.*

22. We use "filers" to designate the initiators of SLAPPs and "targets" for the objects, as explained in Chapter 1.

23. Eight cases were still pending and could not be used; in 110 cases we were unable to obtain the cooperation of any disputants—in some, because of temporal attrition (moved/no forwarding address, bad health, death); in others, where parties were entities ("State of South Dakota," "Kansas City Southern Railway Corp.," etc.), because it was impossible to identify an appropriate, knowledgeable representative. For only 9 cases were we able to contact all four party types (Filers, Targets, Ripple Effects, and Untouchables); in 42, three of the four types; in 34, two of four; and in 38, one of four.

24. The factorial survey method has been applied to model normative beliefs about social equity and distributive justice, decision-making processes, and consumer preferences, among others. For references, see Canan, Hennessy & Pring, note 14 above, at 347, 355.

25. Mather & Yngvesson, note 10 above; Felstiner, Abel & Sarat, *id.*

26. The coding method we started with produced the following breakdowns: urbanization issues, 25 percent; profession/public service, 20 percent; basic resources (air/water/wildlife), 19 percent; business operation, 12 percent; civil rights, 11 percent; domicile (residence or neighbors), 8 percent; taxes and consumer issues, 8 percent.

27. *E.g.*, G. ALMOND & S. VERBA, THE CIVIC CULTURE (1963); H. MCCLOSKY & J. ZALLER, THE AMERICAN ETHOS: PUBLIC ATTITUDES TOWARD CAPITALISM AND DEMOCRACY (1984).

28. Political participation levels are already low in the United States. Estimates are that only 10 percent of the population takes part in political activities other than voting (see sources in Chapter 2).

29. R. DAHRENDORF, THE MODERN SOCIAL CONFLICT (1988).

30. MCCLOSKY & ZALLER, note 27 above.

31. *Id.*

32. *Id.* at 74.

33. J. SULLIVAN ET AL., POLITICAL TOLERANCE IN CONTEXT: SUPPORT FOR UNPOPULAR MINORITIES IN ISRAEL, NEW ZEALAND, AND THE UNITED STATES (1985).

34. *Id.*; J. GIBSON & R. BINGHAM, CIVIL LIBERTIES AND NAZIS: THE SKOKIE FREE SPEECH CONTROVERSY (1985).

35. *E.g.*, J. BRIGHAM, CIVIL LIBERTIES & AMERICAN DEMOCRACY (1984); Grossman, *Teaching Civil Liberties in the Bicentennial Year*, 6 FOCUS ON LEGAL STUDIES 1 (1991); R. EPSTEIN, TAKINGS: PRIVATE PROPERTY AND THE POWER OF EMINENT DOMAIN (1985).

36. MCCLOSKY & ZALLER, note 27 above, at 1.

37. R. DAHRENDORF, note 29 above.

38. *Id.*

Index